Lecture Notes in Computer Science 12653

More information about this subseries at http://www.springer.com/series/7410

Jieren Cheng · Xiangyan Tang ·
Xiaozhang Liu (Eds.)

Cyberspace Safety and Security

12th International Symposium, CSS 2020
Haikou, China, December 1–3, 2020
Proceedings

 Springer

Editors
Jieren Cheng
Hainan University
Haiukou, China

Xiangyan Tang
Hainan University
Haikou, China

Xiaozhang Liu
Hainan University
Haikou, China

ISSN 0302-9743   ISSN 1611-3349 (electronic)
Lecture Notes in Computer Science
ISBN 978-3-030-73670-5   ISBN 978-3-030-73671-2 (eBook)
https://doi.org/10.1007/978-3-030-73671-2

LNCS Sublibrary: SL4 – Security and Cryptology

This Springer imprint is published by the registered company Springer Nature Switzerland AG
The registered company address is: Gewerbestrasse 11, 6330 Cham, Switzerland

Preface

The 12th International Symposium on Cyberspace Safety and Security (CSS 2020) is the latest edition in a series of highly successful international events on cyberspace safety and security previously held as CSS 2019 (Guangzhou, China), CSS 2018 (Amalfi, Italy), CSS 2017 (Xi'an, China), CSS 2016 (Granada, Spain), CSS 2015 (New York, USA), CSS 2014 (Paris, France), CSS 2013 (Zhangjiajie, China), CSS 2012 (Melbourne, Australia), CSS 2012 (Milan, Italy), CSS 2009 (Chengdu, China), and CSS 2008 (Sydney, Australia).

The CSS Symposium aims to provide a leading-edge forum to foster interaction between researchers and developers within the cyberspace safety and security communities, and to give attendees an opportunity to network with experts in this field. It focuses on all areas of cyberspace safety and security, such as authentication, access control, availability, integrity, privacy, confidentiality, dependability, and sustainability. CSS 2020 was held in Haikou, China, during December 1–3, 2020, and organized by Hainan University, China. CSS 2020 attracted 82 high-quality research papers of which 27 were accepted, an acceptance rate of 33%.

The success of CSS 2020 is the result of the behind-the-scenes efforts of selfless individuals and organizations. We would like to thank all the authors. We are also very grateful for the support of the Program Committee members and reviewers, as well as the symposium chairs, without whose hard work the success of CSS 2020 would not have been possible.

Finally, we would like to thank all the contributors and all the conference attendees, the great team at Springer who helped produce the minutes, and the developers and maintainers of EasyChair.

December 2020

Jieren Cheng
Xiangyan Tang
Xiaozhang Liu

Organization

Honorary General Chair

Jieren Cheng   Hainan University, China

General Co-chairs

Chunjie Cao   Hainan University, China
Jin Li   Guangzhou University, China

Program Co-chairs

Xu Yuan   University of Louisiana at Lafayette, USA
Qinghua Zheng   Xi'an Jiaotong University, China

Publication Chairs

Chunyang Ye   Hainan University, China
Xiaoyi Zhou   Hainan University, China
Xiaozhang Liu   Hainan University, China

Publicity Co-chairs

Nan Jiang   East China Jiaotong University, China
Yucong Duan   Hainan University, China
Chunyuan Zhang   Hainan University, China
Zhao Qiu   Hainan University, China

Track Co-chairs

Xiangyan Tang   Hainan University, China
Qi Qi   Hainan University, China
Jun Ye   Hainan University, China
Jianqiang Ma   Hainan University, China
Yu Zhang   Hainan University, China
Chaosheng Tang   Hainan University, China

Steering Committee Chair

Yang Xiang   Swinburne University of Technology, Australia

Program Committee

Chao Chen	James Cook University, Australia
Liqian Chen	National University of Defense Technology, China
Xiaochun Cheng	Middlesex University, UK
Yi He	University of Louisiana at Lafayette, USA
Xinyi Huang	Fujian Normal University, China
Jingbing Li	Hainan University, China
Wenjuan Li	The Hong Kong Polytechnic University, China
Fang Liu	Hunan University, China
Shigang Liu	Swinburne University of Technology, Australia
Xiaozhang Liu	Hainan University, China
Xinwang Liu	National University of Defense Technology, China
Jianfeng Ma	Xidian University, China
Lichuan Ma	Xidian University, China
Weizhi Meng	Technical University of Denmark, Denmark
Jiaohua Qin	Central South University of Forestry and Technology, China
Youyang Qu	Deakin University, Australia
Kui Ren	Zhejiang University, China
Yizhi Ren	Hangzhou University of Electronic Science and Technology, China
Hong Sheng	Beihang University, China
Victor S. Sheng	Texas Tech University, USA
Limin Sun	Chinese Academy of Sciences, China
Shifeng Sun	Monash University, Australia
Willy Susilo	University of Wollongong, Australia
Lei Wang	Hainan University, China
Xianmin Wang	Guangzhou University, China
Xianpeng Wang	Hainan University, China
Yu Wang	Guangzhou University, China
Bailin Xie	Guangdong University of Foreign Studies, China
Naixue Xiong	Tianjin University, China
Ping Xiong	Zhongnan University of Economics and Law, China
Hongyang Yan	Guangzhou University, China
Qiuling Yang	Hainan University, China
Jianping Yin	National University of Defense Technology, China
Dian Zhang	Hainan University, China
Jun Zhang	Swinburne University of Technology, Australia
Peng Zhang	Shenzhen University, China
En Zhu	National University of Defense Technology, China
Tianqing Zhu	University of Technology Sydney, Australia

Organization Committee

Jianping Yin	National University of Defense Technology, China
Xinwang Liu	National University of Defense Technology, China
Jianfeng Ma	National University of Defense Technology, China

Kui Ren	National University of Defense Technology, China
Limin Sun	National University of Defense Technology, China
Sheng Hong	Beihang University, China

Contents

Camdar-Adv: Method for Generating Adversarial Patches on 3D Object

Chang Chen[1,2] and Teng Huang[1,2(✉)]

[1] Institute of Artificial Intelligence and Blockchain, Guangzhou University, Guangzhou, China
huangteng1220@buaa.edu.cn
[2] Peng Cheng Laboratory, Shenzhen, China

Abstract. DNN model is the core technology for sensors of the autonomous driving platform to perceive the external environment. However, it has a certain vulnerability, and the artificial designed adversarial examples can make the DNN model output the wrong results. These adversarial examples not only exist in the digital world, but also in the physical world. At present, researches on autonomous driving platform mainly focus on attacking a single sensor. In this paper, we presnet a method called Camdar-adv for generating adversarial examples, which can attack the optical image sensor based on any 3D object. Specifically, based on a 3D object that can attack LiDAR sensors, a geometric transformation can be used to project it onto the 2D plane. Perturbation can be added on the 2D plane to generate 2D adversarial examples, which can attack the optical image sensor in the black-box setting, without changing the object's geometry.

Keywords: Autonomous driving · Geometric transformation · Adversarial example

1 Introduction

Modern autonomous driving platforms usually use sensors, such as optical image sensor (OIS) and LiDAR, to sense the environmental information. This information will be input into a deep neural network (DNN) model to obtain recognition results, which were used to make driving decisions. As the core technology of autonomous driving platforms, DNN models solve many problems that traditional algorithms can't be done. However, DNN models are easily attacked by adversarial examples [1, 2].

The adversarial examples were discovered by Szegedy et al. [3] in 2013. It is a kind of artificially designed malicious examples that is capable to induce the DNN model to produce erroneous output. Some works that successfully attacked image recognition [4–7] and target detection [8–10] models with adversarial examples printed by printer. Cao [11] and Tu [12] used optimization-based methods to generate 3D adversarial examples, and construct them in the physical world with a 3D printer. They attacked the LiDAR-based detecting system of the autonomous driving platform.

The existence of adversarial examples in the physical world introduces safety risks for autonomous driving platforms. Besides, the robustness of the platform is also affected

© Springer Nature Switzerland AG 2021
J. Cheng et al. (Eds.): CSS 2020, LNCS 12653, pp. 1–8, 2021.
https://doi.org/10.1007/978-3-030-73671-2_1

by the inherent physical defects of the sensors mounted on it. A popular solution is the strategy of OIS + LiDAR sensor fusion [13]. With the help of deep completion technology, several works fused the information perceived by both sensor mentioned above for target detection [14, 15], and obtained excellent advantages in both performance and reliability.

In summary, based on existing research results, it is infeasible to generate adversarial examples that capable of attacking both OIS and LiDAR-based detecting systems. This prompted us to study a new approach to adversarial examples generation. We present Camdar-adv, a method consists of a 3D to 2D projection strategy and a black box attack method, that can generate adversarial patches on the surface of a 3D object. This method allows the 3D adversarial examples, capable of attacking LiDAR, to gain the ability to attack OIS under the scenario of autonomous driving. To improve the practicality of Camdar-adv, we use a score-based black box attack method to generate adversarial examples. Since the method runs without the structure and gradient information of the DNN model, it shall be able to defend against some gradient-related methods [15] theoretically.

We propose a projection strategy that could project the surface information of a 3D object onto a 2D plane from a certain angle of view. Through its inverse operation, project the 2D pattern back to the surface of the 3D object is also feasible.

2 Related Work

2.1 Attacks Against LiDAR-Based System

Attacks against this kind of system are mainly achieved through disturbance of point cloud generation. The process of sensing the environment with LiDAR is as follows: LiDAR emits a continuous array of laser beams in both horizontal and vertical directions. Then obtain the reflected light intensity through the receiver to calculate the distance and coordinates of the reflection point, which were used to generate the original point cloud. The point cloud data will be fed to the DNN model after preprocessing. Finally, the system performs postprocessing on the output information of the DNN model to obtain the final prediction [16].

2.2 OIS-Based Target Detectors

There are two kinds of commonly-used target detectors: FasterRCNN [17] (two-stage strategy) and YOLO [18] (one-stage strategy). FasterRCNN first uses the region proposal network to separate the foreground and background of the picture Semantically and then performs the classification operation. YOLO directly converts the detection problem into a regression problem and uses the default division principle to select a region proposal. Compared with FasterRCNN, the accuracy of YOLO is slightly reduced while the efficiency is greatly improved. Furthermore, YOLO has better real-time performance, so it was used in the traffic signal detection module of the automatic driving platform Apollo and the target detection module for satellite images [19]. Based on the research scenario of autonomous driving, we use YOLO v3 [20], which improved it's detection performance on tiny objects, as the target model.

2.3 Mono Camera and LiDAR Fusion Technology

In signal-level fusion strategy, image information and depth information of point cloud was used directly to predict dense depth information, but this kind of methods require other conditional constraints. [21] requires high-precision ground point cloud data so that currently used HD Map is far from enough to support this algorithm due to its low accuracy. [14] assumes that the target object is stationary, but the vehicle is real-time moving in the situation of autonomous driving. In feature-level fusion, Jaritz et al. [22] perform semantic segmentation on the image and point cloud separately and then fuse the results into the shared decoder. Wang [23] improved the performance of existing image-based depth prediction networks with the help of sparse depth maps of the point cloud. These methods can generally achieve better results than signal-level fusion. But they still rely on the detection capabilities of a single sensor heavily and could be subjected to adversarial attacks in practical application scenarios.

3 The Projection from 2D to 3D

In this section, we introduce our pre-processing method for 3D objects. Specifically, in this step, we map three-dimensional data to two-dimensional data in digital space. After on such operation, we can focus on the generation of adversarial examples at the image level without caring about the geometric characteristics of the object in the next step.

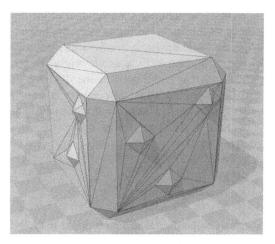

Fig. 1. The 3D object we generated.

3.1 Preparation

Referring to the contour of 3D adversarial examples in [11, 12], we manually created a 3D object O_{adv} with irregular contours using a 3D modeling tool. The shape of O_{adv} is similar to a cube with a side length of 50 cm (see Fig. 1). Our main goal in this article

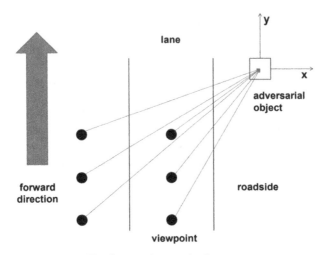

Fig. 2. Attack scenario diagram.

is to propose a general method for generating adversarial patches for 3D objects, so we do not concentrate on specific 3D objects.

The geometric information of O_{adv} is stored in a 3mf format file, which is widely used in the 3D printing industry. We use Meshlab [24] to convert 3mf file into ASCII-encoded ply format, which is convenient for subsequent data processing. According to the definition of ply format, the geometric information of the object is saved in the form of point coordinates and a surface (surrounded by the line of three points). The three-dimensional rectangular coordinate system where the point coordinates are located takes the center of the bottom surface of O_{adv} as the origin. The positive direction of the y-axis of the coordinate system is the same as the direction of the lane, and the z-axis is perpendicular to the ground. Assume the center point of O_{adv} as M, and set the coordinates of the viewpoint $V(x_v, y_v, z_v)$ according to the planned attack scenario. (see Fig. 2) is a schematic diagram of the scene we have prepared. So far, the viewpoints and 3D object involved in the attack scene have been reconstructed in three-dimensional digital space.

3.2 Projection

Based on the attack scenario in the digital space proposed in the previous section, the projection scheme can be split into three steps:

1) Calculate the visible surface of O_{adv} under a certain angle of view.
2) Select a viewing plane according to the angle of view as the mapping plane of the surface information of O_{adv}.
3) Project the points contained in O_{adv} to the viewing plane and combine the visible surface calculated before, the projected object contour could be obtained.

This scheme only makes a simple projection transformation according to the existing mathematical formula, so the compression effect of the focal length of the OIS lens on the object is not under consideration.

The visible surfaces: When we are observing an object, the visible surfaces are those facing us. The surfaces facing away from us can't be observed. Using mathematical symbols, this phenomenon could be precisely described as follows: Suppose the direction vector of the sight is V_{view}. And the normal vector, whose direction always points away from the center of the object, of the nth surface F_n of the object is V_n. If the angle between V_{view} and V_n is greater than 90°, then the nth surface is visible from the viewpoint. The included angle between the two vectors could be judged by their dot product. When the dot product is less than zero, it comes to the conclusion that their included angle is greater than 90°. By analogy, all visible faces $S = \{F_1, F_2,..., F_n\}$ could be calculated.

Projection plane: In the physical world, while an object is captured by OIS, it will be recorded to a 2D image. The recording process can be regarded as a down-sampling process from three-dimensional to two-dimensional. This process can be described by mathematical formulas. Select a plane that passes through the center point of the object, and the direction vector from the viewpoint V is perpendicular to it. It is easy to write out the equation of the surface F through the dot method:

$$A(x - x_0) + B(y - y_0) + C(z - z_0) = 0 \tag{1}$$

While (A, B, C) is any vector that perpendicular to F, and (x_0, y_0, z_0) is the coordinate of any point on F.

Projection of points: In the ply file, each surface is a triangle and composed of three points. Therefore in the projection operation, the logical composition of the surface will not be affected by the projection process. Assuming that the origin coordinates of a point is (x_o, y_o, z_o), and it's new coordinates after projection is (x_p, y_p, z_p). Since the connection between the origin point and the projected point is parallel to the normal vector, a formula can be obtained:

$$(x_p - x_o)/A = (y_p - y_o)/B = (z_p - z_o)/C = 0 \tag{2}$$

The following formula can be obtained by combining formula (1) and formula (2):

$$x_p = ((B^2 + C^2)x_o - A(B \times y_o + C \times z_o + D))/(A^2 + B^2 + C^2)$$

$$y_p = ((A^2 + C^2)y_o - B(A \times y_o + C \times z_o + D))/(A^2 + B^2 + C^2) \tag{3}$$

$$z_p = ((A^2 + B^2)z_o - C(A \times y_o + B \times z_o + D))/(A^2 + B^2 + C^2)$$

With formula (3), the projection coordinates on surface F of all points can be calculated. The information on the visible surface and the point after projection will output to a ply file. The result (see Fig. 3 and Fig. 4) shows the visualization of the projection results in MeshLab. The projection results vary with the angle of view.

So far, we have completed the projection process of the 3D object to the 2D plane under a certain viewpoint.

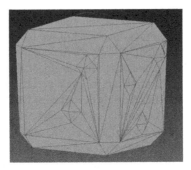

Fig. 3. Projection 1.

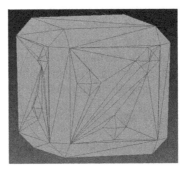

Fig. 4. Projection 2.

4   Conclusion and Prospect

In this paper, we propose an effective deception attack method, Camdar-adv, which can generate adversarial examples on objects with irregular surface, for target detectors. In specific scenarios, our work can enable LiDAR system-oriented 3D adversarial examples to gain the ability to attack the visual perception system. Formed an attack on the single-camera LiDAR fusion technology of the autonomous driving platform. Camdar-adv will further weaken the safety of the autonomous driving platform. The safety of the platform can not be guaranteed by relying solely on the visual optical image sensor and LiDAR. Robust algorithms or more additional hardware are needed.

Currently, Camdar-adv is only capable under a certain perspective, it can not guarantee the effectiveness of the attack in the real world. The relative position between the vehicle and the object keeps changing in the autonomous driving scene. We have started the research on the multi-view target detector attack. This paper only verifies the reliability of the attack in the digital space. To apply the attack to the physical world scenario, more restrictions need to be added in the generation process. We will expand and improve the existing work in the future.

References

1. Carlini, N., Wagner, D.: Towards evaluating the robustness of neural networks. In: IEEE Symposium on Security and Privacy (2017)
2. Sun, M., et al.: Data poisoning attack against unsupervised node embedding methods. arXiv preprint arXiv:1810.12881 (2018)
3. Szegedy, C., et al.: Intriguing properties of neural networks. In: ICLR 2014: International Conference on Learning Representations (ICLR) (2014)
4. Brown, T.B., et al.: Adversarial patch. arXiv: Computer Vision and Pattern Recognition (2018)
5. Liu, A., et al.: Perceptual-sensitive GAN for generating adversarial patches. In: AAAI 2019: Thirty-Third AAAI Conference on Artificial Intelligence, vol. 33, no. 1, pp. 1028–1035 (2019)
6. Kurakin, A., et al.: Adversarial examples in the physical world. In: ICLR (Workshop) (2017)
7. Luo, B., Xu, Q.: Region-Wise Attack: On Efficient Generation of Robust Physical Adversarial Examples. arXiv Preprint arXiv:1912.02598 (2019)
8. Thys, S., et al.: Fooling automated surveillance cameras: adversarial patches to attack person detection. In: 2019 IEEE/CVF Conference on Computer Vision and Pattern Recognition Workshops (CVPRW), pp. 49–55 (2019)
9. Wang, Z., et al.: AdvPattern: physical-world attacks on deep person re-identification via adversarially transformable patterns. In: 2019 IEEE/CVF International Conference on Computer Vision (ICCV), pp. 8340–8349 (2019)
10. Zhao, Y., et al.: Seeing isn't believing: towards more robust adversarial attack against real world object detectors. In: Proceedings of the 2019 ACM SIGSAC Conference on Computer and Communications Security, pp. 1989–2004 (2019)
11. Cao, Y., et al.: Adversarial Objects Against LiDARBased Autonomous Driving Systems. arXiv Preprint arXiv:1907.05418 (2019)
12. Tu, J., et al.: Physically Realizable Adversarial Examples for LiDAR Object Detection. arXiv Preprint arXiv:2004.00543 (2020)
13. Cui, Y., et al.: Deep Learning for Image and Point Cloud Fusion in Autonomous Driving: A Review. arXiv Preprint arXiv:2004.05224 (2020)
14. Ma, F., Cavalheiro, G.V., Karaman, S.: Selfsupervised sparse-to-dense: self-supervised depth completion from lidar and monocular camera. In: 2019 International Conference on Robotics and Automation (ICRA) (2019)
15. Tang, J., Tian, F.-P., Feng, W., Li, J., Tan, P.: Learning guided convolutional network for depth completion (2019)
16. Cao, Y., et al.: Adversarial sensor attack on LiDAR-based perception in autonomous driving. In: Proceedings of the 2019 ACM SIGSAC Conference on Computer and Communications Security, pp. 2267–2281 (2019)
17. Ren, S., et al.: Faster R-CNN: towards real-time object detection with region proposal networks. IEEE Trans. Pattern Anal. Mach. Intell. **39**(6), 1137–1149 (2017)
18. Redmon, J., et al.: You only look once: unified, real-time object detection. In: 2016 IEEE Conference on Computer Vision and Pattern Recognition (CVPR), pp. 779–788 (2016)
19. Van Etten, A.: You Only Look Twice: Rapid MultiScale Object Detection In Satellite Imagery. arXiv Preprint arXiv:1805.09512 (2018)
20. Redmon, J., Farhadi, A.: YOLOv3: An Incremental Improvement. arXiv Preprint arXiv:1804.02767 (2018)
21. Ma, F., Karaman, S.: Sparse-to-dense: depth prediction from sparse depth samples and a single image. In: 2018 IEEE International Conference on Robotics and Automation (ICRA) (2018)
22. Jaritz, M., Charette, R.D., Wirbel, E., Perrotton, X., Nashashibi, F.: Sparse and dense data with CNNs: depth completion and semantic segmentation. In: 2018 International Conference on 3D Vision (3DV) (2018)

23. Wang, J.-G., Zhou, L.-B.: Traffic light recognition with high dynamic range imaging and deep learning. IEEE Trans. Intell. Transp. Syst. **20**(4), 1341–1352 (2019)
24. Cignoni, P., Callieri, M., Corsini, M., Dellepiane, M., Ganovelli, F., Ranzuglia, G.: Meshlab: an open-source mesh processing tool. In: Eurographics Italian Chapter Conference, vol. 2008, pp. 129–136 (2008)

Universal Adversarial Perturbations of Malware

Ruitao Hou(ID), Xiaoyu Xiang(ID), Qixiang Zhang(ID), Jiabao Liu(ID),
and Teng Huang$^{(\boxtimes)}$(ID)

Institute of Artificial Intelligence and Blockchain, Guangzhou University,
Guangzhou 510006, China
huangteng1220@buaa.edu.cn

Abstract. Adversarial malware examples refer to the malwares that can evade the malware detector. Researching adversarial malware examples can help us find the vulnerability of malware detector and improve the defense ability of cyberspace. Considering the huge market share of android system, adversarial malware examples of android are studied in this paper. And an algorithm is proposed to find universal adversarial perturbations of malware. Such perturbation can be inserted the different malwares to generate adversarial examples. Then the effectiveness of algorithm is verified in the experiment. And three classic android malware detectors are used as targets. Experimental results show that universal adversarial perturbations for different machine learning models can be discovered via the proposed algorithm.

Keywords: Adversarial malware examples · Universal adversarial perturbations · Android platform

1 Introduction

Statistics show that as of December 2019, Android application system had about 74.13% of the market [1]. The widespread use of android and its open nature make it possible for the spread of malware, and the security of the Android system is seriously threatened. To solve these problems, researchers are devoted to the study and development of Android malware detection technologies. Among them, Android malware detection tools based on machine learning had wide potential applications due to its high accuracy and adaptability [2,3]. However, studies found that some specific subtle perturbations inserted in examples can cause machine learning algorithms to yield erroneous results with extremely high confidence [4,5]. Such perturbed examples are called adversarial examples.

The concept of adversarial examples was first proposed in 2013, which was discovered by Szegedy et al. [6]. when they studied the image classification model. Erroneous classification results can be output by modifying some specific pixels. Then Grosse et al. found that adversarial examples also exist in malware detection [4]. The basic process is: The original malware is analyzed using decompile

© Springer Nature Switzerland AG 2021
J. Cheng et al. (Eds.): CSS 2020, LNCS 12653, pp. 9–19, 2021.
https://doi.org/10.1007/978-3-030-73671-2_2

tool firstly, and relevant information such as API and hardware application is extracted; Then 0/1 feature vector is constructed based on above information; Finally, the feature vector is modified in a specific way to guide the generation of adversarial examples. Different from adversarial image examples, the generation of adversarial malware examples must satisfy the following conditions: 1) Integrity. Malware modification cannot destroy the executable of the software; 2) Functionality. Malware modification cannot destroy software functions; 3) Penetration. The modified malware can evade detection of malicious code. Therefore, in order to meet the above conditions, the current generation method of adversarial malware examples is mainly through inserting redundant API to the original malware rather than modify the original API.

The existence of adversarial examples shows the vulnerability of machine learning algorithms. Therefore, the research on adversarial examples can be immensely valuable in cyberspace security construction, and it is also helpful for the interpretation of machine learning models, especially deep learning models. At present, a series of research results have been achieved on the research of adversarial image examples and adversarial malware examples. In studies of adversarial image examples, universal adversarial perturbations were discovered by Moosavi-Dezfooli et al., which refers to the perturbation that can be inserted to different images to make the model yields erroneous results [7]. Universal adversarial perturbations are of great significance to further reveal the classification boundary of deep learning. However, in the research on adversarial malware examples, whether there are is still an open question.

Based on the research on universal adversarial perturbations of image, and considering the extremely high market share of Android system, we studied the universal adversarial perturbations of android malware in this paper. Our contributions are shown as follows:

(1) Universal adversarial perturbations of android malware are discovered;
(2) An algorithm of generating universal adversarial perturbations of android malware is proposed;
(3) The proposed algorithm is effective for current classic malware detectors based on machine learning methods.

The rest of the paper is organized as follows. Related works are discussed in Sect. 2; The definition of universal adversarial perturbations of android malware and generation algorithm is proposed in Sect. 3; The effectiveness of the proposed algorithm is verified experimentally in Sect. 4, and conclude with Sect. 5.

2   Related Work

Until now, generation algorithms of adversarial malware examples have been studied extensively. Considering the similarity of adversarial examples on Windows platform and android platform, both generation algorithms will be introduced in this section.

Based on whether the knowledge of target models is known, the scenarios for adversarial malware examples generation can be classified to two types: black-box and white-box. White-box scenario refers to the condition of known target model parameters; otherwise, it is black-box scenario. Under the white-box scenario, Grosse et al. first calculate the forward derivative of each feature value, then the feature value corresponding to the maximum derivative value is selected for modification, and iterate many times until adversarial example is generated [4]. Kolosnjaji et al. proposed a gradient-based adversarial examples generation method, which uses *MalConv* [8], a Windows malware detection model, as the target model. This method iteratively fills the original malware with specific byte-codes [9]. And Demetrio, CHEN, Kreuk et al. also proposed adversarial malware examples generation methods against *MalConv* model [10–12]. Among them, the schemes proposed by Demetrio and CHEN are similar, both of which first calculate the contribution of each part of the bytecode, and then modify the part with greater contribution [10,11]. But Kreuk inserts redundant Sections based on FGSM algorithm to ensure that malicious functions of the original malware are not interfered [12]. Chen et al. use C&W and JSMA algorithms to conduct adversarial attacks on malware detection models *Drebin* and *MaMaDroid* [5]. Referring to the ideas in [5], Al-Dujaili et al. proposed a random adversarial malware examples generation algorithm based on projection gradient descent algorithm, this algorithm can effectively enhance the quantity of adversarial examples [14]; Labaca-Castro et al. conducted an adversarial attack on a CNN-based malware detection model based on gradient descent method [15]. To ensure the functionality and penetration of adversarial examples, each of them needs to undergo sandbox testing and penetration testing. For the white-box scenario, Hu et al. proposed a generation model of adversarial malware examples, MalGAN, based on Generative Adversarial Network (GAN) [16]. The author trained a substitute model to replace the malware detector. However, *MalGAN* needs to obtain the feature dictionary of the detection model in advance, so it has limitations in reality. In addition, the main attack target of *MalGAN* is feed-forward neural networks. In the later period, *MalGAN*'s authors borrowed the idea of *MalGAN* to conduct adversarial examples attack against the detection model based on RNN [17]. Li et al. found that adversarial examples generated by *MalGAN* could not evade the detectors of adversarial examples effectively [18]. Therefore, on the basis of *MalGAN*, they adopted a dual-detector structure, that is, added a special detector of adversarial examples so as to improve the penetration of adversarial examples. Rosenberg et al. designed a universal architecture for adversarial malware examples generation called *GADGET* [19]. *GADGET* can against most machine learning models, such as RNNs, feed-forward networks and some traditional machine learning models. Castro et al. designed an automatic generation method of adversarial examples [20]. This method utilized LIEF tool to insert perturbations at the binary level, including *overlay_append, section_renam, section_add, section_append*, etc. Pierazzi et al. described the relationship between feature space and problem space, and introduced the concept of side-effect feature, which is a by-product of mapping from feature space back to problem space [22]. And they have dened and proved the necessary and sufficient conditions for problem space attacks. Mao et al. proposed a new composite adversarial attack method, which can automatically search for the best combination of attack algorithms and their hyperparameters from the candidate attacks [23].

Overall, researches on adversarial malware examples has yielded substantial results. However, universal adversarial perturbations of malware are still an open question. Therefore, based on universal adversarial perturbations of image, we conducted the research on universal adversarial perturbations of android malware.

3   Algorithm

In this section, the formal definition of universal adversarial perturbations of malware is presented in this phase. And the generation algorithm of universal adversarial perturbations of malware is proposed.

Definition 1. *Universal adversarial perturbations of malware u are feature vectors that satisfy the following conditions:*

$$
\begin{aligned}
&1. \|u\|_p \leq \eta \\
&2. \underset{x \sim \mu}{\mathcal{P}} \left(\mathcal{F}(x + u) \neq \mathcal{F}(x) \right) \geq \alpha
\end{aligned}
\tag{1}
$$

Among them, η represents the scale constraint of u, x is the feature vector of the original malware, μ represents the distribution of malware, $\mathcal{F}$ is a malware detector, $\mathcal{P}$ is a statistical function, α represents the success ratio of u.

It can be seen that universal adversarial perturbations of malware is the feature vector that could make malware be detected as benign.

Algorithm. The purpose of universal perturbation algorithm of malware is to find a perturbation that can satisfy the scale constraints, to enable most software in the malware data set to be detected as benign. The algorithm is shown in Algorithm 1.

According to Algorithm 1, the computation process of universal adversarial perturbations of malware is an iterative cumulative update process based on a single adversarial malware perturbation. Therefore, the single perturbation should be as small as possible to ensure that the scale of universal adversarial perturbations satisfies the constraints. Specifically, for a malware x, the Jacobian matrix $\boldsymbol{M}$ is calculated and the largest partial derivative value is selected, and then recording its index j. If x_j and Δu_j are equal to 0, then assign j to k; otherwise, continue to select the satisfied index j, as shown in line 7 and line 8. Then, assign Δu_k to 1 and add Δu to universal adversarial perturbation u. After that, it is judged whether u satisfies the scale constraint η and can enable the detection error, that is, $\mathcal{F}(x+u)$ is not equal to $\mathcal{F}(x)$, as shown line 5. If possible update the universal perturbation, as shown in step 12. Otherwise, update the universal perturbation increment Δu. Note that before Δu is updated, the current Δu needs to be subtracted from u to ensure that the increments will not be

---

Algorithm 1. Generate universal adversarial perturbations of malware.

Input: Malware dataset, X; Malware Classifier, $\mathcal{F}$; desired l_p norm of the perturbation, η; desired accuracy on perturbed malwares, α;

Output: Universal perturbation of malware, u;

1: **Initialize:** $u \leftarrow 0$;
2: **while** $FoolRate(u) < \alpha$ **do**
3:    **for** each malware $x \in X$ **do**
4:        $\Delta u \leftarrow 0$
5:        **while** F($x+u$) == F(x) && $\| u \|_p \leq \eta$ **do**
6:            $u \leftarrow u - \Delta u$
7:            Compute *Jacobian matrix* $\mathbf{M}$
8:            $k \leftarrow argmin_{j \in [0, len(x)-1], x_j=0, \Delta u_j=0} \mathbf{M}_j$
9:            $\Delta u_k \leftarrow 1$
10:           $u \leftarrow u + \Delta u$
11:       **end while**
12:       $u \leftarrow \boldsymbol{Update}(u, \Delta u)$
13:    **end for**
14: **end while**
15: **return** u

---

repeatedly superimposed. The function Update needs to be executed to *update* the universal perturbation, as shown in Function 1. If $\mathcal{F}(x + u)$ is not equal to $\mathcal{F}(x)$, and the l_p norm of u is less than η, then return current universal adversarial perturbation u; otherwise, subtract the incremental Δu from the universal perturbation u, and restore it to the previous value. After that, it is continued to compute universal adversarial perturbation u. After the update process is completed, whether $FoolRate(u)$ is greater than α should be determined. If it does, the algorithm returns u; otherwise, repeats the above process. The calculation of $FoolRate(u)$ is shown in Eq. (2).

$$FoolRate(u) = \frac{1}{n} \sum_{i=1}^{n} 1_{\mathcal{F}(x+u) \neq \mathcal{F}(x)} \tag{2}$$

Function 1. Update universal adversarial perturbations of malware.

Input: Current universal perturbations u, increment of universal perturbation Δu

Output: Universal perturbation u

1: **if** F($x+u$) $\neq$ F(x) && $\| u \|_p \leq \eta$ **do**
2:    **return** u
3: **else**
4:    **return** $u \leftarrow u - \Delta u$

---

4   Experiment

In this section, we conducted an experimental verification of the generation algorithm of universal adversarial perturbations of malware. The goal is mainly to find universal adversarial perturbation of malware for the classical malware detector. The experiment is shown below.

4.1   Dataset

Open dataset *AndroZoo* is used in this experiment [24]. *AndroZoo* has collected more than 10 million Android software, mainly from the current mainstream Android application market and malware example libraries, such as *play.google.com* [25], *appchina* [26], *VirusShare* [27], etc. Moreover, the software in *AndroZoo* has been analyzed by dozens of malware detection engines and can be easily identified. According to the requirements of this experiment, we used *AndroZoo* to collect 5K benign software from *play.google.com* and *appchina*, and 25K malwares from *VirusShare*.

4.2   Target Models

In order to verify the effectiveness of generation algorithm of universal adversarial examples of malware, three classic android malware detection models are selected as targets, namely *Drebin* [2], *MaMaDroid* [3] and *DLM*. The details of the three models are shown as follows.

Drebin. *Drebin* is a lightweight Android malware detection model. It mainly consists of feature selection and classification algorithm. In terms of feature selection, *Drebin* presets 8 software feature sets, which are composed of permissions, intents, API calls and other information, as shown in Table 1. In order to improve the detection efficiency, lightweight static analysis method is adopted, and then 0/1 feature vector is built based on the preset feature set. For the classification algorithm, considering that the detection of malware is a binary classification problem, the linear SVM model is adopted.

Table 1. Table captions should be placed above the tables.

Feature sets in *Drebin*	
S_1 Hardware features	S_5 Restricted API calls
S_2 Requested permissions	S_6 Used permissions
S_3 App components	S_7 Suspicious API calls
S_4 Filtered intents	S_8 Network addresses

According to the above settings, A Drebin model is trained as target with specific parameters, including: 1) length of feature vector: 3630; 2) classification algorithm: linear SVM. The test results show that the accuracy of the model is above 99%, which can satisfy the experiment requirement.

MaMaDroid. *MaMaDroid* is an Android malware detection model based on app behavior. It first obtains the call graph of the app, and then calculates the frequency of calls between *package* or *family* in app to build Markov chain. Finally, the frequency in the Markov chain is input into the machine learning algorithm. And family refers to the class library provided by jdk; *package* refers to the basic class *package* in *family*.

In this experiment, the random forest algorithm is used as classification method to train the target model. The number of decision trees in the random forest is set to 64, and the depth of these decision trees is set to 81. The test results show that the accuracy of the model is 96%, which can satisfy the experiment requirement.

DLM. *DLM* is an android malware detector based on Deep Neural Network (DNN). Considering that there is no sophisticated such detector, we reproduce the malware detection model in [4], which is a BP Neural Network with 2 hidden layers, and each hidden layer includes 200 neurons. Feature selection is the same as Drebin, and the length of the feature vector is also 3630. The test results show that the accuracy of the model is 98%, which can satisfy the experiment requirement.

4.3 Experimental Results

In this section, we conducted universal adversarial perturbations attacks on *Drebin*, *MaMaDroid*, and *DLM*, respectively. The number of examples in the verification set was set to 20K.

Drebin. The success rate of universal adversarial perturbations for *Drebin* is shown in Fig. 1.

It can be seen from Fig. 1 that the success rate of malicious code universal perturbation increases with the increase of its length. When the length of universal adversarial is equals to 9, the success rate can reach 1. In other words, Drebin can produce a higher error output rate under a small universal perturbation scale.

MaMaDroid. The success rate of universal malware perturbations for *MaMaDroid* is shown in Fig. 2.

As can be seen from Fig. 2, the success rate of universal adversarial perturbations shows a rapid upward trend when the length of universal malware perturbation is between 10 and 20. When the length of universal adversarial perturbations is between 20 and 100, the success rate is shown as a trend of gradual increasing. The success rate of universal adversarial perturbations exceeds 0.95 at a length of 100 for universal perturbation. Therefore, generation algorithm of universal malware perturbation can successfully find such perturbation for *MaMaDroid*.

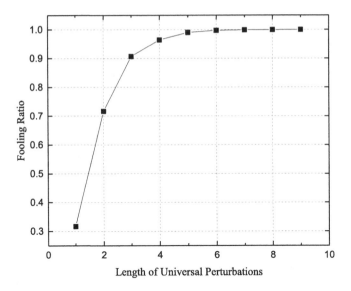

Fig. 1. Fooling Ratio for *Drebin*.

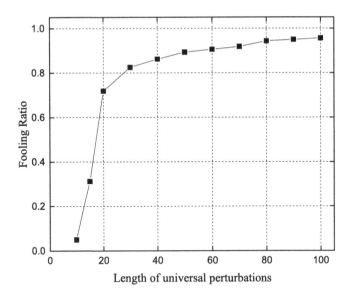

Fig. 2. Fooling ratio for *MaMaDroid*.

DLM. The success rate of universal malware perturbation for *DLM* is shown in Fig. 3.

As shown in Fig. 3, the trend of the success rate of universal adversarial perturbation slows down when the length of universal adversarial perturbation exceeds 25. The success rate of universal adversarial perturbation closes to 1 at a length of 65. Thus, generation algorithm of universal adversarial perturbation is also effective for *DLM* model.

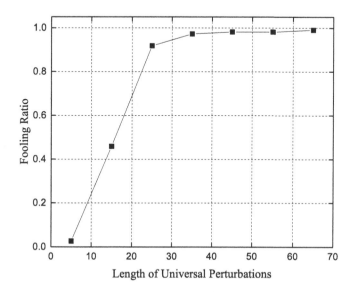

Fig. 3. Fooling ratio for *DLM.*

5   Conclusion

We have studied the issue whether there is a universal adversarial perturbation of malware on android platform in this paper. And universal adversarial perturbation of malware is defined, and generation algorithm of universal adversarial perturbation is proposed. Meanwhile, we take 3 current classic android malware detection models as targets to verify the proposed algorithm. The results show that universal adversarial perturbation of malware exists in android platform, and such perturbations for different detection models can be effectively computed via the proposed algorithm.

References

1. Mobile operating systems' market share worldwide from January 2012 to December 2019. https://www.statista.com/statistics/272698/global-market-share-held-by-mobile-operating-systems-since-2009/. Accessed 16 Apr 2020

2. Arp, D., Spreitzenbarth, M., Hubner, M., et al.: Drebin: Effective and explainable detection of android malware in your pocket. In: The Network and Distributed System Security Symposium (NDSS), pp. 23–26. ISOC, San Diego (2014)

3. Mariconti, E., Onwuzurike, L., Andriotis, P., et al.: Mamadroid: Detecting android malware by building markov chains of behavioral models (2016). arXiv preprint, arXiv:1612.04433

4. Grosse, K., Papernot, N., Manoharan, P., et al.: Adversarial perturbations against deep neural networks for malware classification (2016). arXiv preprint, arXiv:1606.04435

5. Chen, X., Li, C., Wang, D., et al.: Android HIV: a study of repackaging malware for evading machine-learning detection. IEEE Trans. Inf. Foren. Sec. **15**, 987–1001 (2019)

6. Szegedy, C., Zaremba, W., Sutskever, I., et al.: Intriguing properties of neural networks (2013). arXiv preprint, arXiv:1312.6199

7. Moosavi-Dezfooli, S.-M., Fawzi, A., Fawzi, O., et al.: Universal adversarial perturbations. In: Proceedings of the IEEE conference on computer vision and pattern recognition, pp. 1765–1773. IEEE, Puerto Rico (2017)

8. Raff, E., Barker, J., Sylvester, J., et al.: Malware detection by eating a whole exe. In: Workshops at the Thirty-Second AAAI Conference on Artificial Intelligence. AAAI Press, Louisiana (2018)

9. Kolosnjaji, B., Demontis, A., Biggio, B., et al.: Adversarial malware binaries: evading deep learning for malware detection in executables. In: 26th European Signal Processing Conference (EUSIPCO), PP. 533–537. IEEE, Rome (2018)

10. Demetrio, L., Biggio, B., Lagorio, G., et al.: Explaining vulnerabilities of deep learning to adversarial malware binaries (2019). arXiv preprint, arXiv:1901.03583

11. Chen, B., Ren, Z., Yu, C., et al.: Adversarial examples for CNN-based malware detectors. IEEE Access **7**, 54360–54371 (2019)

12. Kreuk, F., Barak, A., Aviv-Reuven, S., et al.: Adversarial examples on discrete sequences for beating whole-binary malware detection (2018). arXiv preprint, arXiv:1802.04528

13. Madry, A., Makelov, A., Schmidt, L., et al.: Towards deep learning models resistant to adversarial attacks (2017). arXiv preprint, arXiv:1706.06083

14. Al-Dujaili, A., Huang, A., Hemberg, E., et al.: Adversarial deep learning for robust detection of binary encoded malware. In: 2018 IEEE Security and Privacy Workshops (SPW), pp. 76–82. IEEE, San Francisco (2018)

15. Labaca-Castro, R., Biggio, B., Dreo Rodose, k.-G.: Poster: Attacking malware classifiers by crafting gradient-attacks that preserve functionality. In: Proceedings of the 2019 ACM SIGSAC Conference on Computer and Communications Security, pp. 2565–2567. Association for Computing Machinery, London (2019)

16. Hu, W., Tan, Y.: Generating adversarial malware examples for black-box attacks based on GAN (2017). arXiv preprint, arXiv:1702.05983

17. Hu, W., Tan, Y.: Black-box attacks against RNN based malware detection algorithms. In: Workshops at the Thirty-Second AAAI Conference on Artificial Intelligence. AAAI Press, Louisiana (2018)

18. Li, H., Zhou, S.-Y., Yuan, W., et al.: Adversarial-example attacks toward android malware detection system. IEEE Syst. J. **1**(4), 653–656 (2019)

19. Rosenberg, I., Shabtai, A., Rokach, L., Elovici, Y.: Generic black-box end-to-end attack against state of the art API call based malware classifiers. In: Bailey, M., Holz, T., Stamatogiannakis, M., Ioannidis, S. (eds.) RAID 2018. LNCS, vol. 11050, pp. 490–510. Springer, Cham (2018). https://doi.org/10.1007/978-3-030-00470-5_23

20. Castro, R.-L., Schmitt, C., Rodosek, G.-D.: ARMED: how automatic malware modifications can evade static detection. In: 5th International Conference on Information Management (ICIM), pp. 20–27. IEEE, Cape Town (2019)
21. Suciu, O., Coull, S.-E., Johns, J.: Exploring adversarial examples in malware detection. In: 2019 IEEE Security and Privacy Workshops (SPW), pp. 8–14. IEEE, San Francisco (2019)
22. Pierazzi, F., Pendlebury, F., Cortellazzi, J., et al.: Intriguing properties of adversarial ML attacks in the problem space. In: 2020 IEEE Symposium on Security and Privacy (SP), pp. 1332–1349. IEEE, San Francisco (2020)
23. Mao, x., Chen, Y., Wang, S., et al.: Composite Adversarial Attacks. In: Thirty-Fifth AAAI Conference on Artificial Intelligence (AAAI). AAAI, Vancouver, Mao et al. proposed a new composite adversarial attack method, which can automatically search for the best combination of attack algorithms and their hyperparameters from the candidate attacks (2021)
24. Li, L., Gao, J., Hurier, M., et al.: Androzoo++: Collecting millions of android apps and their metadata for the research community (2017). arXiv preprint, arXiv:1709.05281
25. Google play. https://developer.android.google.cn/distribute/google-play?hl=zh-cn. Accessed 15 Apr 2020
26. AppChina. http://www.appchina.com. Accessed 12 Apr 2020
27. VirusShare. https://virusshare.com. Accessed 16 Apr 2020

A Semi-supervised Learning Approach for High Dimensional Android Malware Classification

Qiao Shang[1], Ni Li[2,3(✉)], Qi Qi[1(✉)] (ID), and Xiao-Wei Lin[1]

[1] School of Computer Science and Technology, Hainan University, Haikou 570228, China
{qqi,lxw0821}@hainanu.edu.cn
[2] School of Mathematics and Statistics, Hainan Normal University, Haikou 571158, China
lini@hainnu.edu.cn
[3] Key Laboratory of Data Science and Intelligence Education of Ministry of Education, Hainan Normal University, Haikou 571158, China

Abstract. In this paper, we proposed a semi-supervised learning approach to deal with the task of high dimensional Android malware classification. Our approach includes a random projection method for reducing feature dimensionality which would be more efficient than usual feature selection methods in existing work for the task. We also introduced a new method of SGD-based SVM with adapted sampling, which was based on the insight from the confidence and nearest neighbor clustering analysis of input data. The approach was tested on a real-world competition dataset, and effectiveness of the new method was verified by experimental results. By using the new method, we can even obtain a better classification accuracy than the best score produced in the competition.

Keywords: SVM · SGD · Adapted sampling · Classification · Dimensionality reduction · Android malware

1 Introduction

The concerns over malware threats on mobile devices have been raised since smart phones become proliferated over last several years. Traditionally signature-based anti-malware software can't predict new threats from malicious applications. Methods based on machine learning have drawn more attention in recent years.

In machine learning-based methods, it usually needs input data to train a classification model, which will predict a mobile software's label, i.e. malicious or not. The input data can be formed by a vector of Application Interfaces (APIs) called within an Application Package (APK) file. Android platform provides tens of thousands of APIs for developers. The number of key APIs ranges from a few hundred to several thousands [2]. A subset of APIs will be called during

© Springer Nature Switzerland AG 2021
J. Cheng et al. (Eds.): CSS 2020, LNCS 12653, pp. 20–31, 2021.
https://doi.org/10.1007/978-3-030-73671-2_3

the runtime of an application. And those API calls within an APK file can be obtained through reverse engineering.

The learning task here is to classify an android APK file's label based on such a feature vector that indicates which APIs have been used within the application. Recent works in the related field tend to use neural networks or deep learning-based models as in [7,8], these types of models usually have a huge number of parameters to train for, and are generally inefficient especially in a high dimensional input space. A simple neural network model was also presented in [17] with a constrained number of input features. Authors in [12] selected 36 features including features of permission, manifest analysis, and domains, and fed its into a list of classifiers implemented in the WEKA software for predicting android malware. The highest accuracy was 93.63% for the binary classification, and it was achieved by Random Forest (RF). As for feature selection, it is generally hard to select an optimal subset of features, whereas approximate methods exist [11]. Another related work as in [3] applied linear Support Vector Machine (SVM) on multi-modal features including information of permissions, categories, description and the API usage features. Their results showed that API calls carried the most essential behavioral information for android malware detection. A weakness of their method is that the linear SVM model was generated from solving a quadratic optimization problem by a Newton-based method, which will make the training process less efficient when there is a large number of training data. Yuki Maruno et al. [9] also proposed a RF classifier with only API-based features for the task of android malware detection. However, RF-based methods usually suffer from high dimensional data, and are often sensitive to results of feature selection. In their method, features were filtered out by applying a simple suffix-aligned rule based on API names, and their predictive result is hard to reproduce.

We propose a semi-supervised learning approach for android malware classification. The classifier is trained by SVM-based supervised learning in accordance with suggestions from the statistical analysis of input data. Briefly, our approach is mainly comprised of the following components:

- SVM model optimized by Stochastic Gradient Descent (SGD).
- Dimensionality reduction on feature vectors by random projection.
- Confidence analysis of training examples, and nearest neighbor clustering analysis of testing examples without disclosure of its labels .
- Improved SGD-based SVM model with adapted sampling distribution of training examples.

We employed the approach on a real world dataset from the 8th International Cybersecurity Data Mining Competition [1]. Experimental results show that the SGD-based SVM with adapted sampling performs better than the one with a uniform sampling distribution. And it can even yield a better predictive accuracy than the competition winner's best result.

The following Sect. 2 presents the proposed approach, and experimental setting and results will be described in Sect. 3. We will conclude in Sect. 4.

2   Proposed Approach

The semi-supervised learning approach includes a SGD-based SVM classifying model, a procedure of feature dimensionality reduction, and statistical analysis of training and testing data. The purpose is to make the model training more efficient and effective. The basic idea is to maintain geometric characteristic of transformed feature space when reducing the number of features, and to figure out what labeled examples are more important so that SVM during training will lean on those examples more frequently than others.

First, we introduce the method of feature dimensionality reduction. Second, we go into details about methods of statistical analysis of training and testing data, including ones for confidence and nearest neighbor clustering analysis. Then we will present the algorithm of SGD-based SVM with adapted sampling.

2.1   Random Projection

The main method we employed for feature dimensionality reduction is Random Projection (RP) [15]. It is a simple geometric technique for reducing the dimensionality of a set of points in Euclidean space while preserving pairwise distances approximately. The method is especially more suitable for a big data scenario than Singular Value Decomposition (SVD) [6], another widely used method for reducing feature dimensions, because of its efficiency. In our experiments, SVD-based method was also used for comparison with the RP method.

The computation of random projection is indicated by the following formula:

$$S' = S \cdot W^T$$

Where S denotes a training or testing data matrix with row and column dimension as (m, d). The random matrix W consists of r rows and d columns, where r indicates a lower dimensional number. Each element of W is randomly generated from a Gaussian distribution with $\mu = 0$, and $\sigma = 1.0$. W is also divided element-wisely by $\sqrt{d}$ to approximate its rows as orthogonal basis in the r dimensional space. The resulted matrix S' is the transformed lower dimensional data. This random projection method preserves all relative pairwise distances between the input feature vectors with high probability [4].

2.2   Confidence Analysis and Nearest Neighbor Clustering

SVM was designed to find out a discriminating hyperplane in high dimensional feature space to separate two classes with low sample complexity, because that the hyperplane was determined only by the example points, also called support vectors, around the discriminated boundary. In many real world applications, the number of support vectors is expected to be much smaller than the total number of training examples, and only those support vectors are relevant for generating the solution model. Previous works [14,16] usually focused on selecting a subset of training examples in order to speed up the SVM training.

The confidence measure was originally introduced in [16], used for evaluating how likely a training example point could be a support vector. Based on these quantities, a training sample set can be reduced by picking those with high confident values. A reduced sample set can make traditional SVM training more efficient.

Intuitively, imaging that drawing a sphere around a training example as large as possible until it covers a data point from a differently labeled class. Then, the more data points (of the same labels with the centered example point) are contained in the sphere, the less likely the centered training example will be located near the discriminating boundary of a hyperplane.

Given a labeled training sample set X, for each example x, its confidence measure can be deduced by the following steps:

1. Compute a pair-wise Euclidean distance vector containing distances between x and any other data points within X.
2. Sort this distance vector in increasing order, and count from the beginning that the number of elements whose labels are the same as x's until meeting a first different label of data example. Denotes this count as $N(x)$.
3. The confidence measure of x is then in inverse proportion to $N(x)$.

Besides the confidence analysis for training examples, we also want to link this measurement with the testing examples. It's easier for SVM to successfully classify data points located far from the discriminating boundary than those adjacent to.

We also employ the K-Nearest-Neighbor (KNN) method [10] to find the adjacent training examples around every testing data point. Statistical analysis of these neighboring training points can gain us insight for the proximity of testing points to the decision boundary. For example, given the experimental data set in Sect. 3, it showed that many of the adjacent training examples around testing points have small $N(x)$ values. This result inspires us to optimize the training effect by increasing the sampling frequency of training examples with high confidence measurement. Notice that this process is done without the disclosure of labels of testing examples.

2.3   SGD-Based SVM with Adapted Sampling

2.3.1 SGD-Based SVM

SVM [13] is an algorithm for learning the hypothesis of halfspaces with preference for large margin of data points. Assuming that a training sample set consists of m examples of (x_i, y_i), where x_i is a feature vector, and y_i is a corresponding label, then the model parameter w can be obtained by minimizing a regularized empirical loss function (based on the Hinge loss) as followed:

$$\min_{w} \left(\frac{\lambda}{2}\|w\|^2 + \frac{1}{m}\sum_{i=1}^{m} \max\{0, 1 - y_i\langle w, x_i\rangle\} \right) \tag{1}$$

where λ is a regularization parameter.

The optimization problem can be efficiently solved by the method of SGD [5], even there is a large number of training examples. Basically, it randomly picks up an example to calculate an approximate gradient or a sub-gradient if the gradient did not exist, and then using the gradient to iteratively update the model parameter. The update rule of w can be further rewritten as:

$$w^{(t+1)} = -\frac{1}{\lambda t} \sum_{j=1}^{t} v_j \,, \tag{2}$$

where v_j is a sub-gradient of the loss function at $w^{(j)}$ by the chosen random example at iteration j.

2.3.2 Adapted Sampling

Due to the nature of the SGD-based method, its descending route on the geometric surface of the optimization problem is strongly affected by which training example it will select at each of time steps, or even by the order of examples being picked out. These factors are directly influenced by the sampling distribution over training examples. SGD by default would uniformly picked out an example. If the distribution is altered, then it will likely cause the model parameter ending up at a different spot on the geometric surface, which would potentially make an impact on the method's ability of generalization.

The adaptation of sampling distribution is mainly based on results of the confidence analysis of training examples as presented in Sect. 2.2. The smaller value of $N(x)$ an example has, the more confidently it is close to be a support vector. Therefore, for a SVM-based method, high confident examples should be selected more often than others. We also consider the frequency of $N(x)$-indexed examples, and give chances to low confident examples.

Finally, the method of SGD-based SVM with adapted sampling is presented in Algorithm 1.

The algorithm needs a parameter T denoting the total number of iterations, and θ denoting $-\sum_{j=1}^{t} v_j$ as in Eq. 2. A major difference here is the adapted sampling distribution for selecting out training examples contrasting with uniformly choosing.

3   Experiment

This section first describes the process of data preparation for experiment. It then shows results of data analysis including confidence analysis of training examples, and nearest neighbor clustering analysis of testing and training examples. These results form the inspiration of developing a new method of SGD-based SVM with adapted sampling. Last, it will present experimental results of predictive accuracies given by the new method.

Algorithm 1. SGD-Based SVM with Adapted Sampling

Require: T
 1: initialize: $\theta^{(1)} = 0$
 2: **for** $t = 1 \rightarrow T$ **do**
 3:     $w^{(t)} = \frac{1}{\lambda t}\theta^{(t)}$
 4:     Select an example (x_i, y_i) randomly from the adapted sampling distribution
 5:     **if** $y_i\langle w^{(t)}, x_i\rangle < 1$ **then**
 6:         $\theta^{(t+1)} = \theta^{(t)} + y_i x_i$
 7:     **else**
 8:         $\theta^{(t+1)} = \theta^{(t)}$
 9:     **end if**
10: **end for**
11: $\overline{w} = \frac{1}{T}\sum_{t=1}^{T} w^{(t)}$
12: **return** $\overline{w}$

Table 1. Dimensions of prepared data

Data	Dimensions
Training	(30897,37107)
Training-label	(30897,1)
Testing	(30833,37107)
Testing-label	(30833,1)

3.1 Data Preparation

The dataset for experiment was originally from a data mining competition (CDMC 2017) [1]. Training data file includes 30897 rows of API identification numbers (IDs). Each row represents an Android application (aka an APK) comprised of a different number of APIs. There are totally 37107 of unique APIs with its name provided. The label file for training data contains the same number of rows, and each row has either a number 1 for labelling malicious class or -1 for benign class. Testing data file represents 30833 different applications with the same format. Since the competition had closed, the true labeling of the testing data was also released.

In the setting of our experiment, the original training and testing data were extended to full matrices. Each row of application becomes a full scale of API indicators initialized by zeros. Then, the columns corresponding APIs used by the application were filled up by 1s. Dimensions, numbers of rows by columns, of the prepared datasets are shown in Table 1.

The processed datasets of training and testing were essentially high dimensional and sparse matrices, which posed challenges for training SVM models. The motivation was to turn them into dense matrices with lower number of feature dimensions. We employed the RP method as introduced in Sect. 2.1 to transform the datasets. The best random matrix was selected out by cross-validation method, and then it was multiplied by both training and testing datasets separately. We set the reduced feature dimension to number 10000 and 1000, respectively. Then dimensionality reduced datasets were used in the following experiment.

3.2   Confidence and Nearest Neighbor Clustering Analysis

We computed confidence measurement based on $N(x)$ values introduced in Sect. 2.2 for training data. Figure 1 shows histogram of N(x) values for the 10000-feature set, and Fig. 2 shows the counterpart for the 1000-feature set. The density curve lines were formed by the method of smooth spline regression. These two figures show almost the same pattern that a majority of training examples has relatively small $N(x)$ values (aka highly confident data points), and as the $N(x)$ values get increased, the amount of corresponding examples is rapidly decreased.

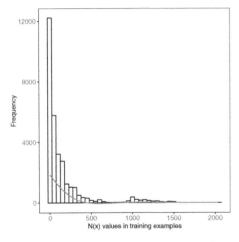 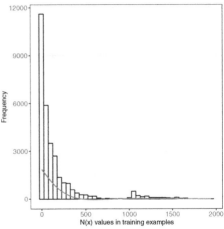

Fig. 1. Histogram of $N(x)$ values with the RP:10000 dataset

Fig. 2. Histogram of $N(x)$ values with the RP:1000 dataset

Next, we used testing examples as centroids to cluster training examples around them on the 10000-feature set. It gathered 10 nearest neighboring training examples for each of testing examples, and computed average $N(x)$ values and Euclidean distances between centroids and neighbored points within every neighborhood. Histogram Fig. 3 shows that many testing examples have a neighborhood of relatively small $N(x)$ values of training examples, and those neighbors are also very close in Euclidean distance to their testing centroids as shown in Fig. 4. Imaging that a large number of testing points are located very closely to the potentially discriminating boundary supported by high confident training points. This phenomenon would wield challenges for SVM-based methods.

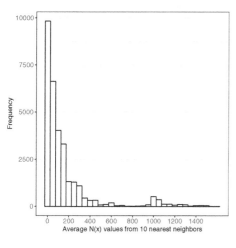
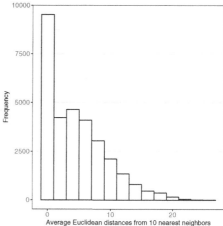

Fig. 3. Histogram of average $N(x)$ values

Fig. 4. Histogram of average Euclidean distances

Based on observations from previous figures, the statistical characteristic of the training and testing datasets suggests that we should put more weights on low $N(x)$ values of training examples than those of high $N(x)$ values generally during SGD processing, in order to deal with the hard phenomenon.

3.3   Prediction of SGD-Based SVM with Adapted Sampling

The statistical analysis of confidence and nearest neighbor clustering of the datasets suggested to alter sampling distribution during SGD processing in order to select high confident training examples more frequently than low confident ones. The adapted sampling distribution was directly converted from a smooth spline regression of frequency data of $N(x)$ values on training examples. The regression curve lines were drawn on Figs. 1 and 2.

Before applying the Algorithm 1, training examples with $N(x)$ values larger than 400 were filtered out. To evaluate the effectiveness of the SGD-based SVM with adapted sampling, we compared it to SGD-based SVM with uniform sampling. Both of models were trained 200 trials, with random shuffle of training examples before each trial. Within every trial, a model was trained with 200 epochs of training set. The λ parameter was fixed to a tuned value during these experiments. Predictive performances were measured by the accuracy rate that is the percentage of testing examples being correctly classified.

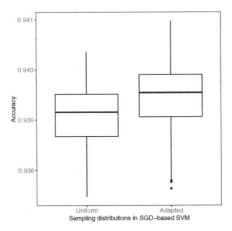

Fig. 5. Box plots of accuracy scores with the RP:10000 dataset

We first show the results of the approach applied on the 10000-feature dataset generated by RP (RP:10000). Figure 5 compares box plots of accuracy scores given by SGD-based SVM with uniform and adapted sampling distributions, and each plot was formed by 200 random trials of results. Also, Fig. 6 shows results with the same setting of experiments as in Fig. 5 but on a different 10000-feature dataset generated by a truncated SVD method (SVD:10000). The purpose of comparing with SVD was to validate the RP method of dimensionality reduction. The detailed statistics of the two sets of box plots are displayed in Table 2.

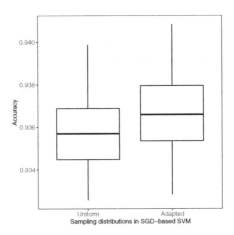

Fig. 6. Box plots of accuracy scores with the SVD:10000 dataset

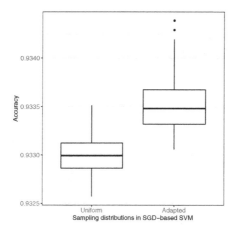

Fig. 7. Box plots of accuracy scores with the RP:1000 dataset

Table 2. Statistics with the box plots

	RP:10000		SVD:10000	
	Uniform	Adapted	Uniform	Adapted
Median	0.93916	0.93955	0.93570	0.93659
Sd	0.00064	0.00062	0.00162	0.00162
Max	0.94036	0.94097	0.93987	0.94084

Adapted sampling in SGD-based SVM boosts predictive performance over that with uniform sampling as shown in both of Figs. 5 and 6. With the RP:10000 dataset, It increased median accuracy score by 0.00039, which should not be undervalued because that the increased amount occupies more than 60% of the relatively small value span of the standard deviation (Sd). It also pushed the maximum score from 0.94036 to 0.94097 which already exceeded the championing result 0.9405 of the competition. The same kind of observations of comparing adapted sampling with uniform sampling can be found out on Fig. 6 as well when experimenting with the SVD:10000 dataset. Additionally, these results also show that the RP is a competitive method of dimensionality reduction in practice compared with the SVD-based method. As shown in Table 2, performances on the RP:10000 dataset generally achieved higher scores and lower standard deviation than its counterparts on the SVD:10000 dataset.

We also experimented with a lower number of feature dimension. Specifically, the same setting of experiment was repeated on a 1000-feature dataset transformed by the RP method, and its results are shown on Fig. 7. The advantage of adapted sampling over uniform sampling in SGD-based SVM is more obvious in the picture than previous ones such that the box framed by upper and lower quartiles of accuracies given by the adapted sampling's is completely located above the box given by the uniform sampling's, although accuracy scores in this setting of feature dimension are relatively smaller than those in the 10000-feature one.

4 Conclusion

In this paper, we presented a semi-supervised learning approach for tackling with high-dimensional Android malware classification tasks, which incorporated components such as feature dimensionality reduction, confidence analysis and nearest neighbor clustering analysis of input data. Within the approach, we also introduced a new model of SGD-based SVM with adapted sampling. Experimental results on a real-world competition's dataset show that the performance of our sampling-adapted SGD-based SVM is statistically better than the original SGD-based SVM with uniform sampling. It can even achieve a more accurate result than the champion's score in the competition.

Acknowledgements. This work was sponsored in part by Hainan University's Scientific Research Start-Up Fund, and the Ministry of Education of China's Scientific Research Fund for the Returned Overseas Chinese Scholars awarded to the corresponding author. This work was also supported by the National Natural Science Foundation of China under the grants No. 11861030, No.61962017, No.61865005, Natural Science Foundation of Hainan Province projects under the grant No.2019RC176, 2019RC088, Hainan Key R&D Program No. ZDYF2019115, and the National Key Research and Development Program of China under the grant No. 2018YFB1404400. The authors of this work was also supported by the State Key Laboratory of Marine Resource Utilization in the South China Sea at Hainan University, and the Key Laboratory of Big Data and Smart Services of Hainan Province.

References

1. The 8th international Cybersecurity Data Mining Competition (cdmc2017) (2017). http://www.csmining.org/cdmc2017/
2. Aafer, Y., Du, W., Yin, H.: DroidAPIMiner: mining API-level features for robust malware detection in android. In: Zia, T., Zomaya, A., Varadharajan, V., Mao, M. (eds.) SecureComm 2013. LNICST, vol. 127, pp. 86–103. Springer, Cham (2013). https://doi.org/10.1007/978-3-319-04283-1_6
3. Ban, T., Takahashi, T., Guo, S., Inoue, D., Nakao, K.: Integration of multi-modal features for android malware detection using linear SVM. In: 2016 11th Asia Joint Conference on Information Security (AsiaJCIS), pp. 141–146. https://doi.org/10.1109/AsiaJCIS.2016.29
4. Blum, A., Hopcroft, J.E., Kannan, R.: Foundations of Data Science. Cambridge University Press, New York (2020)
5. Bottou, L.: Large-Scale Machine Learning with Stochastic Gradient Descent, pp. 177–186. Physica-Verlag HD, Heidelberg, USA (2010). https://doi.org/10.1007/978-3-7908-2604-3_16

6. Golub, G.H., Reinsch, C.: Singular value decomposition and least squares solutions. Num. Math. **14**(5), 403–420 (1970)
7. Kang, J., Jang, S., Li, S., Jeong, Y.S., Sung, Y.: Long short-term memory-based malware classification method for information security. Comput. Electr. Eng. **77**, 366–375 (2019). https://doi.org/10.1016/j.compeleceng.2019.06.014. https://www.sciencedirect.com/science/article/pii/S0045790618328167
8. Lin, Q.G., Li, N., Qi, Q., Hu, J.B.: Classification of IoT malware based on convolutional neural network. In: 2020 International Conference on Service Science (ICSS), pp. 51–57 (2020). https://doi.org/10.1109/ICSS50103.2020.00016
9. Maruno, Y., et al.: Solution for the CDMC 2017. Technical Report, Kyoto Women's University (2017)
10. Peterson, L.E.: K-nearest neighbor. Scholarpedia **4**(2), 1883 (2009). https://doi.org/10.4249/scholarpedia.1883
11. Qi, Q., Li, N., Li, W.: Exploration of heuristic-based feature selection on classification problems. In: Chen, G., Shen, H., Chen, M. (eds.) Parallel Architecture, Algorithm and Programming, pp. 95–107. Springer Singapore, Singapore (2017)
12. Sachdeva, S., Jolivot, R., Choensawat, W.: Android malware classification based on mobile security framework. IAENG Int. J. Comput. Sci. **45**(4), 514–522 (2018)
13. Shalev-Shwartz, S., Ben-David, S.: Understanding Machine Learning: From Theory to Algorithms. Cambridge University Press, New York, USA (2014)
14. Vapnik, V.: Estimation of Dependences Based on Empirical Data. Springer-Verlag New York, New York, USA (2006)
15. Vempala, S.S.: The random projection method, DIMACS series in discrete mathematics and theoretical computer science. In: DIMACS/AMS, vol. 65 (2004). http://dimacs.rutgers.edu/Volumes/Vol65.html
16. Wang, J., Neskovic, P., Cooper, L.N.: Training data selection for support vector machines. In: Wang, L., Chen, K., Ong, Y.S. (eds.) ICNC 2005. LNCS, vol. 3610, pp. 554–564. Springer, Heidelberg (2005). https://doi.org/10.1007/11539087_71
17. Zhou, Q., Feng, F., Shen, Z., Zhou, R., Hsieh, M.Y., Li, K.C.: A novel approach for mobile malware classification and detection in android systems. Multimedia Tools Appl. **78**(3), 3529–3552 (2019). https://doi.org/10.1007/s11042-018-6498-z

Kernel Optimization in SVM for Defense Against Adversarial Attacks

Wanman Li[⊠] and Xiaozhang Liu

Hainan University, Haikou 570228, Hainan, China

Abstract. While malicious samples were widely found in many application fields of machine learning, suitable countermeasures have been researched in the research field of adversarial machine learning. Support vector machines (SVMs), as a kind of successful approach, were widely used to solve security problems, such as image classification, malware detection, spam filtering, and intrusion detection. However, many adversarial attack methods have emerged recently, considering deep neural networks as machine learning models. Therefore, we consider applying them to SVMs and put forward an effective defense strategy against the attacks. In this paper, we aim to develop secure kernel machines against a prevalent attack method that was previously proposed in deep neural networks. This defense approach is based on the kernel optimization of SVMs with radial basis function kernels. To test this hypothesis, we evaluate our approach on MNIST and CIFAR-10 image classification datasets, and the experimental results show that our method is beneficial and makes our classifier more robust.

Keywords: Support vector machines · Kernel optimization · Adversarial machine learning

1 Introduction

During the past several decades, we have seen advances in machine learning. However, with the expansion of machine learning applications, many new challenges have also emerged. In particular, adversarial machine learning, as a machine learning technique, mainly learns the potential vulnerabilities of machine learning in adversarial scenarios and have attracted a lot of attention [1–3]. Adversarial samples have been widely found in the application fields of machine learning, notably image classification, speech recognition, and malware detection [4–6]. Meanwhile, various defensive techniques for the adversarial samples have been proposed recently, including adversarial training, defensive Distillation, pixel deflection, and local flatness regularization [7–10].

As a popular machine learning method, support vector machines (SVMs) were widely used to solve security problems, such as image classification, malware detection, spam filtering, and intrusion detection [11–13]. As described in [14], adversarial attacks against machine learning can be categorized as poisoning attacks and evasion attacks in general. A poisoning attack happens at test time, where the adversary injects a small number of specifically modified samples into the training data, which makes a

J. Cheng et al. (Eds.): CSS 2020, LNCS 12653, pp. 32–42, 2021.
https://doi.org/10.1007/978-3-030-73671-2_4

change in the boundary of the model and results in misclassification. With the rise of various poisoning attack measures against SVMs [15–19], the countermeasures for protecting SVM classifier from poisoning attacks have been developed, one is data cleaning technology [20], and the other is to improve the robustness of learning algorithms against malicious training data [21].

In this paper, we focus mainly on evasion attacks on the SVM classifier. An evasion attack is an attack that evades the trained model by constructing a well-crafted input sample during the test phase. In 2013, Biggio et al. [22] simulated various evasion attack scenarios with different risk levels to enable classifier designers to select models more wisely. However, as time went by, more and more evasion attack methods began to emerge. There are two main directions of evasion attacks to generate adversarial examples. One attack is based on the gradient, which is the most common and most successful attack method. The core idea is to use the input image as the starting and modify the image in the direction of the gradient of the loss function, such as the Fast gradient Sign Method [23], Basic Iterative Method [24], and Iterative gradient Sign Method [25]. Another is to generate adversarial samples based on hyperplane classification, such as the DeepFool algorithm [26]. Although the above methods of generating adversarial examples all consider deep neural networks as machine learning models, in this work, we focus on SVMs. Therefore, we first attempted to apply the above methods of generating adversarial samples to the SVM classifier and proposed corresponding defense strategies.

In this work, our main contribution is to propose an effective defense strategy based on kernel optimization in SVM to protect the classifier against an attack method similar to the method proposed in [26]. The experimental results (in Sect. 4) show that our approach has a very significant defensive effect on the iterative attack based on gradient. Moreover, after using kernel optimization for defense, our classifier becomes more robust. Besides, to our best knowledge, this is the first attempt to apply this adversarial attack, which is proposed in [26] to the SVM model, to generate adversarial examples and achieved good experimental results.

The remaining of this paper is arranged as follows: In Sect. 2, we introduce the relevant knowledge of SVM and the attack approach that we use throughout our work. In Sect. 3, we illustrate our defend method based on kernel optimization in SVM against adversarial examples. Experimental results are presented in Sect. 4, followed by discussion and conclusions in Sect. 5.

2 Preliminary

To better illustrate the proposed procedures, we briefly review the main concepts of the model and the adversarial attack used throughout this paper. We first introduce our notation and summarize the model we utilized in the SVM in Sect. 2.1. Then we describe the major method which was used to generate adversarial samples in Sect. 2.2.

2.1 Support Vector Machine

The SVM model is a prevailing approach of classification between two sets. For illustration, we first describe the main idea of binary SVM, which is to find a hyperplane that well-separated the two classes. In SVM, a hyperplane is a solution that can correctly divide positive and negative class samples based on the principle of structural risk minimization. Thus, the hyperplane equation is univocally represented as $\mathbf{w}^T \cdot \mathbf{x} + b = 0$, where normal vector $\mathbf{w}$ gives its orientation, and b is its intercept displacement.

Assuming that the problem is one of binary classification, we symbol a training dataset as $D = \{(\mathbf{x}_i, y_i)\}_{i=1}^{N}$. Here $\mathbf{x}_i \in \mathbb{R}^d$ is the input feature vector, $y \in \{-1, +1\}$ the output label, respectively, where N is the number of samples, and d is the dimensionality of the input space. The solution of the optimal hyperplane of the SVM model can be expressed as a convex quadratic programming problem with inequality constraints. The Lagrangian multiplier method can be used to obtain its dual problem and then α can be solved by the SMO algorithm. Finally, we can get the discriminant function. In addition, $\mathbf{w}$ can be calculated as $\sum_{i=1}^{N} \alpha_i y_i \mathbf{x}_i$, and the intercept b can be computed as $b = \frac{1}{|S|} \sum_{i \in S} (y_i - \sum_{j \in S} \alpha_j y_j (\mathbf{x}_i, \mathbf{x}_j))$.

Although SVM was initially designed to solve linear classification problems, SVM was extended to nonlinear classification cases by choosing from among different kernel functions [27]. Through the kernel matrix, the training data can be projected to more complex feature space. The process of solving SVM is to solve the following quadratic optimization problem

$$
\begin{aligned}
\min_{\alpha} \ & \tfrac{1}{2} \sum_{i=1}^{N} \sum_{j=1}^{N} \alpha_i \alpha_j y_i y_j k(\mathbf{x}_i, \mathbf{x}_j) - \sum_{i=1}^{N} \alpha_i, \\
s.t. \ & \sum_{i=1}^{N} \alpha_i y_i = 0, s.t. \ \sum_{i=1}^{N} \alpha_i y_i = 0, \\
& \alpha_i \geq 0, \ i = 1, 2..., N,
\end{aligned}
\tag{1}
$$

in which α_i is the Lagrange multiplier corresponding to the training data $\mathbf{x}_i$, $\mathbf{K}(\cdot)$ is the kernel function. If we define a mapping function $\Phi : X \rightarrow \chi$, that is to say, the function maps the training sets into a higher-dimensional feature space, then $\mathbf{K}(\mathbf{x}_i, \mathbf{x}_j)$ can be generalized to $\Phi(\mathbf{x}_i)^T \Phi(\mathbf{x}_j)$, so $\mathbf{w}$, and b can be written as

$$
\mathbf{w} = \sum_{i=1}^{N} \alpha_i y_i \Phi(\mathbf{x}_i),
\tag{2}
$$

$$
b = \frac{1}{|S|} \sum_{i \in S} (y_i - \sum_{j \in S} \alpha_j y_j \mathbf{K}(\mathbf{x}_i, \mathbf{x}_j)),
\tag{3}
$$

where $S = \{i | \alpha_i > 0, i = 1, 2, ...m\}$ the subscript set of all the support vectors. Though it may be too complicated to compute in the feature space, one need not explicitly know, and it only corresponds to the kernel function.

2.2 Attack Strategy

In [26], they proposed the DeepFool algorithm, which is simple as well as an accurate method and based on hyperplane classification to generate adversarial samples. The primary attack method used in our study is similar to this method. In the case where the classifier f is linear, from [26], we know that the minimal perturbation to change the classifier's decision is equal to the distance from the point to the hyperplane classification times the negative gradient of the unit vector of $\mathbf{w}$, where $\mathbf{w}$ is the weight vector of the hyperplane classification. For the nonlinear case, we consider the iterative procedure to find the minimum perturbation vector, as shown in Fig. 1. In some situations, we may not be able to reach the classification hyperplane in one step, like in the case of linearity, and multi-step superposition may be required. Consequently, in a high dimensional space, the minimum perturbation vector of the adversarial sample can be expressed as

$$\varepsilon_\Phi = -\frac{\mathbf{w}_\Phi^T \Phi(\mathbf{x}) + b}{||\mathbf{w}_\Phi||_2^2} \mathbf{w}_\Phi, \tag{4}$$

where $\mathbf{w}$ and b is represented in Eq. (2) and Eq. (3).

In fact, $\mathbf{w}_\Phi$ can also be formally represented by all the support vectors in high dimension space, such as

$$\mathbf{w}_\Phi = \sum_{i \in S} \alpha_i y_i \Phi(\mathbf{x}_i). \tag{5}$$

Of course, $\Phi(\mathbf{x}_i)$ showing no explicit expression, so Eq. (5) is only part of the $\mathbf{w}_\Phi$ formalized representation, cannot be obtained.

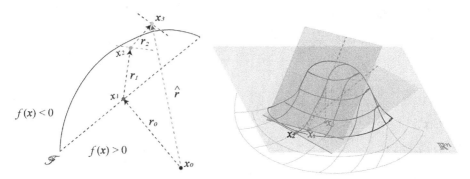

Fig. 1. The minimum perturbation that to classify the positive sample to the negative sample for a nonlinear binary classifier. On the left is the plane figure, on the right is a geometric illustration of the method.

Next, we proposed the adversarial generation method, which is based on kernel. For the nonlinear function $f(\mathbf{x})$, combined with Eq. (3) and Eq. (5), is then defined as follows

$$f(\mathbf{x}) = \mathbf{w}_\Phi^T \Phi(\mathbf{x}) + b$$

$$= \sum_{i \in S} \alpha_i y_i \mathbf{K}(\mathbf{x}_i, \mathbf{x}) + \frac{1}{||S||} \sum_{i \in S} (y_i - \sum_{j \in S} \alpha_j y_j K(\mathbf{x}_i, \mathbf{x})). \tag{6}$$

For an unclassified testing sample, if the value of $f(\mathbf{x})$ is positive, the sample would be classified as a normal example. Otherwise, it would be classified as a malicious sample. The gradient of $f(\mathbf{x})$ with respect to x is thus given by

$$\nabla_{\mathbf{x}} f(\mathbf{x}) = \sum_{i \in S} \alpha_i y_i \nabla_{\mathbf{x}} \mathbf{K}(\mathbf{x}_i, \mathbf{x}). \tag{7}$$

Here, if we use the Radial Basis Function (RBF) as the kernel function, for this kernel $\mathbf{K}(\mathbf{x}_i, \mathbf{x}_j) = e^{-\frac{||\mathbf{x}_i - \mathbf{x}_j||_2^2}{\sigma^2}}$, the gradient is $\nabla_{\mathbf{x}} \mathbf{K}(\mathbf{x}_i, \mathbf{x}) = -\frac{2}{\sigma^2} e^{-\frac{||\mathbf{x}_i - \mathbf{x}||}{\sigma^2}} (\mathbf{x} - \mathbf{x}_i)$. Therefore, the gradient of $f(\mathbf{x})$ can be rewritten as

$$\nabla_{\mathbf{x}} f(\mathbf{x}) = -\frac{2}{\sigma^2} \sum_{i \in S} \alpha_i y_i e^{-\frac{||\mathbf{x}_i - \mathbf{x}||}{\sigma^2}} (\mathbf{x} - \mathbf{x}_i). \tag{8}$$

According to Algorithm 1, we can thus find the adversarial sample.

Algorithm 1 Attack algorithm for RBF-SVM

1: input: Benign example x, classifier f, kernel parameter σ.

2: output: adversarial example $\mathbf{x}_{i+1}$

3: $\mathbf{x}^{(0)} \leftarrow \mathbf{x}$

4: $i \leftarrow 0$ /* Iteration count */

5: **repeat**

6: $\mathbf{r}^{(i)} \leftarrow -\dfrac{f(\mathbf{x}^{(i)})}{\| \nabla f(\mathbf{x}^{(i)}) \|} \nabla f(\mathbf{x}^{(i)})$

7: $\mathbf{x}^{(i+i)} \leftarrow \mathbf{x}^{(i)} + \mathbf{r}^{(i)}$

8: $i \leftarrow i + 1$

9: **until** $sign(f(\mathbf{x}^{(i+1)})) \neq sign(f(\mathbf{x}^{(0)}))$

10: **return** $\mathbf{x}^{(i+1)}$

---

3   The Defense Based on Kernel Optimization

If we choose RBF as the kernel function, according to Eq. (1), the dual problem of SVM can be described as

$$
\min_{\alpha} \; \frac{1}{2} \sum_{i=1}^{N} \sum_{j=1}^{N} \alpha_i \alpha_j y_i y_j e^{-\frac{\|\mathbf{x}_i - \mathbf{x}_j\|_2^2}{\sigma^2}} - \sum_{i=1}^{N} \alpha_i
$$
$$
s.t. \; \sum_{i=1}^{N} \alpha_i y_i = 0
$$
$$
\alpha_i \geq 0, \; i = 1, 2..., N.
$$
(9)

After solving Eq. (9) to obtain the value of α, considering optimize the kernel parameter to improve the ability of defense against adversarial attack. We noted the support vector as $\mathbf{x}_s$ then the discriminant function of support vectors is $f(\mathbf{x}_s) = \mathbf{w}_\Phi^T \Phi(\mathbf{x}_s) + b = \pm 1$. Combining with Eq. (4), correspondingly, we get the minimum perturbation radius of the support vector against the adversarial samples, which is as below

$$
\varepsilon = \frac{1}{\|\mathbf{w}_\Phi\|_2}.
$$
(10)

To make our model more difficult to be attacked, we urgently maximize the minimum perturbation semidiameter. Therefore, the task of defense is to maximize the value of Eq. (10), which can be achieved by minimizing $\|\mathbf{w}_\Phi\|_2^2$. When given the value of α, combined with Eq. (5), the optimization of the kernel parameters to defend the attacks as follows

$$
\min_{\alpha} A(\sigma) = \sum_{i \in S} \sum_{j \in S} \alpha_i \alpha_j y_i y_j e^{-\frac{\|\mathbf{x}_i - \mathbf{x}_j\|_2^2}{\sigma^2}}.
$$
(11)

This is an unconstrained optimization problem, which can be solved by the gradient descent method

$$
\sigma_k = \sigma_{k-1} - \eta A'(\sigma_{k-1}),
$$
(12)

where $A'(\sigma) = \frac{2}{\sigma^3} \sum_{i \in S} \sum_{j \in S} \alpha_i \alpha_j y_i y_j \|\mathbf{x}_i - \mathbf{x}_j\|_2^2 e^{-\frac{\|\mathbf{x}_i - \mathbf{x}_j\|_2^2}{\sigma^2}}$. The Gaussian kernel parameter optimization algorithm for defending against adversarial attack, as shown in Algorithm 2. The initial value of the kernel parameter can be defined as $\sigma^{(0)} = \sqrt{\frac{1}{N(N-1)} \sum_{i=1}^{N} \sum_{j=1}^{N} \|\mathbf{x}_i - \mathbf{x}_j\|_2^2}$, where N is the number of training samples.

In [15], they proposed a simple yet accurate method for computing and comparing the robustness of different classifiers to adversarial perturbations; they defined the average robustness $\hat{\rho}_{adv}(f)$ as follows

$$
\hat{\rho}_{adv}(f) = \frac{1}{D} \sum_{x \in D} \frac{\|\mathbf{\hat{\sigma}}(\mathbf{x})\|_2}{\|\mathbf{x}\|_2}.
$$
(13)

To verify the effectiveness of our defense method, we also use this method to compare the robustness of the classifier under different kernel parameters.

Algorithm 2 Kernel parameter optimization for defense against adversarial attacks

---

Set initial value $\sigma^{(0)}$. Set iteration number $m = 1$.

repeat

Solve the SVM optimization problem in Eq.(9) to obtain $\boldsymbol{\alpha}^{(m)} = (\alpha_1^{(m)}, ..., \alpha_N^{(m)})$.

Set $\alpha_j = \alpha_j^{(m)}, j = 1, ..., N$, and solve the unconstrained optimization

the problem in Eq. (11) using Gradient Descent in Eq. (12) to obtain $\sigma^{(m)}$.

until No significant update for σ.

---

4 Experimental Results

Datasets. For the sake of demonstrating the effectiveness of the kernel optimization defense method, we validated it on MNIST [28] and CIFAR-10[29] image classification datasets, respectively. In these experiments, we only consider a standard SVM with the RBF kernel and choose data from two classes, considering one class as the benign class and a different one as the attack class. The class and number of samples employed in each training and test set are given in Table 1. In order to limit the range of the adversarial example, each pixel of the example in both datasets is normalized to $\mathbf{x} \in [0, 1]^d [0, 1]^d$ by dividing by 255, in which d represents the number of feature vectors. For the MNIST dataset, each digital image represents a grayscale image of $28 * 28$ pixels, which means that feature vectors have $d = 28*28 = 784$ values, while for the CIFAR-10 dataset, each image is a color image with three channels and each channel have $32 * 32$ pixels, which means that feature vectors have $d = 32 * 32 * 3 = 3072$ features. In these experiments, only the kernel parameter σ is considered, and the regularization parameter c of the SVM is fixed to default.

Table 1. Datasets used for training and testing with RBF-SVMs

Dataset	Train size	Test size	Positive	Negative
MNIST	8000	2000	Digit '1'	Digit '7'
CIFAR-10	10000	2000	Cat	Dog

After the process of training, α can be obtained, and we began to the kernel optimization training. According to Sect. 3, we know that the defense method's task is to maximize Eq. (10), that is, to minimize function A in Eq. (11). The gradient descent method is used to evaluate the function A, as described in Algorithm 2. The graph of the value of function A varying with the value of is shown in Fig. 2. We found that the value of the function A grows with the increase of σ on the two datasets. Therefore, the minimum value of the function A is obtained at the initial value of σ on both datasets.

Then we verify the effectiveness of the defense method of σ at different values. We use a method that we proposed in Sect. 2.2 to generate adversarial samples. In order to prevent the gradient from disappearing, we add a small value $\eta = 0.02$ to the disturbance each time we generate adversarial samples. The method used to generate the adversarial sample is shown in Algorithm 2. On the MNIST dataset, we selected the value of σ as 8.6 (initial value of the σ), 20, 40, and 100, respectively, and then compared the generated adversarial samples (as shown in Fig. 3 on the top). On the CIFAR-10 dataset, we selected the value of σ 19.6 (the initial value of σ), 30, 40, and 50, and then compared the resulting adversarial samples (as shown in Fig. 3 on the bottom).

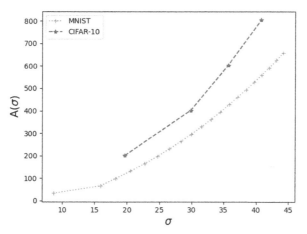

Fig. 2. How the function A changes with different values of σ on MNIST and CIFAR-10 datasets. The picture shows that function A and σ are positively correlated.

Finally, we verified the robustness of the classifier under different values of the kernel parameters. As shown in Fig. 4, after kernel optimization, it significantly increased the robustness of the classifier.

5 Discussion and Conclusion

In this work, we are the first to propose a strategy for protecting SVMs against the adversarial generation method which is based on kernel. In [26], they put forward a technique based on hyperplane classification for generating adversarial examples of deep neural networks. We think a similar approach could also work for SVMs, namely applying it to SVM classifiers. Through experiments, it is confirmed that this method was beneficial on SVM, especially on MNIST dataset, which have been caused by

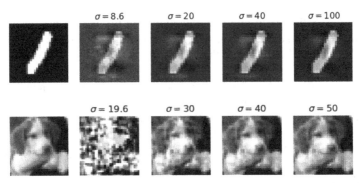

Fig. 3. Different defense effects. The figure on the top was the result obtained on the MNIST dataset. On the top row, the first picture is the original example, representing the digit '1', and the other four pictures are the adversarial samples generated by the initial sample under different kernel parameters, representing the digit '7'. The picture below shows the results of the CIFAR-10 dataset. On the bottom row, the first one is the original example, which represents 'dog'. The other four are the adversarial samples generated by the first one under different σ, which is meant 'cat'.

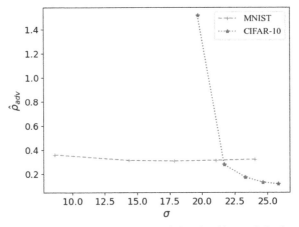

Fig. 4. Relation diagram between the robustness of the classifier and the kernel parameter on MNIST and CIFAR-10 datasets. As the value of σ increases, the robustness of the classifier will decrease. The performance is more obvious on the CIFAR-10 dataset.

nearly 100% misclassification. According to this phenomenon, we proposed a strategy for protecting SVMs against the adversarial attack. This defense approach is based on the kernel optimization of SVM. We extensively evaluate our proposed attack and defense algorithms on MNIST and CIRAR-10 datasets.

According to Fig. 3, we found that when the initial value of the σ, that is, the minimum value of its corresponding function A (see Fig. 2), was taken, there was the largest perturbation required to generate the adversarial sample, which means that the defenses are at their best. This finding holds for both datasets. The experimental results also show that our proposed defense method can effectively increase the price of attackers and achieve a robust performance (see Fig. 4). This gives the classifier's designer a better picture of the classifier performance under adversarial attacks.

In this paper, we first described a practical attack method which has already confirmed to be effective. Then we proposed a defense method which is based on kernel. The experimental results demonstrated that the defense method is useful and effective to the security of SVM. Finally, we believe that our work will inspire future research towards developing more secure learning algorithms against adversarial attacks.

Acknowledgments. This work is supported by the National Natural Science Foundation of China under Grant No. 61966011.

References

1. Vorobeychik, Y.: Adversarial machine learning. In: Synthesis Lectures on Artificial Intelligence and Machine Learning, vol. 12, no. (3) pp. 1–169 (2018)
2. Kumar, R.S.S.: Adversarial machine learning-industry perspectives. In: 2020 IEEE Security and Privacy Workshops (SPW), pp. 69–75. IEEE (2020)
3. Kianpour, M., Wen, S.-F.: Timing attacks on machine learning: state of the art. In: Bi, Y., Bhatia, R., Kapoor, S. (eds.) IntelliSys 2019. AISC, vol. 1037, pp. 111–125. Springer, Cham (2020). https://doi.org/10.1007/978-3-030-29516-5_10
4. Goodfellow, I.: Making machine learning robust against adversarial inputs. Commun. ACM **61**(7), 56–66 (2018)
5. Jati, A.: Adversarial attack and defense strategies for deep speaker recognition systems. Comput. Speech Lang. **68**, 101199 (2021)
6. Islam, M.S.: Efficient hardware malware detectors that are resilient to adversarial evasion. IEEE Trans. Comput. (2021)
7. Papernot, N.: Distillation as a defense to adversarial perturbations against deep neural networks. In: 2016 IEEE Symposium on Security and Privacy (SP), Washington, pp. 582–597. IEEE (2016)
8. Prakash, A.: Deflecting adversarial attacks with pixel deflection. In: Proceedings of the IEEE Conference on Computer Vision and Pattern Recognition, pp. 8571–8580 (2018)
9. Zheng, H.: Efficient adversarial training with transferable adversarial examples. In: Proceedings of the IEEE/CVF Conference on Computer Vision and Pattern Recognition, pp. 1181–1190 (2020)
10. Xu, J.: Adversarial defense via local flatness regularization. In: 2020 IEEE International Conference on Image Processing (ICIP), pp. 2196–2200. IEEE (2020)
11. Ma, Y., Guo, G. (eds.): Support Vector Machines Applications. Springer, Cham (2014). https://doi.org/10.1007/978-3-319-02300-7
12. Gu, J.: A novel approach to intrusion detection using SVM ensemble with feature augmentation. Comput. Secur. **86**, 53–62 (2019)
13. Zamil, Y.: Spam image email filtering using K-NN and SVM. Int. J. Electr. Comput. Eng. **9**(1), 2088–8708 (2019)
14. Biggio, B.: Wild patterns: ten years after the rise of adversarial machine learning. Pattern Recogn. **84**, 317–331 (2018)
15. Biggio, B.: Poisoning attacks against support vector machines. In: 29th International Conference on Machine Learning, pp.1807–1814. arXiv:1206.6389 (2012)
16. Koh,P.W.: Stronger data poisoning attacks break data sanitization defenses. arXiv:1811.00741 (2018)

17. Mei, S.: Using machine teaching to identify optimal training-set attacks on machine learners. In: Proceedings of the Twenty-Ninth AAAI Conference on Artificial Intelligence, pp. 2871–2877 (2015)
18. Xiao, H.: Is feature selection secure against training data poisoning? In: 32th International Conference on Machine Learning, pp. 1689–1698 (2015)
19. Xiao, X.: Adversarial label flips attack on support vector machines. In: ECAI, pp. 870–875 (2012)
20. Laishram, R.: Curie: A method for protecting SVM Classifier from Poisoning Attack. arXiv: 1606.01584 (2016)
21. Weerasinghe, S.: Support vector machines resilient against training data integrity attacks. Pattern Recogn. **96**, 106985 (2019)
22. Biggio, B., et al.: Evasion attacks against machine learning at test time. In: Blockeel, H., Kersting, K., Nijssen, S., Železný, F. (eds.) ECML PKDD 2013. LNCS (LNAI), vol. 8190, pp. 387–402. Springer, Heidelberg (2013). https://doi.org/10.1007/978-3-642-40994-3_25
23. Goodfellow, I.: Explaining and harnessing adversarial examples. arXiv:1412.6572 (2014)
24. Kurakin, A.: Adversarial machine learning at scale. arXiv:1611.01236 (2016)
25. Kurakin, A.: Adversarial examples in the physical world. arXiv:1607.02533 (2016)
26. Moosavi-Dezfooli, S.M.: Deepfool: a simple and accurate method to fool deep neural networks. In: Proceedings of the IEEE Conference on Computer Vision and Pattern Recognition, pp. 2574–2582 (2016)
27. Boser, B.E.: A training algorithm for optimal margin classifier. In: Proceedings of the Fifth Annual Workshop on Computational Learning Theory, pp.144–152 (1992)
28. LeCun, Y.: Gradient-based learning applied to document recognition. Proc. IEEE **86**(11), 2278–2324 (1998)
29. Krizhevsky, A.: Learning multiple layers of features from tiny images. Citeseer (2009)

An Empirical Study on the Status Quo of Higher Vocational Teachers' Informatization Teaching Ability – A Case Study of Hainan Province

Yi-nan Chen[✉], Peng Sun, and Xia Liu

Sanya Aviation and Tourism College, Sanya 572000, Hainan, China

Abstract. In order to understand the status quo of teachers' informatization teaching ability in Hainan higher vocational colleges, this study took teachers in Hainan higher vocational colleges as the survey samples and the survey was conducted from five perspectives including the teachers' awareness of informatization teaching, the design ability of informatization teaching, the implementation ability of informatization teaching, the teachers' demands for informatization training and their satisfaction with informatization environment. Then an empirical research was conducted through SPSS. The results showed that the teachers' satisfaction with the school's informatization environment would positively affect their awareness of informatization teaching, which would then positively affect their design ability of informatization teaching and demands for informatization training. Meanwhile, the teachers' design ability of informatization teaching would positively affect their implementation ability of informatization teaching. In this sense, higher vocational colleges should intensify the school's informatization environment, stipulate related policies to encourage information-based teaching, and provide informatization technology training in diversified manners to improve the teachers' initiative in informatization learning.

Keywords: Higher Vocational Teachers · Informatization · Teaching ability · Empirical research

1 Introduction

With the rise of the Internet, the wave of informatization has swept into the field of education, such as MOOC, micro-class, cloud class, rain classroom, etc. As pointed out in 2018 Education Informatization 2.0 Action Plan, it is necessary to transform from dedicated resources to large resources, from enhancing the students' application ability of informatization technology to enhancing the informatization technology literacy, from the application integration development to the innovation integrated development [1]. It indicates that the informatization technology has been widely applied to the field of education, but in order to adapt to the development of the times, deep-level changes are still in urgent demand, such as cultivating the concept of Internet resources, improving the teachers and students' informatization technology literacy, pioneering and innovation abilities, etc. In the course, the teachers are deemed as the founders of educational

© Springer Nature Switzerland AG 2021
J. Cheng et al. (Eds.): CSS 2020, LNCS 12653, pp. 43–57, 2021.
https://doi.org/10.1007/978-3-030-73671-2_5

informatization while the higher vocational colleges are playing an important role in higher and vocational education. Therefore, it is of great significance to improve the teachers' informatization teaching ability in higher vocational colleges.

The authors, in reference to domestic and foreign literatures, found out that domestic scholar Hu Xiaoyong et al. [2] took the initiative in proposing that the core competence of the teacher profession under the new tendency would lie in the informatization teaching ability, and pointed out the cultivation of informatization teaching ability from three perspectives; Gu Xiaoqing et al. [3] investigated the status quo and problems as encountered in the information-based professional development of teachers; Wang Weijun [4] believed that the teachers' informatization teaching ability should be developed dynamically in a stage-based process; Han Xibin et al. [5] surveyed and studied the informatization teaching ability of teachers in 28 universities and higher vocational colleges across the country. Foreign scholar Koehler et al. [6] proposed the "Technological Pedagogical Content Knowledge" (TPACK) model that deeply integrated subject knowledge, pedagogy and technology together [7], which has thus attracted widespread attentions from the academic community.

Meanwhile, the authors further retrieved related literatures precisely in core journals and periodicals with the key words "informatization teaching ability" in Chinese National Knowledge Infrastructure (CNKI). It is found that related research has been always in the growth and even become the hotspot with the advancement of education informatization in recent years. Up to now, there are totally 164 papers. In the process of sorting the above-mentioned literatures, the authors found that domestic and foreign scholars' research on informatization teaching ability mainly focused on the structure, status quo, problems and influencing factors as encountered by teachers in primary and middle schools, colleges and universities. By contrast, few empirical studies have been carried out on the status quo and the suggestions for improvement of teachers' informatization teaching ability in higher vocational colleges. Therefore, the authors commenced their survey from five perspectives including the teachers' awareness of informatization teaching [8], the design ability of informatization teaching [9], the implementation ability of informatization teaching [10], the teachers' demands for informatization training [11] and their satisfaction with the school's informatization environment [12], then reflected the status quo of the teachers' informatization teaching ability [13, 14] in Hainan's higher vocational colleges through data analysis, and finally provided suggestions for improvement in hope that such study can be referred by other higher vocational colleges to improve their teachers' informatization teaching ability and accelerate the informatization process of vocational colleges as a whole.

2 Description and Statistics

The frequency statistics of demographic variables as performed is shown in Table 1. Among the 201 tested samples, there are 130 females, accounting for 64.7%; the majority samples are of 31–40 years old, 108 people in total, accounting for 53.7%; the teaching age is mainly 5 years and below and 11–15 years, 87 and 58 people respectively, accounting for 72.2%; the majority samples are master graduates, 112 people in total, accounting for 55.7%; meanwhile, most samples have intermediate or no title, 75 and 52 respectively, accounting for 63.2% of the total.

Table 1. Sample allocation (N = 201)

Variable	Property	Frequency	Percentage (%)
Gender	Female	130	64.7
	Male	71	35.3
Age	30 years old and below	62	30.8
	31–40 years old	108	53.7
	41–50 years old	24	11.9
	Above 50 years old above	7	3.5
Teaching age	Above 20 years	9	4.5
	16–20 years	7	3.5
	11–15 years	58	28.9
	6–10 years	40	19.9
	5 years and below	87	43.3
Academic degree	Bachelor's Degree	77	38.3
	Master's Degree	112	55.7
	Doctoral Degree	4	2
	Others	8	4
Professional title	Senior title	7	3.5
	Vice senior title	31	15.4
	Intermediate title	75	37.3
	Primary title	36	17.9
	None	52	25.9

The frequency statistics of the multiple-choice question "Which courses did you mainly undertake?" is shown in Table 2. Among the tested samples, the majority are "professional basic courses", followed by "professional core courses" while the "public basic courses" take the minority.

Table 2. Multiple-choice question "which courses did you mainly undertake?"

Question	Property	Frequency	Percentage
What type of courses did you mainly undertake?	Public basic courses	68	33.80%
	Professional basic courses	121	60.20%
	Professional core courses	87	43.30%

The frequency statistics of the multiple-choice question "Which training have you ever participated in to improve your informatization teaching ability?" is shown in Table 3. Among the tested samples, those who have participated in "school-level training" take the majority, followed by those who have participated in the "provincial (including munici-pal) training" and "no training at all"; fewer have participated in the "national training", the "city-level training" and "Others".

Table 3. Multiple-choice question "Which training have you ever participated in to improve your informatization teaching ability?"

Question	Property	Frequency	Percentage
Which training have you ever participated in to improve your informatization teaching ability?	National training	18	9.00%
	Provincial (including municipal) training	65	32.30%
	City-level training	16	8.00%
	School-level training	105	52.20%
	None	57	28.40%
	Others	8	4.00%

The frequency statistics of the multiple-choice question "What kind of approaches/means/measures have been ever provided by the schools to improve the informatization teaching ability?" is shown in Table 4. "Training" is mostly selected, followed by "teaching support", "establishment of a professional teacher-oriented devel-opment platform/software/system", "technical support"; fewer schools prefer to "provide

Table 4. Multiple-choice question "What kind of approaches/means/measures have been ever provided by the schools to improve the informatization teaching ability?"

Question	Property	Frequency	Percentage
What kind of approaches/means/measures have been ever provided by the schools to improve the informatization teaching ability?	Provide training	152	75.60%
	Support academic visit	32	15.90%
	Carry out school-based research & training	32	15.90%
	Establish a study community	31	15.40%
	Establish a professional teacher-oriented development management department	40	19.90%
	Release policies & measures	44	21.90%
	Issue standard specifications	39	19.40%
	Provide technical support	62	30.80%
	Provide teaching support	70	34.80%
	Provide guarantee measures	49	24.40%
	Establish a professional teacher-oriented development platform/software/system	65	32.30%
	Others	31	15.40%

guarantee measures", "release policies & measures" "establish a professional teacher-oriented development management department", "issue standard specifications", "support academic visit", " carry out school-based research and training", "establish a study community" and "others".

The frequency statistics of the multiple-choice question "What kind of abilities do you expect to improve through informatization teaching ability training?" is shown in Table 5. The "courseware production technology" is mostly selected, followed by "informatization teaching design", "integrated technology pedagogy and competency", "use of subject teaching tool", "application of the informatization teaching/management platform", and then "downloading and application skills of online resources", "modern educational technology theory" and "basic operations of information technology" while "network security application" and "others" are rarely selected.

Table 5. Multiple-choice question "What kind of abilities do you expect to improve through informatization teaching ability training?"

Question	Property	Frequency	Percentage
What kind of abilities do you expect to improve through informatization teaching ability training?	Courseware production technology	130	64.70%
	Integrated technology pedagogy and competency	101	50.20%
	Modern educational technology theory	65	32.30%
	Use of subject teaching tools	92	45.80%
	Network security application	34	16.90%
	Application of the informatization teaching/management platform	91	45.30%
	Basic operations of information technology	65	32.30%
	Downloading and application skills of online resources	78	38.80%
	Informatization teaching design	118	58.70%
	Others	15	7.50%

The frequency statistics of the multiple-choice question "Where should the cultivation of teacher's informatization teaching ability start?" is shown in Table 6. The "design ability of informatization teaching" is mostly selected, followed by "edition and processing of audio and video elements", "PPT and other multimedia courseware production, development and improvement", further followed by "animation production", "development and application of online courses" and "image acquisition and processing" while "modern teaching technology theory", "office software" and "Office" are rarely selected.

Table 6. Multiple-choice question "Where should the cultivation of teacher's informatization teaching ability start?"

Question	Property	Frequency	Percentage
Where should the cultivation of teacher's informatization teaching ability start?	Modern teaching technology theory	86	42.80%
	Design ability of informatization teaching	146	72.60%
	Development and application of online courses	103	51.20%
	PPT and other multimedia courseware production, development and improvement	126	62.70%
	Office	70	34.80%
	Office software	73	36.30%
	Edition and processing of audio and video elements	127	63.20%
	Image acquisition and processing	96	47.80%
	Animation production	108	53.70%

The frequency statistics of the multiple-choice question about the "factors restricting the use of digital resources" is shown in Table 7. The "restrictions of downloading and copyright for resource use" and the "lack of supporting resources required for course teaching activities" are mostly selected, followed by "difficulty in searching for resources suitable for teaching goals due to incomplete and inaccurate resource description" and "difficulty in integrating resources from different sources into online courses" while the factor of "trouble in accessing resources by students" is rarely selected.

Table 7. Multiple-choice question about "factors restricting the use of digital resources"

Question	Property	Frequency	Percentage
Factors restricting the use of digital resources	Trouble in accessing resources by students	71	35.30%
	Restrictions of downloading and copyright for resource use	137	68.20%
	Lack of supporting resources required for course teaching activities	136	67.70%
	Difficulty in integrating resources from different sources into online courses	96	47.80%
	Difficulty in searching for resources suitable for teaching goals due to incomplete and inaccurate resource description	97	48.30%

The descriptive statistics of the application of informatization teaching resources to each teaching/research process is shown in Table 8. The scale is scored at 5 points with 3 as the median. The higher the score, the higher degree of application will be, and vice versa. The results of descriptive statistics show that the average value of course preparation, organization and implementation of teaching, online homework and testing, online Q&A and guidance, teaching evaluation and reflection are all above 3, indicating relatively high application of informatization teaching resources to such activities as mentioned above.

Table 8. Descriptive statistics of the application of informatization teaching resources to each teaching/research process

	Average	Standard deviation	Minimum	Maximum
Course preparation	3.92	0.777	2	5
Organization and implementation of teaching	3.81	0.766	2	5
Online homework and testing	3.73	0.943	1	5
Online Q&A and guidance	3.35	1.005	1	5
Teaching evaluation and reflection	3.43	0.963	1	5

The descriptive statistics of familiarity with the following commonly used teaching tools is shown in Table 9. The scale is scored at 5 points with 3 as the median. The higher the score, the higher the familiarity will be, and vice versa. The results of descriptive statistics show that the average value of information retrieval tools, office software and teaching resource production software are all above 3, indicating that the test objects' high familiarity with the information retrieval tools, office software, and teaching resource production software. Meanwhile, the average value of knowledge management tools is below 3, indicating the testing objects' lower familiarity with such knowledge management tools.

Table 9. Descriptive statistics of familiarity with the commonly used teaching tools

	Average	Standard deviation	Minimum	Maximum
Information retrieval tools	4.34	0.738	1	5
Office software	4.26	0.725	1	5
Teaching resource production software	3.29	0.875	1	5
Knowledge management tools	2.94	0.949	1	5

3 Reliability and Validity Test

The confirmatory factor analysis is adopted to test the questionnaire's structural validity and the analysis model is shown in Fig. 1.

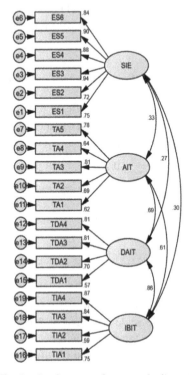

Fig. 1. Confirmatory factor analysis model

Note: ES: environment satisfaction; TA: teaching awareness; TDA: Teaching design ability; TIA: teaching implementation ability; SIE: satisfaction with informatization environment; AIT: awareness of informatization teaching; DAIT: design ability of informatization teaching; IBIT: implementation ability of informatization teaching.

The overall fitting of the confirmatory factor analysis model is shown in Table 10, in which, x2/df = 1.940 < 3, RMSEA = 0.069 < 0.08, RMR = 0.029 < 0.05, IFI = 0.943 > 0.9, TLI = 0.932 > 0.9, CFI = 0.942 > 0.9, the main fitting indexes have all reached the critical value range and it is thereby judged that the model can be fitted as a whole.

Table 10. Overall fitting result of the confirmatory factor analysis model

Fitting index	Critical value	Model fitting index	Fitting judgement
χ^2/df	<3	1.940	Yes
RMSEA	<0.08	0.069	Yes
RMR	<0.05	0.029	Yes
IFI	>0.9	0.943	Yes
TLI	>0.9	0.932	Yes
CFI	>0.9	0.942	Yes

The factor load and Cronbach's α coefficient of the confirmatory factor analysis model are shown in Table 11, from which it can be seen that all factor loads are above 0.5, indicating sound validity test results, and the Cronbach's α coefficients are all above 0.8, indicating sound reliability test results.

Table 11. Factor load and Cronbach's α coefficient

Latent variable	Composing indexes	Factor Load	Cronbach's α Coefficient
Satisfaction with Informatization environment	Satisfaction with Informatization environment 1	0.747	0.934
	Satisfaction with Informatization environment 2	0.722	
	Satisfaction with Informatization environment 3	0.944	
	Satisfaction with Informatization environment 4	0.876	
	Satisfaction with Informatization environment 5	0.902	
	Satisfaction with Informatization environment 6	0.843	
Design ability of informatization teaching	Design ability of informatization teaching 1	0.569	0.812
	Design ability of informatization teaching 2	0.697	
	Design ability of informatization teaching 3	0.807	

(*continued*)

Table 11. (*continued*)

Latent variable	Composing indexes	Factor Load	Cronbach's α Coefficient
	Design ability of informatization teaching 4	0.805	
Implementation ability of informatization teaching	Implementation ability of informatization teaching 1	0.746	0.839
	Implementation ability of informatization teaching 2	0.586	
	Implementation ability of informatization teaching 3	0.839	
	Implementation ability of informatization teaching 4	0.869	
Awareness of informatization teaching	Awareness of informatization teaching 1	0.618	0.820
	Awareness of informatization teaching 2	0.691	
	Awareness of informatization teaching 3	0.807	
	Awareness of informatization teaching 4	0.643	
	Awareness of informatization teaching 5	0.783	

4   Related Analysis

The descriptive statistics and the correlation analysis are carried out on the satisfaction with informatization environment, the awareness of informatization teaching, the design ability of informatization teaching, the implementation ability of informatization teaching, and the demand for informatization teaching ability training with the results shown in Table 12. The scale is scored at 5 points with 3 as the median. The results show that the average values are all above 3 from these five perspectives, indicating the test objects' relatively high scores in respect of their satisfaction with informatization environment, awareness of informatization teaching, design ability of informatization teaching, implementation ability of informatization teaching and training demand for informatization teaching ability. The result of correlation analysis shows a significant positive correlation between any two variables ($p < 0.01$) among such three variables as the satisfaction with informatization environment, the awareness of informatization teaching and the design ability of informatization teaching, a significant positive correlation only between the demand for teaching ability training and the awareness of informatization teaching ($p < 0.001$), but no significant correlation between the demand for informatization teaching ability training and other variables ($p > 0.05$).

Table 12. Descriptive statistics and correlation analysis

	Satisfaction with informatization environment	Awareness of informatization teaching	Design ability of informatization teaching	Implementation ability of informatization teaching	Demand for informatization teaching ability training
Satisfaction with informatization environment	1				
Awareness of informatization teaching	0.296***	1			
Design ability of informatization teaching	0.216**	0.56***	1		
Implementation ability of informatization teaching	0.265***	0.536***	0.732***	1	
Demand for informatization teaching ability training	0.134	0.245***	0.02	0.03	1
Average value M	3.24	4.08	3.66	3.55	4.27
Standard deviation SD	0.762	0.539	0.584	0.622	0.735

Note: * means $p < 0.05$, ** means $p < 0.01$, *** means $p < 0.001$

5 Structural Equation Model

A structural equation model is established to examine the relationship among the satisfaction with informatization environment, the awareness of informatization teaching, the design ability of informatization teaching, the implementation ability of informatization teaching, and the demand for informatization teaching ability training. The structural equation model is shown in Fig. 2.

Note: TIA: teaching implementation ability; ES: environment satisfaction; IAIT: implementation ability of informatization teaching; SIE: satisfaction with informatization environment; DITAT: demand for informatization teaching ability training; AIT: awareness of informatization teaching; DAIT: Design ability of informatization teaching; TA: teaching awareness; TDA: Teaching design ability.

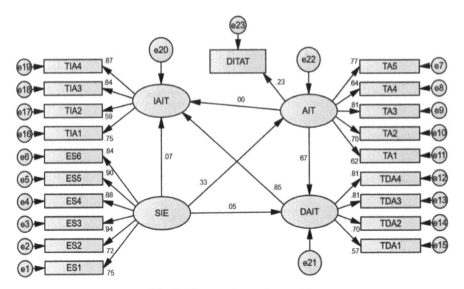

Fig. 2. Structural equation model

The main fitting indexes of the structural equation model are shown in Table 13. Among them, x2/df = 1.971 < 3, RMSEA = 0.07 < 0.08, RMR = 0.032 < 0.05, IFI = 0.934 > 0.9, TLI = 0.923 > 0.9, CFI = 0.934 > 0.9 have all reached the range that can be fitted, so it is judged the structural equation model is acceptable.

Table 13. Overall Fitting result of the structural equation model

Model fitting index	Critical value	Research model	Fitting judgement
χ^2/df	<3	1.971	Yes
RMSEA	<0.08	0.070	Yes
RMR	<0.05	0.032	Yes
IFI	>0.9	0.934	Yes
TLI	>0.9	0.923	Yes
CFI	>0.9	0.934	Yes

The path coefficients of the structural equation model are shown in Table 14. The results show that the satisfaction with informatization environment exerts significantly positive impacts on the awareness of informatization teaching ($\beta = 0.331, t = 4.143, p < 0.001$) but has no significant influence on the design ability of informatization teaching and the implementation ability of informatization teaching ($\beta = 0.052, t = 0.742, p > 0.05; \beta = 0.067, t = 1.182, p > 0.05$). The design ability of informatization teaching exerts significantly positive impacts on the implementation ability of informatization teaching ($\beta = 0.848, t = 7.467, p < 0.001$). The awareness of informatization teaching exerts significantly positive impacts on the design ability of informatization teaching and the demands for informatization teaching ability training ($\beta = 0.667$, t $= 7.501$, p < 0.001; $\beta = 0.234$, t $= 3.103$, p < 0.01), but has no significant influence on the implementation ability of informatization teaching ($\beta = -0.003$, t $= -0.036$, p > 0.05).

Table 14. Path coefficients of the structural equation model

Influence path	β	S.E	C.R	P
Satisfaction with informatization environment → Awareness of informatization teaching	0.331	0.053	4.143	***
Satisfaction with informatization environment → Design ability of informatization teaching	0.052	0.059	0.742	0.458
Awareness of informatization teaching → Design ability of informatization teaching	0.667	0.114	7.501	***
Satisfaction with informatization environment → Implementation ability of informatization teaching	0.067	0.047	1.182	0.237
Awareness of informatization teaching → Implementation ability of informatization teaching	−0.003	0.113	−0.036	0.971
Design ability of informatization teaching → Implementation ability of informatization teaching	0.848	0.111	7.467	***
Awareness of informatization teaching → Demands for informatization teaching ability training	0.234	0.121	3.103	0.002

Note: *** means p < 0.001

6 Conclusion

The top priority of higher vocational education is to cultivate high-skilled talents working at the frontline in that the faculties team will directly affect the quality of talent cultivation in higher vocational colleges. Based on the description of the status quo of faculties engaged in the questionnaire, the females accounted for more than half in terms of gender, those with the master's degree accounted for 55.7%, those with the teaching age of 5 years or below accounted for 77.2%, and those with the intermediate titles took the majority. All these data indicate that there are more young teachers with intermediate titles among the test objects and they have mastered certain information technology abilities. The data of multiple-choice questions indicate that higher vocational colleges usually provide school-level information teaching ability training for the tested objects to improve their ability of information teaching. Moreover, the tested objects are more familiar with information retrieval tools, office software and teaching resource production software but with lower familiarity with knowledge management tools.

A factor analysis of factors such as awareness of informatization teaching, design ability of informatization teaching, implementation ability of informatization teaching, and satisfaction with informatization environment was carried out. The results showed significant positive correlation between any of the two factors among the satisfaction with informatization environment, the awareness of informatization teaching and the design ability of informatization teaching, and the significant positive correlation only between the demand for informatization teaching ability training and the awareness of informatization teaching. A structural equation model was established to verify factors such as the awareness of informatization teaching, the design ability of informatization teaching, the implementation ability of informatization teaching, the satisfaction of informatization environment, and the demand for informatization teaching ability training, etc. The results showed significant positive impacts exerted by the satisfaction of informatization environment on the awareness of informatization teaching, the significant positive impacts exerted by the awareness of informatization teaching on the design ability of informatization teaching and the demands for informatization teaching ability training, and the significant positive impacts exerted by the design ability of informatization teaching on the implementation ability of informatization teaching.

Therefore, higher vocational colleges should enhance the school's informatization construction not only by providing hardware guarantees such as campus network construction and equipment procurement, but also providing software supports such as high-quality network platform, teaching resources construction or sharing, etc. At the same time, the schools should issue relevant policies to encourage and advocate teachers to apply informatization teaching, optimize the informatization environment to improve the teachers' awareness of informatization teaching and promote teachers to actively study and apply informatization skills. In addition, higher vocational colleges can also provide differentiated and multi-level training based on the teachers' informatization competency to better promote the teachers' design and implementation abilities of informatization teaching.

Acknowledgment. Project supported by the Education Department of Hainan Province, project number: Hnjg2020-161.

References

1. Tong,Y.: Research on the problems and countermeasures of educational informatization in China. J. Sichuan Vocat. Tech. Coll. **29**(06), 117–120+162 (2019)
2. Hu, X., Zhu, Z.: Perspectives of teachers education in e-education. China Audiov. Educ. **06**, 25–27 (2003)
3. Gu, X., Zhu, Z., Pang, Y.: Teachers' informatization professional development: status quo and problems. China Acad. J. Electron. Publ. House **01**, 12–18 (2004)
4. Wang, W.: A Study on the Development of Teachers' Informationized Teaching Ability. Northwest Normal University (2009)
5. Han, X., Ge, W.: Investigation and research on the informatization teaching ability of Chinese university teachers. China Higher Educ. Res. **07**, 53–59 (2018)
6. Shah, S., Murtaza, A.: An investigation into the application of educational technology at higher educational institutions. Theory Pract. Lang. Stud. **2**(7), 1420–1429 (2012)
7. Liu, L., Dai, X.: Research on the cultivation of pre-service teachers' informatization teaching ability from the perspective of TPACK theory. Softw. Guide **18**(12), 267–270+276 (2019)

8. Huang, J.: Investigation on the status quo and improvement countermeasures of teachers' informatization teaching ability in higher vocational colleges. Educ. Vocation **16**, 105–108 (2018)

9. Song, M.: Research on the evaluation system and improvement countermeasures of young teachers' informatization teaching ability. China Manag. Informationization **23**(11), 231–233 (2020)

10. Liang, Y., Jiang, L., Zhao, C., et al.: Research on the status quo and development strategy of teachers' informatization teaching ability in vocational colleges -- taking 5 vocational colleges in W City as study cases. e-Educ. Res. **37**(04), 107–113 (2016)

11. Jie, M.: Strategies for young teachers' information-based teaching ability cultivation. Heilongjiang Res. High. Educ. **36**(11), 92–94 (2018)

12. Jiang, Y., Xing, X., Tong, Y.: The status quo, problems and development path of vocational education informatization in 2.0 era. China Educ. Technol. **07**, 119–124 (2020)

13. Liu, X., Ou, Z., Li, Y., et al.: An empirical study on the status quo of public course teachers in hainan vocational college. J. Hainan Radio TV Univ. **20**(02), 150–158 (2019)

14. Chen, Y., Liu, X.: An empirical study on the status quo of public computer teachers in hainan higher vocational colleges. J. Liaoning High. Vocat. **21**(04), 85–89 (2019)

Reliability Optimization and Trust Computing of Composite Wing Based on Sparse PC Method

Li Miao[✉], Wang Lei, and Xu Chao

Beijing Institute of Special Mechanic-Electric, Beijing 100012, China
limiaopla@sina.com

Abstract. The accuracy and efficiency of uncertainty analysis, as well as its trust computing, have key influences on the reliability optimization results, so the research on uncertainty analysis method is particularly important. Although the traditional Monte Carlo method can ensure the accuracy of optimization, it takes too long time, which limits its potential application on engineering. High precision uncertainty analysis and optimization design based directly on the simulation model are usually faced with large amount of calculation problem, and tend to have different accuracy in aircraft design and calculation of simulation analysis model (such as different aerodynamic analysis model of grid density). To guarantee the reliability, trust computing is necessary. Making full use of the integration of these models, as well as reducing the number of calls for high precision model, is one of the effective ways to improve the efficiency of aircraft design. In this paper, the uncertainty analysis method based on PC theory is adopted to optimize the airfoil reliability, which greatly reduces the calculation time and improves the efficiency of optimal design while maintaining the accuracy.

Keywords: Uncertainty analysis · Polynomial-chaos · Reliability analysis

1 Introduction

Due to requirement of lightweight structure, the research and development of aircraft structure design has been closely related to the use of new materials with superior performance [1–5]. Advanced composites have many excellent properties, such as high specific strength and specific modulus, designable properties and easy integral forming. When it is used to aircraft structure, the weight of aircraft structure can be reduced considerably, and its aeroelastic characteristics as well as the flight performance can be improved [6, 7]. The structural design of composite materials is the key to the scientific and reasonable application of composite materials in structure and the reduction of life cycle cost. The point is to make full use of direction of composite performance and design ability of structural performance to achieve comprehensive optimization among structure, performance and cost [8, 9].

© Springer Nature Switzerland AG 2021
J. Cheng et al. (Eds.): CSS 2020, LNCS 12653, pp. 58–66, 2021.
https://doi.org/10.1007/978-3-030-73671-2_6

The whole life cycle of aircraft is full of uncertainties, such as payload, engine thrust, working environment, design parameters and so on. They have an important impact on the performance of aircraft, even the life cycle of using ensures safety and maintenance costs. Therefore, how to improve the reliability of the aircraft, while maintaining its high performance, has become an urgent problem.

In response to above requirements, the method of Design Optimization under Uncertainty combining with trust computing gradually rise. It pays attention to the uncertainty in the initial stage of design, the influence of uncertain factors as a constraint condition or a part of the performance index is directly brought into the optimization design process. The robustness and reliability of the design scheme are comprehensively improved while pursuing optimal performance, which provides a new idea for promoting the product design level and has been widely used in many fields [10, 11]. For uncertainty analysis, the traditional Monte Carlo Simulation method has high accuracy, but too much calculation is needed. As a new method of uncertainty analysis, Polynomial-chaos (PC) method has been widely studied and applied because of its solid mathematical foundation and fast convergence speed [12–14]. The Polynomial-chaos method expresses the random output response as a weighted sum of a series of orthogonal polynomials, it is equivalent to build a random surrogate model of the original random variables, and the uncertainty analysis is carried out directly on the surrogate model, which greatly reduces the calculation compared with Monte Carlo Simulation method.

This paper focuses on the optimization design of aircraft to improve the reliability. In view of above problems, it takes the reliability analysis and trust computing in the project as an example, and is based on PC theory with great potential of engineering application, propose methods and strategies. To improve the accuracy and efficiency of the uncertainty analysis of PC method, and to expand its scope of application, lay a solid foundation for aircraft design with high quality, high level and high efficiency [15].

2 Description of Reliability Optimization Problem for Composite Wing

2.1 Finite Element Analysis Modeling and Parameterization

Wing box is the main load-bearing structure of a wing surface, which mainly includes skin, girder, core and other structural elements. Select airfoil B-8306-b, as shown in Fig. 1.

Fig. 1. Airfoil B-8306-b

Table 1 shows the relevant parameters for establishing the geometric model.

Table 1. Wing geometric parameters

UAV quality	Reference wing area	Top root ratio	Aspect ratio	Sweep angle of quarter chord leading edge
$W = 5$ kg	$s = 0.16$ m^2	$\lambda = 0.67$	$A = 10.15$	$\Lambda_{c/4} = 10°$

The overall shape parameters of the airfoil can be obtained, then 20 control points are selected to parameterize the upper and lower sections of the airfoil, and solid works is used to carry out parameterized modeling. In the design process, since the spars are very close to the leading and trailing edges, the regions between the front and front parts and these between the rear and rear parts can be ignored in modeling, then the simplified wing model is obtained. The obtained wing model was imported into ABAQUS for meshing and finite element analysis.

A 4-node 2D network is used for surface partition and an 8-node 3D network is used for solid partition. The load distributions on the upper and lower surfaces of the wing are shown in Fig. 2(a). If it is not easy to apply load on the model by this curve, considering the actual situation, we can simplify it within the range of accuracy allowed, and the required load is approximately as shown in Fig. 2(b).

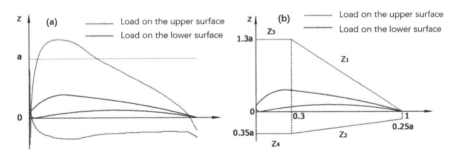

Fig. 2. Load profile

In Fig. 2, a is a constant factor that yields $a = 2.64 \times 10^{-4}$ MPa when balanced against the load on the wings and the weight of the drone. According to the geometric relationship, it can be obtained that the chord length of any section is $c = c_r - \frac{c_r - c_l}{b/2}$, thus, the pressure distribution of the upper surface of the wing z_1, z_3 and the pressure distribution of the lower surface z_3, z_2, z_4 are obtained.

$$z_1 = 4.9 \times \left(1 - \frac{x - 0.195y}{157.135 - 0.1784y}\right) \times 10^{-4} \text{ MPa}$$

$$z_2 = \left(10.37 - \frac{3.77(x - 0.195y)}{157.135 - 0.0784y}\right) \times 10^{-5} \text{ MPa}$$

$$z_3 = 3.432 \times 10^{-4} \text{ MPa}$$

$$z_4 = 9.24 \times 10^{-5} \text{ MPa}$$

Since the wings are fixed to the fuselage, a constraint is created at the root chord section, making both displacement and rotation angles zero. The material used for the core is expanded polyurethane foam, its elastic modulus is $E = 5.7$ MPa, shear modulus is $G = 3$ MPa, the density is 0.04 g/cm^3. The material used in the beam is red pine, its elastic modulus is $E = 10400$ MPa, the density is 0.5 g/cm^3. The material used for the skin is carbon cloth/epoxy resin G803/5224, its single layer thickness is 0.2 mm, the density is 1.4 g/cm^3. The lower skin is in tension due to compression of the upper skin, carbon cloth is a two-dimensional anisotropic material, its tensile and compressive properties are not necessarily the same. In order to achieve the best performance of the wing, the upper and lower surface of the skin can change the direction of ply to achieve the best performance of the skin. When creating composites, the number of layers is a variable 3 layers, and the lamination style is 3 layers orthogonal lamination.

A geometric model of a composite wing is shown in Fig. 3.

Fig. 3. Sketch diagram of composite wing geometry model

2.2 Mathematical Model of Reliability Optimization

By designing the geometric parameters of the airfoil, the optimization problem minimizes the mass of the wing, and satisfies the constraints of maximum thickness stress and maximum strain. Define $X = [x_1, x_2, ..., x_{20}, \alpha]$ as the control point for the airfoil, let the ply closest to the skin on the upper and lower airfoils be the first ply, α is the angle of the first layer of the composite, Y is the average value of the maximum stress, Z is the average value of the maximum strain, P_f is the probability of failure. The mathematical model of reliability optimization design of composite wing is expressed as follows:

$$
\begin{aligned}
&\text{Min } M(X) \\
&\text{s.t. } P_f(Y \geq 15 \text{ MPa}) \leq 0.001 \\
&\qquad P_f(Z \geq 3 \text{ mm}) \leq 0.001
\end{aligned}
\tag{1}
$$

The number of control points on both upper and lower surfaces of the airfoil is 10, totaling 20. Because the three layers are orthogonal, the stacking angle of the other two layers can be obtained by determining the stacking angle of the first layer. In the uncertainty analysis, it is assumed that the stacking angles of the first and third skin layers of the upper and lower airfoils are the same in a three-layer orthogonally laminated skin, and then the uncertainty exists in the stacking angles of the first and third skin layers and in the stacking angle of the second skin layer, therefore, there are two uncertainty variables. 22 variables including 20 airfoil control points and 2 ply angles are used as uncertain variables to optimize the reliability. Let the airfoil control points follow normal distribution, their ordinates are taken as mean values, their variances are 0.015^2 and the range of variation is ± 5 mm, the stacking angle of the first and second layers has an average value of $[90°, 0°]$, a variance of 0.5^2, and a variation range of $\pm 30°$.

For this optimization design problem, although PC method has better mathematical theoretical basis and application conditions, but when facing a high dimension problem, it is easy to appear singular matrix in the calculation, which will produce a very large amount of calculation and reduce the calculation accuracy. In this case, sparse chaotic polynomial method can be used to omit the relatively unimportant orthogonal polynomial, so as to reduce the amount of calculation and avoid the dimension disaster. The PC coefficient is calculate by using that technique of minimum angle regression and serial sample, in the following optimization results, it is difficult to get the results of the full order PC model due to the dimension disaster problem, while the sparse PC method can achieve the desired accuracy by using only 2976 sample points to construct the model, which significantly improves the calculation speed.

3 Sparse PC Method

Polynomial Expansions (PC) method has been widely used in practical engineering because of its solid mathematical foundation and efficient performance of uncertainty analysis. It uses a weighted sum of orthogonal polynomials to construct a surrogate model between random input and random response of the system, the statistical moments, the failure probability and the probability density function of the system response are obtained. The PC method is mainly based on the theory of chaotic polynomial, which can accurately describe the randomness of random variables with arbitrary distribution.

The PC model can be approximated as:

$$y \approx \sum_{i=0}^{P} b_i \phi_i\ x \tag{2}$$

were $\phi_i\ x$ stands for multi-dimensional orthogonal polynomials and can be expressed as the product of each orthogonal polynomial, b_i is the PC coefficient to be solved.

PC method basically assumes that each dimensional random input variable has a complete probability distribution function, and more extensive applicability and application potential. However, in the calculation of PC coefficients, we only use regression method to study the low-dimensional uncertainty analysis problems, but in high-dimensional cases, it is easy to appear the matrix ill-conditioned situation, which seriously affects the calculation accuracy and efficiency. In this paper, the adaptive sparse chaotic polynomial method is used to deal with the correlation of random input variables. This method directly constructs the multivariate orthogonal polynomial by matching the mixed moments of the input variables from zero to a certain order. For the rest of the independent random input variables, the corresponding one-dimensional orthogonal polynomials are constructed by the existing PC method, and then the PC model is constructed by tensor product operation on the orthogonal polynomials above.

The sparse PC approach can be approximated as

$$y \approx \sum_{i=0}^{Q} b_i \Phi_i \ \ x = \sum_{i=0}^{Q} b_i \big[P_c\ x_1, \dots, x_l \ \otimes \ P\ x_{l+1}, \dots, x_d \big]^i \tag{3}$$

where b_i is the unknown PC coefficient, $Q = (d + H)!/(d!H!) - 1$; $P_c(x_1, \cdots, x_l)$ and $P(x_{l+1}, \cdots, x_d)$ are the sets of multivariate orthogonal polynomials corresponding to the correlated random variable $(x_1, \cdots, x_l)$ and the independent random variable $(x_{l+1}, \cdots, x_d)$, respectively. A is a tensor product operating symbol, and $Q + 1$ orthogonal polynomials $\Phi(x)$ of order H are obtained.

4   Results and Analysis

Table 2 is a comparison of the mean values of maximum stresses and displacements and the probabilities of stresses and displacements for the original, deterministic and reliability-optimized airfoils.

Table 2. Optimized result

	Original wing	Reliability optimization	Deterministic optimization
Mass Mean Value(g)	168.7542	152.6123	149.6958
Mean maximum stress (MPa)	17.588	14.871	16.17
Mean maximum displacement (mm)	3.019	2.590	2.808
Pf (mises ≥ 15 Mpa)	1	0.0003	1
Pf (MaxU ≥ 3 mm)	1	0	0
First skin ply angle (°)	90	113	102
Number of model calls	/	581	2976

Several conclusions can be obtained. The first, the deterministic optimization significantly reduces the mean mass of the airfoil, which is about 11.29% less than the original airfoil. However, the failure probability of the stress reaches 1, which is far from meeting the constraints. Compared with the original airfoil, the mean value of mass, maximum stress and maximum displacement are reduced, and the constraints of failure probability are satisfied, which increases the reliability. Secondly, the overlay angles of the original, deterministic and reliability-optimized airfoils show that the overlay angles of anisotropic materials have a great influence on the performance of the airfoil skin, so it is necessary to redesign the overlay angle and mode according to different working conditions. The third, PC method has more obvious computational advantage than Monte Carlo method which needs 10000 times of all. SDD-PC method is less computational advantage in solving high-dimensional problems. The fourth, the effect of the shape of the airfoil section on airfoil performance can be derived from the reliability optimization in Fig. 4 by comparing the cross section with the original airfoil. Although the deterministically optimized airfoil uses less material than the original airfoil, it has a smoother section shape and reduces the stress concentration.

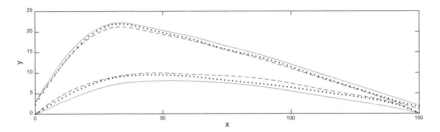

Fig. 4. Airfoil configuration comparison

Figure 4 is a comparison of the shapes of the original airfoil, the deterministically optimized airfoil and the reliability-optimized airfoil.

Figure 5 A stress drawing of the original airfoil, the deterministically optimized airfoil and the reliability-optimized airfoil.

Since the stresses are concentrated on the upper wing surface, Fig. 5 shows the upper wing surface stress distribution. It can see that the stress is mainly concentrated on the wing bending of the upper wing surface, where the wing is thicker and the deformation resistance is strong, so that the stress is easy to concentrate. The leading edge and trailing edge of the wing due to the existence of the beam, the stress is also more concentrated, to cloud the stress is greater than the surrounding skin position, in line with the actual situation.

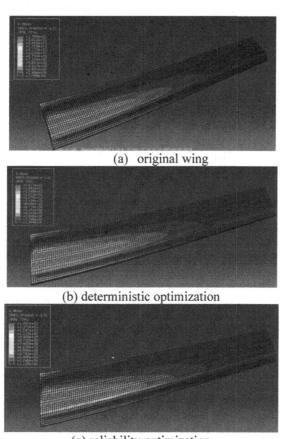

(a) original wing

(b) deterministic optimization

(c) reliability optimization

Fig. 5. Stress drawing of airfoil

5   Conclusion

In this paper, the sparse chaotic polynomial (SSD-PC) method is applied to the robust optimization design for B-8306-b airfoil, and the reliability optimization of airfoil and the trust computing about the optimization is carried out. Under the premise of ensuring accuracy, the efficiency of optimization design is further improved compared with Monte Carlo method and traditional PC method. In addition, compared with the traditional PC method, SSD-PC method can not only perform the uncertainty analysis of correlated random input systems more accurately, but also significantly reduce the amount of calculation and alleviate the dimension disaster.

The effectiveness and great application potential of the input dependent adaptive SSD-PC method are verified by engineering simulations of this paper.

References

1. Molent, L., Haddad, A.: A critical review of available composite damage growth test data under fatigue loading and implications for aircraft sustainment. Compos. Struct. **232**, 111568 (2020)
2. Towsyfyan, H., Biguri, A., Boardman, R., Blumensath, T.: Successes and challenges in non-destructive testing of aircraft composite structures. Chin. J. Aeronaut. (2019)
3. Romano, F., Sorrentino, A., Pellone, L., Mercurio, U., Notarnicola, L.: New design paradigms and approaches for aircraft composite structures. Multiscale Multidiscip. Model. Exp. Des. **2**(2), 75–87 (2018). https://doi.org/10.1007/s41939-018-0034-8
4. Aly, A., Colton, J.: The design and manufacturing of fluidic oscillators for composite aircraft structures. Proc. Inst. Mech. Eng. Part B J. Eng. Manuf. **233**(4), 1250–1259 (2019)
5. Liu, T., Ge, J.B., Peng, G.: Structural design of composite laminates in sunken area. J. Nanjing Univ. Aeronaut. Astronaut. **51**, 41–47 (2019). (in Chinese)
6. Tong, M.B., Liang, H.: Structural strength analysis of aircraft based on multi-scale method. J. Nanjing Univ. Aeronaut. Astronaut. **51**, 16–23 (2019). (in Chinese)
7. Calado, E.A., Leite, M., Silva, A.: Selecting composite materials considering cost and environmental impact in the early phases of aircraft structure design. J. Clean. Prod. **186**, 113–122 (2018)
8. Shroff, S., Acar, E., Kassapoglou, C.: Design, analysis, fabrication, and testing of composite grid-stiffened panels for aircraft structures. Thin-Walled Struct. **119**, 235–246 (2017)
9. Anwar, W., Khan, M.Z., Israr, A., Mehmood, S., Anjum, N.A.: Effect of structural dynamic characteristics on fatigue and damage tolerance of aerospace grade composite materials. Aerosp. Sci. Technol. **64**, 39–51 (2017)
10. Taguchi, G.: Taguchi on Robust Technology Development: Bringing Quality Engineering Up Stream. ASME Press, New York (1993)
11. Du, X., Chen, W.: Towards a better understanding of modeling feasibility robustness in engineering design. J. Mech. Des. **122**, 385–394 (1999)
12. Gao, C.W., Liu, M.J., Green, W.H.: Uncertainty analysis of correlated parameters in automated reaction mechanism generation. Int. J. Chem. Kinetics **52**, 266–282 (2020)
13. Yu, H., Gillot, F., Ichchou, M.: A polynomial chaos expansion based reliability method for linear random structures. Adv. Struct. Eng. **15**(12), 2097–2111 (2012)
14. Xiu, D., Karniadakis, G.: The wiener-askey polynomial chaos for stochastic differential equations. SIAM J. Sci. Comput. **24**, 619–644 (2002)
15. Rackwitz, R., Flessler, B.: Structural reliability under combined random load sequences. Comput. Struct. **9**, 489–494 (1978)

Malware Variants Detection Based on Feature Fusion

Jianbin Mai[1,2,3(✉)], Chunjie Cao[1,2,3(✉)], and Qian Wu[1,3]

[1] Key Laboratory of Internet Information Retrieval of Hainan Province,
Haikou 570228, Hainan, China
[2] College of Cryptography, Hainan University, Haikou 570228, Hainan, China
[3] College of Computer and Cyberspace Security, Hainan University,
Haikou 570228, Hainan, China

Abstract. Being able to detect malware variants is an important problem due to the rapid development and the security threats of new malware variations. Machine learning methods are currently one of the most popular malware variant detection methods, however, most of these methods only use single type of features (e.g. opcode) and shallow learning algorithms (e.g. SVM), which also makes these methods have demonstrated poor detection accuracy and low detection speeds. In this paper, we propose a method that combines multiple features of malware with deep learning methods to optimize the detection of malware variants. To implement the proposed method, we use Deep Convolutional Neural Network (DCNN) and Information Gain (IG) to extract effective features from the grayscale map and disassembly file mapped from the malware, respectively. Then we construct a fusion feature space by combining the different types of extracted features and use it to train a Multilayer Perceptron (MLP) to obtain results. The experimental results demonstrated that our method achieved good accuracy as compared with other common malware detection methods.

Keywords: Malware variants · Deep convolutional neural network · Information gain · Fusion feature space

1 Introduction

With the rapid development of information technology, malware has become one of the main threats to network security. The 2019 safety report from Rising Company shows that the number of malware infections reached 1.125 billion in 2018, an increase of 55.63% over the same period last year. Among then, the number of malware variants has increased by 78% compared to last year's total [1]. One of the main reasons for the exponential growth of malware variants is that malware variants is that malware developers widely use techniques such as obfuscation and encryption to circumvent antivirus detection [2], which makes the original malware appear diversified and polymorphic. And this change has posed severe challenges to the current malware variant detection technology.

© Springer Nature Switzerland AG 2021
J. Cheng et al. (Eds.): CSS 2020, LNCS 12653, pp. 67–77, 2021.
https://doi.org/10.1007/978-3-030-73671-2_7

The rapid growth in the number of malware variants forced researchers to propose detection methods that combine machine learning methods with static or dynamic features of malware, such as malware detection methods based on KNN [3] or RF [4], etc. And this type of method has become one of the common malware detection methods due to its simple operation and high detection efficiency.

However, these methods also face challenges. First of all, most of these methods use a single type of data feature (e.g. opcode) [5]. Since a single type of method will lose some useful information, it may produce unreliable results in the detection. Secondly, most of these methods use shallow learning algorithms (e.g. SVM) [6]. In the case of a large number of data samples, their accuracy and speed will be severely limited.

In this context, the researchers proposed to combine the malware families with static detection to improve the ability of malware variant detection. Research shows that malware variants from the same family usually have similar logic or behavior [7], so determine the similarity between malware by classifying malware families can help determine whether the malware is a variant of a known family.

Based on the above research, we propose a detection method based on the combination of multiple features of malware and malware families. In the proposed method, we use deep convolutional networks and information gain to extract high-dimensional forward image features and useful opcode features from malware grayscale images and malware assembly files mapped from the malware of different families, respectively. Then we combine these two different features to construct a fusion space, and use it to train a multilayer perceptron to get our detection model.

In this paper, we use the malware dataset released by Microsoft [8] as a sample to experiment with the proposed method. In the experiment, we compare the proposed method with the current common methods in the detection accuracy and time of different types of malware to prove the performance of our method.

2   Related Work

In this section, we will introduce relevant research on current malware detection, including detection based on feature analysis, detection based on visualization technology, detection based on deep learning.

2.1   Malware Detection Based on Feature Analysis

Malware detection technologies based on feature analysis methods are mainly divided into static analysis and dynamic analysis. Static analysis mainly uses static information such as the text content of the malware code and the bytecode of the malware as the features of detection and classification [9]. Compared with the traditional heuristic detection method [10], this method has higher efficiency and lower false alarm rate. But its disadvantage is that a single type of feature is easily affected by the obfuscation technique and produces an unreliable detection results. Dynamic analysis method mainly uses the behavior of the malware at runtime as a feature. For example, Kolosnjai et al. [11] proposed that the detection method based on graph matching to analyze the behavior of malicious samples is realized by using dynamic features such as system calls. However, when the execution environment does not comply with the rules, the dynamic signature analysis method may ignore certain types of malware.

2.2 Malware Detection Based on Visualization Technology

In order to prevent the interference of obfuscation technology, the researchers proposed to combine image processing technology with malware detection. Goodall et al. [12] proposed a visualization method of malware behavior that aggregates the results of malware behavior analysis by different malware tools into one environment. This method effectively optimizes the problem of low coverage of single detection tool. Nataraj et al. [13] proposed a method of directly converting executable files into grayscale images, then using GIST [14] to calculate image texture features and combining with machine learning models for detection. But most of these methods face the problem of high time cost when extracting complex image features, so their efficiency will be low in the case of large-scale data samples.

2.3 Malware Detection Based on Deep Learning

In recent years, deep learning has achieved good performance in image understanding and classification [15]. This type of method is characterized by the ability to automatically extract effective high-dimensional features, so some researchers have proposed applying deep learning methods to malware detection. Cui et al. [16] proposed an end-to-end malware variant detection method that combines convolutional neural networks and malware visualization technology, this method effectively improves the accuracy and efficiency of malware variant detection. However, the model proposed by Cui is only a relatively shallow convolution, so the extracted features are still shallow in nature.

3   Features and Models

This section presents our proposed malware variant detection method based on feature fusion, which included: Gray image feature extraction based on deep convolutional network (DCNN), Important opcode feature extraction based on information gain (IG), Design of malware variant detection model based on feature fusion.

3.1   Gray Image Feature Extraction Based on DCNN

Malware visualization can effectively prevent obfuscation technology has already been proven by Nataraj. To improve the ability of our malware variants method, we use the malware grayscale image as one of the features we choose.

Figure 1 shows images of malware from different families. As we can see, malware belonging to the same family usually has similar texture features, while variants of different families have obvious differences. This because most of the new malware are variants of existing malware series, which have similar behavioral logic or the same behavioral purpose. Therefore, we can use this visual similarity to detect malware variants.

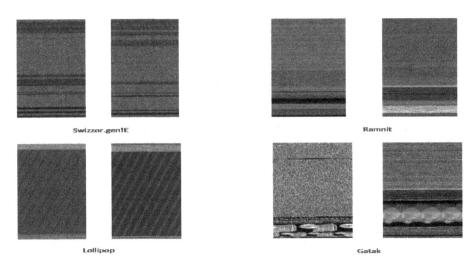

Fig. 1. Grayscale images from different families

Compared with the DBN and SAE, the advantage of DCNN is that it has a network structure with shared receptive fields and weights, which makes convolution not affected by complex features and data reconstruction during data feature extraction. In our method, we combined DCNN to construct a network to extract high-dimensional features from grayscale images based on the visual similarity of malware variants from the same family. Figure 2 shows our 32-layer deep convolutional network based on the VGG-16 framework.

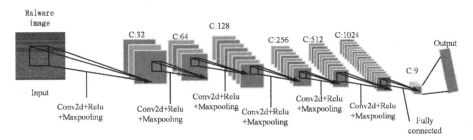

Fig. 2. Deep convolutional network structure in our method

As we can see from Fig. 2, the convolutional layer and sub-sampling layer (pooling layer) of each layer in the deep convolutional network will learn the malware image features, and extract the high-dimensional positive features of the grayscale image after learning. It can be seen that the convolutional layer and sub-sampling layer are the core of the network, the convolutional layer can effectively enhance the characteristics of the input signal and reduce noise, while the sub-sampling layer helps reduce the amount of data processing and only retains useful feature information. And they will be introduced separately below.

Convolutional layer: Its function is to reduce the number of input parameters while maintaining the input characteristics. The relationship between the input and output of the convolutional layer is shown in formula (1):

$$X_j^l = f\left(\sum_{i \in M_J} X_J^{l-1} * K_{iJ}^l + b_j^L\right) \tag{1}$$

In the above formula, f is the activation function in the model, K_{iJ}^l and b_j^L are the deviations of the mapping between the convolution kernel and the feature vector, respectively. As we can see, the output in the convolutional layer is the mapping of the input after dimensionality reduction, and each mapping belongs to the combination of the convolution results from the upper layer input, so the use of convolution can effectively avoid overfitting during training.

Sub-sampling layer: It also called the max pooling layer, its convolution kernel generally uses the maximum pool or average value, and is not affected by the back propagation of the network model. In our method, the relationship between the input and output of the sub-sampling layer in the deep convolutional network is shown in Eq. (2):

$$x_J^l = f\left(down\left(X_J^{l-1}\right) + b_J^l\right) \tag{2}$$

In the above formula, $down$ represents the pooling function, and b is the deviation value of the function. The sub-sampling layer acts to reduce the dimensionality of the feature map, but has little effect on various deformations of the image. Therefore, adding a sub-sampling layer to the model helps to improve the accuracy of the model while avoiding overfitting.

3.2 Important Opcode Features Extraction Based on IG

Opcode is a visual representation of machine code, and it is the most frequent element that appears in assembly view. Many related studies have proved that the detection based on opcode has good results. In this paper, in order to solve the problem that the effective information of the malware is lost due to the use of a single feature, we propose to merge the important opcode features with the malware image texture features during detection.

We use the 3-gram of opcode as the feature, and select all the assembly instructions in the sample for statistics as opcode features, and use the 3-gram method to represent them. Then, in order to ensure that the optimal operation code sequence can be selected, we use the information gain method to sort the operation code sequence after 3-gram processing, and select the first few opcode sequences as features. The feature selection based on information gain technology is shown in Fig. 3.

Information gain is a common method in feature selection, and the value of information gain is closely related to the key characteristics of the feature. Equation (3) is the formula for information gain, the $H(x)$ in the formula represents the entropy and $p(x)$ represents the probability of feature x, their formulas are shown in formula (4) and formula (5) respectively.

$$IG(Y|X) = H(Y) - H(Y|X) \tag{3}$$

Malware
assembly code

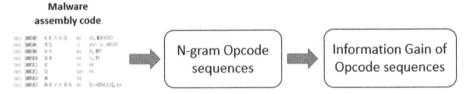

Fig. 3. Feature selection technology based on IG

$$H(X) = -\sum_{i=1}^{n} p(x_i)log_b p(x_i) \qquad (4)$$

$$H(Y|X) = \sum_{x} p(x)H(Y|X = x) \qquad (5)$$

The entropy in formula (3) and (4) can express the uncertainty of the sample, the greater the entropy, the greater the uncertainty of the sample. Therefore, the difference in entropy before and after the division can be used to evaluate the effectiveness of the currently used features for malware classification. As we can see from the above formula, $H(Y|X)$ represents the entropy after division, so the larger value of $H(Y) - H(Y|X)$,the better of the features.

3.3 Malware Detection Model Based on Feature Fusion

Combining the fusion features extracted by different methods described above, we constructed a malware variant detection network as shown in Fig. 4.

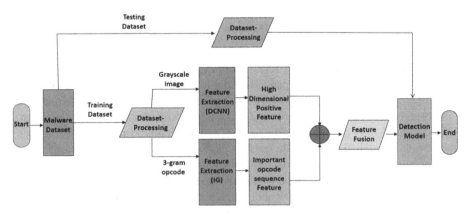

Fig. 4. Feature selection technology based on IG

As we can see in the method, the disassembly file of the malware and the grayscale image mapped from malware are used as training samples. To the disassembly file, we express all the opcodes in the form of 3-gram, and then use IG to extract the combination that has the greatest effect on the model classification accuracy. To the malware grayscale image, we directly input it into the constructed DCNN for learning and then extract the high-dimensional positive features of the malware. After that, we combine the obtained features to generate a fusion feature space, and use the fusion feature space to train a MLP to obtain the final classification of malicious samples.

4 Experimental Evaluation

4.1 Dataset and Experimental Settings

In this experiment, we selected the BIG2015 malware dataset released by Microsoft as the experimental data. The dataset contains 10868 labeled training data and 10873 unlabeled test data. All samples are from nine different malware families for detection. The grayscale images and opcodes used in this experiment come from byte files and disassembly files in the data set.

In our detection model, the adjustment factor r of the DCNN network is set to 5, the initial learning rate lr is set to 0.0005, the maximum number of iterations $epoch$ is 1000, and the training strategy of degenerate learning rate is adopted, which reduces by 10 times every 20 iterations. The dataset in the experiment will be divided into three sets of training, verification and testing. After the model is trained, it will first perform verification optimization on the verification dataset before testing its performance on the test dataset.

The experiment will use Logloss and Accuracy as indicators to evaluate the performance of the model, their mathematical definitions are shown in formula (6) and formula (7) respectively.

$$Logloss = -\frac{1}{N}\sum_{i=1}^{N}\sum_{j=1}^{M} y_{iJ}\log(p_{iJ}) \tag{6}$$

$$Accuracy = \frac{TP + TN}{TP + FP + TN + FN} \tag{7}$$

propose a robust generative adversarial network based on the attention mechanism. By adding the attention mechanism, the features of the original image can be extracted deeply, thereby improving the quality of the image generated by the generator. At the same time, the discriminator and generator are jointly trained in the case of adversarial attack to obtain a more powerful discriminator, this method can effectively improve the robustness of the classifier. And through experimental comparison, it is proved that the attention mechanism component we added has an optimization effect on Rob-GAN, both in terms of the robustness of the discriminator and the quality of the generator.

4.2 Experimental Results

To prove the effectiveness of the proposed method in malware detection, different experiments are designed in this section to verify it. Details as follows: (1) Important operation code extraction experiment based on IG. (2) The performance comparison between our feature fusion model and the single feature model used in our method. (3) Comparison of the average detection results of our method and mainstream malware detection methods on different families of malware using the same feature.

Important Operation Code Extraction Experiment Cased on IG
In our method, the selection of opcode as one of the features will have a certain impact on the final detection result. Therefore, in this experiment, the IG method is used to select important sequence combinations in the opcode based on the 3- gram, representation to improve the accuracy of model detection. The experimental results are shown in Table 1.

Table 1. The top 10 opcode sequence of the IG value

3-gram, opcode sequences	Information Gain
pop push mov	0.516 321 742
push add mov	0.475 326 852
add retn push	0.456 221 274
mov shl push	0.455 932 408
xor cmp mov	0.442 734 186
mov lea mov	0.428 521 746
call jmp xor	0.422 386 145
or and cmp	0.421 356 331
shr jmp add	0.413 198 325
or jmp mov	0.410 325 431

As we can see from the Table 1, we screened out important opcode sequences through IG, and combined these opcode features with the high-dimensional features extracted by DCNN for malware detection.

The Performance Comparison Between Our Feature Fusion Model and the Single Feature Model Used in our Method
Based on the network parameters set in the above experiment and the optimal features obtained, we compare the deep convolutional network that uses grayscale images for classification and the ANN network that uses opcode filtered by IG for classification with our fusion feature method. The experiments in this section will use two indicators of accuracy and loss to measure the effectiveness of these methods on malware variants detection. In addition, two indicators of training time and detection time on the test dataset are used to compare their computational costs. The experimental results are shown in Table 2.

As we can see from the Table 2, the detection accuracy of DCNN method and ANN are 95.4% and 89.3% respectively, and the training time is 14036 1s and 1972 s. In contrast, our feature fusion method sacrifices training time due to the increase in computational cost, but our method has a detection accuracy of 3% and 9% higher than the former when the detection time is not far from the former. It can be proved that

Table 2. The performance comparison between our feature fusion model and the single feature model used in our method

Method	Accuracy (%)	Loss	Training Time cost (s)	Detection Time cost (s)
Our method	98.6	0.085	152631.0	28.0
Grayscale based on CNN	95.6	0.115	140361.0	25.0
Opcode sequences based on ANN	89.4	0.258	1972.0	18.0

our fusion feature method can effectively cover more information of malware, so it has better performance in detection than the detection method based on single feature.

Comparison of Detection Performance Between Our Feature Fusion Method and Other Mainstream Detection Methods Under the Same Feature
To further verify the effectiveness of our proposed feature fusion method, we compare our method with other common malicious code detection models under the same feature. In the experiment, we adopt GIST method and IG method to collect texture features and important operation codes respectively, and then combined with the current common KNN [17], SVM [18], RF [19] and decision tree algorithms for detection.

Table 3. Performance comparison of different malware detection methods

Type	KNN	SVM	RF	Decision tree	Our method
Ramnit	65.2	73.2	94.3	88.0	97.9
Lollipop	72.1	84.1	95.2	84.1	99.2
Kelihos_v3	74.7	93.6	97.5	95.6	98.4
Vundo	83.5	90.5	96.3	90.3	98.2
Simda	11.5	37.5	94.2	73.4	96.0
Tracur	38.3	50.0	92.8	65.3	97.3
Kelihos_v1	60.7	82.5	96.1	90.8	98.4
Obfuscator	69.8	85.8	96.7	93.7	98.5
Gatak	74.4	76.4	93.4	84.2	97.9

Table 3 shows the average detection results of our method and other malware detection methods on nine malware variants from different families in the dataset. As we can see that compared with other malware detection methods based on machine learning, the DCNN used in our proposed method has a stronger ability to express the texture features of the grayscale image of malware. Therefore, the detection accuracy of malware variants is higher and the generalization ability is stronger.

5 Conclusion

This paper proposes a malware variant detection method based on feature fusion. In the method, important opcodes and malware grayscale textures are selected as the features for detection, which effectively solves the problem of single feature method. And because our method combines the DCNN in the deep learning method to process gray-scale image data, our method has a stronger ability to express image texture features than other methods. Therefore, our method performs better in different types of malware variants.

Although the method proposed in this paper effectively improves the ability to detect malware variants, it still needs to be optimized in terms of model calculation cost and detection accuracy. In the next step, we will continue to study in these directions to optimize the model.

Acknowledgements. We acknowledge the support by the National Natural Science Foundation of China (No. 66162019); National Natural Science Foundation of China Enterprise Innovation and Development Joint Fund (No. U19B2044).

References

1. China network security report in 2019. https://it.rising.com.cn/dongtai/19692.html
2. You, I., Yim, K.: Malware obfuscation techniques: a brief survey. In: 2010 International Conferences on Broadband, Wireless Computing, Communication and Applications, pp. 297–300. Communication and Applications, Fukuoka (2010)
3. Ren, Z.J., Chen, G.: Application of entropy visualization method in malware classification. Comput. Eng. **43**(9), 167–171 (2017)
4. Yi, H.D., Xu, Y.N.: Malicious code detection based on random forest. Cyberspace Secur. **9**(2), 70–75 (2018)
5. Ye, Y., Li, T.: A survey on malware detection using data mining techniques. ACM Comput. Surv. **50**(3), 1–40 (2017)
6. Wang T., Xu N.: Malware variants detection based on opcode image recognition in small training set. In: 2017 IEEE 2nd International Conference on Cloud Computing, pp. 328–332, Chengdu (2017)
7. Peng, W., Li, F., Zou, X.: Behavioral malware detection in delay tolerant networks. IEEE Trans. Parallel Distrib. Syst. **25**(1), 53–63 (2014)
8. Microsoft malware classification challenge (big 2015). https://www.kaggle.com/c/malw-are-classification
9. Bo, W., Yan, Y.H.: Malware classification method based on static multiple-feature fusion. Chin. J. Netw. Inf. Secur. **3**(11), 68–76 (2017)
10. Bazrafshan, Z., Hashemi, H., Fard, S.M.: A survey on heuristic malware detection techniques. In: The 5th Conference on Information and Knowledge Technology, pp. 113–120, Shiraz (2013)

11. Kolosnjaji, B., Zarras, A., Webster, G., Eckert, C.: Deep learning for classification of malware system call sequences. In: Kang, B.H., Bai, Q. (eds.) AI 2016. LNCS (LNAI), vol. 9992, pp. 137–149. Springer, Cham (2016). https://doi.org/10.1007/978-3-319-50127-7_11

12. Goodall, J.R., Radwan, H., Halseth, L.: Visual analysis of code security. In: Proceedings of the 7th International Symposium on Visualization for Cyber Security, pp. 46–51. ACM, New York (2010)

13. Nataraj, L., Karthikeyan, S., Jacob, G.: Malware images: visualization and automatic classification. In: Proceedings of the 8th International Symposium on Visualization for Cyber Security, pp. 1–7. ACM, New York (2011)

14. Oliva, A., Torralba, A.: Modeling the shape of the scene: a holistic representation of the spatial envelope. Int. J. Comput. Vision **42**(3), 145–175 (2001)

15. Long, J., Shelhamer, E., Darrell, T.: Fully convolutional networks for semantic segmentation. In: IEEE Conference on Computer Vision and Pattern Recognition, pp. 3431–3440. Boston (2015)

16. Cui, Z., Xue, F., Cai, X.: Detection of malicious code variants based on deep learning. IEEE Trans. Industr. Inf. **14**(7), 3187–3196 (2018)

17. Swetha, M.S., Sarraf, G.: Spam email and malware elimination employing various classification techniques. In: 2019 4th International Conference on Recent Trends on Electronics, Information, Communication & Technology (RTEICT), pp. 140–145. IEEE (2019)

18. Han, H., Lim, S.J., Sun, K.: Enhanced android malware detection: an SVM-based machine learning approach. In: 2020 IEEE International Conference on Big Data and Smart Computing, pp. 75–81. IEEE (2020)

19. Priyadarshan, P., Sarangi, P., Rath, A.: Machine Learning based improved malware detection schemes. In: 2021 11th International Conference on Cloud Computing, Data Science & Engineering (Confluence), pp. 925–931. IEEE (2021)

20. Kawai, M., Ota, K., Dong, M.: Improved malgan: avoiding malware detector by cleanware features. In: 2019 International Conference on Artificial Intelligence in Information and Communication (ICAIIC), pp. 040–045. IEEE (2019)

21. Khan, R.U., Zhang, X., Kumar, R.: Analysis of ResNet and GoogleNet models for malware detection. J. Comput. Virol. Hacking Tech. **15**(1), 29–37 (2018). https://doi.org/10.1007/s11416-018-0324-z

22. Kolter, J.Z., Maloof, M.A.: Learning to detect malicious executables in the wild. In: Proceedings of the 10th ACM SIGKDD International Conference on Knowledge Discovery and Data Mining, pp. 470–478. ACM, New York (2004)

23. Khoshkbarforoushha, A., Khosravian, A., Ranjan, R.: Elasticity management of streaming data analytics flows on clouds. J. Comput. Syst. Sci. **89**, 24–40 (2017)

24. Roundy, K., Miller, B.P.: Binary-code obfuscations in prevalent packer tools. ACM Comput. Surv. **46**(1), 1–32 (2013)

Robust GAN Based on Attention Mechanism

Qian Wu[1,2,3](✉), Chunjie Cao[1,2,3](✉), Jianbin Mai[1,2,3], and Fangjian Tao[1,2,3]

[1] Key Laboratory of Internet Information Retrieval of Hainan Province,
Haikou 570228, Hainan, China
[2] College of Cryptography, Hainan University, Haikou 570228, Hainan, China
[3] College of Computer and Cyberspace Security, Hainan University,
Haikou 570228, Hainan, China

Abstract. Deep neural networks (DNNs) have been found to be easily mislead by adversarial examples that add small perturbations to inputs to produce false results. Different attack and defense strategies have been proposed to better study the security of deep neural networks. But these works only focus on an aspect such as attack or defense. In this work, we propose a robust GAN based on the attention mechanism, which uses the deep latent features of the original image as prior knowledge to generate adversarial examples, and it can jointly optimize the generator and discriminator in the case of adversarial attacks. The generator generates fake images based on the attention mechanism to deceive discriminator, the adversarial attacker perturbs the real images to deceive discriminator, and the discriminator wants to minimize the loss between fake images and adversarial images. Through this training, we can not only improve the quality of adversarial images generated by GAN, but also enhance the robustness of the discriminator under strong adversarial attacks. Experimental results show that our classifier is more robust than Rob-GAN [14], and the generator outperforms Rob-GAN on CIFAR-10.

Keywords: Robust · GAN · Adversarial · Attention mechanism

1 Introduction

In recent years, deep neural networks have achieved great success in image recognition [1], text processing [2], speech recognition [3] and other fields, even widely used in critical security applications, such as malware detection [4], driverless technology [5], aircraft collision avoidance detection [6], etc. These all rely on the security of deep neural networks, which has become the focus of artificial intelligence security. At present, studies have shown that the deep neural network is vulnerable to the disturbance of the original samples with small perturbations [7]. These disturbances can make the system produce wrong judgment results while cannot be perceived by human eyes. Such input samples are called adversarial samples [8]. Adversarial examples can not only pose potential threat by attacking deep neural networks, but also enhance the robustness of models through training models [9]. Therefore, it is necessary to study the generation of adversarial samples.

© Springer Nature Switzerland AG 2021
J. Cheng et al. (Eds.): CSS 2020, LNCS 12653, pp. 78–86, 2021.
https://doi.org/10.1007/978-3-030-73671-2_8

Adversarial samples can be divided into two categories according to the attack target: maliciously-chosen target class (targeted attack) or classes that are different from the ground truth (non-targeted attack). At present, different methods have been proposed to generate adversarial samples. These methods are mainly divided into three categories. The first is gradient-based attack, such as the Fast Gradient Sign Method (FGSM) [8], which uses the linear nature of the deep neural network model in the high-dimensional space to quickly obtain the anti-perturbation, and adds disturbances in the gradient direction of the input vector. However, there is a minimization problem in this way. The second is optimization-based attack. Such as C&W attack [10], by limiting the distance l_0, l_2, l_∞ norms from the real image, the perturbation amplitude of the adversarial sample is reduced. But this method is slow because it can only focus on one instance at a time. The third is generative-network based attack. Such as Natural GAN [11], which generates adversarial examples of text and images by GAN and makes the generated adversarial examples more natural. These methods are also used in black box attack. Although the generation speed of these methods is fast, the disturbance is usually larger than the above two types of methods, and it's easy to be found.

Contrary to adversarial attacks, adversarial defenses are techniques that enable the model to resist adversarial samples. Compared with attacks, defenses are more difficult. Nevertheless, a large number of defense methods are still proposed, mainly in two aspects: the passive defenses, including input reconstruction, confrontation detection, and the active defenses, including defense distillation [12] and adversarial training [13].

However, the researches in these networks only focus on one aspect of attack or defense, and do not consider improving attack and defense simultaneously within a framework.

Our contribution in this work is:

A robust generative adversarial network based on the attention mechanism (Atten-Rob-GAN) is proposed. By introducing the attention mechanism to extract the original image features and use them as the input of generator G, the network can learn the relationship between the deep features of the image. Fake images generated by G are inputted into the discriminator D, while the adversarial images obtained from the attacker interference with the original images are also inputted into D. The adversarial training and GAN training are coordinated to obtain a powerful classifier, while improving the training speed of GAN and the quality of the generated images.

2   Materials and Methods

In this section, we will first introduce the definition of the problem, then briefly describe the framework of the Atten-Rob-GAN algorithm, and the method used to generate attacked images, finally explain the network in detail, concluding the formula and training details used in our framework.

2.1   Problem Definition

$x \in R^n$ is the original sample feature space, and n is the feature dimension. (x_i, y_i) is the i-th instance in the training set, which is composed of a feature vector $x_i \in X$

generated from an unknown distribution $x_i \sim P_{real}$ and the corresponding ground truth label $y_i \in Y$. Let $x_{fake} \in R^n$ be the feature space of false sample, and n is the feature dimension. (x_{fake_i}, l_i) is the i-th sample pair in the false sample data set, x_{fake_i} obeys an unknown distribution P_{fake}, and l_i is the corresponding prediction label. x_{adv} is the original image preprocessed by the PGD attack. The discriminator encourages x_{fake} to approximate x_{adv} within the perturbation range, so that P_{fake} is close to P_{real}.

2.2 The Atten-Rob-GAN Framework

Figure 1 shows the overall framework of Atten-Rob-GAN, which mainly includes three parts: feature extractor F, generator network G, and discriminator D. The output $F(x)$ of the feature extractor F which input is the real image and the noise vector z are concatenated vectors to form $F(x)^*$. The generator G receives $F(x)^*$ to generates the fake image x_{fake}. The discriminator D receives the image x_{adv} and the generator output x_{fake}, and distinguishes them, predict the category when the judgment is true.

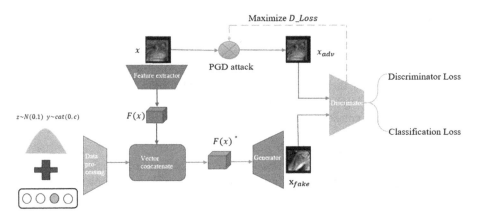

Fig. 1. The network architecture

The Loss Function
This work uses the same loss function as in Rob-GAN [14], the discriminator judges the source and category of the image, $P(S|X), P(C|X) = D(X)$. The only difference is that the generator G adds the deep features of the original image for feature fusion as input, $X_{fake} = G((c, z) + F(X_{real}))$. The loss function has two parts:
Discriminator Loss:

$$L_s = E[\log P(S = real|X_{real})] + E[\log P(S = fake|X_{fake})] \tag{1}$$

Classification Loss:

$$L_{c_{real}} = E[\log P(C = c|X_{real})] \tag{2}$$

$$L_{c_{fake}} = E[\log P(C = c|X_{fake})] \tag{3}$$

Train the discriminator D to maximize $L_s + L_{c_{real}}$, and train the generator G to minimize $L_s - L_{c_{fake}}$.

2.3   The Method of Generating Adversarial Examples Datasets

Projected Gradient Descent (PGD)
Madry et al. proposed an attack used in adversarial training called "Projected Gradient Descent" (PGD) [15] in 2017. Here, the PGD attack refers to initializing a search for an adversarial instance at a random point within the allowed norm sphere, and then running several basic iterative methods [16] to find adversarial examples. Given an example x, whose ground truth label is y, the PGD attack calculates the adversarial disturbance δ by using the projection gradient descent to solve the following optimization:

$$\delta := \mathop{argmax}_{||\delta|| \leq \delta_{max}} l(f(x + \delta; w), y) \tag{4}$$

Where $f(.; w)$ is the network parameterized by the weight w, $l(., .)$ is the loss function, and we choose $||.||$ as the l_∞ norm. The PGD attack is the strongest attack in first-order gradient attack. Using this attack to conduct adversarial training will make the defense more successful.

2.4   Implementation

Network Architecture
Next, we briefly introduce the network structure of Atten-Rob-GAN. For a fair comparison, we copied all the network architectures of the generator and discriminator from Rob-GAN. Other important factors, such as learning rate, optimization algorithm, and the number of discriminator updates in each cycle also remain unchanged. The only modification is that we added an attention mechanism to the input of the generator, the feature extractor (see Fig. 3).

Generator
The specific network structure of the generator is shown in Table 1:

Table 1. The specific structure of Atten-Rob-GAN generator

Layers	Types	Input channel number	Output channel number	Activation function	Up-sample
1	Linear	128	64×16		
2	Block1	64×16	64×8	ReLU	True
3	Block2	64×8	64×4	ReLU	True
4	Block3	64×4	64×2	ReLU	True
5	Block4	64×2	64×1	ReLU	False
6	BatchNorm2d	64	64	ReLU	
7	Conv2d (3 * 3)	64	3	tanh	

The first layer of the generator is a fully connected layer that the input is 128 noise, and the output is a $4^2 \times 64 \times 16$ image, where 4^2 is the size of the feature map, and 64

× 16 is the number of channels. Then there are 4 residual blocks, a batch regularization, and the last layer is a convolutional layer with the size of a 3 * 3 convolution kernel.

Discriminator
The specific network structure of the discriminator is shown in Table 2:

Table 2. The specific structure of Atten-Rob-GAN discriminator

Layers	Types	Input channel number	Output channel number	Activation function	Down-sample
1	Optimized block	3	64 × 2		True
2	Block2	64 × 2	64 × 2	ReLU	True
3	Block3	64 × 2	64 × 2	ReLU	False
4	Block4	64 × 2	64 × 2	ReLU	False
5	Activation	64 × 2	64 × 2	ReLU	
6	Linear	64 × 2	1 (sources) 10 (classes)		

The first layer of the discriminator is the optimized residual block, its detailed information is shown in Fig. 2. Then there are 3 residual blocks, an activation layer, a fully connected layer. The last fully connected layer has two types, in one case, the number of output channels is 1 when judging true or false image, and the other is that the number of output channels is the number of categories when judging the image category.

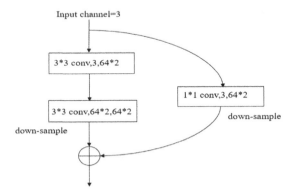

Fig. 2. Optimized block

Feature Extractor Based on Attention Mechanism

Here, we first extract the image features by reducing the dimension of the original image through a network structure completely symmetrical to the generator network, then introduce the attention mechanism (SE module [17]) to extract the spatial relationship in the image's shallow features and channel feature relationship to form deep features, so that the image can learn the weight coefficients of different channel features, thus the model can make more discerning about the characteristics of each channel. Figure 3 shows the detailed process of feature extractor F.

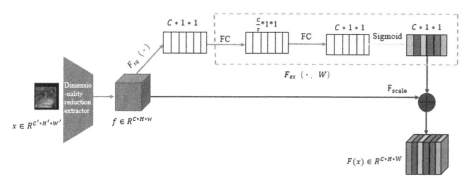

Fig. 3. Feature extraction (SE [17])

Training Details

We conduct experiments on the MNIST [18] and CIFAR-10 [19], where we use the training set to train Rob-GAN and Atten-Rob-GAN respectively, and evaluate the test set. After the model training is completed, the test set is input to the discriminator for testing, and the accuracy of the model is used as the measurement standard. The Adam optimizer with a learning rate of 0.0002 and $\beta_1 = 0$, $\beta_2 = 0.9$ is used to optimize the generator and discriminator. We sample the noise vector from the normal distribution and use label smoothing to stabilize the training.

Implementation Details

In our experiment, we use Pytorch for implementation and run on NVIDIA GeForce RTX 2080 Ti * 2. We train Atten-Rob-GAN to be 200 eopchs, batch size is 64, learning rate is 0.0002, attenuation by 50% every 50 steps, and PGD attack intensity is assumed to be 0.0625.

3   Results and Discussion

3.1   Robustness of Discriminator

In this experiment, we compared the robustness of the discriminator trained by Atten-Rob-GAN with Rob-GAN. As shown in [14], the robustness of Rob-GAN under adversarial attacks even surpasses the state-of-the-art adversarial training algorithm [15]. In the comparison of [20], adversarial training was considered to be the latest level of robustness. Since Rob-GAN is equivalent to Atten-Rob-GAN without an attention mechanism component to extract feature, for fair comparison, we keep all other components the same. In order to test the robustness of the model, we choose the widely used l_∞ PGD attack [15], but using other gradient-based attacks is also expected to produce the same results. As defined in (8), we set l_∞ disturbance as $\delta_{max} \in np.range(0, 0.01, 0.02, 0.03, 0.04)$. In addition, we scale the image to $[-1, 1]$ instead of $[0, 1]$, because the last layer of the generator has $tanh()$ output, so we need to modify it accordingly. We display the results in Table 3, all results are the average results after 5 runs.

Table 3. Accuracy of our model under l_∞ PGD-attack.

Datasets	Defenses	δ_{max} of l_∞ attack				
		0	0.01	0.02	0.03	0.04
CIFAR 10	Rob-GAN [14]	78.99%	69.54%	58.47%	50.78%	35.51%
	Ours	**88.37%**	**79.49%**	**66.94%**	**51.53%**	**36.35%**
MNIST	Rob-GAN [14]	52.43%	50.59%	49.37%	47.35%	45.05%
	Ours	**61.31%**	**57.32%**	**53.92%**	**49.20%**	44.91%

We can observe from Table 3 that our model has a higher classification success rate than Rob-GAN without attack, which proves that our classifier is more accurate after training. At the same time, under the attack intensity of [0, 0.04], our accuracy is higher than Rob-GAN's classifier on CIFAR-10, which proves that our model can obtain a more robust classifier. In the case of an attack intensity of 0.04 on MNIST, our result is slightly lower than that of Rob-GAN. The reason may be that the number of experiments is too few, and the calculated mean result is not universal.

3.2 Quality of Generator

Finally, we evaluate the quality of the generator trained on the CIFAR-10 dataset by comparing it with the generator obtained by Rob-GAN. Figure 4 shows the adversarial images generated on the two models. We can clearly observe that the image quality generated by Atten-Rob-GAN is significantly better than Rob-GAN, and even brighter than the original image.

(a) The real images   (b) Images generated by our model   (c) Images generated by Rob-GAN

Fig. 4. Different generated images.

4 Conclusion

We propose a robust generative adversarial network based on the attention mechanism. By adding the attention mechanism, the features of the original image can be extracted deeply, thereby improving the quality of the image generated by the generator. At the same time, the discriminator and generator are jointly trained in the case of adversarial attack to obtain a more powerful discriminator, this method can effectively improve the robustness of the classifier. And through experimental comparison, it is proved that the attention mechanism component we added has an optimization effect on Rob-GAN, both in terms of the robustness of the discriminator and the quality of the generator.

Acknowledgements. We acknowledge the support by the National Natural Science Foundation of China (No. 66162019); National Natural Science Foundation of China Enterprise Innovation and Development Joint Fund (No. U19B2044).

References

1. Krizhevsky, I.S., Hinton, G.E.: ImageNet classification with deep convolutional neural networks. Commun. ACM **60**(6), 84–90 (2017)
2. Bahdanau, D., Cho, K., Bengio, Y.: Neural machine translation by jointly learning to align and translate. In: 3rd International Conference on Learning Representations, pp. 11–17. ICLR, San Diego (2015)
3. Hinton, G., Deng, L., Yu, D., et al.: Deep neural networks for acoustic modeling in speech recognition: the shared views of four research groups. IEEE Sig. Process. Mag. **29**(6), 82–97 (2012)
4. Yuan, Z., Lu, Y.Q., Wang, Z.G., Xue, Y.B.: Droid-Sec: deep learning in android malware detection. In: ACM SIGCOMM 2014 Conference, pp. 371–372. ACM, Chicago (2014)
5. Eykholt, K., Evtimov, I., Fernandes, E., et al.: Robust physical world attacks on deep learning models. In: Proceedings of the IEEE Conference on Computer Vision and Pattern Recognition, pp. 1625–1634. IEEE Computer Society, Salt Lake City (2018)
6. Majumdar, R., Kunčak, V. (eds.): CAV 2017. LNCS, vol. 10426. Springer, Cham (2017). https://doi.org/10.1007/978-3-319-63387-9
7. Cubuk, E.D., Zoph, B., Schoenholz, S.S., Le, Q.V.: Intriguing properties of adversarial examples. In: 6th International Conference on Learning Representations (ICLR), pp. 106–118. ICLR, Vancouver (2018)

8. Goodfellow, I.J., Shlens, J., Szegedy, C.: Explaining and harnessing adversarial examples. In: 3rd International Conference on Learning Representations, pp. 65–78. ICLR, San Diego (2015)

9. Tramèr, F., Kurakin, A., Papernot, N., GoodfellowI, B.D., McDaniel, P.: Ensemble adversarial training: attacks and defences. In: 5th International Conference on Learning Representations, pp. 123–142. ICLR, Toulon (2017)

10. Carlini, N., Wagner, D.: Towards evaluating the robustness of neural networks. In: IEEE Symposium on Security and Privacy, vol. 0, pp. 39–57. IEEE, San Jose (2017)

11. Zhao, Z., Dua, D., Singh, S.: Generating natural adversarial examples. In: 6th International Conference on Learning Representations, pp. 108–115. ICLR, Vancouver (2018)

12. Papernot, N., Mc Daniel, P., Wu, X., Jha, S., Swami, A.: Distillation as a defense to adversarial perturbations against deep neural networks. In: 2016 IEEE Symposium on Security and Privacy (SP), pp. 582–597. IEEE, San Jose (2016)

13. Wu, Y., Bamman, D., Russell, S.: Adversarial training for relation extraction. In: Proceedings of the 2017 Conference on Empirical Methods in Natural Language Processing, pp. 1778–1783. ACL (2017)

14. Liu, X., Hsieh, C.: Rob-GAN: generator, discriminator, and adversarial attacker. In: Proceedings of the IEEE Conference on Computer Vision and Pattern Recognition, pp. 11226–11235. IEEE Computer Society, Long Beach (2019)

15. Madry, A., Makelov, A., Schmidt, L., Tsipras, D., Vladu, A.: Towards deep learning models resistant to adversarial attacks. In: 5th International Conference on Learning Representations, pp. 1538–1549. ICLR, Toulon (2017)

16. Kurakin, A., Goodfellow, I., Bengio, S.: Adversarial examples in the physical world. In: 5th International Conference on Learning Representations, pp. 995–1012. ICLR, Toulon (2017)

17. Hu, J., Li, S., Albanie, S., Sun, G., Wu, E.: Squeeze-and-excitation networks. IEEE Trans. Pattern Anal. Mach. Intell. **42**(8), 2011–2023 (2018)

18. LeCun, Y., Cortes, C.: MNIST handwritten digit database. Proc. IEEE **86**(11), 2278–2324 (1989)

19. Krizhevsky, A., Nair, V., Hinton, G.: CIFAR-10 (Canadian institute for advanced research). http://www.cs.toronto.edu/~kriz/cifar.html

20. Athalye, A., Carlini, N., Wagner, D.: Obfuscated gradients give a false sense of security: circumventing defenses to adversarial examples. In: 35th International Conference on Machine Learning, ICML 2018, vol. 1, pp. 436–448. IMLS, Stockholm (2018)

Training Aggregation in Federated Learning

Li Hu, Hongyang Yan[✉], and Zulong Zhang

School of Artificial Intelligence and Blockchain, Guangzhou University,
Guangzhou, People's Republic of China

Abstract. Federated learning is a new machine learning paradigm for distributed data. It enables multi-party cooperation to train global models without sharing their private data. In the classic federated learning protocol, the model parameters are the interaction information between the client and the server. The client can update the local model according to the global model parameters, and the server can aggregate the updated model parameters of each client to obtain a new aggregation model. However, in the actual federated learning scenario, there are still privacy problems caused by model stealing attack in collaborative learning using model parameters as interactive information. Therefore, we use knowledge distillation technology to avoid the model stealing attack in federated learning, and on this basis, we propose a novel aggregation scheme, which can make the output distribution of each customer refine the aggregation results through model training. Experiments show that the scheme can achieve normal convergence while ensuring privacy security, and reduce the number of interactions between client and server, thus reducing the resource consumption of each client participating in federated learning.

Keywords: Collaborative learning · Knowledge distillation · Heterogeneous · Communication

1 Introduction

Federated learning [1–3] is a collaborative machine learning algorithm for Non-IID data [4,5], which enables multiple parties to collaboratively train a shared global model without sharing data. At the beginning of each round of training, the central server will transmit the current global model to all parties, and all parties will train the model on local data. Then the server will collect model update information from all parties and update the central global model.

The main purpose of participating in federated learning is to obtain better models without sharing local data. The prototypical federated learning architecture [2,6] uses model parameters as the interactive information between the clients and the server, and then the server performs weighted average aggregation to update the global model. However, there are three problems with the model parameters as the interactive information:

© Springer Nature Switzerland AG 2021
J. Cheng et al. (Eds.): CSS 2020, LNCS 12653, pp. 87–94, 2021.
https://doi.org/10.1007/978-3-030-73671-2_9

1. When model parameters are used as interactive information, malicious clients may steal model parameters from victims, which may lead to privacy leakage.
2. The model structure trained by each client must be the same to be aggregated. However, in real scenarios, the agents participating in federated learning may have different training model structures due to different requirements [7,8].
3. When there are many users participating in federated training, the required communication will increase sharply, because each user has many model parameters, which will affect the efficiency of federated aggregation.

In response to the above problems, existing related articles [9–11] propose to use the output of the model as interactive information. However, articles [9,10] both directly aggregate the logit value by weighted average, while the article [11] designs an robust mean estimation algorithm to achieve aggregation, but none of these methods of aggregation explains whether the final aggregation result is the optimal result. Inspired by these solutions, this paper proposes to use knowledge distillation technology [12–14] and let the logit value output by the client aggregate by itself, that is, train the model on the server to aggregate the updated value uploaded by each client. Experiments have proved that this aggregation method can also achieve high convergence accuracy. At the same time, the number of interactions with the client is greatly reduced for its convergence, which will significantly reduce the amount of communication in the federated learning scenario. And it can explain from the perspective of knowledge distillation that each client participating in the training can obtain better results.

Figure 1 gives a high-level overview of this scheme. The model of each client is different. What is uploaded is the prediction distribution of the public data set. A model is trained on the server to aggregate the prediction distribution uploaded by the client. The generated model then predicts the public data set, and the prediction results broadcast to each client updates its local model, and so on, until the average accuracy of each client model converges, and then stops federated learning.

The main contributions of this work are summarized as follows:

- We design a collaborative learning approach with training for aggregation to achieve federated learning with heterogeneous model architectures.
- We further verify federated learning aggregation by training (FLAT) can improve the computation efficiency and reduce communication overhead.

Organization. The remainder of this paper is organized as follows. In Sect. 2, we present our detailed designs of mutual federated learning framework. The system evaluation and experimental results are presented in Sect. 3. Section 4 concludes this paper.

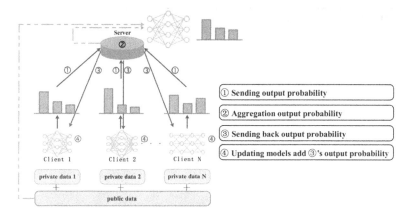

Fig. 1. The illustration of FLAT framework.

2 The Detail for Federated Learning Aggregation by Training

In this section we will introduce the details of our proposal. Algorithm 1 describes the process (called FLAT). We learn from the idea of knowledge distillation [12,15] and use the output of the model as the interactive information between the client and the server to achieve federated learning.

Each client initializes its own model parameter $\theta_k^0 (k \in \{1, 2, ...n\})$, and the models are heterogeneous between clients, that is, they have different model structures and sizes. User k has a dataset D_k containing N_k samples $X_k = \{x_{ki}\}_{i=1}^{N_k}$, of the M class, with the corresponding label set of $Y_k = \{y_{ki}\}_{i=1}^{N_k}, y_{ki} \in \{1, 2, ..., M\}$, at the same time, each client has a dataset D containing N samples $X = \{x_i\}_{i=1}^{N}$, of the M class, with the corresponding label set of $Y = \{y_i\}_{i=1}^{N}, y_i \in \{1, 2, ..., M\}$. In the first round, each client updates the model parameters based on the local datasets D_k and D, and obtains $\theta_k^1 = \theta_k^0 - \triangledown L(D_k \bigcup D; \theta_k^0)$, where $L(D_k \bigcup D; \theta_k^0)$ is about θ_k^0 loss function on the dataset $D_k \bigcup D$, and α is the learning rate. Each party then predicts dataset D based on locally updated parameters and uploads the prediction $\overline{Y}_k^1 = f(\theta_k^1, X)$ to the server, $f(\theta_k^1, X)$ represents the probability distribution of input X passing through the model with parameters θ_k^1. The server aggregates by training a model (model parameter is θ^0) and gets a new predictive distribution $\widetilde{Y}^1$ of public dataset D. Each client obtains $\widetilde{Y}^1$ through the server broadcast, and updates themself model through the dataset $D_k \bigcup D \bigcup (X, \widetilde{Y}^1)$.

3 Experiment Evaluation

The framework FLAT is evaluated based on popular image datasets: MNIST [16], that is a widely used in the FL [17,18]. In the MNIST training dataset with 60,000 samples, and in the MNIST testing dataset with 10,000 samples.

Algorithm 1. Federated Learning Aggregation by Training(FLAT)

Input:

  D_k : private dataset for each client k ,($k \in \{1, 2, ..., n\}$)

  D : public dataset for all clients and server

  α : the learning rate of training

Output:

  θ_k^t : model parameters for each client k ,($k \in \{1, 2, ..., n\}$)

 1: **Initialize :**

  each client initialize θ_k^0 by themselves

  server initialize θ^0 by all clients

 2: t = 0

 3: **repeat**

 4:   **Client:**

  $\overline{D} = D$

 5:   **for** each client $k \in \{1, 2, ..., n\}$ **do**

 6:    **if** $t == 0$ **then**

 7:     $\tilde{D}_k = D_k \bigcup D$

 8:     $\theta_k^{t+1} = \theta_k^t - \alpha \bigtriangledown L(\tilde{D}_k; \theta_k^t)$

 9:    **else**

10:     $\theta_k^{t+1} = \theta_k^t - \alpha \bigtriangledown L(\tilde{D}_k; \theta_k^t)$

11:    **end if**

12:    $\overline{Y}_k^t = f(\theta_k^{t+1}, X)$

13:    send $\overline{Y}_k^t$ to server

14:    server get dataset $\overline{D} = \overline{D} \bigcup (X, \overline{Y}_k^t)$

15:   **end for**

16:   **Server:**

17:   get dataset $\overline{D}$

18:   $\theta^{t+1} = \theta^t - \alpha \bigtriangledown L(\overline{D}; \theta^t)$

19:   $\tilde{Y}^{t+1} = f(\theta^{t+1}, X)$

20:   send $\tilde{Y}^{t+1}$ to each client

21:   client k get dataset $\tilde{D}_k = D_k \bigcup D \bigcup (X, \tilde{Y}^{t+1})(k \in \{1, 2, ..., n\})$

22: **until** t>100

First, we verify FLAT algrithm in same neural network with two hidden layers. After determining the optimal hyperparameter, we then verify FLAT algrithm in different neural network, which is taken from the tensorflow tutorial [19].

We tested the test accuracy of 3 clients and 20 clients with tagged public data, and their models are the same. As shown in Fig. 2(a), the results were consistent with the original federated learning effect, and the increase in the number of clients would improve the performance of federated learning. In order to verify the effectiveness of our scheme, we compared the results of federated distillation (FD) with 20 clients. In the training process of federated distillation,

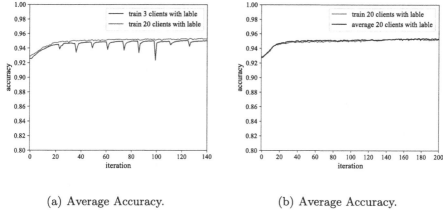

(a) Average Accuracy.   (b) Average Accuracy.

Fig. 2. The variation trend of Average Accuracy. On the left is the FLAT scheme using tagged public data to compare 3 clients and 20 clients. On the right, 20 clients are trained with labeled public data to compare the FLAT scheme and the FD scheme.

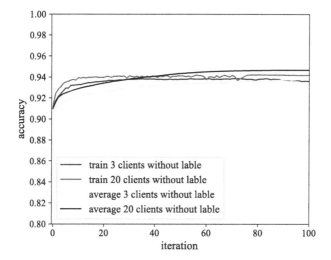

Fig. 3. Convergence behavior about the FLAT scheme and the FD scheme using unlabeled public data to train 3 and 20 clients.

the probability distribution uploaded by each client was weighted averaged, as shown in Fig. 2(b), and we found that we could also achieve the optimal accuracy. And we tested the test accuracy of 3 clients and 20 clients with untagged public data. Each client with 2,000 private data and 10,000 untagged public data, server just with 10,000 untagged public data. We can see Fig. 3, public data with or without tags will have the same effect.

At the same time, we found that when our scheme achieves the optimal accuracy, the number of rounds required for interaction between the client and the server is much less than that of the federated distillation solution. Table 1 lists the specific differences. It can be seen that when the number of clients is 3 and the public data has tags, our solution only needs 62 rounds of interaction to achieve the best test accuracy of 95.19%, while the federated distillation scheme requires 188 rounds of interaction to achieve the best test accuracy of 95.29%. That is to say, at this time, within the range of less accuracy loss, the number of interactions required by our solution is 1/3 of the FD solution, which can greatly reduce the resource consumption of the client participating in federated learning. We also compared the unlabeled cases of the public data sets. The experimental results show that the number of interactions required by our solution is 1/2 of the FD solution when the public data set is not labeled, although the accuracy is more lost when 20 clients participate in federated learning, but the accuracy loss is within an acceptable range.

Table 1. The number of interactions between clients and server when the model reaches the Top-1 accuracy (%) on the mnist dataset. FD - FLAT measures the difference in the number of interactions and accuracy between the FD and FLAT.

Number of clients	With Lable			Without Lable		
	FLAT	FD	FD - FLAT	FLAT	FD	FD - FLAT
3	62(95.19)	188(95.29)	126(0.01)	83(93.88)	170(93.89)	87(0.01)
20	150(95.32)	176(95.38)	26(0.06)	83(94.23)	169(94.72)	86(0.49)

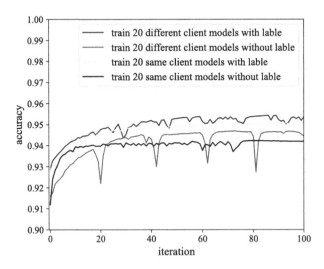

Fig. 4. Use different models to train 3 and 20 clients to compare the convergence behavior of the FLAT scheme with labeled public data and unlabeled public data.

Then we test on different models, so that the number of layers in the model is different (maybe 2–3 layers), and the number of neurons in each layer is different (there may be 32, 64, 128, 256, 512, 1024). After that we use the labeled public data set and the unlabeled public data set to train 20 clients for testing. We found that changing the model structure can still converge normally. As shown in Fig. 4, when the model becomes larger, the accuracy of the model obtained by convergence is also higher.

4   Conclusion

In this paper, we have proposed a novel while effective federated learning framework, targeting to achieve that the user model can be heterogeneous and the privacy of user can be protected, while reducing the user's resource consumption during the federated learning process. Here we learned from the knowledge distillation method of interacting information with model output as knowledge, and further improved the existing federated learning aggregation scheme. Through experiments, we found that FLAT can realize good convergence while greatly reducing the resource consumption of the client.

Acknowledgement. The research leading to these results has received funding from China Postdoctoral Science Foundation (2020M682658).

References

1. McMahan, B., Moore, E., Ramage, D., Hampson, S., y Arcas, B.A.: Communication-efficient learning of deep networks from decentralized data. In: Artificial Intelligence and Statistics, pp. 1273–1282 (2017)
2. McMahan, H.B., Moore, E., Ramage, D., y Arcas, B.A.: Federated learning of deep networks using model averaging
3. Yang, Q., Liu, Y., Chen, T., Tong, Y.: Federated machine learning: concept and applications. ACM Trans. Intell. Syst. Technol. **10**(2), 1–19 (2019)
4. Zhao, Y., Li, M., Lai, L., Suda, N., Chandra, V.: Federated learning with Non-IID data
5. Sattler, F., Wiedemann, S., Müller, K.-R., Samek, W.: Robust and communication-efficient federated learning from Non-IID data
6. Mohri, M., Sivek, G., Suresh, A.T.: Agnostic federated learning. arXiv preprint arXiv:1902.00146
7. Liu, Y., et al.: Fedvision: an online visual object detection platform powered by federated learning. arXiv: Learning
8. Choudhury, O., et al.: Differential privacy-enabled federated learning for sensitive health data. arXiv: Learning
9. Li, D., Wang, J.: FedMD: Heterogenous federated learning via model distillation. arXiv preprint arXiv:1910.03581
10. Jeong, E., Oh, S., Kim, H., Park, J., Bennis, M., Kim, S.-L.: Communication-efficient on-device machine learning: federated distillation and augmentation under Non-IID private data. arXiv preprint arXiv:1811.11479

11. Chang, H., Shejwalkar, V., Shokri, R., Houmansadr, A.: Cronus: robust and heterogeneous collaborative learning with black-box knowledge transfer. arXiv preprint arXiv:1912.11279
12. Hinton, G., Vinyals, O., Dean, J.: Distilling the knowledge in a neural network. arXiv preprint arXiv:1503.02531
13. Zhang, Y., Xiang, T., Hospedales, T.M., Lu, H.: Deep mutual learning. In: Proceedings of the IEEE Conference on Computer Vision and Pattern Recognition, pp. 4320–4328 (2018)
14. Wang, J., Bao, W., Sun, L., Zhu, X., Cao, B., Philip, S.Y.: Private model compression via knowledge distillation. In: Proceedings of the AAAI Conference on Artificial Intelligence, vol. 33, pp. 1190–1197 (2019)
15. Chen, H.: Data-free learning of student networks. In: Proceedings of the IEEE International Conference on Computer Vision, pp. 3514–3522 (2019)
16. Lecun, Y., Bottou, L.: Gradient-based learning applied to document recognition. Proc. IEEE **86**(11), 2278–2324 (1998)
17. Caldas, S., et al.: Leaf: a benchmark for federated settings
18. Kairouz, P., et al.: Advances and open problems in federated learning. arXiv preprint arXiv:1912.04977
19. Team, T.: Tensorflow convolutional neural networks tutorial. http://www.tensorflow.org/tutorials/deepcnn

A Robust Digital Watermarking
for Medical Images Based on PHTs-DCT

Dan Yi[1], Jing Liu[3], Jingbing Li[1,2(✉)], Jingjun Zhou[1], Uzair Aslam Bhatti[4],
Yangxiu Fang[1], and Saqib Ali Nawaz[1]

[1] College of Information and Communication Engineering, Hainan University,
Haikou, Hainan, People's Republic of China
{Yidan,juingzhou,FangYangXiu}@hainanu.edu.cn
[2] State Key Laboratory of Marine Resource Utilization in the South China Sea,
Hainan University, Haikou, Hainan, People's Republic of China
[3] Research Center for Healtcare Data Science, Zhejiang Lab, Hangzhou, Zhejiang,
People's Republic of China
liujinglj@zhejianglab.edu.cn
[4] School of Geography (Remote sensing and GIS Lab), Nanjing Normal University,
Nanjing, China

Abstract. In recent years, digital watermarking technology has been
widely used to solve the protection of privacy issues in medical images.
However, the existing algorithms are failed to solve the protection problems against geometric attacks. To solve this problem, a robust digital
watermarking algorithm for medical images based on PHTs-DCT is proposed in this paper. For embedding watermark, DCT is applied to reduce
the redundant data of the image, then the coefficients are calculated via
PHTs and the DCT to construct a binary feature sequence. Moreover,
the watermark information is encrypted by Logistic mapping, and the
zero watermark is constructed and stored in a third party medical image
protection database. Extensive experiments have shown that the proposed algorithm has good robustness to geometric attacks and common
attacks, especially anti-translation, rotation, and compression attacks.

Keywords: Medical image · Zero-watermarking · PHTs-DCT ·
Logistic map · Feature extraction

1 Introduction

With the development of medical technology, medical images are playing an
increasingly important role in the process of medical diagnosis of patients. The

---

This work was supported in part by the Hainan Provincial Natural Science Foundation
of China under Grant 2019RC018 and by the Natural Science Foundation of China
under Grant 62063004 and 61762033, in part by the Hainan Provincial Higher Education Research Project under Grant Hnky2019-73, and in part by the Key Research
Project of Haikou College of Economics under Grant HJKZ18-01.

© Springer Nature Switzerland AG 2021
J. Cheng et al. (Eds.): CSS 2020, LNCS 12653, pp. 95–108, 2021.
https://doi.org/10.1007/978-3-030-73671-2_10

medical image not only contains the basic personal information of the patient but also contains private information that reflects the patient's health status. When medical images are transmitted and stored on the network, patients' private information may be leaked or maliciously attacked [5,8]. Therefore, the data integrity and copyright protection of medical images in the transmission and processing process are very important. Using digital watermarking technology can effectively solve this problem [14,15].

Digital watermarking technology has the characteristics of concealment, hidden position security, and robustness. According to the watermark detection process, digital watermarks can be divided into plain text watermarks and blind watermarks. Plain text watermarks require original data during the detection process, while blind watermark detection only can be done with a key and does not modify the original image. To ensure the security and integrity of watermarks and medical images, we use blind watermarking technology, so that medical images have better security and ensure visual quality. In recent years, watermarking algorithms have developed rapidly in medical images. Discrete Cosine Transformation (DCT) [2,10,12], SIFT feature points [9,16], Zernike moments (ZMs) [6,7] and pseudo-Zernike (PZMs) [17] are commonly used feature extraction algorithms. Lin [4] proposed a text image zero watermarking algorithm based on wavelet transform and signal energy. The text file is converted into the corresponding binary image, and then the binary image is subjected to triple wavelet transform, and combined with the relationship of signal energy to construct a zero watermark. So that the watermark algorithm has a better solution to the problems of embedding capacity and invisibility. Zhao et al. [19] proposed a mapping-based zero watermarking scheme for 2D vector graphics. The watermark is not embedded in the original vector graphics but is constructed or extracted by mapping the two most important characters (length ratio and angle) to a point image that can also be saved in vector format. This method is robust enough to geometric transformation, shearing and adding attacks, and has high accuracy and computational efficiency. However, these methods still have some major following problems:

(1) The adopted watermark embedding strategy is too simple to effectively resist some common signal processing operations.
(2) The algorithm has high computational complexity and numerically unstable.

In response to the above problems, Kang et al. [1] proposed a robust and invisible blind image watermarking scheme based on discrete cosine transform and singular value decomposition. Combining the DCT with DWT, the best embedding strength of a specific overlay image is obtained through estimation based on the least-squares curve fitting. The polar coordinate harmonic transforms (PHTs) proposed by YAP et al. [18] include polar complex exponential transform (PCET), polar cosine transform (PCT), and polar sine transform (PST) which helps to generate a set of features for images which are invariant to rotation. Compared with other orthogonal moments, they have lower noise sensitivity and lower computational complexity, and the numerical value of the polar coordinate harmonic transformation is stable, which can accurately obtain high-order moments.

Li et al. [3] evaluated the invariance performance and image representation ability of Zernike moments (ZMs), pseudo-Zernike (PZMs), and polar harmonic transformation (PHTs) algorithms. The results show that the performance of PHTs is better than that of ZMs and PZM. Singh et al. [11] proposed a method to quickly calculate PHTs by establishing the recurrence relationship between the radial and angular parts of the transform kernel function. They use of 8-way symmetric/antisymmetric features improved the speed of the algorithm.

On the basis of PHTs performance, we proposed a robust digital watermarking algorithm for medical images based on PHTs-DCT. Our algorithm takes the advantage of PHTs in creating distinguishability with good balance and DCT's ability to resist conventional attacks, traversal, and robust features such as feature extraction of medical images. Encrypt the watermark via logistic mapping, associate the feature vector with the encrypted binary watermark to obtain a binary logical sequence, and store the binary. Then, the feature vector of the medical image to be tested is extracted by PHTs-DCT transformation, and the watermark is extracted by correlating it with the binary sequence stored in the third party. This algorithm combines the feature vector of medical image, cryptography, hash function and zero-watermark technology to solve the shortcoming of the traditional digital watermarking method that cannot protect the medical image itself.

The main contribution of the present research is:

(1) Using blind watermark technology, the watermark can be embedded and extracted without changing the visual quality of the original medical image.
(2) By combining the feature vector of medical image, cryptography, hash function and zero-watermarking technology, it better solved the shortcoming of the traditional digital watermarking method cannot protect the medical image itself.
(3) It solved the problem of poor robustness of ordinary algorithms and has good performance in resisting geometric attacks such as translation, rotation, and compression.

2   The Fundamental Theory

2.1   Polar Harmonic Transforms (PHTs)

Polar harmonic transforms is a kind of orthogonal invariant moment [13], which is defined on the unit circle by projecting the image to the orthogonal kernel function, as shown in Fig. 1. According to the form of the kernel function, polar harmonic transforms can be divided into polar complex exponential transforms (PCET), polar cosine transforms (PCT) and polar sine transforms (PST). The formula for PHTs with order n and the number of repetitions m is as follows:

$$A_{nm} = \lambda \int_0^{2\pi} \int_0^1 f(r,\theta) V_{nm}^*(r,\theta) r \, dr \, d\theta \tag{1}$$

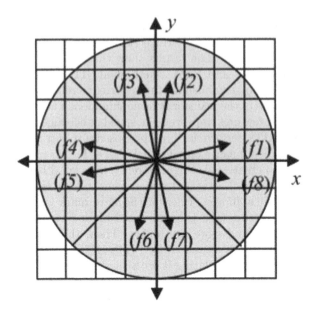

Fig. 1. Mapping of the square image into a unit disk

Among them, $n, m = 0, \pm 1, \pm 2, \ldots$. The kernel function $V^*_{nm}(r, \theta)$ is the complex conjugate of function $V_{nm}(r, \theta)$. The definition of formula $V_{nm}(r, \theta)$ is as follows:

$$V_{nm}(r, \theta) = R_n(r)e^{jm\theta} \tag{2}$$

The radial part of the kernel function and the parameter λ is expressed as:

$$PCET : R_n(r) = e^{j2\pi n r^2}, \lambda = \frac{1}{\pi} \tag{3}$$

$$PCT \quad and \quad PST : R_n(r) = \begin{cases} \cos\left(\pi n r^2\right), PCT \\ \sin\left(\pi n r^2\right), PST \end{cases} \tag{4}$$

$$\lambda = \begin{cases} \frac{1}{\pi}, n = 0 \\ \frac{2}{\pi}, n \neq 0 \end{cases} \tag{5}$$

The radial part of the kernel function satisfies the orthogonal condition:

$$\int_0^1 R_n(r) \left[R_{n,}(r)\right]^* r dr = \frac{1}{2}\delta nn' \tag{6}$$

Where, if $n = n'$ then $\delta nn' = 1$, otherwise $\delta nn' = 0$.

Besides, the complete kernel function $V_{nm}(r, \theta)$ satisfies the orthogonal condition:

$$\int_0^{2\pi} \int_0^1 V_{nm}(r, \theta) \left[V_{nm}(r, \theta)\right]^* r dr d\theta = \pi \delta nn' \delta mm' \tag{7}$$

2.2   Logistic Map

Logistic mapping is derived from a demographic dynamics system and is a kind of chaotic mapping that has been studied extensively. Its mathematical expression is as follows:

$$X_{k+1} = \mu x_k (1 - x_k) \tag{8}$$

It can be seen from the formula that this system equation is a nonlinear iterative equation. Among them, $0 \leq \mu \leq 4$, μ is the control parameter, $x_k \in (0, 1)$ is the system variable, and k is the number of iterations. When $3.569945 \leq \mu \leq 4$, the system enters a chaotic state. The closer μ is to 4, the stronger the chaos.

3   The Proposed Algorithm

3.1   Feature Extraction

At present, most medical image watermarking algorithms embed digital watermarks in pixels or transform coefficients. A slight geometric transformation will cause the pixel values or transform coefficient values to change, which leads to poor resistance to geometric attacks. If the visual feature vector reflecting the geometric characteristics of the image can be found, the watermark image can be verified by comparing the visual feature vector. To find this feature vector, we randomly select a normal human brain image (512 pixels × 512 pixels) for PHTs-DCT transformation, and perform different attacks on the human brain medical image, as shown in Fig. 2. According to the human visual characteristics (HVS), low and intermediate frequency signals have a greater impact on human vision and represent the main characteristics of medical images. Therefore, we select a 4*8 matrix in the low-frequency coefficient part of the transformed matrix and use the hash function to obtain a stable binary sequence, which is the eigenvector.

In the experiment, we randomly selected a large number of medical images for testing. Figure 3 shows some selected medical images. We calculated the normalized correlation coefficients between images, as shown in Table 1. It can be seen from the table that the correlation coefficients between different images are small, and the NC value with itself is 1.00.

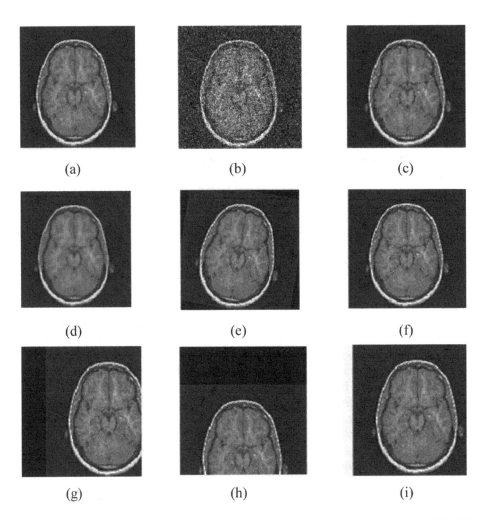

Fig. 2. Different attacks on the brain: (a) Original image; (b) Gaussian noise (5%); (c) JPEGcompression (5%); (d) Median filter [5 × 5] (10times); (e) Rotation (clockwise, 10°); (f) Scaling (×0.8); (g) Translation (25%, right); (h) Translation (30%, down); (i) Cropping (12%, X direction)

Table 1. Values of the correlation coefficients between different images (32 bits)

Image	(a)	(b)	(c)	(d)	(e)	(f)	(g)	(h)
(a)	1.00	−0.06	−0.06	−0.10	−0.03	0.31	−0.09	−0.06
(b)	−0.06	1.00	−0.10	0.09	−0.06	0.06	0.39	0.26
(c)	−0.06	−0.10	1.00	0.09	0.56	0.06	0.12	−0.10
(d)	−0.10	0.09	0.09	1.00	−0.10	0.39	0.33	0.35
(e)	−0.03	−0.06	0.56	−0.10	1.00	−0.10	−0.09	−0.06
(f)	0.31	0.06	0.06	0.39	−0.10	1.00	−0.09	0.06
(g)	−0.09	0.39	0.12	0.33	−0.09	−0.09	1.00	0.12
(h)	−0.06	0.26	−0.10	0.35	−0.06	0.06	0.12	1.00

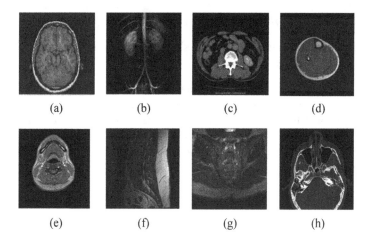

Fig. 3. The original medical images: (a) Brain, (b) Lung, (c) Abdomen, (d) Leg, (e) Neck, (f) Lumbar spine, (g) Sacroiliac, (h) Maxilla

3.2 Watermarks Encryption

The watermark encryption process is shown in Fig. 4. A chaotic sequence $X(j)$ is generated from the initial value x_0. The chaotic sequence is converted into a binary sequence using a hash function, and the position space of the watermark pixel is XOR scrambled according to the sequence of the binary sequence. Finally, the chaotic scrambled watermark $BW(i,j)$ is obtained. In this experiment, the initial value of the chaos coefficient is 0.2, the growth parameter is 4, and the number of iterations is 1023.

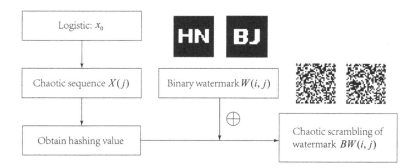

Fig. 4. Watermark encryption process

3.3   Watermark Embedding

The watermark embedding flowchart is shown in Fig. 5, which is mainly divided into the following steps:

Step 1. Use DCT transform to reduce the data redundancy of the original medical image and improve the computational efficiency.
Step 2. Applied PHTs-DCT transform to extract the image feature sequence.
Step 3. Select the 4*8 matrix at the low frequency.
Step 4. Obtain a binary feature sequence through the perceptual hash.
Step 5. Encrypt watermark by chaotic sequence.
Step 6. XOR the binary sequence with the encrypted watermark to obtain the logical key.

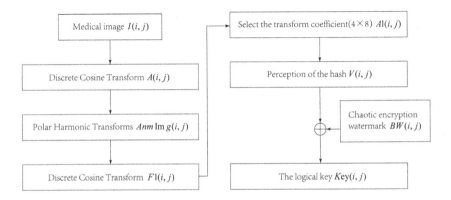

Fig. 5. Watermark embedding process

3.4   Watermarking Extraction

The watermark extraction flow is shown in Fig. 6, the main steps are as follows:

Step 1. Use DCT transform to reduce the data of the attacked medical image, and then carry out PHTs-DCT transform.
Step 2. Obtain the binary feature sequence with the same method as the watermark embedding.
Step 3. XOR the binary feature sequence and the logical key to get the extracted watermark.

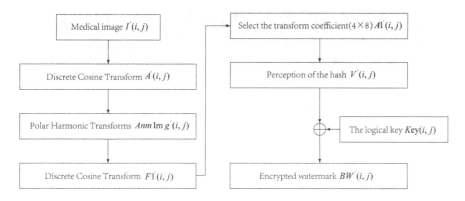

Fig. 6. Watermark extraction process

3.5 Watermarks Restoration

The watermark decryption flow chart is shown in Fig. 7. The binary feature sequence is obtained using the same method as the watermark encryption, and the chaotically scrambled watermark $BW'(i,j)$ location space is XORed and restored according to the binary sequence. The watermark $W'(i,j)$ is calculated. By calculating the correlation coefficient NC of the original watermark $BW(i,j)$ and the restored watermark $W'(i,j)$ to determine the ownership of the medical image and the embedded watermark information.

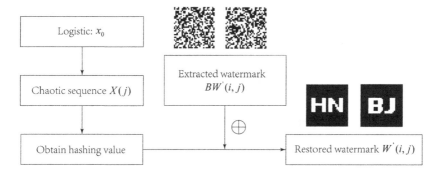

Fig. 7. Watermark decryption process

4 Experiments and Results

4.1 Settings

In the experiment, we choose MATLAB 2018b as the simulation platform, using 512 pixels × 512 pixels medical image as the test image, and the original watermark size is 32 pixels × 32 pixels. The PHTs algorithm takes the exact coefficient

(a)   (b)   (c)   (d)   (e)

Fig. 8. (a) Original medical image; (b) Original watermark image; (c) Chaotic scrambled watermark image; (d) Rotation (clockwise, 12°); (e) Extracted watermark

n = m = 10 to construct a zero-watermark image. Taking Fig. 2(a) as an example, select HN as the text watermark image and perform a rotation attack on the original medical image (rotate 12° clockwise), and the extracted watermark result is shown in Fig. 8. Now with NC = 0.74, the watermark can be extracted accurately.

The peak signal-to-noise ratio (PSNR) is generally used for validation between the maximum signal and the background noise and is usually used as an objective evaluation standard for medical image quality. We set the pixel value of each point of the image as $I(i,j)$, and represent the digital image with a square matrix, that is, $M = N$, and the formula is:

$$PSNR = 10 \lg \left[\frac{MN \max_{i,j}(I(i,j))^2}{\sum_i \sum_j (I(i,j) - I'(i,j))^2} \right] \tag{9}$$

Use the Normalized Correlation Coefficient (NC) to compare the similarity between the embedded original watermark and the extracted watermark. The mathematical expression is as follows:

$$NC = \frac{\sum_i \sum_j W_{(i,j)} W_{(i,j)}}{\sum_i \sum_j W_{(i,j)}^2} \tag{10}$$

$W(i,j)$ and W'(i,j) respectively represent the feature vectors of the original watermark image and the watermark image to be tested, and the length is 32 bit.

4.2   Attacks Results

We use Gaussian noise, JPEG compression, median filtering and other geometric attacks (such as rotation, translation) to process the encrypted medical image. Table 2 shows the PSNR and NC values of the watermark extracted under different types of attacks. It can be seen from the Table 2 that in all attacks at different strengths, the NC values of the extracted watermarks are all greater than 0.5, indicating that the method proposed in this paper has a better ability to resist various common and geometric attacks.

Table 2. Different attacks based on NC and PSNR values using the PHTs-DCT

Attack	Parameter	PSNR	NC
Gaussian noise (%)	5	14.32	0.90
	10	10.59	0.81
	20	9.78	0.81
	30	8.79	0.81
	40	8.20	0.74
JPEG compression (%)	1	26.28	0.90
	5	28.44	0.90
	10	31.29	0.90
	40	35.46	0.90
	80	37.82	1.00
Median filter (20 times)	3×3	33.81	0.90
	5×5	27.46	0.81
	7×7	25.50	0.81
Rotational attack (°)	4	19.02	0.90
	8	16.21	0.90
	12	15.22	0.74
	18	14.68	0.63
Scaling	0.3	-	0.90
	0.6	-	0.90
	2.0	-	1.00
	20	-	1.00
Translation (%) (right)	5	14.52	0.90
	20	11.98	0.74
	30	10.84	0.81
Translation (%) (down)	5	15.11	0.90
	20	13.78	0.90
	30	12.72	0.90
Cropping ratio (%) (Y direction)	1	-	0.90
	3.5	-	0.79
	4	-	0.65
Cropping ratio (%) (X direction)	6	-	0.90
	15	-	0.74
	21	-	0.56

4.3   Comparison with Other Algorithms

We compared the proposed PHTs-DCT algorithm with the DCT and PHTs algorithms. Table 3 shows the NC values of the three algorithms under different

Table 3. Proposed algorithm comparison with PHTs and DCT

Attacks strength	PSNR (db)			NC		
	PHTs	DCT	PHTs-DCT	PHTs	DCT	PHTs-DCT
Gaussian noise (30%)	8.79	8.79	8.79	0.79	0.57	0.81
JPEG Compression (5%)	28.44	28.44	28.44	0.88	0.90	0.90
Median filter 7 × 7 (20times)	25.45	25.45	25.45	1.00	0.72	0.81
Rotation 12° (Clockwise)	15.22	15.22	15.22	0.18	0.54	0.74
Scaling (×0.3)	-	-	-	0.67	0.90	0.90
Translation 30% (right)	10.84	10.84	10.84	0.25	0.90	0.81
Translation 30% (down)	12.73	12.73	12.73	0.27	0.14	0.90
Cropping 3.5% (Y axis)	-	-	-	0.28	0.40	0.79
Cropping 15% (X axis)	-	-	-	-	0.88	0.74

attacks. It can be seen from Table 3 that the PHTs algorithm performs well in the three common attacks of Gaussian noise, JPEG compression, and median filtering, but performs poorly for various geometric attacks. The DCT algorithm performs better than the PHTs-DCT algorithm when panning to the right and X-axis cutting. When performing JPEG compression and scaling attacks, it has the same NC value as the PHTs-DCT algorithm. In other attacks, the NC value of the PHTs-DCT algorithm is higher than the DCT algorithm. In general, the proposed algorithm performs well under any type of attack and is overall better than the DCT algorithm and the PHTs algorithm.

5   Conclusion

In this paper, we proposed a robust digital watermarking algorithm for medical images based on PHTs-DCT. Use the properties of logistic map to scramble and encrypt the watermark in the frequency domain. Then extract feature vectors to embed the watermark by performing PHTs-DCT transformation on the medical image, and associate the feature vector with the binary watermark to obtain a binary logical sequence to construct a zero-watermark image. At last, perform PHTs-DCT transformation to extract the feature vector of the medical image to be tested, and associate it with the binary sequence stored in the third party to extract the watermark. The experimental results show that the proposed algorithm can realize the embedding and extraction of watermarks without changing the pixel values of the original image, can resist various common attacks and geometric attacks during transmission. And it can better protect the copyright of medical images, which is robust and invisible.

References

1. Kang, X.B., Zhao, F., Lin, G.F., Chen, Y.J.: A novel hybrid of DCT and SVD in dwt domain for robust and invisible blind image watermarking with optimal embedding strength. Multimed. Tools Appl. **77**(11), 13197–13224 (2018). https://doi.org/10.1007/s11042-017-4941-1

2. Ko, H.J., Huang, C.T., Horng, G., Wang, S.J.: Robust and blind image watermarking in DCT domain using inter-block coefficient correlation. Inf. Sci. **517**, 128–147 (2019)

3. Li, L., Li, S., Wang, G., Abraham, A.: An evaluation on circularly orthogonal moments for image representation. In: International Conference on Information Science and Technology, pp. 394–397. IEEE (2011)

4. Lin, Q.W.: DWT and signal energy based zero-watermarking algorithm for text image. In: Advanced Materials Research, vol. 631, pp. 1313–1317. Trans Tech Publications (2013)

5. Liu, J., Li, J., Ma, J., Sadiq, N., Bhatti, U.A., Ai, Y.: A robust multi-watermarking algorithm for medical images based on DTCWT-DCT and Henon map. Appl. Sci. **9**(4), 700 (2019)

6. Lutovac, B., Daković, M., Stanković, S., Orović, I.: An algorithm for robust image watermarking based on the DCT and Zernike moments. Multimed. Tools Appl. **76**(22), 23333–23352 (2017). https://doi.org/10.1007/s11042-016-4127-2

7. Munib, S., Khan, A.: Robust image watermarking technique using triangular regions and Zernike moments for quantization based embedding. Multimed. Tools Appl. **76**(6), 8695–8710 (2017). https://doi.org/10.1007/s11042-016-3485-0

8. Navas, K.A., Sasikumar, M.: Survey of medical image watermarking algorithms (2007)

9. Pang, J.P., Wang, A.L., Zhu, X.F., Guo, L., Liu, F.P.: A holographic image robust watermarking algorithm based on DWT-sift and neural network model. In: IOP Conference Series Materials Science and Engineering, vol. 563, p. 052088 (2019)

10. Parah, S.A., Sheikh, J.A., Akhoon, J.A., Loan, N.A., Bhat, G.M.: Information hiding in edges: a high capacity information hiding technique using hybrid edge detection. Multimed. Tools Appl. **77**(1), 185–207 (2016). https://doi.org/10.1007/s11042-016-4253-x

11. Singh, C., Kaur, A.: Fast computation of polar harmonic transforms. J. Real-Time Image Process. **10**(1), 59–66 (2012). https://doi.org/10.1007/s11554-012-0252-y

12. Singh, R., Ashok, A., Saraswat, M.: An optimized robust watermarking technique using CKGSA in DCT-SVD domain. IET Image Process. **14**(10), 1015–10261026 (2020)

13. Singh, S.P., Urooj, S.: A new computational framework for fast computation of a class of polar harmonic transforms. J. Signal Process. Syst. **91**(8), 915–922 (2019). https://doi.org/10.1007/s11265-018-1417-0

14. Sk, A., Masilamani, V.: A novel digital watermarking scheme for data authentication and copyright protection in 5G networks. Comput. Electr. Eng. **72**, 589–605 (2018)

15. Tang, Z.Z., et al.: Robust image hashing via random Gabor filtering and DWT. Comput. Mater. Continua **55**(2), 331–344 (2018)

16. Wang, S., Cui, C., Niu, X.: Watermarking for DIBR 3D images based on sift feature points. Measurement **48**, 54–62 (2014)

17. Wang, X.Y., Hou, L.M.: A new robust digital image watermarking based on pseudo-Zernike moments. Multidimension. Syst. Signal Process. **21**(2), 179–196 (2010). https://doi.org/10.1007/s11045-009-0096-1

18. Yap, P.T., Jiang, X., Kot, A.C.: Two-dimensional polar harmonic transforms for invariant image representation. IEEE Trans. Pattern Anal. Mach. Intell. **32**(7), 1259–1270 (2009)
19. Zhao, H., Du, S., Zhang, D.: Zero-watermark scheme for 2D vector drawings based on mapping. In: 2013 International Conference on Information Science and Cloud Computing Companion, pp. 601–605. IEEE (2013)

A Robust Zero Watermarking Algorithm for Medical Images Based on Tetrolet-DCT

Wenfeng Cui[1], Jing Liu[3], Jingbing Li[1,2(✉)], Yangxiu Fang[1], Xiliang Xiao[1], Uzair Aslam Bhatti[4], and Saqib Ali Nawaz[1]

[1] School of Information and Communication Engineering, Hainan University, Haikou, Hainan, People's Republic of China
FangYangXiu@hainanu.edu.cn
[2] State Key Laboratory of Marine Resource Utilization in the South China Sea, Hainan University, Haikou, Hainan, People's Republic of China
[3] Research Center for Healthcare Data Science, Zhejiang Lab, Hangzhou, Zhejiang, People's Republic of China
liujinglj@zhejianglab.edu.cn
[4] School of Geography (Remote Sensing and GIS Lab), Nanjing Normal University, Nanjing, China

Abstract. The rapid development of the information age of big data has promoted the development of traditional medicine and online diagnosis, as well as aroused concerns about the privacy of patient information. Aiming at the hidden dangers of copying, cutting, tampering, etc. in the dissemination of medical images, combined with the characteristics of medical images, this paper proposed a novel zero-watermarking algorithm based on Tetrolet-DCT, focusing on how to improve its security. Logistic map chaotic encryption is performed on the watermark, the Tetrolet-DCT transform is used to extract the visual feature of medical image, and the watermark information is embedded and extracted by combining the zero-watermarking technology. Experimental data show that the algorithm proposed in this paper can effectively extract the watermark without any changing of the medical image, and has a higher NC value under conventional attacks and geometric attacks. it has better invisibility and robustness.

Keywords: Zero Watermark · Tetrolet-DCT · Medical image · Robustness

1 Introduction

With the rapid development of the Internet and information technology, images, texts, videos, etc. containing important information are constantly updated and widely spread in various fields. In this process, they may be subject the problems of copying, cutting, and malicious tampering. Once tampered, it is easy to cause serious consequences, especially in the special medical field [1, 2]. Digital watermarking technology can solve this problem well.

Digital watermarking mainly realize copyright protection by embedding important information in digital media such as images, text, and audio [3]. Generally, a complete

© Springer Nature Switzerland AG 2021
J. Cheng et al. (Eds.): CSS 2020, LNCS 12653, pp. 109–119, 2021.
https://doi.org/10.1007/978-3-030-73671-2_11

digital watermarking system includes three parts: watermark embedding, watermark extraction and watermark detection [4]. According to the hidden position of the watermark, digital watermarks are divided into spatial watermarks and frequency domain watermarks. LSB algorithms and patchwork algorithms are classical spatial watermarking algorithms, and transform domain watermarking algorithms are mainly based on DCT, DWT, DFT transform [5]. However, the wavelet transform can only reflect the zero-dimensional singularity of the signal. To represent and process image data more effectively, multiscale geometric analysis has gradually become a research hotspot. In the last years, researchers have proposed a series of multi-scale geometric analysis tools, such as ridgelet, curvelet, contourlet, brushlet, wedgelet, bandlet, shearlet, tetrolet, and so on. The multi-scale geometric analysis shows strong advantages and potential in the fields of image compression, denoising, enhancement, and feature extraction [6].

Medical image is a special form of image. In modern medicine, it is regarded as an important basis for diagnosis, and it is generally not allowed to be modified artificially to avoid misdiagnosis [7]. The existing watermarking algorithms for general digital images are generally less robust when applied to medical images, and basically cannot resist geometric attacks [8, 11]. Therefore, this paper proposed a novel algorithm based on Tetrolet-DCT, which combined the concept of zero watermark [14] and can quickly achieve watermark embedding and extraction on the premise of ensuring the invisibility and robustness of watermark information. Compared with wavelet transform, curving transform, contour transform and ridgelines, this method is more effective for medical images [12, 13].

2 Basic Theory

2.1 Tetrolet Transform

In 2009, Jens Krommweh proposed Tetrolet transform for sparse image representation, which is a new Haar wavelet transform, and its basic idea is simple, fast and effective. The construction of this transform is similar to wedglet transform, and Haar function is applied in the edge part, which can be expressed sparsely. Compared with wavelet, curvelet and contourlet, the transformed image coefficients are more concentrated, which can get better image quality.

Tetrolet transform was first applied to the four-frame jigsaw puzzle. The image was divided into 4×4 blocks, disregarding rotations and reflections there are five different shapes. In each 4×4 blocks, the imposition combination is performed according to the geometric information. And 22 kinds of square combinations and 117 different combinations of rotation and reflection are considered. The decomposition steps are as follows:

Suppose an image size is a $= a(a[i, j])_{i,j=0}^{N-1}$, where $N = 2J$, $J \in N$ which can be decomposed at the rth level $r = 1, 2, 3 \ldots, J$.

Step 1: Decompose the image into 4×4 blocks.

Step 2: Decompose each block by tetrolet to obtain 2×2 low-pass subbands and 12×1 high-pass subbands, then find the most sparse tetrolet representation in each block.

The low-pass subband coefficient is

$$a^{r,(c)}[s] = \sum_{(m,n)\in I_s^{(c)}} [0, L(m, n)]a^{r-1}[m, n] \tag{1}$$

The high-pass subband coefficient is

$$w_l^{r,(c)} = \left(\sum_{(m,n)\in I_s^{(c)}} \varepsilon[0, L(m, n)]a^{r-1}[m, n]\right)_{s=0}^3 \tag{2}$$

Where r is the decomposition series, c is 117 combinations, $C = 1, 2, ..., 117, \varepsilon[l, m]$.

Step 3: Decompose the next layer and rearrange the low-pass coefficients and high-pass coefficients of each block to a 2×2 block.

Step 4: Save the Tetrolet decomposition coefficient (high pass part).

Step 5: Repeat steps 1–4 for the low-pass part until the decomposition is complete. Figure 1 shows the decomposition process:

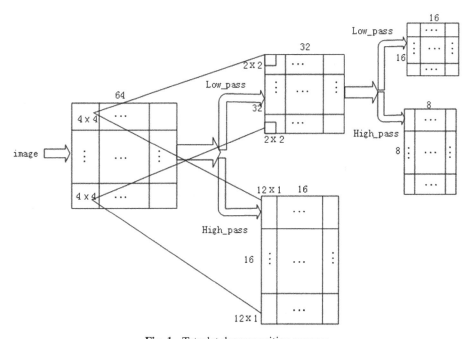

Fig. 1. Tetrolet decomposition process

As a result, Tetrolet can adapt to the geometric characteristics of the image, so the Tetrolet transform can maintain the edge and texture of the image very well, and it is very effective in image compression, denoising and nonlinear approximation.

2.2 DCT Transform

Discrete Cosine Transform (DCT) is a classic frequency domain algorithm, which is widely used in digital watermarking and image processing.

It has the advantages of fast calculation speed and high resistance to compression attacks and is compatible with international data compression standards JPEG and MPEG. According to the visual characteristics of human eyes, the characteristics of the image are mainly in the middle and low frequency of the image, so the watermark information can be embedded in the middle and low-frequency region of the image in DCT domain. A two-dimensional DCT transform is as follows:

$$F(u, v) = c(u)c(v) \sum_{x=0}^{M-1} \sum_{y=0}^{N-1} f(x, y)\cos\frac{\pi(2x+1)u}{2M}\cos\frac{\pi(2y+1)v}{2N} \tag{3}$$

Among them, $u = 0, 1, ..., M - 1, v = 0, 1, ..., N - 1$;

$$c(u) = \begin{cases} \sqrt{\frac{1}{M}} & u = 0 \\ \sqrt{\frac{2}{N}} & u = 1, 2, \ldots, M - 1 \end{cases}, \quad c(v) = \begin{cases} \sqrt{\frac{1}{N}} & v = 0 \\ \sqrt{\frac{2}{M}} & v = 1, 2, \ldots, N - 1 \end{cases} \tag{4}$$

2.3 Logistic Map

Logistic map, also known as the wormhole model, is a very simple and classic chaotic system, which is widely used in the encryption field. The mathematical expression is:

$$x_{n+1} = \mu x_n(1 - x_n) \tag{5}$$

Where μ is the branch parameter. And when $3.5699456 < \mu \le 4$, the logistic map is chaotic.

According to the formula, the chaotic sequence is very sensitive to the initial value. When $\mu = 4$, the probability distribution function of the Logistic chaotic sequence $\rho(x)$ is:

$$\rho = \frac{1}{\pi\sqrt{x(1-x)}}, 0 < x < 1 \tag{6}$$

It shows that the Logistic sequence is ergodic. In this paper, we set $\mu = 4$.

3   Proposed Watermarking Algorithm

3.1   Feature Extraction

We first decompose the original medical image (512 pixel × 512 pixel) by tetrolet and get the low-frequency subband and high-frequency subband. The low-frequency subband is decomposed to the next level, and the high-frequency subband is saved. We know that the image features are mainly in the low-frequency part, while the high-pass part mainly shows the texture and geometric details in all directions.

Then DCT is applied to the low-frequency part of tetrolet decomposition to obtain the feature of thr medical image. The 8-bit low and medium frequency coefficients of DCT are taken as the feature vector.

Table 1. Coefficients of medical image under different attacks (correlation coefficient: 1.0e + 04)

Image attacks	PSNR (dB)	C(1, 1)	C(1, 2)	C(1, 3)	C(1, 4)	C(1, 5)	C(1, 6)	C(1, 7)	C(1, 8)	Symbol sequence	NC
The original image	–	3.642	0.055	−1.609	−0.049	−0.016	−0.028	0.244	−0.015	11000010	1
Gaussian noise (3%)	16.24	3.812	0.048	−1.507	−0.044	−0.013	−0.025	0.234	−0.014	11000010	1
JPEG compression 30%	34.83	3.642	0.056	−1.607	−0.049	−0.019	−0.027	0.245	−0.015	11000010	1
Medianfilter [5 × 5] 10 times	28.56	3.663	0.054	−1.582	−0.052	−0.010	−0.023	0.240	−0.008	11000010	1
Scaling(×0.75)	–	2.732	0.041	−1.206	−0.036	−0.012	−0.021	0.183	−0.012	11000010	1
Movement (down 4%)	15.28	3.545	0.053	−1.572	−0.043	−0.048	−0.035	0.267	−0.008	11000010	1
Rotation (clockwise 10°)	15.60	3.512	0.137	−1.705	−0.085	−0.122	−0.096	0.136	−0.030	11000010	0.81
Y Cropping(10%)	–	3.343	0.052	−1.463	−0.043	−0.086	−0.032	0.243	−0.015	11000010	0.83

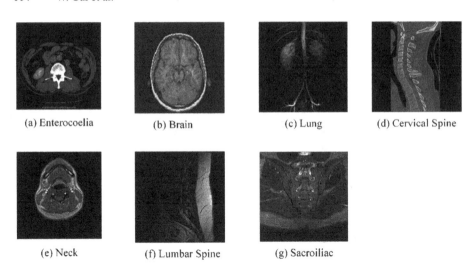

(a) Enterocoelia   (b) Brain   (c) Lung   (d) Cervical Spine

(e) Neck   (f) Lumbar Spine   (g) Sacroiliac

Fig. 2. Different original medical images for watermarking

Through experiments, we found that although the coefficients of the medical image changed after various attacks, the positive and negative signs of the coefficients did not change (see Table 1).

To verify the feasibility of this method, we selected 7 different medical images for comparison experiments and found that the NC value of different images is much less than 0.5, indicating that the correlation is very small, and the NC values between the same pictures are all 1.00 (see Table 2). In consequence, this method is feasible for feature extraction.

Table 2. Correlation test of seven different medical images

NC	enterocoelia	Brain	Lung	Cervical spine	Neck	Lumbar spine	Sacroiliac
enterocoelia	1.00	−0.07	−0.13	0.25	0.20	0.13	0.34
Brain	−0.07	1.00	0.18	−0.06	0.02	−0.06	0.29
Lung	−0.13	0.18	1.00	0.25	0.32	−0.12	0.08
Cervical spine	0.25	−0.06	0.25	1.00	−0.20	0.00	−0.34
Neck	0.20	0.02	0.32	−0.20	1.00	−0.07	0.36
Lumbar spine	0.13	−0.06	−0.12	0.00	−0.07	1.00	−0.08
Sacroiliac	0.34	0.29	0.08	−0.34	0.36	−0.08	1.00

3.2 Encryption and Embedding of the Watermark

Figure 3 shows the encryption process of the watermark. First, the watermark image (32 pixel × 32 pixel) is binarized to obtain $W(i, j)$. Secondly, a chaotic sequence is generated through the logical initial value $X(j)$, then carry out the ascending dimension and symbol operation on the sequence to obtain the binary encryption matrix $C(i, j)$. Then perform XOR operation on $W = (i, j)$ and $C(i, j)$ to get the encrypted watermark $BW(i, j)$.

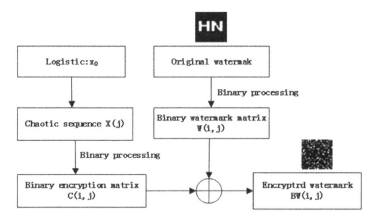

Fig. 3. Watermark encryption process

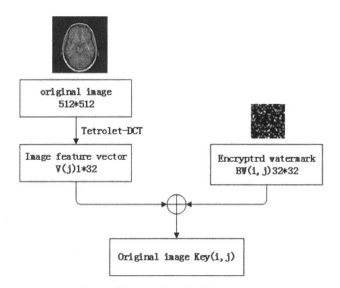

Fig. 4. Watermark embedding process

Figure 4 is the watermark embedding process. First, perform the Tetrolet-DCT transform on the medical image (512 pixel × 512 pixel) to obtain a 32 bit dimensional feature vector V(j), then perform XOR operation on V(j) and BW(i,j) to get the key of the original medical image K(i,j).

3.3 Watermark Extraction and Restoration

Figure 5 is a flow chart of watermark extraction and restoration. First, perform feature extraction on the attacked image to obtain32 bit dimensional feature vector V'(j), and then perform an XOR operation with K(i,j) of the original medical image to extract the watermark BW'(i,j) contained in the attacked image.

Then the watermark matrix BW'(i,j) and the binary matrix C(i,j) are XOR to obtain the restored watermark matrix W'(i,j).

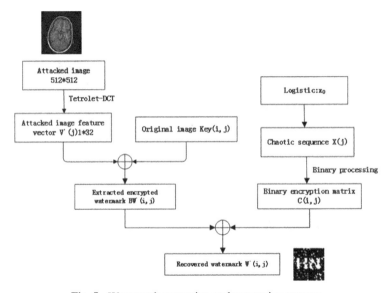

Fig. 5. Watermark extraction and restoration process

3.4 Watermark Evaluation

The performance evaluation of watermarking mainly has two indicators: imperceptibility and robustness.

Imperceptibility means that after the watermark is embedded in the original image, it does not affect the quality of the carrier image, and compared with the original image. It is difficult for the human visual system to find the difference. The peak signal-to-noise ratio(PSNR) is as follows:

$$PSNR = 10\log_{10}\left[\frac{MN\max_{i,j}(I(i,j))^2}{\sum_i \sum_j (I(i,j) - I'(i,j))^2}\right] \quad (7)$$

Watermark robustness is used to judge the anti-attack ability of the watermark, which is judged by comparing the correlation between the extracted watermark and the original watermark. The formula for calculating the normalized correlation coefficient (NC) is as follows:

$$NC = \frac{\sum_i \sum_j W(i,j)W'(i,j)}{\sum_i \sum_j W^2(i,j)} \tag{8}$$

4 Experiments and Results

4.1 Experimental Data

In this paper, the Matlab R2016a platform is used for simulation, and 512 pixel × 512 pixel brain medical image and a meaningful 32 pixel × 32 pixel watermark are selected for experiments.

Table 3. Experimental data of various attacks on test images

Attacks	Parameter	PSNR	NC
Gaussian noise	5%	14.30	0.95
	10%	11.87	0.95
	15%	10.61	0.93
Median filtering	[3 × 3], 20 times	33.82	1.00
	[5 × 5], 20 times	27.46	1.00
	[10 × 10], 20 times	25.45	1.00
JPEG	1%	26.28	1.00
	5%	28.44	1.00
	10%	31.29	1.00
Rotation (clockwise)	6°	17.24	0.81
	10°	15.60	0.81
	20°	14.68	0.73
Scaling	×0.22	–	0.70
	×0.75	–	1.00
	×2.50	–	1.00
Move vertically	6%	15.03	1.00
	15%	14.28	0.76
	20%	13.78	0.65
Cropping Y direction	2%	–	0.95
	9%	–	0.83
	15%	–	0.66

The experimental data are as follows:

Generally, when the NC value is more than 0.5, it indicates that the extracted watermark is valid. The higher the NC value, the better the quality of the extracted watermark. It can be seen that the algorithm in this paper has good robustness. The data in Table 3 shows that the algorithm used in this paper has strong anti-attack performance in traditional attacks, especially in geometrical attacks such as median filtering, JPEG compression, scaling, rotation and shearing. It has the better anti-attack performance.

4.2 Performance Comparison with Other Algorithms

Table 4 shows the comparison between the algorithms in this paper and reference 15.

Table 4. Comparison results between different algorithms

Attacks	Parameter	DWT-DCT		Tetrolet-DCT	
		PSNR (dB)	NC	PSNR (dB)	NC
JPEG attack	1	26.28	0.94	26.28	1.00
	5	28.43	0.94	28.43	1.00
	10	31.29	0.94	31.29	1.00
Median filtering/10 times	[3, 3]	33.99	0.94	33.99	1.00
	[5, 5]	28.55	0.94	28.55	1.00
	[7, 7]	26.39	0.89	26.39	1.00
Gussian noise/%	2	17.77	0.89	17.77	1.00
	10	11.89	0.83	11.87	0.95
	20	9.81	0.83	9.78	0.87
Movement (down)/%	5	18.99	0.94	15.10	1.00
	10	16.19	0.94	14.73	1.00
	15	15.33	0.94	14.28	0.75
Rotation (clock wise)/°	5	18.00	0.76	18.00	0.81
	10	15.59	0.76	15.59	0.81
	15	14.86	0.68	14.86	0.81

We can find that when compared with reference [15], the proposed algorithm in this paper has advantages in traditional attacks such as JPEG compression, median filtering, and Gaussian noise. Anti-attack is more stable than DWT-DCT.

5   Conclusion

In the medical image field, this paper proposed a robust zero-watermarking algorithm based on Tetrolet-DCT, which used Tetrolet-DCT and logistic mapping to embed and extract watermark. Compared with DWT, Tetrolet has advantages in image compression, denoising, and nonlinear approximation. And robust watermarking algorithm is most commonly used for digital copyright protection and is widely used in the fields of medical images, bill anti-counterfeiting, and digital signatures, etc., which improves the security of information. Experiments show that the watermark information can be extracted effectively without any changing of the original image. The proposed algorithm is robust and can resist geometric attacks well.

Acknowledgement. This work was supported in part by the Hainan Provincial Natural Science Foundation of China under Grant 2019RC018 and by the Natural Science Foundation of China under Grant 62063004 and 61762033, in part by the Hainan Provincial. Higher Education Research Project under Grant Hnky2019-73, and in part by the Key Research Project of Haikou College of Economics under Grant HJKZ18-01.

References

1. Parah, S.A., Sheikh, J.A., Ahad, F., Loan, N.A., Bhat, G.M.: Information hiding in medical images: a robust medical image watermarking system for E-healthcare. Multimedia Tools Appl. **76**(8), 10599–10633 (2015). https://doi.org/10.1007/s11042-015-3127-y
2. Nyeem, H., Boles, W., Boyd, C.: A Review of Medical Image Watermarking Requirements for Teleradiology. J. Digit. Imaging **26**, 326–343 (2013)
3. Ya-Kun, W.U., Chun-Hong, D.I.: A survey of digital watermarking techniques. J. Liaoning Univ. (Natural ences Edition) **37**, 202–206 (2010)
4. Balasamy, K., Ramakrishnan, S.: An intelligent reversible watermarking system for authenticating medical images using Wavelet and PSO. Clust. Comput. **22**(2), 4431–4442 (2018). https://doi.org/10.1007/s10586-018-1991-8
5. Guihua, X.: Research on the Key Technologies of Digital Watermarking., Vol. Doctor. 132. Nanjing University of Aeronautics and Astronautics (2009)
6. Analysis, I.-S.: Cai-Lian L, J.S.Y.K. Natural Science J. Hainan University **29**, 275–283 (2011)
7. Krommweh, J.: Tetrolet transform: A new adaptive Haar wavelet algorithm for sparse image representation. J VIS COMMUN IMAGE R **21**, 364–374 (2010)
8. Hung-Jui, K., Cheng-Ta, H., Gwoboa, H., Shiuh-Jeng, W.: Robust and blind image watermarking in DCT domain using inter-block coefficient correlation. INFORM Sci. **517** (2020)
9. Xu, Z., Xuan, Y.: Image watermarking algorithm based on DCT and Arnold transform. Int. J. Reasoning-Based Intell. Syst. **9** (2017)
10. Xu, Z.J., Wang, Z.Z., Lu, Q.: Research on image watermarking algorithm based on DCT. Procedia Environ. Sci. **10**, 1129–1135 (2011)
11. Mastan Vali, S.K., Naga Kishore, K.L., Prathibha, G.: Notice of retraction robust image watermarking using tetrolet transform, pp. 1–5. IEEE (2015)
12. Zhang, D.X., Xun, L.N., Liu, K.F., et al.: Research on Stationary Tetrolet Transform Algorithm. Zidonghua Xuebao/Acta Automatica Sinica **44**, 2041–2055 (2018)
13. Muhammad, F.K., Syed, M.G.M., Imran, N.: A novel zero-watermarking based scheme for copyright protection of grayscale images. Mehran Univ. Res. J. Eng. Technol. **38** (2019)
14. Zhang, S., Zhang, H.: Research on zero watermarking algorithm for hyper-chaos-based image. Appl. Res. Compu. **36** (2019)
15. Domain, J., Li, J., Duan, Y., Guo, Z.: A robust zero-watermarking algorithm for encrypted medical images in the DWT-DCT encrypted domain. Int. J. Simul. Syst. Sci. Tech. (2016)

HOUGH-DCT Based Robust Watermarking for Medical Image

Ruiqi Mo[1], Jing Liu[3], Jingbing Li[1,2(✉)], Yulin Wang[1], and Jingjun Zhou[1]

[1] School of Information and Communication Engineering,
Hainan University, Haikou 570228, China
juingzhou@hainanu.edu.cn
[2] State Key Laboratory of Marine Resource Utilization in the South China Sea,
Hainan University, Haikou 570228, China
[3] Research Center for Healthcare Data Science Zhejiang Lab, Hangzhou, Zhejiang, China
liujinglj@zhejianglab.edu.cn

Abstract. The patients' case files may be maliciously tampered with during network transmission. Once the patients' medical record information is altered by criminals, serious medical accidents will occur. To solve the problem of information leakage, a robust medical image watermarking algorithm based on Hough transform and discrete cosine transform (HOUGH-DCT) is proposed. This method combines the feature vector of medical image, cryptography, hash function and zero watermark technology, and it makes up for the shortcoming that the traditional digital watermark method cannot protect the medical image. It has strong robustness and invisibility which can protect the patient's private information and medical image data security at the same time. Experimental results show that the algorithm can embed the watermark information at a faster speed without changing the medical image information and extract the watermark safely with better invisibility and robustness.

Keywords: Medical image · HOUGH-DCT · Zero watermarking · Robust

1 Introduction

With the advent of the information age, especially the popularity of the Internet, digital technology improve dramatically. But it also brings a lot of information leakage problems [1]. For example, medical information, medical images are easily tampered with during transmission. From the perspective of security, it is necessary to introduce digital watermarking technology [2, 3] into the medical care system. Medical images are the personal privacy of patients. In order to protect these information, experts use the robustness and invisibility of digital watermarking to hide the patient's personal information in medical images. When the information needs to be verified, it can be done by extracting the watermark [4]. Digital watermarks have the following characteristics: invisibility, digital works embedded in digital watermarks, it will not cause a significant drop in quality, and it is not easy to be noticed. Robustness, the watermark can still be extracted

© Springer Nature Switzerland AG 2021
J. Cheng et al. (Eds.): CSS 2020, LNCS 12653, pp. 120–131, 2021.
https://doi.org/10.1007/978-3-030-73671-2_12

by the watermark extraction algorithm after the watermark carrier is attacked [5]. Medical images are important evidence for doctors to diagnose. Therefore, any operation that may modify medical information should be avoided. Wen quan et al. proposed the concept of "zero watermark" for the first time, that is, the important features of the original image are used to construct the watermark information, and the contradiction between the robustness of invisible watermark and the irreversible distortion of the original image is solved well without modifying the image features [6, 7]. Mr. P.V. Hough proposed the Hough transform in 1959, which is a reliable method for straight line detection and a good feature extraction method. Hough transform has excellent robustness and excellent anti-interference ability [8]. Traditional image watermarking methods have poor robustness, and the image watermarking information is easy to change when it get attacked.

Therefore, this paper proposes a robust watermarking algorithm for medical images based on Hough transform and discrete cosine transform (HT-DCT). This method uses Hough transform and discrete cosine transform to extract visual feature vectors of medical images for watermark embedding and extraction, and uses logical map to encrypt watermark, which greatly improves the security and robustness of medical images. Experimental results show that the proposed method is robust to geometric attacks and conventional attacks without changing the original medical images.

2   The Fundamental Theory

2.1   Hough Transform (HT)

Hough transform is an effective algorithm for finding straight lines in digital image technology [9]. It first maps the target point of the rectangular coordinate system to the polar coordinate system for accumulation, that is, first all points on any straight line on the rectangular coordinate system plane are accumulated to the same point in the polar coordinate system, and then by looking for the polar coordinate, the peak of the midpoint set is used to find the long straight line feature. Since this point set is obtained through cumulative statistics, it can tolerate the discontinuity of the straight line. The basic idea of Hough's transformation is point-line duality. In the image space XY, all straight lines passing through the point (x, y) satisfy the equation:

$$y = px + q \tag{1}$$

Where p is the slope and q is the intercept.

Equation (1) can also be written as.

$$q = -px + y \tag{2}$$

Equation (2) can be regarded as a straight line that passes the point (p, q) in the parameter space PQ. It can be seen that the collinear points in the image space correspond to the intersecting lines in the parameter space. That is, all straight lines that intersect at the same point in the parameter space have collinear points corresponding to them in the image space. The Hough Transformation transforms the detection problem in the image space into the parameter space according to these relationships, and completes the detection task by performing simple accumulation statistics in the parameter space [10]. Equation (1) When the straight line is close to the vertical direction, both p and q will be close to infinity and the calculation will be greatly increased. Therefore, we can use the polar coordinate equation of the straight line:

$$\rho = x \cos \theta + y \sin \theta, 0 \leq \theta \leq \pi \tag{3}$$

ρ is the distance from the origin to the straight line and θ is the angle between the normal of the straight line and the x-axis

As shown in Fig. 1(a). When all the feature points on a straight line in the image space are mapped in this way, there will be many sinusoids in the parameter space, and all these sinusoids pass through the unit (ρ, θ), so that the parameters of this straight line are determined by The coordinates of the unit (p, θ) are expressed, as shown in Fig. 1(b)

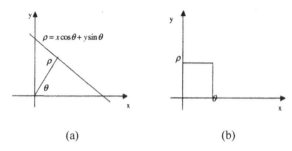

(a)   (b)

Fig. 1. Hough transform diagram: (a) Linear equation (b) Hough transform of a single point.

2.2 Discrete Cosine Transform

Discrete cosine transform can divide the image into different frequencies for work, including low frequency, high frequency and intermediate frequency coefficients [11]. After the image undergoes the discrete cosine transform, most of the energy is concentrated in the low frequency part. When applied to an M × N image or matrix, the two-dimensional discrete cosine transform (DCT) is as follows:

$$F(u, v) = c(u)c(v) \sum_{x=0}^{M-1} \sum_{y=0}^{N-1} f(x, y) \cos \frac{\pi(2y+1)v}{2N} \tag{4}$$

$$u = 0, 1, \cdots, M - 1; \quad v = 0, 1, \cdots, N - 1;$$

In the formula:

$$c(u) = \begin{cases} \sqrt{1/M} & u = 0 \\ \sqrt{2/M} & u = 1, 2, \cdots, M - 1 \end{cases}$$

$$c(v) = \begin{cases} \sqrt{1/N} & v = 0 \\ \sqrt{2/N} & v = 1, 2, \cdots, N - 1 \end{cases} \tag{5}$$

In the formula, M × N indicates the size of the image, and the formula shows that the sign of the DCT coefficient is related to the phrase of the component.

2.3 Logistic Map

Chaos is a deterministic and random-like process that appears in nonlinear dynamic systems. This process is non-periodic, non-convergent but bounded, and has an extremely sensitive dependence on the initial value. Using this property, chaotic mapping can be Provide a large number of uncorrelated, random and deterministic signals that are easy to generate and reproduce [12].

The logistic map is one of the most famous chaotic maps, which is a simple dynamic nonlinear regression with chaotic behavior [13, 14]. Its mathematical definition can be expressed as follows:

$$x_{k+1} = \mu x_k (1 - x_k) \tag{6}$$

Where x_k belongs to $(0, \ 1), 0 < u \leq 4$, Experiments show that when $3.5699456 < u < = 4$, the logistic map enters the chaotic state and the Logistic chaotic sequence can be used as a good key sequence.

3 Watermarking Algorithm

3.1 Acquire the Feature Vector of Medical Images

After HT-DCT transformation of medical images, low frequency coefficients are removed. The extraction method is as follows:

Step 1: Use the Canny algorithm to extract the edge of the original medical image I (i, j) to obtain the BW(i,j) edge set;

$$BW(i, j) = edge((i, j), ' Canny');$$

Step 2: Perform Hough transform on BW edge set points to obtain coefficient matrix H (i, j);

$$[H, T, R] = HOUGH(BW(i, j));$$

Step 3: Perform DCT transformation on the coefficient matrix H (i, j) to obtain the coefficient matrix F (i, j);

$$F(i, j) = DCT2(H(i, j));$$

After a lot of simulation, we found that the low-frequency coefficients after HT-DCT transformation may change, but the signs of the coefficients remain unchanged. So we perform perceptual hash binarization on this part of the coefficient. Let "1" represent the coefficient greater than or equal to zero, and "0" represent the coefficient less than zero. The hash coefficient is shown in the Table 1.

Table 1. Change of HT-DCT coefficients under attacks for the original images.

Image manipulation	PSNR (dB)	F(1, 1)	F(2, 1)	F(3, 1)	F(4, 1)	F(5, 1)	F(6, 1)	F(7, 1)	F(8, 1)	Symbol sequence	NC
The original image		3.03	−1.31	−1.74	1.32	−0.92	0.37	0.38	−0.33	1001 0110	1
Gaussian noise (0.3%)	25.33	3.32	−1.44	−1.86	1.40	−0.98	0.39	0.38	−0.33	1001 0110	0.86
JPEG attack (80%)	37.16	3.03	−1.32	−1.74	1.33	−0.92	0.37	0.37	−0.34	1001 0110	1
Median filter [3 × 3]	28.59	2.57	−1.11	−1.46	1.10	−0.77	0.31	0.31	−0.28	1001 0110	0.94
Rotation (clockwise 2°)	22.48	3.08	−1.33	−1.76	1.31	−0.87	0.34	0.33	−0.34	1001 0110	0.76
Scaling (×2)		6.67	−2.88	−3.72	2.79	−1.99	0.1	0.69	−0.55	1001 0110	0.75
Movement (right 4%)	14.67	3.07	−1.37	−1.69	1.31	−0.93	0.45	0.29	−0.34	1001 0110	0.79

HT-DCT coefficient unit: $1.0e + 003$.

As shown in the Table 1, the hash perception coefficients of the attacked medical images are basically the same. Therefore, we can use the coefficient symbols as the feature vectors of the medical images.

3.2 Watermark Embedding

The specific steps are as follows (see Fig. 2.):

Step 1. The medical image could be processed by HT-DCT.

Step 2. Select the transform coefficient (32×1).

Step 3. Obtain 32-bit binary feature sequence of medical image.

Step 4. Use Logistic Map to scrambling the original watermarking image.

Step 5. Get the watermarking extraction key sequence though XOR operation.

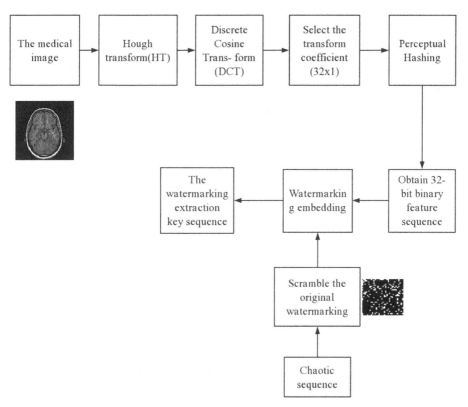

Fig. 2. The watermarking embedding process

3.3 Watermark Extraction

The specific steps are as follows (see Fig. 3.):

Step 1. The attacked medical image could be processed by HT-DCT.

Step 2. Use the same method to get the 32-bit binary feature sequence of the attacked medical image.

Step 3. XOR the binary feature sequence of the attacked medical image and the watermark extraction key sequence.

Step 4. Reverse the scrambled watermark image.

Step 5. Calculate the NC value of the watermark after the attack.

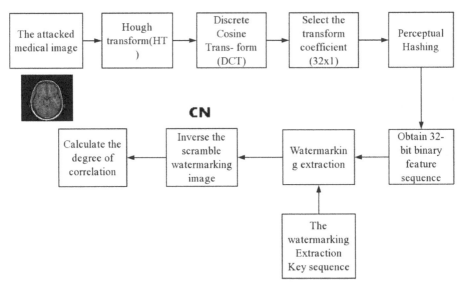

Fig. 3. The watermarking extraction process

3.4   Watermark Evaluation

We use the following formula to evaluate the normalized correlation coefficient between the attacked watermark $W'(i,j)$ and the original watermark $W(i,j)$.

$$NC = \frac{\sum_i \sum_j W(i,j)W'(i,j)}{\sum_i \sum_j W^2(i,j)} \qquad (7)$$

The peak signal-to-noise ratio formula is as follows:

$$PSNR = 10\lg\left[\frac{MN \max\limits_{i,j}(I_{(i,j)})^2}{\sum_i \sum_j (I_{(i,j)} - I'_{(i,j)})^2}\right] \qquad (8)$$

PSNR value indicates the degree of image distortion, and the larger the PSNR value, the smaller was the distortion of the image. Where $I_{(i,j)}$ and $I'_{(i,j)}$ represent the gray values of the original medical images and the coordinates of the embedded watermark images (i,j), respectively, M and N represent the pixel values of image rows and columns.

4   Experiments and Results

We use matlab 2016a as the simulation platform in this experiment, and choose the brain slice image (512 × 512) as the original medical image, and the letter image (32 × 32) as the watermark, as hown in Fig. 4(a) and Fig. 4(b). The encrypted watermark is completely different from the watermark to ensure the security of the information. Shown in Fig. 4(c). In this experiment, the initial value of the chaotic coefficient was set to 0.2, the growth parameter was 4, and the iteration number was 32.

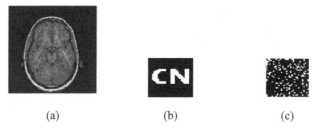

(a)   (b)   (c)

Fig. 4. Watermarks and their chaotic encrypted images: (a) Original image, (b) Watermark, (c) Watermark of chaotic encryption.

4.1 General Attacks

Median Filtering Attack

As shown in the Fig. 5(a), we performed a median filter attack on the original medical image (parameters [3 × 3], filtering repeat time 10), the picture after the attack is still clear, and the watermark also detects a higher NC value,as shown in Fig. 5(b), NC = 0.94, which shows that the proposed algorithm is robust to median filtering attacks (Table 2).

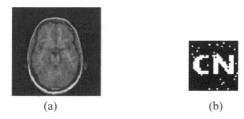

(a)   (b)

Fig. 5. Median filtered watermarked images and extracted watermarks: (a) Median filtering [3 × 3], 10 times (b) Extracted watermarking.

Table 2. PSNR and NC values under median filtering attack.

Parameter	[3 × 3]			[5 × 5]			[7 × 7]		
Times	5	10	20	5	10	20	5	10	20
PSNR (dB)	29.53	25.59	27.95	25.36	24.53	23.87	22.88	22.20	21.48
NC	0.89	0.94	0.90	0.76	0.77	0.70	0.76	0.70	0.75

Gaussian Noise Attack

We use different degrees of Gaussian noise to attack the original medical image. As shown in the Fig. 6 and Table 3, the watermark extracted from the image after the 1% Gaussian noise attack is seriously distorted, and the NC value is only 0.44.

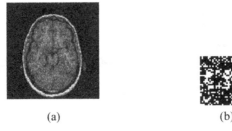

(a)   (b)

Fig. 6. Image attacked by Gaussian noise and extracted watermarks: (a) the Gauss noise intensity 1%, (b) Extracted watermarking.

Table 3. The PSNR and NC values under Gaussian noise

Noise intensity/%	0.1	0.3	0.5	1
PSNR(dB)	30.03	25.30	23.22	20.48
NC	0.88	0.82	0.82	0.44

JEPG Compression Attack

The original medical image is attacked by different JPEG compression ratios as shown in Fig. 7 and Table 4. As seen from Table 4, the PSNR values increased followed with the compression ratio. When the JEPG compression rate reached 80%, the NC value is still as high as 1.00. The algorithm is robust to JEPG attacks.

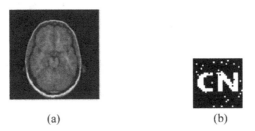

(a)   (b)

Fig. 7. JPEG compressed 40% watermarked images and extracts watermarks: (a) JPEG compression quality 40%, (b) Extracted watermarking.

Table 4. The PSNR and NC values under compression

Compression quality	5%	10%	20%	40%	60%	80%
PSNR(dB)	26.70	29.27	30.06	34.09	35.35	37.16
NC	0.82	0.61	0.86	0.82	0.86	1

4.2 General Attacks

Rotation Attack

As shown in the Fig. 8, when the medical picture is rotated by 2, the watermark can still be extracted clearly, and the NC value is 0.76. The quality of the watermark increases with the degree of rotation, and when it increases to 10°, the extracted watermark is still clear It can be seen that the NC value is 0.81 (Table 5). This shows that the method is robust to rotating attacks.

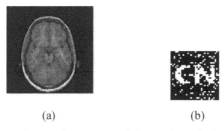

(a)   (b)

Fig. 8. Watermark image and extraction watermark in rotation (clockwise 2°): (a) Parameter is 2°, (b) Extracted watermarking.

Table 5. The NC value under rotation attack (clockwise).

Parameter /°	2	3	4	6	8	10
PSNR(dB)	22.48	20.46	19.07	17.27	16.23	15.61
NC	0.76	0.75	0.80	0.74	0.75	0.81

Scaling Attack

We carry out different degrees of scaling attacks on medical images and extract watermarks. From the Fig. 9 and Table 6, we can see that when the scaling factor is 2, the NC value of the watermark is 0.75. This shows that this method is robust against scaling attacks.

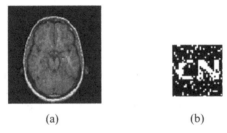

(a)   (b)

Fig. 9. Watermark image and extraction watermark in scaling: (a) Parameter is 2, (b) Extracted watermarking.

Table 6. The NC value under scaling attack (clockwise).

Zoom (×)	0.8	1	1.4	1.8	2
NC	0.95	1	0.75	0.80	0.75

Moving Attack

As shown in the Fig. 10 and Table 7, when the medical image moves to the right (4%), the extracted watermark can still be identified, and the NC value is 0.79. Therefore, it can be shown that the algorithm has good robustness to mobile attacks.

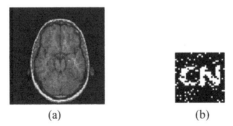

(a)   (b)

Fig. 10. Movement (right) 4% watermark image and extract watermark: (a) Movement (right) 20%, (b) Extracted watermarking.

Table 7. The PSNR and NC values under moving attack.

Movement (right)/%	2	4	6
PSNR(dB)	16.06	14.67	14.35
NC	0.86	0.79	0.55

5 Conclusion

This paper proposes a robust medical image watermarking algorithm based on Hough transform and discrete cosine transform (HT-DCT). This method uses HT-DCT to extract the visual feature vector of the medical image to embed and extract the watermark and the chaotic map to tamper with the watermark to improve the security of the watermark information. Experimental results prove that the algorithm not only improves the security of the medical image watermark information, but it has good robustness under both conventional attacks and geometric attacks.

Acknowledgement. This work was supported in part by the Hainan Provincial Natural Science Foundation of China under Grant 2019RC018 and by the Natural Science Foundation of China under Grant 62063004 and 61762033, in part by the Hainan Provincial Higher Education Research Project under Grant Hnky2019–73, and in part by the Key Research Project of Haikou College of Economics under Grant HJKZ18–01.

References

1. Wu, D.Y., Zhao, J., Wang, G.P.: An image zero watermarking technology based on improved singular value and sub-block mapping. Acta Optics 1–20 (2020)
2. Chen, M.Q., Niu, X.X., Yang, Y.X.: Research progress and application of digital watermarking. J. Commun. **22**(5), 71–79 (2001)
3. Sun, S.H., Lu, Z.M.: Digital watermarking processing technology. Acta Electron. Sin. **28**(8), 85–90 (2000)
4. Cheng S.: Research on digital watermarking algorithm for medical image. Nanjing University of Posts and Telecommunications (2013)
5. Gong, A., Li, C.Y., Chen, G.: Digital watermarking technology and application. Comput. Inf. Technol. 91–93 (2010)
6. Wen, Q., Sun, T.F., Wang, S.X.: The concept of zero watermark and application. J. Electron. **31**(2), 214–216 (2003)
7. Ye, D.P.: Zero-watermark copyright protection scheme based on binary image construction. Comput. Appl. Res. **24**(8), 239–241 (2007)
8. Yi, L.: Fast hough transform line detection based on classification. Microcomput. Inf. **23**(11), 206–208 (2007)
9. Sun, F.R., Liu, J.R.: Fast hough transform algorithm. J. Comput. 1102–1109 (2001)
10. Zhang, H.Z., Zhang, L.X.: Hough transform to extract the target boundary. Comput. Appl. 117–119 (2003)
11. Candès, E., Demanet, L., Donoho, D., Ying, L.: Fast discrete curvelet transforms. Multiscale Model. Simul **5**(3), 861–899 (2006)
12. Li, J.H., Hou, J.J.: Fragile digital watermarking algorithm in DCT domain based on Logistic chaotic mapping. Chin. J. Electron. 2134–2137 (2006)
13. Liao, X.F.: Analysis and improvement of image encryption algorithm based on Logistic chaotic system. Softw. Guide **16**(5), 39–41 (2017)
14. Yuan, L., Kang, B.S.: Image scrambling algorithm based on Logistic chaotic sequence and bit exchange. Comput. Appl. **29**(10), 2681–2683 (2009)

The Blind Separation of Cockpit Mixed Signals Based on Fast Independent Component Analysis

Zhengmao Wu[1(✉)], Sihai Li[1], Jing Sun[2], and Mingrui Chen[1,2,3]

[1] Sanya Aviation and Tourism College, Sanya 572000, Hainan, China
[2] Yueyang Vocational Technical College, Yueyang 414000, Hunan, China
[3] Hainan University, Haikou 570228, Hainan, China

Abstract. Cockpit Voice Recorder (CVR) records all the sound signals related to the accident in the cockpit before the crash. Accurate analysis of the cockpit voice signal is the basis for exploring the real reason behind the flight accident, which often starts from the separation of cockpit mixed signals. In this paper, a Fast Independent Component Analysis (FastICA) method for mixed signal separation is proposed. The basic idea of the method, three classical assumptions and the independence criteria of separation results are presented. The FastICA algorithm is analyzed theoretically, and the blind separation experiment of cockpit mixed signals is realized in this paper. The simulation experiment result shows that although FastICA algorithm is complex in theory, the realize of this algorithm is concise and clear, which can quickly and effectively separate these signals, and provide research basis for accurate analysis of the causes of aircraft accidents in the later stage.

Keywords: Cockpit voice recorder · Independent component analysis · Blind signal separation · FastICA · Python

1 Introduction

Cockpit Voice Recorder (CVR) and Flight Data Recorder (FDR) of modern civil aviation aircraft are generally referred to as flight recorders, which are commonly known as "Black Box" [1]. Flight Recorders are mandatory installation of airborne accident investigation equipment in civil aviation. Through four independent channels, the CVR records the voice information in the cockpit in the last 2 h or 30 min, including land air communication, crew intercom, audio warning, etc. In fact, CVR not only records the voice information, but also records the sound of switch button and engine noise. These sound information reflects the objective working state of the aircraft and its systems, as well as the pilots' perception and emotional description of what happened in the cockpit [2].

CVR is often the "First Witness" of civil aviation aircraft accidents. To explore the real causes behind aircraft accidents, looking for the CVR of the crashed aircraft and separating various information in the cockpit is known as the starting point of the investigation. At present, the professional decoding system of CVR is mainly used in

© Springer Nature Switzerland AG 2021
J. Cheng et al. (Eds.): CSS 2020, LNCS 12653, pp. 132–143, 2021.
https://doi.org/10.1007/978-3-030-73671-2_13

China to distinguish and hear through human ears. Obviously, when a variety of sounds are mixed together, it will greatly affect the effect of hearing discrimination [3].

Independent Component Analysis (ICA) is a very effective signal analysis tool proposed in recent years. It can be used to extract useful original independent signals from mixed signals or separate them. Although it is not a long time since ICA appeared, it has been paid more and more attention in theory and application, and has become a hot spot of research at home and abroad [4]. Among many ICA algorithms, the fixed point algorithm (FastICA) is widely used in signal processing because of its fast convergence and good separation effect. Based on some basic statistical characteristics of the original signal, such as statistical independence and non Gaussian distribution, the algorithm can estimate the original signal which is statistically independent and mixed by unknown factors. Since the blind separation of signals does not require prior knowledge of known sources, it has many potential uses [5].

In this paper, we try to use the popular Scikit-learn tool to implement FastICA algorithm and complete the blind separation experiment of mixed signals. Scikit-learn (module named sklearn) is an open source machine learning tool based on Python language. It uses Numpy, SciPy and Matplotlib libraries to implement efficient algorithm applications, and covers almost all mainstream machine learning algorithms [6, 7].

2 ICA Background and Its Basic Principle

2.1 Question Prototype - Cocktail Party Question

In a noisy cocktail party, n people speak in one room at the same time, and there may be background music. M microphones are placed in different positions of the room. Each microphone can simultaneously collect the overlapping voice of each person's voice at every moment. Because the distance between each microphone and each person is different, the overlap of sounds received by each microphone is also different. How to separate the speaker's voice from the mixed sound signals observed by multiple microphones has become a standard research topic in Blind Signal Separation (BSS). A. J. Bell's research on this problem has become one of the milestones in the development of ICA algorithm. This research can distinguish the speech of 10 speakers, which fully shows the great potentiality of ICA [8].

2.2 Mathematical Description

Suppose N unknown and statistically independent signal sources $S_i(t)$ constitute a column vector $S(t) = [S_1(t), S_2(t), \cdots, S_N(t)]^T$. Let A be an M × N-dimensional matrix, which is generally called a mixed matrix. Let $X(t) = [x_1(t), x_2(t), \cdots, x_M(t)]^T$, which is a column vector composed of M observable signals $X_i(t)$. It is the signal received by M sensors after the source signal S(t) is mixed by the mixing matrix A. The matrix form can be expressed as follows:

$$X(t) = A\,S(t), \ M \geq N \tag{1}$$

The proposition of Independent Component Analysis is: assuming that the signal source is a real random variable and the source signals are statistically independent, only one Gaussian distribution is allowed and the signal number M is the same as the observed signal number N, that is M = N. The mixed matrix A is full rank, that is, the inverse matrix A^{-1} exists. In the case of no noise, the unknown source signal S(t) should be obtained or separated according to the known observed signal X(t). This constitutes the problem of noise free Blind Signal Separation [9].

2.3 Problem Solving Thought

The basic idea of ICA is to find an N × N -dimensional inverse mixing matrix $W = (w_{ij})$. X(t) can get N-dimensional output column vector $Y(t) = [y_1(t), y_2(t), \cdots, y_N(t)]^T$ after W transformation. There are:

$$Y(t) = WX(t) = WAS(t) \tag{2}$$

If WA = I (I is an N × N-dimensional unit array) or $W = A^{-1}$ can be realized by learning, then Y(t) is an estimation of the original signal vector S(t), so as to achieve the goal of source separation.

The key of ICA is to establish an objective function which can measure the independence of separation results and find the optimal separation algorithm under the premise of maximizing or minimizing the objective function.

There are two inherent uncertainties in Blind Signal Separation: one is the uncertainty of the sequence of output vectors, that is, it is impossible to determine which component of the original signal source corresponding to the extracted signal; the other is the uncertainty of the output signal amplitude, that is, it can not be recovered to the true amplitude of the signal source. However, since the main information is contained in the output signal, these two uncertainties do not affect the application of BSS [10].

2.4 Classical Hypothesis of ICA

In order to realize independent component analysis, ICA gives the following three assumptions.

1. It is assumed that the components $S_i(t)$ of the source signal vector S(t) are statistically independent.
2. It is assumed that only one component of the source signal vector S(t) is a Gaussian random variable, because the stronger the non Gaussian property, the better the independence of the signal source.
3. Suppose that the mixed matrix A is a square matrix, that is, M = N.

2.5 The Independence Criterion of Separation Results

The research of ICA algorithm can be divided into two categories: iterative estimation method based on information theory criterion and algebraic method based on statistics. In principle, they all make use of the independence and non Gaussian of the source signal. In the research of methods based on information theory, scholars from various countries have proposed a series of estimation algorithms from the perspectives of maximum entropy, minimum mutual information, maximum likelihood and maximum negative entropy, such as FastICA algorithm, Infomax algorithm, Maximum likelihood estimation algorithm, etc. The methods based on statistics mainly include second-order cumulant, fourth-order cumulant and so on. The following mainly introduces the independence criterion of maximizing negative entropy [11].

According to the central limit theorem, if a random variable X is the sum of many independent random variables, as long as each independent random variable has finite mean and variance, and regardless of the distribution of independent random variables, the distribution of sum of the variable X tends to Gaussian distribution more than that of single independent component. Therefore, the problem of judging whether the output components are independent can be transformed into the problem of calculating the maximum non Gaussian property of the output components [12].

Let the probability density of the output random vector Y be p(y), and the entropy H of the random vector Y is defined as:

$$H(y) = -\int p(y)\log(p(y))dy \tag{3}$$

Information entropy is the information measure of random variables. The more random, the greater the entropy.

Negative entropy N(y) is defined as:

$$N(y) = H(y_{gauss}) - H(y) \tag{4}$$

Where y_{gauss} is a Gaussian variable with the same variance as y.

There is a basic conclusion of information theory: among the random variables with the same variance, the random variables with Gaussian distribution have the largest information entropy, but the stronger the non Gaussian, the smaller the information entropy. It can be seen from formula (4) that when y is a Gaussian signal, N(y) value is 0; when y is a non Gaussian signal, N(y) value is greater than 0, and the stronger the non Gaussian property of y is, the greater the N(y) value is. The maximization of negative entropy N(y) is the maximization of non Gaussian property. Therefore, negative entropy can be used as the objective function to measure the independence of separation results.

In practical application, because the probability density function of Y is difficult to know, so N(y) is difficult to calculate directly, only approximate calculation can be used. The following is the expression of estimating negative entropy by the mean value of function G in reference [13].

$$N(y_i) = K\left[E\{G(y_i)\} - E\{G(y_{yauss})\}\right] \tag{5}$$

When the algorithm is used, the function $G(y_i)$ is a non quadratic function and K is a normal number. For details, please refer to the selection principle in reference [13].

3 FastICA Algorithm Flow

FastICA algorithm is proposed and developed by the Computer and Information Science Laboratory of Helsinki University of Technology in Finland. The algorithm finds a unit vector W through systematic learning and makes its projection $W^T X$ have the maximum non Gaussian property. There are two main steps in running FastICA algorithm: first, the observed signal is preprocessed, that is, removing the mean and whitening; secondly, the FastICA algorithm is run to make the output Yi have the maximum mutual independence and complete the signal separation [14].

3.1 Observation Signal Preprocessing

Firstly, the observed data X is normalized, that is, the mean value m = E{x} is subtracted, so that the observed signal becomes a zero mean vector. Normalization pretreatment can simplify ICA algorithm.

Secondly, the whitening process is to transform the observed signal X linearly $\tilde{X} = VX$ so that the components after whitening are uncorrelated with each other and are unit variance $E\left\{\tilde{X}\tilde{X}^T\right\} = I$. Whitening is usually realized by Principal Component Analysis (PCA). The whitening matrix is $V = \Lambda^{-\frac{1}{2}}U^T$. Where is the diagonal matrix $\Lambda = \mathrm{diag}(d_1, d_2, \cdots, d_n)$ composed of n eigenvalues of correlation coefficient matrix R, and U is the matrix composed of eigenvectors corresponding to n eigenvalues.

In addition to the uncorrelated processing of observation signal X, whitening processing can also reduce the dimension. Generally speaking, ICA algorithm converges faster and gets better stability after whitening. The estimation matrix A needs to estimate n^2 parameters, while the estimation of orthogonal matrix only needs to estimate n(n − 1)/2 parameters, which greatly reduces the computational complexity of ICA algorithm.

3.2 Estimate Separation Matrix W and Extract Independent Components

Let W_i be a column vector of the separation matrix W, which is the whitened data with zero mean and unit covariance. Suppose that a source signal to be estimated is $y_i = w_i^T \tilde{x}$. Substituting it into Eq. (5), we can get the following result:

$$N(y_i) = N\left(w_i^T \tilde{x}\right) = K\left[E\left\{G\left(w_i^T \tilde{x}\right)\right\} - E\left\{G(y_{yauss})\right\}\right]^2 \tag{6}$$

In this way, the criterion of negative entropy can be understood as follows: if we try to find a W_i so that $N(y_i)$ reaches a maximum, we can obtain an independent component $S_i(t) = Y_i(t)$. Because $E\left\{G(y_{yauss})\right\}$ is a constant, finding the maximum of the negative entropy of $y_i = w_i^T \tilde{x}$ is equivalent to finding the maximum of $E\left\{G(w_i^T \tilde{x})\right\}$. Under the constraint conditions $E\left\{G(w_i^T \tilde{x})\right\} E\left\{(w_i^T \tilde{x})^2\right\} = E\left\{w_i^T w_i\right\} = 1$, the following cost function is constructed: $F(w_i) = E\left\{G(w_i^T \tilde{x}) + \lambda[E(w_i^T w) - 1]^2\right\}$.

In order to obtain the maximum value $F(w_i)$, let $f(w_i) = \frac{\partial F(w_i)}{\partial w_i}$ be 0. The following iterative formula is obtained by solving w_i by Newton iteration method.

$$w_i(k + 1) = w_i(k) - \frac{f(w_i(k))}{f'(w_i(k))} \tag{7}$$

Because $f'(w_i(k)) = E\left\{\tilde{x}^T \tilde{x}g'(w_i^T \tilde{x})\right\} - \beta I = E\left\{g'(w_i^T \tilde{x})\right\} - \beta I$ and $\beta I = E\left\{w_i^T \tilde{x}g(w_i^T \tilde{x})\right\}$.

In this way, the iterative formula is written as follows:

$$w_i(k+1) = w_i(k) - \frac{E\{\tilde{x}g(w_i^T(k)\tilde{x})\} - \beta w_i(k)}{E\{g'(w_i^T(k)\tilde{x})\} - \beta I} \quad (8)$$

It can be further written as follows:

$$w_i(k+1) = E\{\tilde{x}g(w_i^T(k)\tilde{x})\} - E\{g'(w_i^T(k)\tilde{x})\}w_i(k) \quad (9)$$

According to iterative formula (9), w_i can be obtained recursively, and an independent component can be separated by further calculation of $w_i^T\tilde{x}$. It should be noted that: after each iteration, w_i should be normalized, that is, to ensure that the separated results have unit energy; for the extraction of multiple independent components, after extracting each component, the independent component should be subtracted from the observation signal, and the above separation process should be repeated until all independent components are completely separated [15].

4   Simulation Results and Performance Analysis

The following are two groups of experimental results of mixed signal separation using FastICA algorithm. The simulation environment is Spyder under anaconda3, and the programming language is Python 3.7. The standard library and third-party modules of Python are mainly used, including Numpy, Wave, Matplotlib and Sklearn. The Numpy is an extended library of Python language, which supports a large number of dimensional array and matrix operations, and also provides a great deal of mathematical function libraries for array operations. The Wave module provides a convenient interface for processing wave sound format files. The Wave module does not support compression/decompression, but it supports mono/stereo. The Sklearn (scikit-learn) module is a common third-party module in machine learning. The Sklearn module encapsulates common machine learning methods, including regression, dimensional reduction, classification, clustering and so on [6, 16, 17]. The citation methods of main modules and ICA function in the program are as follows:

```
import numpy as np
import wave
import matplotlib.pyplot as plt
from sklearn.decomposition import FastICA
……

ica = FastICA(n_components=4) # There are 4 independent
components
```

4.1   Simple Signal Separation

In the first experiment, four common signals are randomly mixed and separated by FastICA algorithm. The four common signals are sine wave, sawtooth wave, square wave and random signal, as shown in Fig. 1.

The four signal sources are mixed according to the randomly generated matrix, and the mixed signals are shown in Fig. 2.

After being unmixed by ICA algorithm, the signal is separated, the separated signals are shown in Fig. 3.

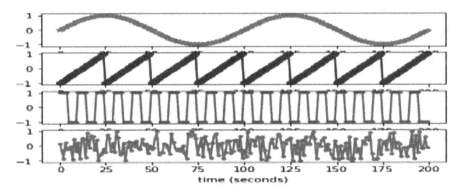

Fig. 1. Four basic signal waveforms

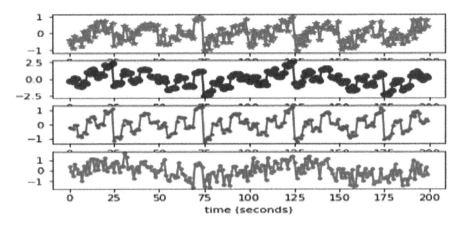

Fig. 2. Mixed waveforms of four basic signals

According to the waveform results after separation in Fig. 3, FastICA algorithm can basically separate mixed signals, but the sequence, amplitude and phase of signals after separation have changed, which just verifies two uncertainties of ICA algorithm: one is the uncertainty of output signal sequence and the other is the uncertainty of output signal amplitude. The number of iterations is 5 in the experiment. The unmixed matrix is as follows.

```
[[ -0.84404744   -8.49932598   -2.81939283    7.89626743]
 [ -3.72387623   -2.64310061  -11.19695028    3.32051678]
 [ -2.60734638   -6.90860045   -1.64240691    1.2761872 ]
 [ -6.76356312   -7.31836801   -5.37749473    5.08481377]]
```

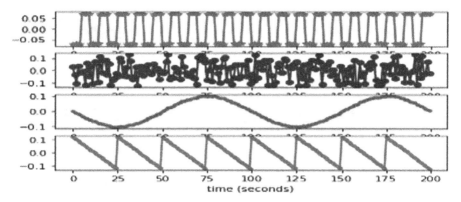

Fig. 3. Separated waveforms of four mixed basic signals

4.2 Cockpit Mixed Signal Separation

In the second experiment, four sound signals in the cockpit were randomly mixed and separated by FastICA algorithm.

The original sound signal comes from Boeing 737–800 simulator, which is a typical aircraft of modern civil aviation. It includes crew voice, fire alarm, overspeed warning and other warning sounds, as shown in Fig. 4.

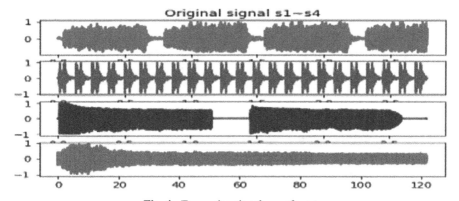

Fig. 4. Four voice signal waveforms

The signal is mono channel, the sampling frequency is 48000 Hz, and the sampling depth is 2 bytes. Then the four original sound signals are randomly mixed, and the shortest length is intercepted after mixing, as shown in Fig. 5.

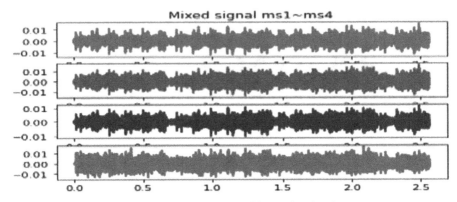

Fig. 5. Mixed waveform of four voice signals

The separated voice signal is shown in Fig. 6. The number of iterations of the algorithm in this experiment is 3, the unmixed matrix is as follows.

```
[[-0.0512429    0.62484974  -0.16021129   0.53013271]
 [-0.0567761    0.31123055  -0.32071436   0.79515322]
 [-0.32054797   0.32310568  -0.50733082   0.10109215]
 [-0.05578936   0.38942496  -0.56083011   0.13901414]]
```

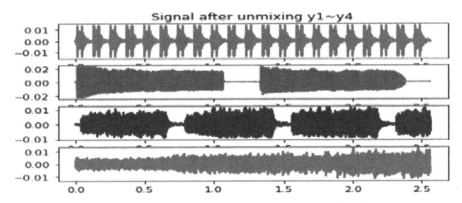

Fig. 6. Separated waveforms of four mixed voice signals

According to the waveform results after separation in Fig. 6, FastICA algorithm can also quickly and accurately separate the mixed sound signals in the cockpit, but the sequence of signals and the amplitude of output signals also change after separation, and these two changes have little impact on the analysis of the causes of aircraft accidents.

Figure 7, 8, 9 and 10 below shows the scatter diagram of the separated signal and the original signal. The horizontal axis is the original signal s_i ($i = 1$–4), and the vertical axis is the separated signal y_i ($i = 1$–4). It is realized by scatter function in Matplotlib module, which can more intuitively illustrate the separation degree of the separated signal and the original signal.

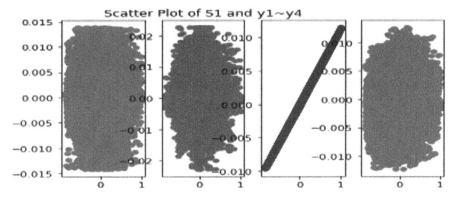

Fig. 7. Scatter plot of original signal S1 and separated signal

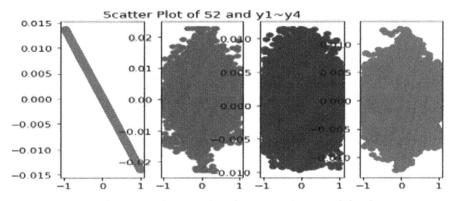

Fig. 8. Scatter plot of original signal S2 and separated signal

In Fig. 7, 8, 9 and 10, if the scatter plot of si and yi is approximately a straight line, that is, the separated signal is linearly related to the original signal, then yi is the separated signal of si. The more the figure of si and yi presents as a straight line, the better the separation effect of mixed signal is. If the scatter plot of si and yi is non-linear, then yi is not a separate signal of si. In addition, if the scatter diagram of si and yi is approximately a straight line with an acute angle to the horizontal axis, then yi is the separated signal of si with the same phase; if the scatter diagram of si and yi is approximately a straight line with an obtuse angle with the horizontal axis, it means that yi is also the separated signal of Si, but the phase of the two signals is opposite.

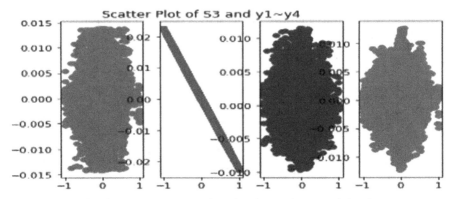

Fig. 9. Scatter plot of original signal S3 and separated signal

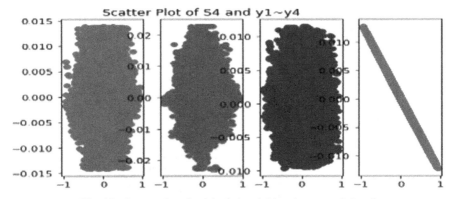

Fig. 10. Scatter plot of original signal S4 and separated signal

5 Conclusion

Based on the ICA algorithm in machine learning, this paper proposes a FastICA algorithm, which is used to separate cockpit mixed signal. The number of iterations and separation results of computer simulation experiments' results show that FastICA is a fast and effective algorithm and it can be a powerful tool to separate or extract the independent information from the observed signals. The separated voice information provides an important research basis for accurate analysis of the causes of aircraft accidents in the later stage. In addition to Blind Signal Separation, we will verify the feasibility of the FastICA algorithm in image processing, language recognition, communication, biomedical signal processing, brain functional imaging research, fault diagnosis, feature extraction, financial time series analysis and data mining.

Acknowledgement. This research was financially supported by Hainan Natural Science Foundation Surface Project (20166236).

References

1. Federal Aviation Administration: Advisory Circular AC20-186. FAA, Washington, D.C. (2016)
2. National Transportation Safety Board: Safety Recommendation Report: Extended Duration Cockpit Voice Recorders. ASR-18–04. NTSB, Washington (2018)
3. European Union: Commission Regulation (EU) 2015/2338: Official Journal of the European Union, L 330, 16 December 2015, pp. 1–11 (2015)
4. Acharya, D.P., Panda, G.: A review of independent component analysis techniques and their applications. IETE Tech. Rev. **5**(6), 320–332 (2014)
5. Nikam, S., Deosarkar, S.: Fast ICA based technique for non-invasive fetal ECG extraction. In: 2016 Conference on Advances in Signal Processing (CASP), pp. 60–65 (2016)
6. SHOGUN-TOOLBOX Homepage. http://www.shogun-toolbox.org. Accessed 18 Oct 2020
7. D'Angiulli, A., Devenyi, P.: Retooling computational techniques for EEG-based neurocognitive modeling of children's data, validity and prospects for learning and education. Front. Comput. Neurosci. **13**, 4 (2019)
8. Feifei, X., Stefan, G., Birger, K., et al.: Joint estimation of reverberation time and early-to-late reverberation ratio from single-channel speech signals. IEEE/ACM Trans. Audio Speech Lang. Process. (TASLP) **27**(2), 255–267 (2019)
9. Zhang, K., Wei, Y., Wu, D., Wang, Y.: Adaptive speech separation based on beamforming and frequency domain-independent component analysis. Appl. Sci. **10**(7), 2593 (2020)
10. Mohanaprasad, K., Singh, A., Sinha, K., Ketkar, T.: Noise reduction in speech signals using adaptive independent component analysis (ICA) for hands free communication devices. Int. J. Speech Technol. **22**(1), 169–177 (2019). https://doi.org/10.1007/s10772-019-09595-9
11. Karrupusamy, P., et al. (eds.): Speech separation using deep learning. In: ICSCN 2019, LNDECT 39, pp. 319–326 (2020)
12. Gao, T., Li, J.: The research and simulation of blind source separation algorithm. Int. J. Adv. Pervasive Ubiquitous Comput. (IJAPUC) **8**(3), 1–36 (2016)
13. Hassan, N., Ramli, D.A.: A comparative study of blind source separation for bioacoustics sounds based on FastICA PCA and NMF. Procedia Comput. Sci. **126**, 363–372 (2018)
14. Lei, P., Chen, M., Wang, J.: Speech enhancement for in-vehicle voice control systems using wavelet analysis and blind source separation. IET Intel. Transp. Syst. **13**(4), 693–702 (2019)
15. Sundararajan, T.V.P., Sampath, P., Kiruthika, T., Dharani, E.: Separation of different voices in speech using fast Ica algorithm. Int. J. Eng. Manag. Res. (IJEMR) **6**(6), 364–368 (2016)
16. Hao, J., Ho, T.K.: Machine learning made easy: a review of scikit-learn package in python programming language. J. Educ. Behav. Stat. **44**(3), 348–361 (2019)
17. GITHUT Homepage. https://github.com/LiangjunFeng/Machine-Learning/blob/master/9. FastICA.py. Accessed 21 Oct 2020

A Zero-Watermarking Algorithm for Medical Images Based on Gabor-DCT

Xiliang Xiao[1], Jing Liu[3], Jingbing Li[1,2(✉)], Yangxiu Fang[1], Cheng Zeng[1], Jiabin Hu[1], and Uzair Aslam Bhatti[4]

[1] School of Information and Communication Engineering, Hainan University, Haikou, Hainan, People's Republic of China
{FangYangxiu,18085208210009}@hainanu.edu.cn
[2] State Key Laboratory of Marine Resource Utilization in the South China Sea, Hainan University, Haikou, Hainan, People's Republic of China
[3] Research Center for Healthcare Data Science, Zhejiang Lab, Hangzhou, Zhejiang, People's Republic of China
liujinglj@zhejianglab.edu.cn
[4] School of Geography (Remote sensing and GIS Lab), Nanjing Normal University, Nanjing, People's Republic of China

Abstract. The development of digital age accelerated the development of digital medical systems, but it also inevitably brings security problems of the transmission and storage of medical images in the network. The wide use of digital watermarking technology in medical images has effectively improved such problems, but the research on the medical image watermarking algorithm is still less and immature. How to improve the invisibility and robustness of watermark information is a difficult problem in the medical image watermarking algorithm. In this paper, a zero watermarking algorithm for medical images based on Gabor-DCT is proposed. The watermark information first encrypted by a Logistic chaotic map and then combined with the medical image feature vector extracted by the Gabor-DCT algorithm to improve the robustness of the watermark information. At last, the watermark is extracted and embedded by zero watermark technology, which improved the invisibility of the watermark information. Experimental results show the proposed algorithm can effectively resist both common attacks and geometric attacks, and has good invisibility and robustness.

Keywords: Gabor · DCT transform · Zero watermark · Chaotic sequence · Robustness

This work was supported in part by the Hainan Provincial Natural Science Foundation of China under Grant 2019RC018 and by the Natural Science Foundation of China under Grant 62063004 and 61762033, in part by the Hainan Provincial Higher Education Research Project under Grant Hnky2019-73, and in part by the Key Research Project of Haikou College of Economics under Grant HJKZ18-01.

J. Cheng et al. (Eds.): CSS 2020, LNCS 12653, pp. 144–156, 2021.
https://doi.org/10.1007/978-3-030-73671-2_14

1   Introduction

The modern medical system has entered the process of digitalization. A large amount of patient information is disseminated and stored on the Internet in the form of text and images, which facilitates the medical system. But it also brings more security risks due to the insecurity of the Internet [11,14]. Patients' information are easily be attacked and destroyed during the transmission of the network, or even stolen, with poor security. The development of digital watermarking technologies [8,17] provides good solutions to such problems. Combining medical images with watermarks, and embedding patients' information in the medical image in the form of watermarks can better protect patients' information, which can greatly improve the safety and stability of medical images spreading on the network [1,10].

The concept of digital watermarking was first formally proposed by Tirkel et al. They added the watermark information to the least significant bit (LSB). The method is simple, and the robustness is poor, especially in terms of resistance to geometric attacks [13]. At present, the research in the field of medical image watermarking is still immature. Generally, the embedding and extraction of watermarking are mainly concentrated in the spatial domain and the transform domain [6]. The spatial domain refers to directly embedding watermark information in medical images, while the transform domain refers to transforming the image, and then embedding the watermark information in the transformed data. Medical images are generally divided into regions of interest (ROI) and regions of non-interest (RONI). [4] R. Eswaraiah and E. Sreenivasa Reddy proposed a medical image watermarking technology that can locate the tampered position and restore the ROI by combining the watermark information and the ROI.And the information is embedded in the boundary area and RONI. Divide the region of interest into blocks, find the mean and variance, and determine the tampered position of the region of interest. Then use the restoration data embedded in RONI to restore the ROI. This algorithm can be very effective. Good positioning restores the ROI area information, but it is performed in the airspace. If it is subjected to geometric attacks, its robustness is poor, as the information embedded in the edge area and RONI will also be destroyed. The transform domain methods include DCT transform, Fourier transform, wavelet transform, etc. [7,15], which have better hiding and robustness for watermark information and are more popular by researchers. Siddharth Singh et al. proposed an NSCT-DCT-SVD medical image watermarking algorithm. The algorithm decomposed the medical image and watermark into six subbands by NSCT, and then performed DCT transformation on any subband, and applied SVD on the coefficients after DCT transformation. Decompose, and finally add the weight of the two singular values to realize the embedding of the watermark [12], which has high invisibility and robustness. Compared with the spatial domain, the watermark embedding in the transform domain is more robust and effective, but whether it is the spatial algorithm in [4] or the transform domain algorithm in [12], they all need to change the pixel value or transform coefficient to realize the embedding of the watermark. This may affect the visual characteristics of the images, which is not desirable for medical images. The development of zero watermark [5,16] solved this problem very well. It has better robustness and invisibility by finding the feature invariant vector of the image and combining it with the watermark.

Gabor texture features are mostly used in face recognition, expression recognition, fingerprint recognition, image index, etc. [3,9]. Since the Gabor transform can extract texture features, it is also used in the watermarking algorithm. [2] In this paper, a Gabor transform-based watermarking algorithm is proposed. The watermark information is hidden by changing the DGT coefficients to represent the special low frequency. However, this method will affect the visual characteristics of medical images. In the field of medical image watermarking, there is little research on Gabor transform to extract texture features. In this paper, the texture features obtained by Gabor filter in different scales and directions are combined with DCT, which greatly improved the robustness of the watermark image against various common attacks and geometric attacks.

2   Basic Theory

2.1   Gabor Texture Features

Gabor transform is a windowed Fourier transform, which is obtained by Gaussian function and the complex sine function. It is similar to human visual cell response, sensitive to image edge, and has good direction and scale selectivity. Compared with the traditional Fourier transform, Gabor wavelet transform has good time-frequency localization characteristics, and is insensitive to illumination. It can adapt to a certain degree of image rotation and deformation.

By generating a set of self-similar Gabor filters(as shown in Fig. 1), texture features in different scales (frequencies) and different directions can be extracted(as shown in Fig. 2). If the input medical image is $I(x, y)$ and the size is $M \times N$, then its Gabor wavelet transform is as follows:

$$W_{uv}(x, y) = \sum_{x_1}^{d_1} \sum_{y_1}^{d_2} I(x - x_1, y - y_1) g_{uv}(x_1, y_1) \tag{1}$$

where $W_{uv}(x, y)$ are the texture feature image after the Gabor wavelet transform, and d_1, d_2 are the template size of Gabor filter, which u represent a certain scale (frequency),and v represent a certain direction. $g_{uv}(x, y)$ are a group of self similar filters after scale transformation and rotation transformation of the mother wavelet $g(x, y)$.

The expression of mother wavelet is as follows:

$$g(x, y) = \frac{1}{2\pi\sigma_x\sigma_y} \exp\left(-\frac{1}{2}\left(\frac{x^2}{\sigma_x} + \frac{y^2}{\sigma_y}\right)\right) \exp(2\pi jwx) \tag{2}$$

Where, σ_x and σ_y are the standard deviation of Gaussian function on two coordinate axes, w are the frequency of complex sine function, and the value of σ_x, σ_y is related to bandwidth and inversely proportional to w.

$$\begin{cases} g_{uv}(x,y) = \alpha^{-u} g(x',y'), & \alpha > 1 \\ x' = \alpha^{-u}(x \cos \theta + y \sin \theta) \\ y' = \alpha^{-u}(-x \sin \theta + y \cos \theta) \end{cases} \quad (3)$$

Where α^{-u} is the scale modulation factor (u, v are integers), $\alpha = \left(\frac{U_h}{U_l}\right)^{-\frac{1}{S-1}}$, $\theta = \frac{v\pi}{K}$, S is the number of scales, K is the number of directions, $u = 0, 1, 2, \ldots, S - 1, v = 0, 1, 2, \ldots, K - 1, U_h$ is the highest spatial frequency, U_l is the lowest spatial frequency.

Fig. 1. Gabor filter kernels with different directions and scales

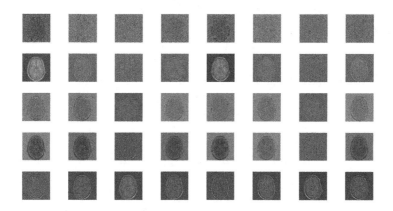

Fig. 2. Texture features of brain images with different directions and scales

The Gabor filter banks are used to extract the texture feature maps of medical images $W_{uv}(x,y)$ in different scales and directions. As the feature dimension is too high, the feature vector G_{uv} (row vector) of each texture feature map is generally obtained by averaging in blocks, and the Eigenvector matrix H (total $S \times K$ row, texture feature vector with one scale and one direction for each row) is constructed:

$$H = \begin{bmatrix} G_{00} \\ G_{10} \\ G_{20} \\ \cdots \\ G_{(S-1)(K-1)} \end{bmatrix} \tag{4}$$

2.2   Discrete Cosine Transform

Since the discrete cosine transform (DCT) was proposed in 1974, it has been loved and recognized by many scholars. It is widely used in image processing, digital signal, and other fields. It is similar to discrete Fourier transform, but only uses the real part. Discrete cosine transform (DCT) can concentrate the data energy in the upper left corner, that is, the low-frequency region, which has the characteristic of "energy concentration". It can realize data compression. Discrete cosine transform is used in standard JPEG, MJPEG and MPEG compression. The expression of 2D-DCT is as follows:

$$F(u,v) = c(u)c(v) \sum_{x=0}^{M-1} \sum_{y=0}^{N-1} f(x,y) \cos \frac{\pi(2x+1)u}{2M} \cos \frac{\pi(2y+1)v}{2N} \tag{5}$$

Among them, $u = 0, 1, \ldots, M-1$; $v = 0, 1, \ldots, N-1$;

$$c(u) = \begin{cases} \sqrt{\frac{1}{M}}, & u = 0 \\ \sqrt{\frac{2}{M}}, & u = 1, 2, \ldots, M-1 \end{cases} \qquad c(v) = \begin{cases} \sqrt{\frac{1}{N}}, & v = 0 \\ \sqrt{\frac{2}{N}}, & v = 1, 2, \ldots, N-1 \end{cases} \tag{6}$$

x, y is the spatial domain sampling value; u, v is the frequency domain sampling value.

2.3   Logistic Map

The logistic map is a kind of nonlinear mapping. Given the initial value and parameters, the chaotic sequence can be obtained:

$$x_{k+1} = \mu \cdot x_k \cdot (1 - x_k) \tag{7}$$

where, μ is the growth parameter and k is the number of iterations, $0 \le \mu \le 4$, $x_k \in (0,1)$. At that time, $3.5699456 < \mu \le 4$, the logistic map was chaotic. In this paper, $\mu = 4$, the number of iterations is set $k = 32$.

3   Algorithm Process

Embedding the watermark information into the spatial domain of medical images, once the image is destroyed, the embedded watermark information will be greatly affected, and the watermark restoration effect is generally poor. However, by embedding the watermark information into the feature vector which can represent the image features in the transform domain, zero watermark can be embedded and extracted when the feature vector does not change much when the image is destroyed, so as to improve the invisibility and robustness of the watermark.

3.1   Watermark Encryption

As shown in Fig. 3, firstly, the chaotic sequence is generated by chaotic mapping function. Then binary encryption matrix is obtained by binarization of perceptual hash, and the chaotic encrypted watermark is get by XOR of binary watermark $W(i, j)$ of 32 pixels × 32 pixels and $C(i, j)$.

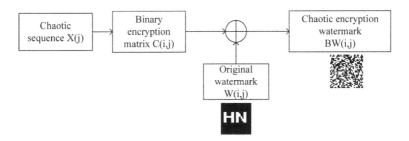

Fig. 3. Watermark encryption process

3.2   Watermark Embedding

For watermark embedding, the original medical image $I(i, j)$ with 512 pixels × 512 pixels is transformed by Gabor to get the feature matrix $H(i, j)$. And then DCT transform is applied to get the feature vector $V(j)$. The chaotic encryption watermark $BW(i, j)$ and the feature vector are XOR to get the logical secret key $key(i, j)$, which is retained and used in watermark extraction, as shown in Fig. 4.

$$key(i, j) = V(j) \oplus BW(i, j) \tag{8}$$

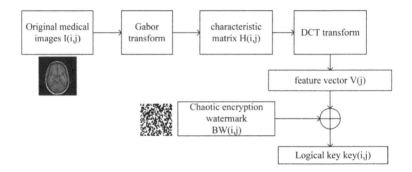

Fig. 4. Watermark embedding process

3.3   Watermark Extraction

As shown in Fig. 5, watermark extraction is the inverse process of watermark embedding. According to the embedding method, the feature vector $V'(j)$ of the image to be tested is extracted, and then XOR processing is performed between $V'(j)$ and the logical secret key $key(i,j)$ to obtain the encrypted watermark $BW'(i,j)$. At the same time, $BW'(i,j)$ do XOR with the binary encryption matrix $C(i,j)$ which was obtained when embedding the watermark to obtain the restored watermark $W'(i,j)$

$$W'(i,j) = C(i,j) \oplus BW'(i,j) \tag{9}$$

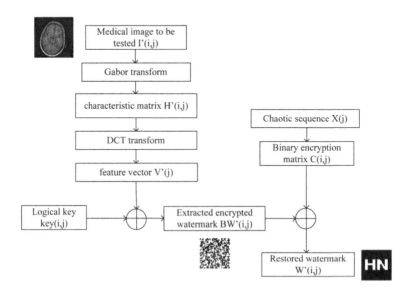

Fig. 5. Watermark extraction

3.4   Performance Metrics

The distortion degree of the medical image can be expressed by the peak signal-to-noise ratio (PSNR/dB), and the restoration degree of the watermark can be expressed by normalized correlation coefficient (NC);

$$PSNR = 10\log\left[\frac{MNmax_{i,j}(I(i,j))^2}{\sum_i\sum_j(I(i,j)-I'(i,j))^2}\right] \tag{10}$$

$$NC = \frac{\sum_i\sum_j W(i,j)W'(i,j)}{\sqrt{\sum_i\sum_j W(i,j)^2}\sqrt{\sum_i\sum_j W'(i,j)^2}} \tag{11}$$

The lower the $PSNR$ value is, the greater the distortion is, and the closer the NC value is to 1 ,the better the watermark restoration is.

4   Experiments and Results

Experiments were performed using Matlab r2015b for all medical images.This paper selects a 512 pixels × 512 pixels medical image brain as the cover image of the watermark. First,a Gabor transformed are performed to obtain feature matrix H, and then do the DCT transformed to the feature matrix H, and the first 32-bit DCT coefficients in the upper left corner are obtained through the Z-scan method. The 32-bit binary sequences obtained by the coefficient sign judgment (the coefficient is positive to be 1, and the coefficient is negative to be 0) is used as the feature vector of the medical images.

As shown in Fig. 6, four different medical images are selected. Table 1 shows the feature vectors extracted from each medical image by Gabor-DCT. It can be seen from the Table 1 that the feature vectors extracted from different medical images are different.

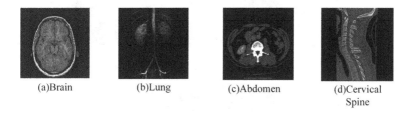

| (a)Brain | (b)Lung | (c)Abdomen | (d)Cervical Spine |

Fig. 6. Different medical images

Table 1. Feature vectors of different medical images.

Different medical images	Feature sequences
(a) Brain	1100 0011 1000 1010 0001 0001 1010 0110
(b) Lung	1111 1111 1000 1110 1011 0101 0100 1000
(c) Abdomen	1100 0110 1110 1010 0001 0100 1011 1011
(d) Cervical spine	1011 1010 1111 1010 1011 0101 1110 1010

Table 2. PSNR and NC values based on Gabor-DCT under common attacks.

Conventional attack	Gaussian noise			JPEG compression			Median filter (Thirty times)		
	1%	5%	10%	1%	10%	20%	3×3	5×5	7×7
PSNR/dB	20.45	14.31	11.85	26.28	31.29	33.81	33.78	26.92	24.96
NC	0.90	0.80	0.74	1.00	0.90	1.00	1.00	1.00	0.90

4.1 Common Attacks

There are three kinds of common attacks in the experimental: Gaussian noise attacks, JPEG compression attacks and median filtering attacks. Table 2 shows the PSNR and NC values under different attacks intensities.

From Table 2, when the Gaussian noise is 10%, the NC value is 0.74. When the JPEG compression quality is 1%, the NC value is 1.00. For 30 times of 7×7 median filtering, the NC value is still as high as 0.90. At the same time, it can be seen from Fig. 7 that the watermark is still visible after each attacks, that is, the algorithm proposed in this paper can well resist common attacks, especially in the aspect of JPEG compression attacks and median filtering attacks.

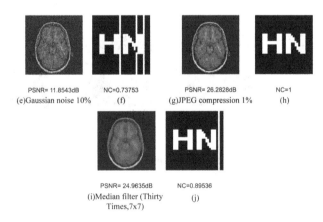

PSNR= 11.8543dB   NC=0.73753
(e)Gaussian noise 10%   (f)

PSNR= 26.2828dB   NC=1
(g)JPEG compression 1%   (h)

PSNR= 24.9635dB   NC=0.89536
(i)Median filter (Thirty Times,7x7)   (j)

Fig. 7. Medical image after the common attacks and the restored watermark

4.2 Geometric Attacks

Geometric attacks (rotation, scaling, translation, clipping) have a great impact on images. How to improve the robustness of images under geometric attacks have always been a difficult problem. Table 3 shows the test results of the algorithm after several geometric attacks.

Table 3. PSNR and NC values for geometric attacks based on Gabor-DCT.

Geometric attacks	Attack strength	PSNR/dB	NC
Rotation (clockwise)	5°	18.00	1.00
	10°	15.60	1.00
	20°	14.60	0.71
Scaling attack	0.5	/	0.70
	0.8	/	0.90
	2.0	/	0.89
Translation attack (left)	5%	14.48	1.00
	15%	12.86	1.00
	25%	11.42	0.89
Translation attack (right)	5%	14.51	1.00
	15%	12.90	1.00
	25%	11.30	0.81
Crop (Y direction)	5%	/	1.00
	10%	/	0.80
	25%	/	0.61
Crop (X direction)	5%	/	1.00
	15%	/	1.00
	25%	/	0.81

(1) Rotation attacks: When the medical image is rotated 20 degrees, as shown in (k) and (l) in Fig. 8, the PSNR value is very low, but the NC value is 0.71, which still can restore the watermark well, indicating that the algorithm has good robustness against rotation attacks.

(2) Scaling attacks: When the medical image is reduced to 0.5 times, the NC value is 0.71 when the medical image is magnified by 2 times, as shown in (m) and (n) in Fig. 8, the NC value is 0.89 , and the watermark restoration degree is high. It shows that the algorithm is robust to scaling attacks.

(3) Translation attacks: When the left shift and right shift of medical images are all 25%, the NC values are above 0.80. As shown in (o), (p), (q) and (r) in Fig. 8, they are 25% left shift, 25% right shift and corresponding restored watermark. Therefore, the algorithm is robust to translation attacks.

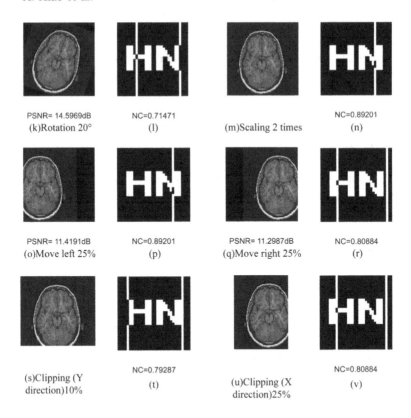

PSNR= 14.5969dB
(k)Rotation 20°

NC=0.71471
(l)

(m)Scaling 2 times

NC=0.89201
(n)

PSNR= 11.4191dB
(o)Move left 25%

NC=0.89201
(p)

PSNR= 11.2987dB
(q)Move right 25%

NC=0.80884
(r)

(s)Clipping (Y direction)10%

NC=0.79287
(t)

(u)Clipping (X direction)25%

NC=0.80884
(v)

Fig. 8. Medical image and the restored watermark under geometric attacks.

(4) Crop attacks: As it can be seen in Table 3, compared with the ability to resist X-axis crop, the anti Y-axis crop ability of this algorithm is worse, but the NC value is still greater than 0.50 when the Y-axis is 25% cropped, and the NC value is as high as 0.81 when the X-axis is 25% which indicates that the algorithm has a good anti crop ability. In Fig. 8, (s) and (t) are the watermarks cut by 10% and restored by Y-axis, (u) and (v) are the watermarks cut by 25% and restored by X-axis respectively.

Combined with Table 3 and Fig. 8, it can be seen that the algorithm in this paper has a good ability to resist geometric attacks.

4.3 Algorithm Comparison

This paper compared the DCT algorithm and the Gabor-DCT algorithm. It can be seen from Table 4 that under common attacks, the watermark restoration effect of the DCT algorithm and Gabor-DCT algorithm is similar, and the NC value is close. However, under geometric attacks, the anti-rotation, translation, and crop of the Gabor-DCT algorithm are performing better than the DCT algorithm. Hence the Gabor-DCT algorithm is better than DCT in the anti-geometric attacks.

Table 4. Comparison of different algorithms.

	Attack	PSNR/dB		NC	
		DCT	Gabor-DCT	DCT	Gabor-DCT
Conventional attack	Gaussian noise 10%	11.85	11.85	0.78	0.74
	JPEG compression 1%	26.28	26.28	1.00	1.00
	Median filter 7 × 7 (Thirty times)	24.96	24.96	1.00	0.90
Geometric attacks	Rotation 20° (clockwise)	14.60	14.60	0.51	0.71
	Scaling 2 times	/	/	1.00	0.89
	Translation 20% (left)	12.07	12.07	0.33	1.00
	Translation 25% (right)	11.30	11.30	−0.08	0.81
	Clipping 25% (Y direction)	/	/	0.63	0.61
	Clipping 25% (X direction)	/	/	−0.21	0.81

5   Conclusion

In this paper, Gabor texture feature extraction is combined with DCT algorithm to obtain a Gabor-DCT based zero watermarking algorithm for medical images. The algorithm extracted texture information of different scales and directions through Gabor transform, and used the "energy concentration" feature of the DCT algorithm to concentrate the extracted texture information. Then applied the extracted medical image features to associate with the watermark, and combined the cryptographic ideas to design the watermark algorithm. Experimental results show that the algorithm has strong robustness to both common attacks and geometric attacks, and can effectively protect the security of medical image information.

References

1. Brar, A.S., Kaur, M., Kaur, S.: Medical Image Watermarking. Lap Lambert Academic Publishing, Sunnyvale (2012)
2. Chen, J.Y., Tao, L.: An efficient image watermarking scheme based on Gabor transform. Guangdianzi Jiguang/J. Optoelectron. Laser **16**(11), 1363–1367 (2005)
3. Lee, C.-J., Wang, S.-D.: Fingerprint feature extraction using Gabor filters. Electron. Lett. **35**(4), 288–290 (1999)
4. Eswaraiah, R., Sreenivasa Reddy, E.: Medical image watermarking technique for accurate tamper detection in ROI and exact recovery of ROI. Int. J. Telemed. Appl. **2014**, 984646 (2014)
5. Jian-Hu, M.A., Jia-Xing, H.E.: A wavelet-based method of zero-watermark. J. Image Graph. (2007)
6. Kavadia, C., Lodha, A.: A review on spatial and transform domain digital watermarking techniques. Int. J. Adv. Res. Comput. Sci. **04**(08), 20–22 (2013)
7. Kundur, D., Hatzinakos, D.: Digital watermarking using multiresolution wavelet decomposition. In: Proceedings of the 1998 IEEE International Conference on Acoustics, Speech and Signal Processing, ICASSP 1998 (Cat. No.98CH36181), vol. 5, pp. 2969–2972 (1998)

8. Liu, J., He, X.: A review study on digital watermarking. In: International Conference on Information and Communication Technologies (2006)
9. Lyons, M., Akamatsu, S., Kamachi, M., Gyoba, J.: Coding facial expressions with Gabor wavelets. In: Proceedings Third IEEE International Conference on Automatic Face and Gesture Recognition, pp. 200–205 (1998)
10. Nyeem, H., Boles, W., Boyd, C.: A review of medical image watermarking requirements for teleradiology. J. Digit. Imaging **26**(2), 326–343 (2013). https://doi.org/10.1007/s10278-012-9527-x
11. Perlman, R., Kaufman, C., Speciner, M.: Network security: private communication in a public world. Pearson Education India (2016)
12. Singh, S., Singh, R., Singh, A.K., Siddiqui, T.J.: SVD-DCT based medical image watermarking in NSCT domain. In: Hassanien, A.E., Elhoseny, M., Kacprzyk, J. (eds.) Quantum Computing: An Environment for Intelligent Large Scale Real Application. SBD, vol. 33, pp. 467–488. Springer, Cham (2018). https://doi.org/10.1007/978-3-319-63639-9_20
13. van Schyndel, R.G., Tirkel, A.Z., Osborne, C.F.: A digital watermark. In: Proceedings of 1st International Conference on Image Processing, vol. 2, pp. 86–90 (1994)
14. Williams, P.A.: Medical data security: are you informed or afraid? Int. J. Inf. Comput. Secur. **1**(4), 414–429 (2007)
15. Xiao, M., Wan, X., Gan, C., Du, B.: A robust DCT domain watermarking algorithm based on chaos system. Proc. SpIE **7495**, 183 (2009)
16. Yaxun Zhou, Wei Jin: A novel image zero-watermarking scheme based on DWT-SVD. In: 2011 International Conference on Multimedia Technology, pp. 2873–2876 (2011)
17. Zhuang, J.Z.: Digital watermarking technology. Computer Knowledge and Technology (2009)

Analysis on Influencing Factors of Electricity Sales for Electric Data Security

Hailing He[1,2], Wei Zou[1,2], Qinghong Guo[1,2], Wenxian Wu[1,2], and Kejiang Xiao[3(✉)]

[1] State Grid Hunan Electric Power Limited Company Power Supply Service Center (Metrology Center), Changsha 410004, China
[2] Hunan Province Key Laboratory of Intelligent Electrical Measurement and Application Technology, Changsha 410004, China
[3] Hubei Research Center for Educational Informationization, Faculty of Artificial Intelligence in Education, Central China Normal University, Wuhan 430079, China

Abstract. Electricity has become one of the most important energy in human social. A reliable analysis of the influencing factors of electricity sales will help strengthen the electricity companies, related national energy departments' control and security over the expected electricity consumption across the country. In this paper, we analyze the relationship between different types of electricity sales and a variety of potential factors, including immediacy factors, leading factors and the influencing of Chinese New Year by using Pearson correlation coefficient, dynamical time warping. Through the result of experiment, we found that the influencing factors are different for different electricity usage categories. And some factors have lagging effects on electricity sales, so we need to comprehensively consider immediacy factors and leading factors when forecasting electricity sales. At the same time, we also found that Chinese New Year also has a significant impact on electricity sales, thus Chinese New Year is also is also an important factor affecting electricity sales.

Keywords: Electricity sales · Pearson correlation coefficient · Dynamic time warping

1 Introduction

Electricity is almost related to all aspects of human life, such as smart home, data security and so on. Accurate forecasting of electricity sales is conducive to make rational use of resources. Overestimating the electricity consumption will lead to more supply than actual needs, resulting in waste of resources. And underestimating the electricity consumption will lead to less supply than the actual demand, which will not guarantee normal production and life. In order to enable policymakers to make reasonable plans which can strengthen the control of operating cost in the power sector, it's necessary to make an accurate analysis of electricity consumption. One of the prerequisites for accurate prediction is to understand the mechanism of electricity consumption. And the factors that influence electricity consumption plays an important role of this study.

© Springer Nature Switzerland AG 2021
J. Cheng et al. (Eds.): CSS 2020, LNCS 12653, pp. 157–171, 2021.
https://doi.org/10.1007/978-3-030-73671-2_15

Many scholars have been studying the related factors of energy consumption for data security. Initially, people discovered a causal relationship between economic growth and energy consumption [1, 2]. But due to the different economic and industrial structures in different regions, it is not reliable to generalize their influence mechanism [3].

However, it is too rough to use a single factor to analyze the overall electricity consumption. Therefore, some scholars study the influencing factors of different types of electricity, such as industrial electricity [4] and residential electricity [5, 6].

Except for this problem, there are also some factors with time lag or lead that affect electricity consumption [7]. But few studies have analyzed it.

In this paper, we first decompose the original data by using the X13-ARIMA-SEATS algorithm to obtain trend items, seasonal items and stochastic term. Then analyze the correlation between different type electricity consumption and instantaneous factors, obtaining the relationship between them. The results obtained by comparing different types of electricity consumption are also more comprehensive and accurate. To analyze the lagged effect, we analyze the lead-lap relationship between electricity consumption and leading factors by dynamic time warping (DTW). Finally, analyze the effect of Chinese New Year, a special festival unique to China.

The following is a summary of contributions to this paper:

(1) Use X13-ARIMA-SEATS algorithm to separate the original data into trend term, seasonal term and stochastic term, which improves the model's ability to perceive electricity trends.
(2) Analyze the correlation between different type electricity sales and immediacy factors, so as to obtain effective immediacy factors.
(3) Analyze the lead-lap relationship between electricity sales and leading factors by DTW. It is concluded that forecasting electricity sales requires comprehensive consideration of leading factors and immediate factors.
(4) Analyze the impact of Chinese New Year and add it to influence factors.

2 Related Work

Electricity is one of the most important energy for human, so people realize the importance of studying electricity.

There are some great studies for economy and electricity usage. Zhang [1] review the relationship between electricity usage and economic growth in China from the time, the regional and the industrial dimension comprehensively. Fang [2] took China's electricity consumption from 1995 to 2016 as the research object and used the multi-period ST-LMDI model to analyze. Jiang [6] use the Logarithmic Mean Divisia Index method, finding that economic growth is the main factor affecting non-residential electricity consumption and different regions have different impacts due to differences in technological level and industrial structure. But the data they used in these studies are all annual data. It is difficult to discover the causal relationship between variables from annual data alone.

Some scholars have conducted more detailed research on other factors. Previous studies have found a correlation between weather and electricity consumption [8–10]. Xu [5] analyzed the impact on electricity consumption in residential buildings through income, family size, education level and other characteristics such as the occupants and found that there may indeed be an impact. Guo [11] summarized the influencing factors that affect residential electricity consumption, such as the number of family members, social status of the family, family economic situation, level of education, age composition of family members, the type of a house, and analyzed the residents' electricity consumption behavior from the perspective of social psychology.

The time lag effect is widespread in the field of economics and security, and there are also lag variables in electricity consumption analysis. Liu [12] develops a function of energy consumption, population growth, economic growth and urbanization process, and provides fresh empirical evidences for urbanization and energy consumption for China over the period 1978–2008 through the use of ARDL testing approach and factor decomposition model. And the results of the bounds test show that there is a stable long run relationship amongst total energy consumption, population, GDP and urbanization level when total energy consumption is the dependent variable in China. But there are few special analyses on the leading or lagging factors that affect electricity sales.

3   An Overview

Considering the raw data due to season, weather factors such as electricity curve form variety, to a certain extent masked the trend of electricity, so we first strip its original electricity curve trend, seasonal item and random item by X13-ARIMA-SEATS algorithm, which can improve the perception ability of the model to the electricity sales trend when analyzing the electricity sales.

Then consider the correlation between the immediacy factor and the amount of electricity sales by each category. We mainly use Pearson correlation coefficient (PCC) and line graph to analyze.

In addition to the immediacy factor, we also consider the influence of the leading factor on the electricity sales. Leading factors mainly include manufacturing Purchasing Manager's Index (PMI), non-manufacturing PMI and net capacity increase of industrial expansion. In this paper, we use the Dynamic Time Warping (DTW) algorithm to study the lead-lag relationship between relevant factors and electricity sales data, and the lead-lag period of output factors and electricity sales data, which provides a factor basis for forecast of electricity sales. Such as PMI, net capacity increase of business expansion and other factors and the leading and lagging analysis between the electricity supply in different industries. The inclusion of leading factors in the analysis of electricity sales is conducive to enhance the identification ability of the analysis model for inflection point.

In addition, Chinese New year is a special holiday in China. Due to the unfixed date of Chinese New Year, and the vacation time of Chinese New Year is long and it has a long impact time, these will have different degrees of impact on electricity sales in different regions and different industries. Accordingly the Chinese New Year factor is also needed to be considered as an influencing factor. In this paper, we use the method of function fitting to analyze the impact of the Spring Festival on electricity sales (Fig. 1).

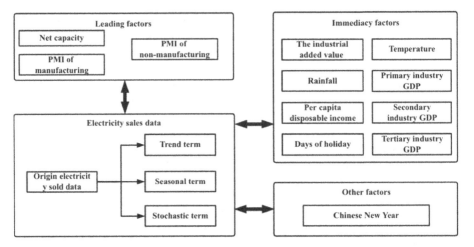

Fig. 1. Analysis framework.

4 Analysis on Influencing Factors of Electricity Sales

4.1 X13-ARIMA-SEATS

We use X13-ARIMA-SEATS to decompose the electricity sales curve at first and obtain the trend term, seasonal term and random term. Here are the detailed steps of X13-ARIMA-SEATS.

Mark the original sequence as Y_t, we filter it linearly and obtain the trend term T_t

$$T_t = \left(\frac{1}{2}Y_{t-6} + Y_{t-5} + \cdots + Y_t + \cdots + Y_{t+5} + \frac{1}{2}Y_{t+6}\right)/12 \tag{1}$$

Let Y_t minus T_t to get SI_t, perform a moving average on SI_t to get the seasonal term S_t.

$$\widehat{S_t} = (SI_{t-24} + 2SI_{t-12} + 3SI_t + 2SI_{t+12} + SI_{t+24})/9 \tag{2}$$

$$S_t = \widehat{S_t} - (\frac{1}{2}\widehat{S}_{t-6} + \widehat{S}_{t-5} + \cdots + \widehat{S}_t + \cdots + \widehat{S}_{t+5} + \frac{1}{2}\widehat{S}_{t+6})/24 \tag{3}$$

Then get stochastic term I_t by Y_t minus T_t and S_t. Through the above algorithm, the electricity sales sequence can be decomposed into three sub-sequences of trend, seasonal and random items. And the relationship between them can be expressed as

$$Y_t = T_t + S_t + I_t \tag{4}$$

4.2 Pearson Correlation Coefficient

PCC is a statistical method that measures linear correlation between two variables [13]. It has a value between $+1$ and -1. A value of $+1$ is total positive linear correlation, 0 is no linear correlation, and -1 is total negative linear correlation. PCC has been widely used in many applications to name a few, such as time-delay estimation, pattern recognition, data analysis. The calculation formula of PCC is as follows:

$$r = \frac{\sum XY - \frac{\sum X \sum Y}{N}}{\sqrt{\left(\sum X^2 - \frac{(\sum X)^2}{N}\right)\left(\sum Y^2 - \frac{(\sum Y)^2}{N}\right)}} \tag{5}$$

X and Y are the two variables we used, N is the number of samples, r is the value of result (PCC value). r is the ratio of the covariance to the standard deviation of two variables, so the linear variation does not affect the result of PCC (Fig. 2).

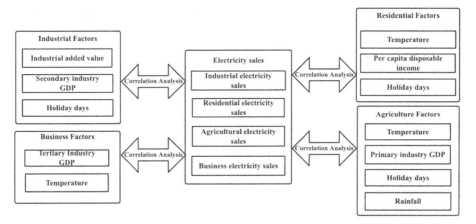

Fig. 2. Pearson correlation coefficient.

4.3 Dynamic Time Warping

Dynamic Time Warping (DTW) is a is one of the algorithms for measuring similarity between two temporal sequences, which may vary in speed. For instance, similarities in walking could be detected using DTW, even if one person was walking faster than the other, or if there were accelerations and decelerations during the course of an observation. DTW has been applied to temporal sequences of video, audio, and graphics data — indeed, any data that can be turned into a linear sequence can be analyzed with DTW. A well-known application has been automatic speech recognition, to cope with different speaking speeds [14]. Other applications include speaker recognition and online signature recognition. It can also be used in partial shade matching application.

We use DTW to obtain the leading factors. Here are the detailed steps of leading study.

(1) Take the trend term of net capacity increase and electricity sales from January 2015 to August 2019 for the industry respectively, the former is denoted as $\{N_i | i \in 1, 2, \ldots, 45\}$, and the latter as $\{Q_i | i \in 1, 2, \ldots, 45\}$.

(2) Use the DTW algorithm to calculate the shortest normalized path $D(N, Q)$ between the trend item of electricity sales and the trend item of net capacity increase.

(3) Mark leading month 0, leading month 1, ..., leading month m as N_iQ_i, $N_{i+1}Q_{i+1}$, ..., $N_{i+m}Q_{i+m}$, and the occurrence times in the shortest regular path are denoted as C_0, C_1, ..., C_m. Take the largest leading month as 12, then the industry's net increase in capacity in the leading months $L = \max\{C_i|i = 0, 1, \ldots, 12\}$.

5   Experiment

5.1   Data Set

The research area of this paper is Hunan. Hunan Province has developed rapidly in recent years and ranked 8th in China's GDP in 2018. With the rapid growth of GDP, the demand for electricity in Hunan Province is also increasing year by year. In order to help the development of the power industry in Hunan Province, it is necessary to conduct a reliable analysis of the electric industry in Hunan Province (Table 1).

Table 1. Data source.

Data	Source	Note
Net capacity	Website of National Bureau of Statistics/Database on Economic and Social Development/The news media	External data
Manufacturing PMI		
Non-manufacturing PMI		
Per capita disposable income		
Primary industry GDP		
Secondary industry GDP		
Tertiary industry GDP		
The industrial added value		
Temperature	The weather sites	
Days of holiday	National holiday Office	
Rainfall	The weather sites	
Five types of electricity usage	Internal System	Internal data
Industry expansion		

Experimental data are divided into external data and internal data. The external data include net capacity, manufacturing PMI, non-manufacturing PMI, per capita disposable income, GDP of primary industry, GDP of secondary industry, GDP of tertiary industry, the industrial added value, temperature, days of holiday and rainfall. And we can obtain these data from public website, such as website of National Bureau of Statistics, database on Economic and Social Development and the news media. The internal data include five types of electricity use and industry expenses, and they come from the internal systems of electricity companies.

5.2   Curve Decomposition

After obtaining the electricity sales data, we use X13-ARIMA-SEATS to strip the trend, seasonal and stochastic term of the original electricity sales curve. Here is the result of striping (Fig. 3).

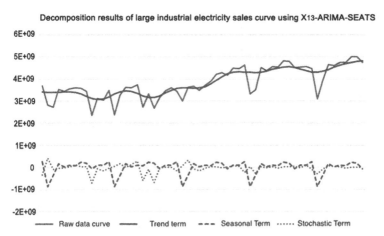

Fig. 3. Decomposition results of large industrial electricity curve using X13-ARIMA-SEATS.

5.3   Immediacy Factors

5.3.1   Large Industrial Electricity

(1)   The industrial added value (Fig. 4)

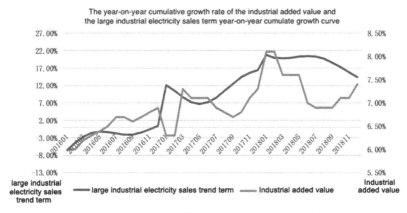

Fig. 4. The year-on-year cumulative growth rate of the industrial added value and the large industrial electricity sales term year-on-year cumulative growth curve.

Through data exploration, it is found that there is a large correlation between the electricity sales of Hunan's large industry and the industrial added value. The Pearson correlation coefficient between the industrial added value in large industry and electricity sales is 0.57.

In order to grasp the details of the data, we analyze the trend term of large industry and industrial added value which has been got the trend term of large industry. The Pearson correlation coefficient between the trend item of large industrial electricity sales and industrial added value is 0.72. There is a strong correlation between the two, so the industrial added value can be regarded as an important factor of large industrial electricity sales.

(2) Secondary industry GDP

The Pearson correlation coefficient between the GDP of secondary industry and large industrial electricity sales is 0.66. And Fig. 5 is the year-on-year cumulative growth rate of the secondary industry's GDP and the trend term of large-scale industrial power sales year-on-year cumulative growth curve. Through the above analysis, we can know there is a strong correlation between GDP of secondary industry and large industrial electricity sales and the GDP of secondary industry can be used as an important influence factor of large industrial electricity sales.

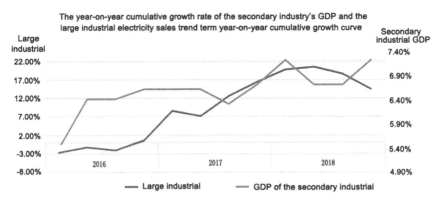

Fig. 5. The year-on-year cumulative growth rate of the secondary industry's GDP and the large industrial electricity sales trend term year-on-year cumulative growth curve.

The immediacy influencing factors of large industrial electricity sales include the industrial added value and the GDP of secondary industry. In Hunan Province, the correlation between the electricity sales of large industries and the number of days on holidays is relatively low, at −0.10, which is not considered for the time being.

5.3.2   Residential Electricity

(1)   Temperature

After analysis, it is found that there is an inconsistency between the electricity sales of Hunan residents and the temperature data. Further business understanding is that the electricity lags behind the weather data by one month due to the impact of the meter reading routine, that is, the supply and sale period is different (Fig. 6).

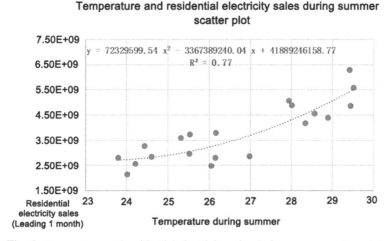

Fig. 6.   Temperature and residential electricity sales during summer scatter plot.

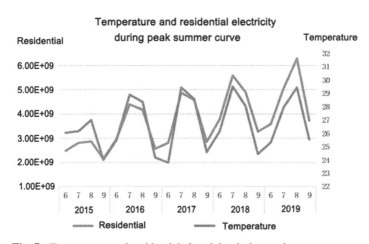

Fig. 7.   Temperature and residential electricity during peak summer curve.

We first use this principle to restore the electricity sales data and weather data of residents and urban residents. Then, in order to ensure the refined analysis of residents, the following is the correlation analysis of temperature and residential electricity sales for peak summer and winter peaks (Fig. 7).

During the peak summer period, there is a strong correlation between electricity and temperature. The Pearson correlation coefficient is 0.86, and the coefficient of determination of the fitting function between temperature and electricity is 0.77. And During the peak winter, the Pearson correlation coefficient between temperature and electricity is -0.87, showing a negative correlation between the two.

(2) Disposable income per capita

The Pearson correlation coefficient between disposable income per capita and resident electricity sales is 0.79. There is a strong correlation between the two, so the disposable income of residents can be used as an influencing indicator for electricity sales (Fig. 8).

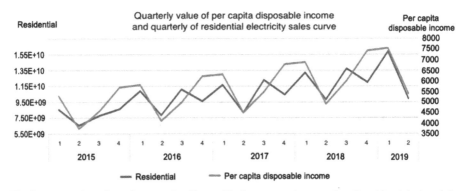

Fig. 8. Quarterly value of per capita disposable income and quarterly of residential electricity sales curve.

The immediacy influencing factors of resident electricity sales include the temperature and disposable income per capita. In Hunan Province, the correlation between the resident electricity sales and the number of days on holidays is relatively low, at -0.08, which is not considered for the time being (Fig. 9).

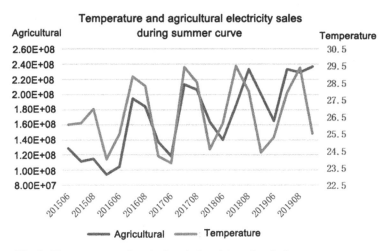

Fig. 9. Temperature and agricultural electricity sales during summer curve.

5.3.3 Agriculture Electricity

Through the analysis of agricultural electricity sales and related factors, we found that the relationship between agricultural electricity and temperature during peak summer is relatively clear. The Pearson correlation coefficient between the two is 0.59, and the peak winter is related to Pearson in other months. The coefficients are respectively: -0.28, 0.21, that is, from the perspective of linear correlation in other months, the relationship between the two is not obvious.

5.3.4 Business Electricity

(1) Temperature

Though the analysis of business electricity sales and related factors, it is found that there is a strong correlation between temperature and business electricity sales (Fig. 10). After analysis, the relationship between general industrial and commercial electricity sales and temperature during the peak winter period is relatively clear, PCC between business electricity sales and temperature is -0.73, showing a strong negative correlation.

The PCC between peak summer and other months are 0.32 and -0.07 respectively, which means that the relationship between the two is not obvious from the perspective of linear correlation in other months.

(2) Tertiary industry GDP

The PCC between business electricity sales and GDP of tertiary industry is 0.48, there is a certain relevance between the two. The main immediacy factors that need to be considered in affecting electricity sales include temperature and GDP of tertiary industry.

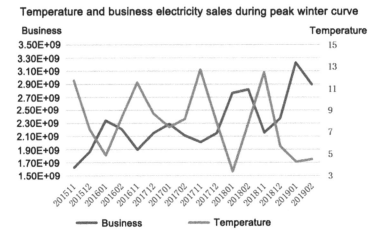

Fig. 10. Temperature and business electricity sales during peak winter curve.

5.3.5 Leading Factors

Leading factors mainly include manufacturing PMI, non-manufacturing PMI, and the net increase in capacity of industry expansion. The inclusion of leading indicators enhances the ability of electricity sales analysis and forecasting models to identify turning points (Fig. 11).

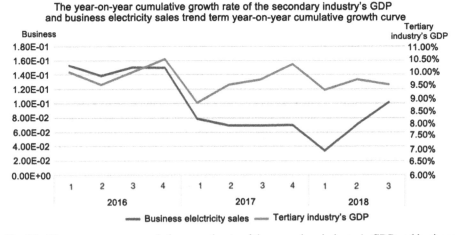

Fig. 11. The year-on-year cumulative growth rate of the secondary industry's GDP and business electricity sales trend term year-on-year cumulative growth curve.

Manufacturing PMI is an index compiled and compiled through the statistical summary and compilation of the monthly survey results of corporate purchasing managers. It is an internationally-used leading index for monitoring macroeconomic trends and has a strong predictive and early warning effect.. PMI usually uses 50% as the demarcation point of economic strength. When PMI is higher than 50%, it reflects the expansion of manufacturing economy; when PMI is lower than 50%, it reflects the contraction of manufacturing economy. The non-manufacturing business activity index is a diffusion index compiled based on the monthly changes in the total amount of business activities completed by a company (such as the number of customers, sales, engineering and other physical quantities). Since there is no synthetic non-manufacturing comprehensive PMI index, the current international business activity index is usually used to reflect the overall changes in the development of the non-manufacturing economy, usually 50% is used as the demarcation point of economic strength, and higher than 50% reflects non-manufacturing Economic expansion, less than 50% reflects non-manufacturing economic contraction.

The business expansion installation business is the general term for the business process of the electric power enterprise and security from the user application to the actual electricity usage. The business expansion installation has a variety of business types, among which the business types that mainly affect the electricity forecast include: new installations (new users according to needs Establishing a relationship between power consumption and power companies), increasing capacity (adding new capacity on the basis of the original agreed capacity), reducing capacity (reducing the capacity stipulated in the contract), and canceling households (terminating power supply and consumption) Contract, stop all electricity consumption) etc. The net capacity increase of the business expansion refers to the business expansion and new installation, the capacity increase minus the business expansion and reduction, and the account sales capacity. The analysis shows that the net increase in capacity has a certain leading effect on the sales of electricity. The change in the net increase in capacity is a slow growth process and will reach stability after several months (Fig. 12).

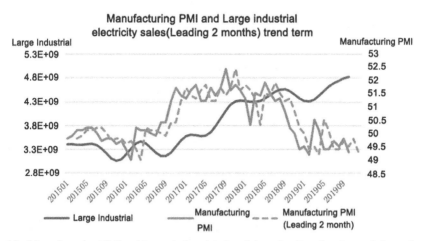

Fig. 12. Manufacturing PMI and Large industrial electricity sales (Leading 2 months) trend term.

We obtain manufacturing PMI leading large industrial electricity sales trend item for 2 months and non-manufacturing PMI leading general industrial and commercial electricity sales trend item 4 months by using DTW (Fig. 13).

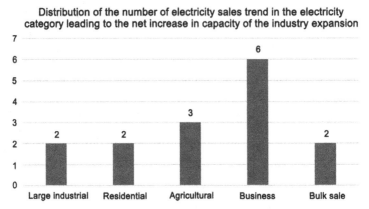

Fig. 13. Distribution of the number of electricity sales trend term in the electricity category leading to the net increase in capacity of the industry expansion.

5.3.6 Other Factors

Chinese New Year

We analyze the impact of the Spring Festival on the electricity sales of large industries. As can be seen from the figure above, Chinese New Year has an obvious impact on the electricity sales of large industries. And the relationship function between the two is computed as follows.

$$y = 0.000066x^2 + 0.000458x + 0.289276 \tag{6}$$

the coefficient of determination of the function is 0.85, the model fits well (Fig. 14).

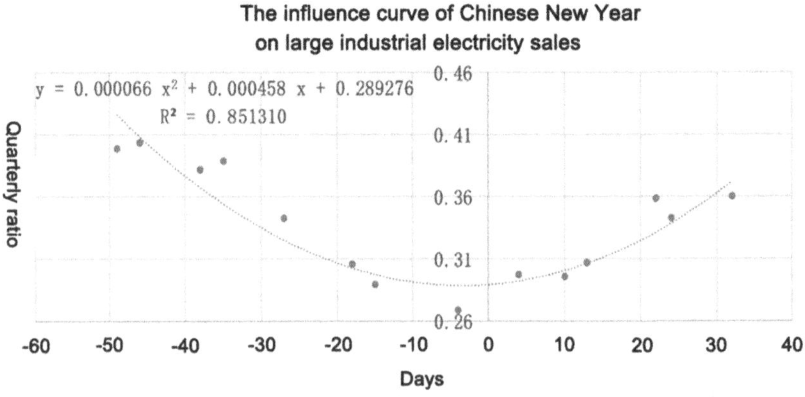

The influence curve of Chinese New Year on large industrial electricity sales

$y = 0.000066\ x^2 + 0.000458\ x + 0.289276$

$R^2 = 0.851310$

Fig. 14. The influence curve of Chinese New Year on large industrial electricity sales.

6 Conclusion

This paper uses X13-ARIMA-SEATS, PCC, DTW and other algorithms to study the influencing factors of five types of electricity sales, and finally the immediate factors and leading factors that impact the electricity sales are got. The work of this article can provide great help for the forecast of electricity sales to protect electric data security. And this will help policy makers formulate more reasonable policies to promote the development of the electric industry and electric security.

Acknowledgement. This work was supported in part by the National Natural Science Foundation of China under Grant No. 61803391, and in part by the Hunan Provincial Natural Science Foundation of China under Grant No. 2019JJ50803.

References

1. Zhang, C., Zhou, K., Yang, S., Shao, Z.: On electricity consumption and economic growth in China. Renew. Sustain. Energy Rev. **76**, 353–368 (2017)
2. Fang, D., Hao, P., Hao, J.: Study of the influence mechanism of China's electricity consumption based on multi-period ST-LMDI model. Energy **170**, 730–743 (2019)
3. Zhang, Y., Da, Y.: The decomposition of energy-related carbon emission and its decoupling with economic growth in China. Renew. Sustain. Energy Rev. **41**, 1255–1266 (2015)
4. Steenhof, P.: Decomposition of electricity demand in China's industrial sector. Energy Econ. **28**(3), 370–384 (2006)
5. Xu, X., Xiao, B., Li, C.: Critical factors of electricity consumption in residential buildings: an analysis from the point of occupant characteristics view. J. Clean. Product. **256**, 120423 (2020)
6. Jiang, S., Zhu, Y., He, G., Wang, Q., Lu, Y.: Factors influencing China's non-residential power consumption: estimation using the Kaya–LMDI methods. Energy **201**, 117719 (2020)
7. Liu, Y.: Exploring the relationship between urbanization and energy consumption in China using ARDL (autoregressive distributed lag) and FDM (factor decomposition model). Energy **34**(11), 1846–1854 (2009)
8. Engle, R., Granger, C., Rice, J., Weiss, A.: Semiparametric estimates of the relation between weather and electricity sales. J. Am. Stat. Assoc. **81**(394), 310–320 (1986)
9. Franco, G., Sanstad, A.: Climate change and electricity demand in California. Clim. Change **87**(1), 139–151 (2008)
10. Chan, A.: Developing future hourly weather files for studying the impact of climate change on building energy performance in Hong Kong. Energy Build. **43**(10), 2860–2868 (2011)
11. Guo, Z., Zhou, K., Zhang, C., Lu, X., Chen, W., Yang, S.: Residential electricity consumption behavior: Influencing factors, related theories and intervention strategies. Renew. Sustain. Energy Rev. **81**, 399–412 (2018)
12. Liu, Y.: Exploring the relationship between urbanization and energy consumption in China using ARDL (autoregressive distributed lag) and FDM (factor decomposition model). Energy **34**(11), 1846–1854(2009)
13. Schober, P., Boer, C., Schwarte, L.: Correlation coefficients: appropriate use and interpretation. Anesth. Analg. **126**(5), 1763–1768 (2018)
14. Müller, M.: Dynamic time warping. Information Retrieval for Music and Motion, pp. 69–84 (2007). https://doi.org/10.1007/978-3-540-74048-3_4

A Regularization-Based Positive and Unlabeled Learning Algorithm for One-Class Classification of Remote Sensing Data

Yan Zhang ⓘ, Tianjiao Yang⁽⊠⁾ ⓘ, and Chenguang Zhang ⓘ

College of Science, Hainan University, Haikou 570228, China

Abstract. Given some pixels with user-defined land cover types as labeled positive and negative samples, traditional remote sensing classification methods are sufficient to obtain optimal classification results. However, in many cases, only the positive pixels that users are interested in are labeled, and the negative samples are too diverse to be labeled. Such classification problems are referred to as one-class classification. Traditional learning methods are not suitable for one-class classification problems because labeled negative samples are required for these methods. In this paper, we propose a regularization-based positive and unlabeled learning method called RPUL for one-class classification of high-spatial-resolution aerial photographs. RPUL uses the implicit mixture model of restricted Boltzmann machines (IRBM) as the base framework of the classifier. With the help of a regularization term embedded into the loss function, an additional restriction is imposed on the negative class conditional PDF to ensure that it is as far from the positive class conditional PDF as possible. Thus, although no labeled negative training samples are available, the negative class conditional PDF can be estimated directly to obtain a binary classifier for the detection of the class of interest. The experimental results indicate that the new method provides high classification accuracy and outperforms state-of-the-art methods, including the cost-sensitive positive and unlabeled learning (CSPUL) and Gaussian domain descriptor methods.

Keywords: Remote-sensing · Positive and unlabeled data · Regularization term · Restricted boltzmann machines (RBM)

1 Introduction

Remote sensing technology has been widely used in various urban and environmental applications, such as land use change monitoring, water quality measurement and vegetation mapping. In general, remote sensing technologies rely on the classification and detection of targets in remote sensing images. Target detection refers to the technical process of distinguishing target and nontarget areas in an image and can essentially be seen as a process of machine learning: learn and construct a statistical classification model on the set of positive and negative labeled data and use this model to obtain the class label of other unlabeled pixels.

© Springer Nature Switzerland AG 2021
J. Cheng et al. (Eds.): CSS 2020, LNCS 12653, pp. 172–183, 2021.
https://doi.org/10.1007/978-3-030-73671-2_16

In recent years, with the development of machine learning and image processing technologies, remote sensing object detection methods have provided relatively good detection results. However, in some applications, we may be interested in only specific target areas and not other areas, which may incur the absence of negative labelled data [1–5]. For example, if the goal of a project is to detect roads from remote sensing data and update the information of an existing transport system, we may be reluctant to label forests and agricultural areas in the images as labeled negative training data. Moreover, even if we can afford the time and labor cost, it is still difficult to obtain a proper negative training dataset due to the high diversity of negative classes, particularly when high-spatial-resolution images are used. The classification problem in which the training data include only labeled positive training samples (target region) and not negative labeled training samples (non-target region) is called the one-class learning problem in machine learning [6, 7]. For this type of problem, traditional supervised classification methods are usually inefficient because traditional supervised classifiers require the classes in the remote sensing image to all have labeled training pixels. Thus, it is necessary to develop a stable and efficient remote sensing image target region detection method for cases where the training set contains only positive labeled samples.

At present, two strategies are used to address the one-class classification problem in the literature. The first strategy completely ignores unlabeled data and trains a classifier on only positive labeled data. Typical approaches of this type include the Gaussian model (GM) [7], one-class support vector machine (OCSVM) [8, 9] and support vector data description (SVDD) [10]. The GM assumes that the positive data are sampled from a Gaussian distribution. After density estimation of the positive labeled data, GM discriminates the positive class from the other classes by specifying an appropriate threshold. The disadvantage of GM is its inability to determine a suitable threshold. Moreover, when the data feature dimensionality is high, density estimation is usually very difficult. SVDD and OCSVM regard the original point as the only negative training case and find a hyperellipsoid that can exactly accommodate all positive examples or a hyperplane to separate the positive labeled data from the original point with the maximum margin. The disadvantage of these two methods is that their classification results are sensitive to the parameter values, so careful parameter tuning is required. The second strategy is semi-supervised learning, where unlabeled data are added to the learning process to compensate for missing negative labeled data. Representative works include semi-supervised one-class SVM (S^2OC-SVM) [11], 1-SVMs [13], positive and unlabeled learning method (PUL) [3] and cost-sensitive positive and unlabeled learning method (CSPUL) [13]. S^2OC-SVM and 1-SVMs improve the classifier by introducing manifold regular terms into the learning goal to make the labels smoother. However, the classification outcome is still sensitive to the parameter values. PUL and CSPUL are state-of-the-art methods for one-class classification. They use the estimated class prior to learning a classifier on positive and unlabeled data directly, where the unlabeled data play a similar role as the negative labeled data. However, the two-step strategy makes the classification precision strongly dependent on the class prior estimated in their first step.

In this paper, we propose a PUL method based on regularization, which is formalized as the Bhattacharyya coefficient (BC). The BC is a measure of the amount of overlap between two statistical samples or populations and is widely used in research on feature extraction and selection, image processing, speaker recognition, and phone clustering. We use the BC to impose an additional restriction on the unknown negative class conditional PDF to ensure that it is as far from the positive class conditional PDF as possible. Since the positive class conditional PDF and the mixture PDF of both the positive class and negative class can be estimated from the positive data and the unlabeled data, respectively, such a learning strategy makes it possible to obtain an estimate of the negative class conditional PDF. Moreover, we adopt an implicit mixture model of restricted Boltzmann machines (IRBM) to depict the data distribution to avoid the problem of simultaneously estimating the value of unknown class priors and unknown density functions. Thus, RPUL is established by embedding the BC between two class conditional densities into the risk function, i.e., the KL divergence between samples and the IRBM model, as a regularization item.

In contrast to other one-class methods, RPUL makes no assumptions about the data generation mechanism and requires no processing steps to estimate the threshold or class prior. We apply RPUL to classify data extracted from three scenes of a high-spatial-resolution image under the assumption that only positive data and unlabeled data are available for training. The experimental results illustrate the superiority of the proposed method compared with other state-of-the-art strategies.

2 The Proposed Approach

2.1 Preliminaries

Bhattacharyya Coefficient. The BC between two probability densities $p_1(\mathbf{v})$ and $p_2(\mathbf{v})$, with $\mathbf{v} \in R^d$, is defined as

$$B = \int_{R^d} \sqrt{p_1(\mathbf{v})p_2(\mathbf{v})}d\mathbf{v}. \tag{1}$$

Clearly, the value of B is always confined within the interval $[0, 1]$.

Implicit mixture model of RBMs (IRBM) [14]. The IRBM is a mixture model of RBMs with the mixed weights implicitly parameterized.

Let $\mathbf{v} \in R^d$ be a vector of visible (observed) variables and $\mathbf{h}$ be a vector of hidden variables. Let K be the number of components (classes): K is two in this paper since we discuss only situations with two classes. Let $\mathbf{q}$ be a K-dimensional binary vector with only one element being one. Further, if $q_1 = 1$ and $q_2 = 0$, then the current $\mathbf{v}$ is a case of the positive class; otherwise, it is a case of the negative class. The energy function for IRBM is

$$E(\mathbf{v}, \mathbf{h}, \mathbf{q}) = \frac{1}{2}\sum_i (v_i - c_i)^2 - \sum_j h_j d_j - \sum_k q_k \sum_{i,j} W_{ijk} v_i h_j \tag{2}$$

$$c_i = \sum_k q_k C_{ik}, d_j = \sum_k q_k D_{jk} \tag{3}$$

where W, C and D are the weight parameters, the visible unit biases and the hi-den unit biases, respectively, and k represents the component index. The joint distribution for the mixture model is

$$p_{\text{model}}(\mathbf{v}^s, \mathbf{h}^s, \mathbf{q}^s) = exp\big(-E(\mathbf{v}^s, \mathbf{h}^s, \mathbf{q}^s)\big)/Z \tag{4}$$

where

$$Z = \sum_{\mathbf{v},\mathbf{h},\mathbf{q}} exp(-E(\mathbf{v}, \mathbf{h}, \mathbf{q})) \tag{5}$$

is the partition function of the implicit mixture model. The components of IRBM are standard RBMs. The energy function of the kth component derived from (2) is

$$E_k(\mathbf{v}, \mathbf{h}) = E(\mathbf{v}, \mathbf{h}, q_k = 1) \tag{6}$$

The corresponding distribution function of the kth component is

$$p_{\text{model}}(\mathbf{v}^s, \mathbf{h}^s | q_k = 1) = exp\big(-E_k(\mathbf{v}^s, \mathbf{h}^s)\big)/Z_k$$
$$Z_k = \sum_{\mathbf{v},\mathbf{h}} exp(E_k(\mathbf{v}, \mathbf{h})) \tag{7}$$

Let $\theta = \{W, C, D\}$ be the set of model parameters. Given a set of N training cases $\{\mathbf{v}^1, ..., \mathbf{v}^N\}$, the learning process of IRBM is to maximize the log likelihood of $L = \sum_{n=1}^{N} \log p_{\text{model}}(\mathbf{v}^n; \theta)$ or to minimize the Kullback–Leibler (KL) distance between the empirical data distribution and the model distribution $KL(p_{data}(\mathbf{v})||p_{\text{model}}(\mathbf{v}\ ; \theta))$, where $p_{data}(\mathbf{v}) = \frac{1}{N} \sum_{i=1}^{n} \delta(\mathbf{v} - \mathbf{v}^n)$ and $\delta(\mathbf{v} - \mathbf{v}^n)$ is 1 only when $\mathbf{v} = \mathbf{v}^n$; otherwise, it is 0. IRBM can be trained by a contrastive divergence-like algorithm by sampling the conditional distributions $p(\mathbf{h}, \mathbf{q}|\mathbf{v})$ and $p(\mathbf{v}|\mathbf{h}, \mathbf{q})$. Sampling $p(\mathbf{h}, \mathbf{q}|\mathbf{v})$ is not straightforward and performed in two steps. First, the K-way discrete distribution $p(\mathbf{q}|\mathbf{v})$ is computed (see below) and sampled. Then, given $q_k = 1$, the kth component RBM is selected and its conditional distribution $p(\mathbf{h}|\mathbf{v})$ is sampled. $p(\mathbf{q}|\mathbf{v})$ is given by

$$p(q_k = 1|\mathbf{v}) = \frac{exp(-F(\mathbf{v}, q_k = 1))}{\sum_m exp(-F(\mathbf{v}, q_m = 1))} \tag{8}$$

where

$$F(\mathbf{v}, q_k = 1) = \frac{1}{2} \sum_i (v_i - c_i)^2 - \sum_j \log\left(1 + exp\left(\sum_i W_{ijk} v_i\right)\right) \tag{9}$$

2.2 Learning Framework

Notation

Let $\mathcal{Y} = \{+1, -1\}$ be the set of possible labels. Without loss of generality, we suppose only the first l cases in $\{\mathbf{v}^1, ..., \mathbf{v}^N\}$ are labeled with positive label $+1$ and the rest are unlabeled. Let $P = \{\mathbf{v}^1, ..., \mathbf{v}^l\}$ be the set of positive samples, and let $U = \{\mathbf{v}^{l+1}, ..., \mathbf{v}^N\}$ be the set of unlabeled samples.

Method

The goal of our method is to learn the posterior probability function $p(q_1 = 1|\mathbf{v})$. According to Bayes' rule,

$$p(q_1 = 1|\mathbf{v}) = \frac{p(\mathbf{v}|q_1 = 1)p(q_1 = 1)}{p(\mathbf{v})}. \tag{10}$$

Then, the positive conditional density function $p(\mathbf{v}|q_1 = 1)$, the mixture density $p(\mathbf{v})$ and the class prior $p(q_1 = 1)$ must be estimated. As the IRBM was adopted as the data description model, estimation of the class prior is replaced by estimation of the negative class conditional density function. However, because of the lack of labeled negative data, estimation of the negative class conditional density is not straightforward. To address this problem, we introduce the BC to obtain supernumerary information about the negative class conditional density to compensate for the absence of negative labeled data. This approach is reasonable. In fact, minimizing the BC between the conditional densities of two class, i.e., the amount of overlap, would lead to a negative class conditional density that is far from the positive class conditional density. Then, in the area far from the negative data, it holds that $p(\mathbf{v}|q_1 = 1)p(q_1 = 1)$ is approximately equal to $p(\mathbf{v})$. Notably, approximating $p(\mathbf{v}|q_1 = 1)p(q_1 = 1)$ as $p(\mathbf{v})$ is the starting point of the state-of-the-art one-class method [13] for estimating the class prior.

Finally, the proposed framework of RPUL is formulated to minimize

$$\begin{aligned} Z(\theta) = \ &KL(p_{\text{data}}(\mathbf{v}|q_1 = 1), p(\mathbf{v}|q_1 = 1; \theta_1)) \\ &+ KL(p_{\text{data}}(\mathbf{v}), p(\mathbf{v}; \theta)) + \mu B(p(\mathbf{v}|q_1 = 1; \theta_1), p(\mathbf{v}|q_2 = 1; \theta_2)) \end{aligned} \tag{11}$$

where $\theta = \{\theta_1, \theta_2\}$ is the set of model parameters and θ_k is the set of parameters of the kth component of IRBM. $KL(\bullet)$ is the Kullback–Leibler divergence. The first two items on the right side of the equal sign measure the degree of fit between the positive data and the first positive component of IRBM and the degree of fit between the unlabeled data and the complete IRBM, respectively. The final item is the BC regularization item, which ensures that the second component of IRBM captures the negative class conditional density precisely, as mentioned in the previous analysis. The trade-off between the data fit items and the regularization item is positive parameter μ, which is fixed at 0.1 in this paper.

Solution

As in the training process of IRBM, gradient descent is employed to solve optimization problem (11). To make the notation concise, the three terms on the right side of the equal sign of (11) are denoted by $KL_1(\theta_1)$, $KL_2(\theta)$, and $B(\theta)$. Given the samples $\mathbf{v}^s \in U$, the estimate of $B(\theta)$ is computed by

$$B(\theta) = \sum_{\mathbf{v}^s} \sqrt{f(\mathbf{v}^s; \theta_1)g(\mathbf{v}^s; \theta_2)}. \tag{12}$$

Then, the derivative of $B(\theta)$ with respect to θ_k is

$$\frac{\partial B}{\partial \theta_k} = \frac{-1}{2\sqrt{p(q_1 = 1)p(q_2 = 1)}} \left[\begin{array}{l} \sum_{\mathbf{v}^s} p(\mathbf{v}^s)\sqrt{p(q_1 = 1|\mathbf{v}^s)p(q_2 = 1|\mathbf{v}^s)} \dfrac{\partial F_k(\mathbf{v}^s)}{\partial \theta_k} \\[2mm] - \left(\dfrac{\sum_{\mathbf{v}^s} p(\mathbf{v}^s)\sqrt{p(q_1 = 1|\mathbf{v}^s)p(q_2 = 1|\mathbf{v}^s)}}{\sum_{\mathbf{v}} p(\mathbf{v})p(q_k = 1|\mathbf{v})} \right) \\[2mm] \left(\sum_{\mathbf{v}} p(\mathbf{v})p(q_k = 1|\mathbf{v})\dfrac{\partial F_k(\mathbf{v})}{\partial \theta_k} \right) \end{array} \right] \tag{13}$$

where θ is omitted for brevity and $F_k(\mathbf{v}) = F(\mathbf{v}, q_k = 1)$. To compute the terms associated with the variable $\mathbf{v}$ of (13) exactly, we would need to sum over the joint space of all possible visible variables, which is an intractable task. Fortunately, we can address this problem using the CD learning algorithm, which has been found to be effective for training a variety of energy-based models. Based on the CD algorithm, we sample the mixed probability density $p(\mathbf{v})$ to compute the corresponding expectation terms and then obtain the approximation to the derivative of $B(\theta)$:

$$\frac{\partial B(\theta)}{\partial \theta_k^n} \approx \frac{-1}{2\sqrt{p(q_1 = 1)p(q_2 = 1)}} \left[\begin{array}{l} \sum_{s=l}^{l+u} p_{data}(\mathbf{v}^s)\sqrt{p(q_1 = 1|\mathbf{v}^s)p(q_2 = 1|\mathbf{v}^s)} \dfrac{\partial F_k(\mathbf{v}^s)}{\partial \theta_k^n} \\[3mm] - \left(\dfrac{\sum_{s=l}^{l+u} p_{data}(\mathbf{v}^s)\sqrt{p(q_1 = 1|\mathbf{v}^s)p(q_2 = 1|\mathbf{v}^s)}}{\sum_{s=l}^{l+u} p((\mathbf{v}^s)^-)p(q_k = 1|(\mathbf{v}^s)^-)} \right) \\[3mm] \left(\sum_{s=l}^{l+u} p((\mathbf{v}^s)^-)p(q_k = 1|(\mathbf{v}^s)^-)\dfrac{\partial F_k((\mathbf{v}^s)^-)}{\partial \theta_k^n} \right) \end{array} \right] \tag{14}$$

where $(\mathbf{v}^s)^-$ is obtained by the negative phase, which are the values of the visible variables after M steps of alternating sampling and $p(\mathbf{h}, \mathbf{q}|\mathbf{v})$ and $p(\mathbf{v}|\mathbf{h}, \mathbf{q})$. Otherwise, given $\mathbf{v}^s$, if the sampled $q_1 = 1$, let $s_k = 1$; else, let $s_k = 2$. Similarly, given $(\mathbf{v}^s)^-$, we can obtain the value of $(s_k)^-$. The derivative of F_k in (14) can be computed approximately as follows:

$$\frac{\partial F_k(\mathbf{v}^s)}{\partial W_{ijk}} = -p(h_j|\mathbf{v}^s, q_k = 1)v_i^s \approx \begin{cases} -h_j^s v_i^s, & k = s_k \\ 0, & k \neq s_k \end{cases}, \tag{15}$$

$$\frac{\partial F_k((\mathbf{v}^s)^-)}{\partial W_{ijk}} = -p(h_j|(\mathbf{v}^s)^-, q_k = 1)(v_i^s)^- \approx \begin{cases} -(h_j^s)^-(v_i^s)^-, & k = s_k^- \\ 0, & k \neq s_k^- \end{cases}, \tag{16}$$

$$\frac{\partial F_k(\mathbf{v}^s)}{\partial C_{ik}} = \begin{cases} -v_i^s + c_i, & k = s_k \\ 0, & k \neq s_k \end{cases}, \tag{17}$$

$$\frac{\partial F_k((\mathbf{v}^s)^-)}{\partial C_{ik}} = \begin{cases} -(v_i^s)^- + c_i, & k = s_k^- \\ 0, & k \neq s_k^- \end{cases} \tag{18}$$

$$\frac{\partial F_k(\mathbf{v}^s)}{\partial D_{jk}} = -p(h_j|\mathbf{v}^s, q_k = 1) \approx \begin{cases} -h_j^s, & k = s_k \\ 0, & k \neq s_k \end{cases}, \tag{19}$$

$$\frac{\partial F_k((\mathbf{v}^s)^-)}{\partial D_{jk}} = -p(h_j|(\mathbf{v}^s)^-, q_k = 1) \approx \begin{cases} -(h_j^s)^-, & k = s_k^- \\ 0, & k \neq s_k^- \end{cases} \tag{20}$$

The derivative of $KL_1(\theta_1)$ with respect to θ_1 and the derivative of $KL_2(\theta)$ with respect to θ can be computed by CD algorithm, as done in the preliminaries. After the derivatives are computed, the parameters of our model are iteratively updated as follows:

$$\theta_{new} = \theta_{old} - \eta\Delta\theta, \tag{21}$$

where η is the learning rate and

$$\Delta\theta = \frac{\partial(\mu B + KL_1 + KL_2)}{\partial\theta}. \tag{22}$$

Finally, for any given sample $\mathbf{v}$, following Bayes' decision theory, if $p(q_1 = 1|\mathbf{v}) > p(q_2 = 1|\mathbf{v})$, the label is positive. Otherwise, the label is negative, and $p(q_1 = 1|\mathbf{v})$ can be computed via formula (8).

Note that the computation of (22) simply involved applying the CD algorithm to the P set and U set, and the time complexity of the proposed method is the same as that of IRBM.

3   Experiments

In this section, we investigate the performance of the proposed RPUL for one-class classification of remote sensing data. The cost-sensitive LPU method (called CSLPU below) proposed in [13] is a state-of-the-art alternative learning method for the same positive/unlabeled scenario, and the Gaussian domain descriptor (GDD) methods are commonly used one-class classifiers. Hence, these methods are also compared with the proposed RPUL in our experiments.

3.1 Dataset Description

The initial dataset used in this paper was RIT-18 [15, 16], which is composed of very-high-resolution aerial photographs (4.7 cm GSD) acquired by an unmanned aircraft system (see Fig. 1). The dataset includes 6 VNIR spectral bands and 18 labeled object classes. The 2nd, 14th, 15th and 16th classes were chosen as positive classes in this paper because they are the first four classes that have a sufficient number of pixels (at least 1%

of the total pixels). The size of the photographs is 9393 × 5642, with a total of 52995306 pixels. We slid a 5 × 5 pixel template over the image and extracted 88 features for each pixel, including the mean, variance, homogeneity, contrast, and second moment of the six bands. All features were rescaled to the range [0, 1].

RPUL and CSLPU require positive and unlabeled data for training, whereas GDD and SVDD require only positive data. In general, more labeled training data results in higher accuracy but also increases the required labeling effort. In our experiments, for each class extraction, we randomly selected only 50 pixels of a class as labeled positive training samples: the labeled pixels were less than 9e−5% of the entire image. Additionally, for RPUL and CSLPU, we randomly selected an additional 1000 pixels from the entire image as the unlabeled dataset. As mentioned in the introduction, the classification results of GDD strongly depend on the tuned model parameters: high classification accuracy on the testing dataset is difficult to guarantee if these parameters are tuned with only positive data. To investigate the optimal performance, we used 1000 randomly selected background pixels of other classes in addition to the previously prepared positive labeled samples to tune the parameters. Finally, the remaining pixels of the photographs formed the test dataset. Moreover, to obtain statistically reliable results, ten different random realizations of the training data were considered for each classification, and the classification results were evaluated in terms of the overall accuracy (OA), F-measure (F), recall (R) and kappa coefficient (K) [17].

Fig. 1. RGB visualization of the RIT-18 dataset. This dataset has six spectral bands.

3.2 Model Development

RPUL. The RPUL model was developed in MATLAB. Typically, we used models with 200 latent variables. The value of the parameter μ in (22) was fixed at 0.1; the learning rate in (21) was set to 1e−3; and the weight decay was set to 1e−2. A momentum term was also used: 0.9 of the previous accumulated gradient was added to the current gradient. A temperature parameter was introduced to scale the free energies, similar to the training process of IRBM: the parameter was set to 100. We trained the model using the entire sample in both the P set and the U set until the class labels of the data did not change or the number of iterations reached 2000.

CSLPU. The CSLPU model was implemented in MATLAB. We used a Gaussian radial basis function (RBF) kernel and followed the empirical approach in [6] to tune the parameters. The number of basis functions was set to 300. The regularization parameter was tuned in the range $[-3, 10]$ on a log scale with a step size of 1. The kernel width was tuned in the range that was computed by first estimating the median value of the distances from all samples to the randomly selected centroids and multiplying the median value by the numbers in the interval $[-2, 10]$ on a log scale with a step size of 1. Moreover, CSLPU needs the class prior to be known first. We used the method in [13] to estimate the class prior, with the parameters tuned under the same settings as those used for CSLPU.

GDD. The GDD model was implemented via dd_tools. We used the simple Gaussian target distribution and tuned two parameters: the error on the target class in the range $[0.1, 1]$ with a step size of 0. 1 and the regularization parameter in the range $[0.1, 1]$ with a step size of 0.1. As for SVDD, only the samples in the P set were used to train the classifier using the tuned parameters.

3.3 Experimental Results

Every experiment was repeated ten times with randomly selected positive and unlabeled samples. Figure 2 shows the classification maps of one of the experiments of Fig. 1 for each land type, where (a) is the benchmarks, i.e., the true pixel labels, and (b), (c) and (d) are the classification results of RPUL, CSLPU and GDD, respectively. In general, RPUL provides the best classification results in the extraction of a single land type from the aerial photograph. Note that such good classification results are obtained in the situation with only 50 positive labeled pixels and no negative labeled pixels for training. Therefore, with the help of the regularization item, RPUL can learn additional information about the unknown negative training samples from the positive and unlabeled samples to construct a proper classifier even without the labeled negative training samples. CSLPU also provides relatively good results, particularly for water areas, but GDD produces poor results. Both RPUL and CSLPU used unlabeled samples to build the classifier, which may be the reason that they have better classification results than GDD. Moreover, CSLPU is slightly inferior to RPUL. The main reason is likely that the distribution of the positive class in the training set is not identical to the distribution in the unlabeled set since we selected only 50 positive samples as labeled samples; therefore, CSLPU might not be able to obtain an optimal estimate of the class prior to train the classifier. Table 1 compares the accuracy, F-measure, recall and kappa coefficient of the three methods for different land types. The results in Table 1 show that RPUL and CSLPU had similar best evaluation values and GDD provided the worst classification results, even with the parameters tuned on the set of additional negative labeled samples and positive labeled samples.

(a) Benchmark   (b) RPUL   (c) CSLPU   (d) GDD

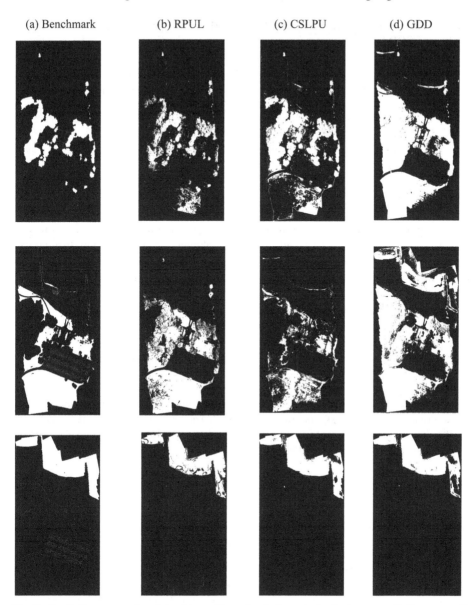

Fig. 2. Prediction maps of each land type. From the first row to the last row, prediction maps of tree, grass and water. White: positive; black: negative.

Table 1. The accuracy (OA), F-measure (F), recall (R) and kappa coefficient (K) of RPUL, CSLPU and GDD for all land types

Land Types	RPUL				CSLPU				GDD			
	OA	F	R	K	OA	F	R	K	OA	F	R	K
Tree	0.93	0.96	0.96	0.67	0.90	0.94	0.90	0.64	0.77	0.85	0.75	0.36
Grass	0.86	0.90	0.89	0.63	0.89	0.93	0.98	0.61	0.74	0.82	0.72	0.43
water	0.98	0.98	0.99	0.91	0.98	0.99	0.99	0.90	0.97	0.98	0.99	0.88

4 Conclusion

In this paper, we addressed the problem of one-class classification of remote sensing data by proposing a new BC-based positive and unlabeled learning algorithm. In contrast to other one-class methods, the proposed method makes no assumptions about the data generation mechanism and does not need a processing step to estimate the threshold or the class prior. Moreover, the proposed method is a semi-supervised learning method that requires only a small set of labeled positive data for classifier training. The experimental results indicated that the new algorithm achieves high classification accuracy, outperforming the CSPUL, SVDD, and GDD methods. In future work, we will apply the learning strategy to a generative adversarial network to further improve the performance of LPU methods.

Acknowledgment. This work is supported by Hainan Provincial Natural Science Foundation of China (Project No. 119MS004), the National Natural Science Foundation of China (61650303) and the Undergraduate Bilingual Course Construction Project of Hainan University "Advanced Mathematics" (Project No. hdsyk201903).

References

1. Rao, T., Rajinikanth, T.: Supervised classification of remote sensed data using support vector machine. Global J. Comput. Sci. Technol. **14** (2014)
2. Wenkai, L., Qinghua, G.: A new accuracy assessment method for one-class remote sensing classification. IEEE Trans. Geosci. Remote Sens. **52**, 4621–4632 (2014)
3. Wenkai, L., Qinghua, G., Elkan, C.: A positive and unlabeled learning algorithm for one-class classification of remote-sensing data. IEEE Trans. Geosci. Remote Sens. **49**, 717–725 (2011)
4. Xueqing, D., Wenkai, L., Xiaoping, L.: One-class remote sensing classification: one-class vs. binary classifiers. Int. J. Remote Sens. **39**, 1890–1910 (2018)
5. Kristen, J., Andreas, S.: Positive and unlabeled learning algorithms and applications: a survey. In: International Conference on Information, Intelligence, Systems and Applications (IISA) (2019)
6. du Plessis, M.C., Niu, G., Sugiyama, M.: Analysis of learning from positive and unlabeled data. In: Advances in Neural Information Processing Systems, MIT Press, Montreal, Quebec, Canada, pp. 703–711 (2014)
7. David, M.: Tax, One-class classification, Concept-learning in the absence of counter-examples. In: ASCI dissertation series, Delft Univ.Technol., Delft,The Netherlands (2001)

8. Schölkopf, B., Williamson, R.C., Smola, A.J., Shawe-Taylor, J., Platt, J.C.: Support vector method for novelty detection. In: NIPS, MIT Press, Colorado, USA, pp. 582–588 (1999)
9. Guerbai, Y., Chibani, Y., Hadjadji, B.: The effective use of the one-class SVM classifier for handwritten signature verification based on writer-independent parameters. Pattern Recogn. **48**, 103–113 (2015)
10. Tax, D.M., Duin, R.P.: Support vector domain description. Pattern Recogn. Lett. **20**, 1191–1199 (1999)
11. Goh, K.-S., Chang, E.Y., Li, B.: Using one-class and two-class SVMs for multiclass image annotation. IEEE Trans. Knowl. Data Eng. **17**, 1333–1346 (2005)
12. Mũnoz-Marí, J., Bovolo, F., Gomez-Chova, L., Bruzzone, L., Camp-Valls, G.: Semisupervised one-class support vector machines for classification of remote sensing data. IEEE Trans. Geosci. Remote Sens. **48**, 3188–3197 (2010)
13. du Plessis, M.C., Sugiyama, M.: Class prior estimation from positive and unlabeled data. IEICE Trans. Inf. Syst. **97**, 1358–1362 (2014)
14. V. Nair, G.E. Hinton, Implicit mixtures of restricted Boltzmann machines. In: Advances in Neural Information Processing Systems, pp. 1145–1152 (2009)
15. Kemker, R., Salvaggio, C., Kanan, C.: Algorithms for semantic segmentation of multispectral remote sensing imagery using deep learning, arXiv preprint arXiv:1703.06452 (2017)
16. Guoping, Y., Yingli, Z.: Target detection method of remote sensing image based on deep learning. In: Cross Strait Radio Science & Wireless Technology Conference (CSRSWTC) (2020)
17. Stehman, S.: Estimating the kappa coefficient and its variance under stratified random sampling. Photogram. Eng. Remote Sens. **62**, 401–407 (1996)

SDSBT: A Secure Multi-party Data Sharing Platform Based on Blockchain and TEE

Hong Lei[1] , Yun Yan[1] , Zijian Bao[1] , Qinghao Wang[1,2]($\boxtimes$) ,
Yongxin Zhang[1,2] , and Wenbo Shi[2]

[1] Oxford-Hainan Blockchain Research Institute, Chengmai 571924, China
{leihong,yanyun,zijian,qinghao,yongxin}@oxhainan.org
[2] Department of Computer Science and Engineering, Northeastern University,
Shenyang 110001, China
shiwb@neuq.edu.cn
https://www.oxhainan.org

Abstract. With the rise of big data analytics and artificial intelligence, an increasing number of enterprises and individuals are concerned about the security and privacy of the shared data. However, it is still challenging to achieve a data sharing scheme, which meets the security, privacy, security, and credibility requirements. This paper proposes SDSBT, a multi-party data sharing platform based on blockchain and the trusted execution environment (TEE), which effectively and securely realizes the data sharing among multiple parties. SDSBT achieves the properties including privacy-preserving, identity authentication, application security, and accountability. The security analysis and experimental results show that the scheme is secure and practical.

Keywords: Blockchain · TEE · SGX · Data sharing · Privacy protection

1 Introduction

With the development of big data analytics and artificial intelligence, data is becoming more and more valuable and has become the core asset of some enterprises and government agencies. One of the fundamental enabling components for the big data analytics and artificial intelligence is the abundance of data. Thus, it is essential to share data between multiple parties for the abundance of data [1,2]. However, as more information on individuals is shared and analyzed, data providers are getting increasingly concerned about data security and privacy issues. How to effectively coordinate all parties to complete data sharing with a secure and privacy-preserving way is one of the current research hotspots [3–11].

This study is supported by Oxford-Hainan Blockchain Research Institute, the National Science Foundation of China (No. 61472074, U1708262) and the Fundamental Research Funds for the Central Universities (No. N172304023).

J. Cheng et al. (Eds.): CSS 2020, LNCS 12653, pp. 184–196, 2021.
https://doi.org/10.1007/978-3-030-73671-2_17

Recently, many scholars propose schemes to solve the security problems in data sharing. Zhao et al. [7] proposed a data sharing model for the Internet of things(IoT) scenario, which used the attribute-based encryption to achieve fine-grained access control of ciphertext and guarantee the data privacy. However, the efficiency and security of the scheme need to be further improved. In [8], the authors implemented a lightweight data sharing platform, which used the data integrity verification to enhance security. But the scheme did not consider the security of the data processing. Wu et al. [9] proposed a human intelligence, artificial intelligence, and organizational intelligence (HAO) governance method to achieve the requirements of data standard governance. However, the security properties of data storage were not considered.

Blockchain is a public and decentralized ledger, which is tamper-proof and traceable. One rising way is to use the blockchain technology to enhance the security of data sharing. Wang et al. [10] proposed a data sharing platform, which employs the tamper-proofing and traceability of the blockchain to ensure the correctness of data. In [11], Wang et al. construct a blockchain-based data sharing network, which implements the secure data sharing. However, both of the schemes store the source data in the blockchain, which is visible to everyone. Thus the data privacy can not be protected.

The trusted execution environment (TEE) technology implements the secure container to protect the integrity and confidentiality of the internal data [12], which can provide powerful support for the blockchain-based data sharing schemes. In this paper, we designed a multi-party data sharing platform, which meets the privacy, security, and credibility requirements of the data sharing, by combining TEE and blockchain. We build the data sharing platform based on TEE and run the data computation in the secure container to protect the data privacy. The secure container can also guarantee the correctness of the internal computation, thus the security of data sharing is ensured from the hardware level. Moreover, we store the data sharing log in the blockchain to provide a basis for data confirmation and to realize the functions of retrospective and accountability afterward.

In summary, in this paper, we make the following contributions:

1. We propose a data sharing platform SDSBT based on blockchain and TEE, which achieves privacy-preserving, identity authentication, application security, and accountability properties.
2. Through simulation and analysis of experiments, the feasibility of the scheme in this paper is confirmed.

The structure of the paper is as follows: in Sect. 2, the related background is provided, including TEE, Intel SGX Software Guard Extensions (SGX), and Blockchain technology. In Sect. 3, we describe the current system architecture, threat model, and design goals. In Sect. 4, we propose the system design. In Sect. 5, the security of the platform is analyzed. In Sect. 6, we conduct the corresponding experimental analysis. The paper is concluded in Sect. 7.

2 Background

To better understand our scheme, the related backgrounds are presented, including the basic concept of TEE, SGX, and blockchain technology.

2.1 Trusted Execution Environment (TEE)

The trusted execution environment (TEE) technology can provide the secure container to prevent potentially malicious users from controlling or observing the internal data [12]. To achieve the secure container, TEE needs to guarantee the data isolation between the trusted environment and the normal environment. A common scheme is providing the physical memory isolation and the extra access checks, so that the normal environment cannot directly access the data in the trusted environment. Currently, the popular TEE solutions include SGX(SoftwareGuard Extensions) based on Intel x86 architecture, TrustZone based on ARM Architecture, and MultiZone [13] based on open-source framework RISC-V.

At present, TEE [14] technology is used in many fields to improve privacy protection and security properties. Chen et al. [15] used TEE to defense causative attacks and achieve data privacy in federated learning systems. Sebastian et al. [16] use TEE technology to enhance the security of IoT devices and provide the implementation of the proposed architecture on the platform supporting ARM TrustZone.

2.2 Intel Software Guard Extensions

Intel software guard extensions (SGX) is one of the most popular TEE products in commodity CPUs, which is employed in various fields [17–19]. It provides the new CPU instructions on the Intel CPU architecture to guarantee the integrity and confidentiality for the security-sensitive computing performed on the SGX-enabled machine where the privileged softwares (e.g., kernel, hypervisor, and so on) are malicious [20].

Essentially, the new instructions are coupled with a pre-partitioned memory called enclave page cache (EPC), which is the secure memory protected by the hardware. Users can employ the instructions to create the secure container called enclave for their applications in EPC [21], and the access to the enclave will be performed additional checks to protect the security. To ensure the reliability of the SGX-enabled platform, SGX implements the remote attestation to prove to the remote parties that the particular application is loaded in the enclave, and the enclave is running in the real SGX-enabled platform. Comparing to the other TEE schemes, the trusted computing base (TCB) of SGX is smaller, which only contains the CPU and EPC. Any privileged software, such as OS, hypervisor, BIOS, SMM, etc., is not included in its TCB.

Note that we employ SGX as the TEE instance to implement the simulation experiment of our schemes. Thus the characteristic of TEE is obeyed to SGX in the paper.

2.3   Blockchain Technology

Blockchain is a public, distributed ledger, which can record transactions in a verifiable and immutable way. It is jointly maintained by the nodes in the blockchain system, and the nodes constitute a vast P2P network. The consistency of the ledger is guaranteed by the consensus algorithm, which is the basis for quickly reaching a consensus on the blockchain data among highly dispersed nodes. The consensus algorithm allows the transactions to be securely stored and verified without any centralized authority. A blockchain is a growing list of records, called blocks, that are linked using cryptography technology. Each block contains a hash value of the previous block, a timestamp, and transaction data (generally represented as a Merkle tree).

3   Problem Statement

3.1   System Model

As shown in Fig. 1, the blockchain-based TEE secure multi-party data sharing platform is mainly divided into four parts: data providers, data users, cloud servers, and a blockchain.

- **Data providers.** The data provider uploads data to cloud servers and shares it into the data sharing platform.
- **Data users.** The data user uses the data sharing platform to access the desired data.
- **Cloud servers.** The cloud server is responsible for the secure transmission of data, secure calculations, and interaction with the blockchain.
- **Blockchain.** The blockchain and the associated smart contracts are used for storing transaction information and driving the transaction process.

3.2   Threat Model

In our assumption, the data user is an unreliable role. It will try to steal the real data. Besides, the platform is also not enough security. It may be compromised by the adversary. Moreover, we assume the TEE is normally trustworthy, i.e., the adversary cannot compromise it. The handled data can be protected by the enclave. We also assume that the adversary cannot control the blockchain, such as tampering with the data, blocking the consensus algorithm.

3.3   Design Goals

As SDSBT is designed to provide a trusted sharing environment for users, it should meet the following goals: privacy-preserving, identity authentication, application security, and accountability.

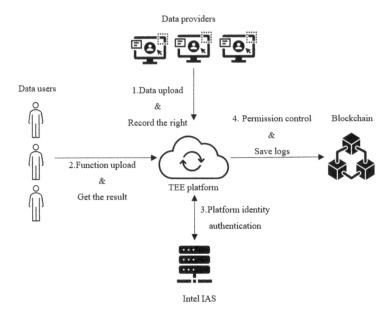

Fig. 1. System model

(1) *Privacy-Preserving*: during the sharing process, the platform and data users cannot infer the user's real data.

(2) *Identity Authentication*: in our scheme, unauthorized users cannot participate in the sharing process.

(3) *Application Security*: it is difficult for the adversary to steal or corrupt the sharing data in runtime.

(4) *Accountability*: in our scheme, once a role violates the protocol, it will be found and blamed.

4   SDSBT System Design

In this section, we will systematically elaborate on the infrastructure and interaction process of our platform. For the convenience of illustration, as well as given the fact that SGX is currently the most widely used TEE technology, we will adopt SGX to replace the term TEE in this section. We use SGX to construct the main part of the platform and design five layers. At the same time, SDSBT strictly controls user access rights. It provides users with access controls at the contract layer and read permissions at the data sharing layer, which reduces the risk of the platform.

4.1   The Infrastructure of SDSBT

As shown in Fig. 2, the overall architecture can be divided into five layers: contract layer, data transmission layer, data operation layer, data sharing layer, and storage layer.

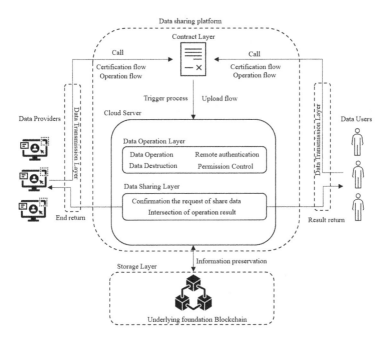

Fig. 2. The platform infrastructure.

Contract Layer. The TEE contract layer mainly implements the driving function of the data sharing process. The data sharing parties complete the data sharing process by calling the contract. The contract layer mainly provides data/code upload functions, platform authentication, and authentication result generation and triggers the platform for data processing.

Data Transmission Layer. In the entire data sharing platform, the basic step is to transmit the local data of the data owner to the cloud platform in a secure and reliable manner, and to ensure that there will be no private copy or storage of data on the platform level during the transmission process, or data leakage caused by malicious third-party attacks.

To achieve this, we first use the enclave of the cloud platform to construct a TLS secure transmission channel from the cloud to the data owner. Then, we conduct the hash value of the code to build the secure channel, and store it in the blockchain to guarantee the data owner can check the authenticity of the data security transmission function.

Data Operation Layer. The data operation layer is the core of the entire secure multi-party data sharing platform. It is a cloud data computing sub-platform built by the SGX server cluster to fulfill the functional requirements of data users.

The data consumer needs to upload the verified function code into the data operation layer. Next, the data operation layer puts the code and the original data into the SGX for execution to obtain the operation result, and then deletes the original data after the execution.

Data Sharing Layer. The data sharing layer mainly completes the sharing process between users and users, ensures users complete the whole sharing strategy according to the established sharing process, and at the same time sends instructions for storing data in the blockchain to the storage layer.

Storage Layer. The storage layer is the underlying blockchain, which utilizes its secure and traceable feature to save the transaction information on the chain and provide the transaction verification mechanism.

4.2   Interactive Process of SDSBT

In this sub-section, we propose the interaction flow in Fig. 3. There exist data providers and data users, denoted as s_i and u_i ($i > 0$), respectively. We further indicate the remote authentication result by r_i, the original data set by D_i, the function code for the data user by P_i, the basic information of the platform hardware by O_i, the result of the operation by Ans, the end of the operation by f_o, the end of the transaction for the data user by f_{tu}, the end of the transaction for the data supplier by f_{ts}, the overall transaction information by inf, and the contract execution operation by Con.

User Registration Process (Step 1). The data user registers on the data sharing platform, including data attributes and user information. The platform assigns a user ID and a monotonic counter to the registered data owner and maintains a table in the database as a retrospective basis.

Function Upload and Attestation Process (Step 2 − Step 6). The data user sends the function code to the contract layer and calls the command to trigger the attestation in the contract. At this time, the contract layer drives the SGX data operation layer for local and remote attestation to the authentication agency. Then the remote authentication agency calls IAS(Intel Attestation Server) to complete the remote attestation of the device and function code, and returns the attestation result to the contract driver layer. The data sharing parties confirm the attestation result. Then the verification process can be expressed as follows, where the n means the total number of O_i and the m means the total number of P_i:

$$\sum_{i=1}^{n}\sum_{j=1}^{m}(O_i + P_j) \xrightarrow[ISA]{Con} \sum_{k=1}^{t} r_k, i \in (0, n], j \in (0, m], t \in (0, t] \tag{1}$$

$$\sum_{k=1}^{t} r_k \xrightarrow{Con} s_i \tag{2}$$

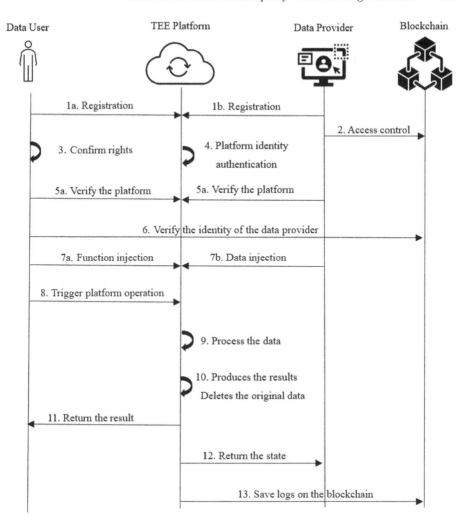

Fig. 3. Diagram of platform interaction process.

Data Upload and Computation Process (Step 7 – Step 9). After receiving the authentication result, the data sharing parties upload the corresponding data and code by calling the contract. The contract layer passes the code and data to the SGX data operation layer. After that, the data operation layer performs data processing and ensures that original data is deleted in time during the processing. Then the data upload and computation process can be expressed as:

$$\sum_{i=1}^{n} D_i \xrightarrow{Con} O, i \in (0, n] \tag{3}$$

$$\sum_{i=1}^{n}\sum_{j=1}^{m}(D_i + P_j) \xrightarrow{O} Ans + f_o, i \in (0, n], j \in (0, m] \tag{4}$$

$$f_o \xrightarrow{Con} u_i \& s_i \tag{5}$$

Data Share and Destruction Process (Step 10 – Step 12). After the data operation is completed, the data sharing layer will return the data operation result to the data consumer and the data completion status to the data provider. After that, the data operation layer and the data sharing layer will automatically delete the intermediate data.

Then the transaction process can be expressed as:

$$f_{ts} \xrightarrow{s_i} Con \tag{6}$$

$$f_{tu} \xrightarrow{u_i} Con \tag{7}$$

$$f_{tu} + f_{ts} \xrightarrow[Ans]{Con} u_i \tag{8}$$

Certificate Preservation Process (Step 13). After the data sharing layer completes the transaction recording, it will save the agreed content of the operation information on the chain so that the platform users can trace back the related information when needed.

Then the process of saving the certificate can be expressed as follows, where the "*Hash*" means the hash function:

$$f_{tu} + f_{ts} \xrightarrow[Hash]{T} inf \tag{9}$$

$$inf \xrightarrow{Hash} P \tag{10}$$

5   Security Analysis

During the process, the data owner needs to ensure that the original data cannot be obtained by the data user without authorization [21]. As a data sharing platform, our system can provide measures for owners to secure data, including data privacy-preserving for data owners, identity authentication for data users, application security for sharing platform, and accountability for malicious users.

Privacy-Preserving. In our system, data users cannot access the real data without procession, such as encryption, aggregation. We isolate the sharing platform and the data computing platform. The former is responsible for interacting with the data consumer and the latter is used to operate on target data as required by the data user, e.g., to return a result of aggregation. As a result, the data user cannot get the real data.

Identity Authentication. Our system provides an identity authentication mechanism for both parties of the process. In the first step, all the users should register in the sharing platform, where each user owns a unique identity in the system. In the next sharing process, each communication data is attached to the ID of a user. Data owners and data users can confirm the identity of the other party based on the ID.

Application Security. To achieve the security of the application, we adopt the TEE to operate the data. The pre-made code and uploaded code on the platform are displayed and attested to provide code security for the data owner. Then, all the computing resources and computing objects are placed in the TEE environment to ensure the safe and reliable operation of data and code, thereby ensuring the security of the application.

Accountability. To further implement the punishment for malicious users, we take advantage of the blockchain, which is not tampered with. The entities' operations during the sharing process are recorded by the blockchain system. Once someone breaks the sharing rules, e.g., delay the submission time, others can use the records in the blockchain to claim the malicious.

6   Experimental Evaluation

We implement the simulation experiment to evaluate the performance of the cloud server, which is the only part with "nonlinear" performance overhead in our scheme (we will explain that why the performance overhead is "nonlinear" in the following paragraph). Specifically, we run a typical calculation that searching for target data in the datasets of different sizes. The cloud server runs on the SGX-enabled PC with Ubuntu 16.04 LTS operating system, a 3.6 GHz Intel(R) Core(TM) CPU i3-9100F, and 8 GB RAM. The source dataset of the experiment includes the metadata of 1.7 million arXiv scholarly papers gathered by Cornell University [22].

The secure memory size of TEE is limited, and the oversubscription of memory may result in extra overhead. For example, SGX only supports secure memory that is smaller than 128 MB, and it requires additional operations to oversubscribe the secure memory by evicting and loading enclave pages securely, which will result in significant overhead. Thus, the calculation of different data volumes in the TEE may bring "nonlinear" performance overhead. To test the performance overhead caused by the use of TEE, we compare the computation time of the searching operations executed in the enclave with the time of the same operations performed out of the enclave in different dataset sizes (e.g., 1M, 10M, 100M, 500M, and 1G) derived from the arXiv metadata. Figure 4 shows that the former is slightly more than the latter in 1M, 10M, 100M sizes, which is because the programs in the enclave need to execute the additional encryption and decryption operations. Moreover, with the 500M and 1G sizes, the former is obviously more than the latter. It is because processing the excessive data will oversubscribe the secure memory, which will generate frequent scheduling operations to bring the extra performance overhead. Thus, a possible future work is that employing the collaboration of multiple cloud servers to reduce the computational overhead of the single node.

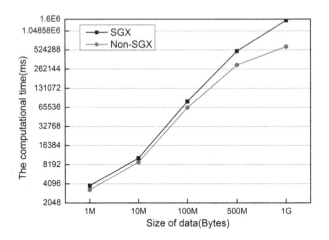

Fig. 4. Experimental results

7   Conclusion

In order to address the security challenges in existing blockchain-based data sharing schemes, we propose a secure multi-party data sharing platform combining blockchain and TEE (i.e., SDSBT). In SDSBT, the tamper-proof features of smart contracts not only ensure the security of the platform itself but also provide users with a reasonable code review path. The operational security of the data sharing platform is guaranteed through the trusted TEE server cluster and the overall performance of the platform is improved through separating the transaction layer and the operation layer. TEE improves the security of our system, but it also imposes certain performance limitations. Through experiments, we have shown that the performance difference between using TEE and not using TEE is significant for a large amount of data due to the limited secure memory of SGX.

Future Work. With the increasing market demand for data sharing, the demand for secure data sharing platforms and the platform visits will continue to increase. Under such circumstances, we need to consider more about the security and usability of the platform.

In terms of the platform security, we mainly consider further enhancing the security capabilities of TEE, due to it suffers the side-channel attacks. For example, we can consider using Oblivious Random Access Machine (ORAM) to further enhance memory protection [23] to resist side-channel attacks. In addition, it is also promising to consider the fusion of trusted computing, secure multi-party computing and SGX [24–26] to achieve stronger security.

In terms of the platform usability, from the perspective of the arnchitectural design of the platform, in order to meet the requirements of security, computing and usability of the users in the future, we will optimize the interactive architecture of the platform and further distinguish on-chain management and off-chain computation functions to enhance its security and efficiency.

References

1. Lu, Y., Huang, X., Zhang, K., Sabita, M., Zhang, Y.: Blockchain empowered asynchronous federated learning for secure data sharing in internet of vehicles. IEEE Trans. Veh. Technol. **69**(4), 4298–4311 (2020). https://doi.org/10.1109/TVT.2020.2973651
2. Imran, M., Ian, Z., Mehran, A., Justin, L., Ni, W.: PrivySharing: a blockchain-based framework for privacy-preserving and secure data sharing in smart cities. Comput. Secur. **88**, 101653 (2020). https://doi.org/10.1016/j.cose.2019.101653
3. Hoon, W., Geong, S., Xu, J., Varsha, C.: PrivateLink: privacy-preserving integration and sharing of datasets. IEEE Trans. Inf. Forensics Secur. **15**, 564–577 (2020). https://doi.org/10.1109/TIFS.2019.2924201
4. Ma, H., Zhang, R., Yang, G., Song, Z., He, K., Xiao, Y.: Efficient fine-grained data sharing mechanism for electronic medical record systems with mobile devices. IEEE Trans. Dependable Secur. Comput. **17**(5), 1026–1038 (2020). https://doi.org/10.1109/TDSC.2018.2844814
5. Shen, J., Zhou, T., He, D., Zhang, Y., Sun, X., Xiang, Y.: Block design-based key agreement for group data sharing in cloud computing. IEEE Trans. Dependable Secur. Comput. **16**(6), 996–1010 (2019). https://doi.org/10.1109/TDSC.2017.2725953
6. Li, H., Zhu, H., Du, S., Liang, X., Shen, X.: Privacy leakage of location sharing in mobile social networks: attacks and defense. IEEE Trans. Dependable Secur. Comput. **15**(4), 646–660 (2018). https://doi.org/10.1109/TDSC.2016.2604383
7. Zhao, Z., Wang, J., Zhu, Z., Sun, L.: Attribute-based encryption for data security sharing of internet of thing. J. Comput. Res. Dev. **56**(6), 1290–1301 (2019). https://doi.org/10.7544/issn1000-1239.2019.20180288
8. Lu, X., Cheng, X.: A secure and lightweight data sharing scheme for internet of medical things. IEEE Access **8**, 5022–5030 (2020). https://doi.org/10.1109/ACCESS.2019.2962729
9. Wu, X., Dong, B., Du, X., Yang, W.: Data governance technology. Ruan Jian Xue Bao **30**(9), 2030–2856 (2019). https://doi.org/10.13328/j.cnki.jos.005854
10. Wang, J., Wei, S., Dai, K.: Research on open data sharing system based on blockchain in the area of financial services system for science and technology. Modern Comput. 22,52–58+78 (2018). https://doi.org/10.3969/j.issn.1007-1423.2018.22.01
11. Wang, J., Gao, L., Dong, A., Guo, S., Chen, H., Wei, X.: Block chain based data security sharing network architecture research. J. Comput. Res. Dev. Ruan Jian Xue Bao **54**(4), 742–749 (2017). https://doi.org/10.7544/issn1000-1239.2017.20160991
12. TEE Committee (formerly Device Committee). https://globalplatform.org/technical-committees/trusted-execution-environment-tee-committee/

13. Newsome, T.: Megan Wachs. RISC-V External Debug Support, SiFive (2019). https://riscv.org/specifications/debug-specification/
14. Yan, Z., Venu, G., Zheng, Q., Wang, Y.: Access special section editorial: trusted computing. IEEE Access. **8**, 25722–25726 (2020). https://doi.org/10.1109/ACCESS.2020.2969768
15. Chen, Y., Luo, F., Li, T., Xiang, T., Liu, Z., Li, J.: A training-integrity privacy-preserving federated learning scheme with trusted execution environment. Inf. Sci. **522**, 69–79 (2020). https://doi.org/10.1016/j.ins.2020.02.037
16. Jonathan, D., Utkarsh, A., Ali, T., Adam, H.: DER-TEE: secure distributed energy resource operations through trusted execution environments. IEEE IoT J. **6**(4), 6476–6486 (2019). https://doi.org/10.1109/JIOT.2019.2909768
17. Shen, T., Jiang, J., Jiang, Y., et al.: DAENet: making strong anonymity scale in a fully decentralized network. IEEE Trans. Dependable Secure Comput. (2021)
18. Wu, L., Cai, H.J., Li, H.: SGX-UAM: a secure unified access management scheme with one time passwords via Intel SGX[J]. IEEE Access **9**, 38029–38042 (2021)
19. Schwarz, F., Rossow, C.: SENG, the SGX-enforcing network gateway: authorizing communication from shielded clients. In: 29th USENIX Security Symposium (USENIX Security 20),pp. 753–770 (2020)
20. Why use Arm architecture? Performant. Efficient. Compatible. https://developer.arm.com/architectures
21. Intel Corporation. Intel® software guard extensions (Intel® SGX). Intel Labs (2013). https://software.intel.com/sgx
22. ArXiv dataset and metadata of 1.7M+ scholarly papers across STEM. https://www.kaggle.com/Cornell-University/arxiv
23. Adil, A., Kyungtae, K, Muhammad, S., Byoungyoung, L.: Obliviate: A Data oblivious filesystem for intel SGX. In: 25th Annual Network and Distributed System Security Symposium, NDSS, San Diego, California, USA, 18–21 February 2018
24. Sasy, S., Gorbunov, S.. Fletcher, C.W.: ZeroTrace: oblivious memory primitives from Intel SGX. In: 25th Annual Network and Distributed System Security Sy.mposium, NDSS, San Diego, California, USA, 18–21 February 2018
25. Bahmani, R., et al.: Secure multiparty computation from SGX. In: Kiayias, A. (ed.) FC 2017. LNCS, vol. 10322, pp. 477–497. Springer, Cham (2017). https://doi.org/10.1007/978-3-319-70972-7_27
26. Zegzhda, D.P., Usov, E.S., Nikol'skii, A.V., Pavlenko, E.Y.: Use of Intel SGX to ensure the confidentiality of data of cloud users. Autom. Control Comput. Sci. **51**(8), 848–854 (2017). https://doi.org/10.3103/S0146411617080284

BID-HCP: Blockchain Identifier Based Health Certificate Passport System

Yuwen Zhang, Yang Liu[✉], and Cheng Chi

China Academy of Information and Communications Technology, Beijing 100191, China
liuyang7@caict.ac.cn

Abstract. The COVID-19 outbreak severely affected daily life. The World Health Organiza-tion stated that quarantine was the most effective way to control the spread of the epidemic before the vaccine was developed, but this also led to economic recession. At present, there is an urgent need for solutions to ensure the normal schedule of life while reducing the spread of the epidemic. Several contact tracking solutions have been proposed in the market, but they all have certain limitations, such as health certificates do not recognize each other, and user information is leaked. This paper proposes a health passport system based on blockchain identifier (BID-HCP), which ensures that uninfected people travel normally through a unified health certificate passport. What's more, the method separates the user's location information from the user's identity effectively, which protects the user's privacy and efficiently analyzes the high-risk areas of the epidemic.

Keywords: Blockchain · Health certificate passport · Digital identity

1 Introduction

Coronavirus disease 2019 (COVID-19) is a serious infectious disease. The disease has spread globally, with a surge in the number of confirmed cases and deaths from COVID-19 in Europe, Asia, North America and other countries. As of June 20, 2020, 8,776,456 people have been diagnosed and 492,910 have died worldwide. According to the current epidemiological investigation, the incubation period of COVID-19 is 1–14 days. It also has the characteristics of incubation period infection, asymptomatic infection and infection in the general population. In addition, it can be spread through respiratory droplets, close contact and aerosols. All the above shows that COVID-19 is extremely spreading and difficult to control. According to the characteristics of infectious diseases, isolation, and restrictions on the movement of people are the most effective means to control the spread of the epidemic as the world has not yet developed a relevant vaccine. Affected by the epidemic, schools, shopping malls, companies and large enterprises have ceased their normal activities. The suspension of production and economic activities has seriously affected economic development, causing economic halt or even regression. The prolonged epidemic has caused many companies to close. Recently, Hermes World-wide (HERMS), Chanel, Gucci and other famous luxury goods companies have also

J. Cheng et al. (Eds.): CSS 2020, LNCS 12653, pp. 197–209, 2021.
https://doi.org/10.1007/978-3-030-73671-2_18

announced the suspension of production. According to Moody's Analytics, the global real GDP will fall by 4.5% this year due to COVID-19 [1].

In order to accelerate economic recovery and reproduction, most countries have adopted contact tracing technology to prevent and control the spread of the epidemic. Early tracking was mainly carried out through personnel investigations, which was time-consuming and labor-intensive and may be inaccurate in tracking. Nowadays, the widespread application of smart phones provides convenience for tracking activities [2]. The user's trace can be tracked through the Bluetooth technology and GPS positioning technology of the smart phone, but this method has problem of leaking user privacy. This paper proposes a blockchain identifier based heath certificate passport solution (BID-HCP) to protect citizens' healthy travel and gradually realize economic recovery while reducing the risk of information leakage.

2   Related Work and Demand Analysis

The current international economic development is highly dependent on global tourism and global trade, but with the outbreak of the epidemic, related activities must be suspended. The WHO has given that when no effective vaccine has been developed, the most effective way to control the spread of the epidemic is contact tracing and isolation. Contact tracing refers to tracing potential patients who have been in contact with a confirmed patient to help them obtain care and treatment, thereby preventing the further spread of the virus. Many countries have stopped commercial activities to control the spread of the epidemic [3]. For example, during the outbreak of the epidemic, China adopted a total blockade of Wuhan, an area where the epidemic was severe, and prohibited the entry and exit of people in Wuhan. This measure of isolating infected people has controlled the spread of the epidemic to a certain extent. Subsequently, this measure was adopted almost nationwide to restrict the movement and gathering of people by stopping commercial activities. Therefore, China's epidemic prevention and control work has achieved great results. However, such measures have severely affected production and economic activities, causing companies to suspend production, and the economy has experienced a serious economic downturn. How to ensure normal economic activities while effectively controlling the epidemic is an important issue currently facing. Many countries and companies around the world have taken corresponding measures to help resume production and realize the recovery of economic activities.

China introduced a health code system during the resumption of work and production [4–6]. The health code system determines the user's health information by collecting key data elements in various scenarios. In order to realize the unification of the nationwide code system, the health code system defines a set of unified identification code mapping rules to realize mutual recognition between different systems and ensure that residents are recognized by one code nationwide. The health code uses the user registration method to complete the user information. When registering, the user first needs to fill in some of their own key information in the health code system, and then the health code system relates to the hospital information, and finally combines the first two to determine the user's health status. User information mainly contains four parts. One is the user's own health information, including current body temperature, whether he has fever, cough and other symptoms related to COVID-19. The second is whether the user has been in contact with people with abnormal physical conditions recently. The third is to directly contact the information of confirmed patients, including whether they have been in contact with confirmed patients or suspected patients of the new crown within 14 days. The fourth is the user's trace. The system collects the user's trace automatically, and through the mobile phone number to confirm whether the user has visited high-risk areas. The above four aspects of information can basically determine the status of the user's own health code. Finally, the above-mentioned health information is entered into the information system, a unified interface is provided to connect with the hospital, and the hospital determines the user's health status. The health code displays the user's health status in the color of the QR code. The QR code of people who are the COVID-19 virus carrier is displayed in red. The QR code of potential patients who have been in contact with the virus patient is displayed in yellow, and the QR code of ordinary residents is displayed in green. Only the people with green QR code can pass through the pre-set checkpoint. This method can only ensure that healthy residents can travel normally and carry out economic activities, but it cannot predict high-risk areas, and the privacy protection of user information is not strong enough.

Singapore launched the TraceTogether solution [7], which uses Bluetooth technology to detect nearby users within a short distance, and exchanges the TraceTogether ID of users in the nearby range. Then the record stores in the mobile terminal to realize contract tracking. This solution requires users to download and install the application. The mobile terminal always needs to keep the Bluetooth device open, actively broadcast and discover nearby device information, and store the close contact record information in the user's mobile terminal. The program introduces encryption technology, all recorded data is encrypted, and it is not uploaded through the network casually. Only those who test positive for COVID-19 will share information with the Ministry of Health to track close contacts, which ensures the privacy of users to a certain extent. The Ministry of Health can quickly trace the close contacts of the patient through the ID information saved in the terminal of the confirmed patient, and notify those who have been in close contact with the patient through TraceTogether. So the user who have been contact with patients can receive treatment as soon as possible, which also blocks the source of infection to a certain extent. The TraceTogether solution does not collect the user's location information, records the user with a random ID, and does not disclose personal identification information. The phone number bound to the ID is stored on a dedicated server and only read when necessary. The ID information stored in the phone will be automatically deleted after 21 days. This method has a certain protective effect on the user's privacy, but from a technical point of view, the Bluetooth device interface has security risks such as eavesdropping and interference. Furthermore, it's power consumption, because Bluetooth is in a long-term communication state.

The world's two major technology giants Google and Apple also adopted a Bluetooth short-range communication solution, which is similar to TraceTogether [8]. Google and Apple created COVID-19 exposure tracking apps for mobile phones to help track the spread of the COVID-19 virus. The application can be used on android and IOS mobile phones, and realizes the mutual detection of Bluetooth between different systems. The solution also relies on Bluetooth technology to identify the device information of other people who have been in contact with residents, and directly anonymously records and exchanges device information within the Bluetooth range through smart phones insteading of the central database. Finally, ID comparisons are used to confirm whether the user has been in contact with patients carrying the Covid-19 virus, and to conduct contact investigations to reduce the spread of the virus. According to a poll conducted by the "Washington Post", nearly three-fifths of Americans said that they are unwilling or unable to use Google or Apple contact tracking technology because of concerns about privacy leakage. Both of the above methods use Bluetooth to exchange identity IDs to achieve close contact tracking of COVID-19 patients. The program seems to be feasible, but according to experts, the program must ensure that more than 60% of the population are using the program to achieve the purpose of prevention and control effectively. Moreover, this solution has technical problems, high power consumption, and it is impossible to infer the susceptible area.

Mohaned Toky proposed a scheme framework based on blockchain [9]. The system consists of four subsystems: infection verification subsystem, blockchain platform, p2p mobile application and Mass-Surveillance System. The infection verification subsystem simulates the epidemic infection mode through digital simulation technology. The blockchain platform serves as a database to store the infection model data of each case. The P2P mobile application system provides information such as visual infection risk assessment results, prediction data, and infection case detection. The Mass-Surveillance System monitors the user's trace and whether have had contact with the COVID-19 patients. Through the creation of new blocks (new cases) in the blockchain and interactive query of P2P mobile application data, unknown infection cases can be automatically detected. This program can be used to automatically detect infection cases in real time and estimate the risk of COVID-19 infection. Based on the private and security advantages of the blockchain system, the program proposes a concept of epidemic prevention measures, control and tracking plans, and combines the advantages of P2P mobile applications to realize the prediction of unknown infection cases. However, the solution is still under development, and it is not clear how the crowd detection system works, and the incentive model is not clear.

The above methods almost have the problem of user privacy leakage. The bluetooth technology itself is vulnerable to malicious attacks and extremely power-intensive. Although the QR code consumes a small amount of power and collects data only when it is used, but the collected data will eventually be concentrated in the hands of a centralized service provider, which may be at risk of leaking user data. Existing technical solutions have certain limitations [10, 11], and they cannot guarantee normal travel, prediction of high-risk areas, and track potential patients while ensuring privacy. Through the comparative analysis of various programs, this article summarizes the existing problems as follows:

(1) Inadequate Interoperability Considerations. In response to the prevention and control of the COVID-19 epidemic, patient tracking through information technology is a commonly adopted measure in most countries. Each country and region have actively proposed corresponding solutions based on existing technologies, but each solution has certain regional applicability and cannot guarantee cross-regional use. There is still no interoperability between these existing solutions. Therefore, a global health certificate passport system is needed to ensure the normal development of transnational business.

(2) Lack of Privacy Protection. The current solutions may leak user privacy to a certain extent. Currently, users are paying more and more attention to personal privacy protection, but in order to track close contacts, data sharing is necessary, which leads to the leakage of users' personal information. In the above-mentioned scheme, the user is not willing to use it because of concerns about privacy leakage, which makes it difficult to achieve the purpose of tracking. Data sharing and privacy protection are contradictory, but they must exist at the same time. There is no effective means to solve such problems.

(3) Bluetooth Tracking Technology Restricted. Bluetooth tracking technology is an effective tracking method that uses Near Field Communication (NFC) to achieve close contact record. However, like all wireless communication technologies, the technology itself has security vulnerabilities and is vulnerable to various threats. For example, it is easy for communication information to be eavesdropped, and even other personal information in the user's device is stolen. More importantly, the power consumption of Bluetooth is serious.

(4) Health Certificate without Contact Tracking Insufficiency. The health code in the above scheme only provides a health certificate for the user's travel, and lacks tracking of the user's close contact with the patient. Bluetooth technology can effectively track and record close contacts of COVID-19 carriers, but it does not provide users with health certificates, nor can guarantee normal travel. The existing scheme does not have both health certificate and contact tracking functions.

This paper proposes a health certificate passport system based on blockchain identifier (BID-HCP). Specifically, the use of blockchain technology to achieve credible authentication of digital objects, by defining a set of universal health passport data structure and interaction mechanism to ensure that users can carry out economic activities on a global scale. At the same time, it can also analyze high-risk areas through the user's track, and provide notificaiton services for COVID-19 potential carriers through user authorization.

3 System Design

The blockchain identifier based health certificate passport (BID-HCP) can provide users with a globally unified health certificate, which can ensure that residents get back to a normal daily lives, and then realize economic recovery gradually. This solution uses blockchain technology to construct a unified identity authentication system, a permissions management and information interaction mechanism based on the identity, which can provide health status certificates to the demander while minimizing the leakage of user privacy. The method of separating the user's trace data from the user's personal information is adopted to minimize the leakage of user privacy. It then analyzes the risk level of each region by using big data processing and other technologies. At the same time, contact matching can be performed through user-authorized behaviors, which can locate high-risk groups quickly. In this part, we will introduce the architecture, data model, participating roles, and the interaction process between them based on the blockchain.

Sharing of User Health Information. The global health certificate passport system based on the blockchain requires all participants to register a digital identity, including public keys, encryption protocols and service endpoints. The digital identity is used to identify the user uniquely. The public key is used to authenticate the user's identity, and the user with the corresponding private key is the owner of the identity. The service endpoint is used for interactive sharing of information. Then, the health certificate signed by the testing agency is transferred among different participants in the form of authorized access, thereby realizing the credible health information sharing on a global scale.

Privacy Protection and Contact Trace. The COVID-19 testing agency obtains the trace information of users who are carriers of the COVID-19 virus and publishes it to the service endpoint. The authorized location service provider subscribes and synchronizes the data from the service system controlled by testing angency. After that, the location service provider analyzes the trace data based on big data technology to predict high-risk areas and infer people who may be infected. Finally, the user can submit their own trace information stored on the mobile phone to the location service provider for determining whether they are high-risk infection group, and accept the COVID-19 nucleic acid testing as soon as possible.

3.1   The Functional Architecture of BID-HCP

BID-HCP system provides a reference functional architecture for the mutual recognition of health certificates among different systems, including a common data model and an interaction method (see Fig. 1). In order to ensure that the health certificate can be used on a global scale, the World Health Organization (WHO) is introduced to release the information of the globally recognized COVID-19 nucleic acid testing agency and the health certificate data model.

The BID-HCP system consists of a blockchain layer, an information service layer, and an entity layer. The blockchain layer is the base of the entire system, and each

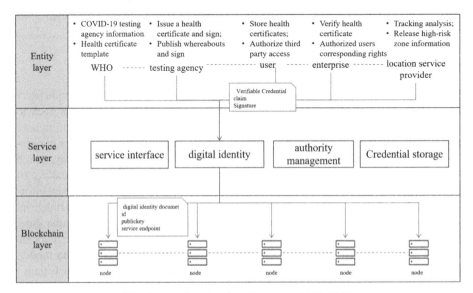

Fig. 1. The functional architecture of BID-HCP

blockchain node stores the digital identity document. The most important thing in the document is the correspondence between the digital identity and the public key, which is mainly used for digital identity verification. The information service layer establishes a secure identity authentication and data exchange mechanism for each participant, which is composed of information service interface, digital identity, data authority management and credential storage modules. The entity layer is composed of health certificate passport participants, and defines the role and data template of each participant.

In this article, the participants in the BID-HCP system are composed of user, WHO, testing agency, enterprise, and location service provider. Each of the participants has an identifier and associated identity description documents on the blockchain. The identity documents include four elements: identity ID, public key, service information URL, and self-declared signature. The public key is used for identity verification and credential verification when interacting with other roles.

The user (terminal) is the applicant for the health passport. Generally, it is a mobile phone application through which the user can register a digital identity. At the same time, the mobile terminal has the ability to communicate with the location service provider, and record trace information. The trace information is mainly used for contact trace analysis.

The World Health Organization (WHO) mainly conducts qualification assessment of COVID-19 nucleic acid testing agency. Only agencies with corresponding qualifications can provide users with COVID-19 nucleic acid testing services, and have the right to issue health certificates. As well, WHO provides a universal health certificate data template to ensure that the health passport can be used globally.

The testing agency with COVID-19 testing qualification can issue a global health certificate passport.

Enterprise is the user of the health certificate passport. The user presents the health certificate issued by the testing agency to the enterprise. After the enterprise has passed the verification, the user will be granted the right to applied for, such as taking an airplane.

Location service providers have the ability to provide geographic location record. In order to protect user privacy, the location information generated by the user during the activity needs to be returned to the user and stored in the user's mobile terminal. Generally, the geographic location service providers need to register on the chain before communicating with the user terminal,, which can prevent malicious attacks.

3.2 BID: Digital Identity Code and Data Structure Model

The identification coding scheme of this scheme (BID) adopts the Decentralized Identifiers (DIDs) [12, 13] scheme formulated by the International World Wide Web Consortium (W3C), and the coding rule is did:bid:specification. Among them, did is the identification prefix specified by the W3C, bid is a self-developed blockchain registration method, and specification is a customized identification coding scheme for bid. In this scheme, the custom part is the first 12 bits of the hash value of the public key. Each role verified by KYC before registering as a corresponding role to ensure the authenticity of the information. The BID is consist by the BID document and verifiable credential (see Fig. 2). The BID document is used to describe how to use BID credibly, which consist by publick key, authentication protocol and service endpoint. The verifiable credential are used to indicate the different identities possessed by the entity.

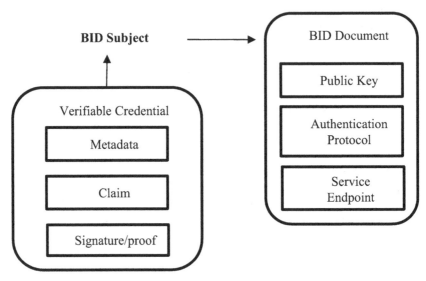

Fig. 2. The structure of BID

The following are the digital identity data model, health certificate data model, and travel data model.

The Digital Identity Data Model:

```
    "id":"did:bid:6cc796b8d6e2fbebc9b3cf9e",
    "type": "Secp256k1",
    "publicKeyHex":
"4b4042665b3235a12fb49730ff620fef1c96e9efa5c90119abd2e8acfe856053"
    "service":
    {
       "id": "did:bid:6cc796b8d6e2fbebc9b3cf9e#resolver",
       "type": "DIDResolve",
       "serviceEndpoint": "https://who.covid-19"//Data exchange interface
    }
    "proof":
    {
       "type": "Secp256k1",
       "creator": "did:did:bid:6cc796b8d6e2fbebc9b3cf9e#keys-1",
       "signatureValue": "QNB13Y7Q9...1tzjn4w=="
    }
```

The Health Certificate Data Model:

id: did:bid:hash(covid-19 passport data)
covid-19 passport :

{
id: did:bid:6cc796b8d6e2fbebc9b3cf9e #Indicates the owner of the health certificate
passport NO: 12345678
covid-19 test result: health
test date: 20200620
Expiry date: 7days
inspection institution: Peking Union Medical College
}
Signature: QNB13Y7Q9...1tzjn4w #Signed by the testing agency to prove that the health certificate is authentic

The Track Data Model:

id: did:bid:hash(track data)
"id": "bid:6cc796b8d6e2fbebc9b3cf9e", #creater
"version": 1,
"created": "2019-10-23T09:14:17.961Z",
"updated": "2019-10-23T09:14:17.961Z",
"COVID-19 track data":
[
{
"location": "beijing ",
"date": "20200708 8:00-9:00",
}
{
"location": "beijing ",
"date": "20200708 8:00-9:00",
}
...
{
"location": "beijing ",
"date": "20200708 8:00-9:00",
}
]
Signature:QNB13Y7Q9...1tzjn4w #Signed by the testing agency to prove that the track is true and effective

3.3 The Workflow of BID-HCP

The registration and use process of the BID-HCP system is mainly divided into three steps. The first step is the digital identity registration, the second step is the health certificate passport application, and the third step is the use process of the health certificate passport. The specific process is as follows (Fig. 3).

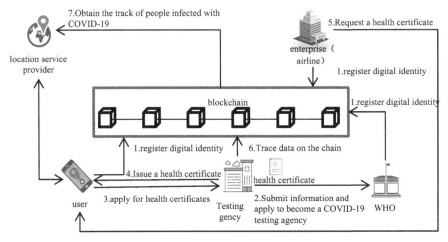

Fig. 3. Flow chart of BID-HCP

(a) **The Process of Registration of Various Roles**

The first step, the user downloads the blockchain wallet through the mobile terminal and generates a public and private key pair, then submits the user information to register the identity through the terminal application, finally publishes the identity and corresponding documents on the blockchain for subsequent interactive verification work. Similarly, other roles also need to register digital identities and publish the corresponding documents on the blockchain.

The second step, the testing agency applies to the WHO to become an international health certification testing agency for COVID-19. After the WHO has reviewed the information of the testing agency, it will expose the testing agency's digital identity to its service information site.

(b) **Health Certificate Passport Application Process**

The third step, enterprises and users query the identity information of testing institutions with COVID-19 testing qualifications through the service information interface of WHO. After obtaining the identity information, the user further queries the detailed information of the testing agency on the chain, including the location of the testing agency, and finally goes to the location for COVID-19 nucleic acid testing. The fourth step, if the user is a non-virus carrier, the testing agency will issue a health certificate for the user based on the universal health certificate model provided by the WHO and the personal identification information provided by the user for the user to travel. The health certificate is stored in the service system of the testing agency and the user's mobile phone terminal. In order to protect the user's privacy, the health certificate is stored off-chain instead of on the blockchain.

(c) **Use Process of Health Certificate Passport**

The fifth step, the enterprise requests the user to access the health certificate. The user obtains the company's public key to verify the company's identity by accessing the document on the chain. If the verification is correct, the enterprise can access health certificate owned by user. After obtaining the health certificate, the enterprise queries the public key of the testing agency on the blockchain to verify whether the health certificate is issued by a qualified testing agency. If the verification is passed, the user is granted the corresponding rights, such as taking an airplane.

(d) **Contract Tracking Process**

The sixth step, if the user is a COVID-19 carrier, the testing agency will issue a COVID-19 virus carrier diagnosis for him. At the same time, the testing agency requires the user to provide its trace information and publish the user's trace without exposing user privacy. In order to prove the authenticity of the trace information, the testing agency will sign the trace data with its own private key.

The seventh step, after the testing agency publishes the track of the COVID-19 virus carrier on the server, the location service provider obtains the track of the COVID-19 virus carrier through the subscriber. Then the location service provider analyzes the trace data base big data technology, infer the high-risk areas of the COVID-19 epidemic, and publish the information on its exposed servers. The location service provider matches the user's trace information with the user's authorization. If the matching is successful, they will be classified as a high-risk group, and remind them to perform nucleic acid testing as soon as possible.

4   Challenges and Analysis

The BID-HCP system solves the problem of information sharing between different subjects to a certain extent. The digital island between each system is opened through the health certificate passport. To a certain extent, this solution also protects the privacy of users. However, in terms of technology and management, there are still certain unresolved problems, and further research work is needed.

Blockchain Performance Challenges. The trace data of COVID-19 carriers is stored on the chain, which will cause data expansion. Later, the mode of on-chain and off-chain storage can be considered. Specifically, the trace data is stored off-chain, and the fingerprint of the off-chain data is stored on the chain. Using the form of data fingerprints can not only save storage space, but also ensure that the off-chain data has not been tampered with through on-chain fingerprint verification.

Mobile Phone Storage Space Challenge. In order to prevent the leakage of private data, the verifiable credentials are stored in the mobile terminal, which occupies a large amount of storage space on the mobile phone. Later, it's available using the proxy storage mode to store the verifiable credentials in the proxy server. However, there is a problem that the proxy server grasps user information, which may leak user information. It's a new challenge that the agency service provider can save user data but not disclose user information.

Location Information Leakage Challenges. It's obvious that location service provider will store the user's geographic location information when the user application interacts with base station, and there is a risk of user privacy leakage. Therefore, it is necessary to formulate user location information security protection management measures to restrict the behavior of location service providers, and protect user privacy.

5 Conclusion

In order to effectively control the spread of the COVID-9 epidemic, a variety of contact tracking applications based on smart phone terminals have been proposed on the market, but these methods expose users' privacy and leads to low user participation. At present, all countries are on the brink of economic recession, and it is necessary to come up with a method that can effectively prevent and control the spread of the epidemic, as well as protect the lives of residents and restore the economy. This article proposes a blockchain identifier based health certificate passport system (BID-HCP) that protects users' privacy while ensuring users' normal travel and resumption of production. On the other hand, this research saves the user's trace data in the mobile terminal, which is controlled by the user, and the data is shared to the demander through authorization, which protects the user's privacy. At present, the BID-HCP system has been deployed and verified in Hubei and some other places, through integration with the National Industrial Internet identification resolution system.

References

1. Zandi, M.: Handicapping the Paths for the Pandemic Economy. Moody's Analytics, June 2020
2. Li, J., Guo, X.: COVID-19 contact-tracing apps: a survey on the global deployment and challenges. Journal (2020)
3. Salathé, M., Althaus, C.L., Neher, R., et al.: COVID-19 epidemic in Switzerland: on the importance of testing, contact tracing and isolation. Swiss Med Wkly (2020)
4. GBT 38961–2020: Personal health information code-Reference model. Standards Press of China, Beijing (2020)
5. GBT 38962–2020: Personal health information code-Data format. Standards Press of China, Beijing (2020)
6. GBT 38963–2020: Personal health information code-Application interface. Standards Press of China, Beijing (2020)
7. Jason, B., et al.: BlueTrace: a privacy-preserving protocol for community-driven contact tracing across borders. Singapore (2020)
8. Apple Inc, Google LLC.: Exposure Notifification-Bluetooth Specification, May 2020
9. Mohamed, T., Ella, H.A.: COVID-19 Blockchain Framework: Innovative Approach (2020)
10. Xu, H., Zhang, L., Onireti, O., Fang, Y., Buchanan, W., Imran, M.: BeepTrace: Blockchain-enabled Privacy-preserving Contact Tracing for COVID-19 Pandemic and Beyond (2020)

11. Angelopoulos, Marios, C., Damianou, A., Katos, V.: DHP Framework: Digital Health Passports Using Blockchain - Use case on international tourism during the COVID-19 pandemic. arXiv:abs/2005.08922 (2020)

12. Decentralized Identifiers (DIDs) v1.0. https://www.w3.org/TR/did-core/. Accessed 30 Aug 2020

13. Verifiable Credentials Data Model 1.0. https://www.w3.org/TR/vc-data-model/. Accessed 30 Aug 2020

Research on Global Map Construction and Location of Intelligent Vehicles Based on Lidar

Biyao Wang, Yi Han$^{(\boxtimes)}$, and Jing Jin

School of Automobile, Chang'an University, Xi'an 710064, China

Abstract. The research and application of lidar in the establishment of high-precision maps and path planning of intelligent driving vehicles are being developed as a technical support for intelligent driving technology. In this paper we mainly focus on the research and application of lidar real-time positioning and map building technology in intelligent driving vehicles, including the preprocessing of raw data required by Simultaneous Localization and Mapping (SLAM), the front-end algorithm of SLAM, the back-end optimization of SLAM and the final algorithm experiment. In the front-end algorithm of SLAM, we propose a boundary line feature extraction scheme based on the traditional curvature feature point extraction method and Random Sample Consensus (RANSAC) algorithm, and realize point cloud registration and pose estimation based on optimized Iterative Closest Point (ICP). In the back-end processing algorithm, we propose a sparse algorithm of graph nodes for selection, and propose boundary verification based on an improved loop detection and relocation strategy design. The results showed that the algorithm in this paper was less affected by noise, which considerably saves time in the operation of the loop frame determination algorithm and improves the safety of the intelligent vehicle in the process of driving.

Keywords: Intelligent driving car · Lidar · Real time positioning · Map building

1 Introduction

Currently, with the development of science and technology, the improvement and pursuit of vehicle performance, intelligence, safety and comfort, and transportation efficiency are constantly changing and strengthening [1]. People's pursuit and exploration of vehicle intelligence have become the driving force for the development of the intelligent driving industry. Among them, safety, efficiency and economy are driving the development of intelligent driving [2].

The construction of high-precision maps and the acquisition of real-time accurate positions are important contents of unmanned vehicle environmental perception, and

Supported by the National Key R&D Program of China under Grant 2018YFB1105304, and National Natural Science Foundation of China under Grant U1664264, and National Natural Science Foundation of China under Grant U1864204.

J. Cheng et al. (Eds.): CSS 2020, LNCS 12653, pp. 210–224, 2021.
https://doi.org/10.1007/978-3-030-73671-2_19

have an important impact on the path planning and decision-making control of unmanned vehicles. At present, the most widely used sensors in the environmental perception of intelligent driving vehicles are laser sensors, GPS and visual sensors. Depending on different application environments [3, 4], the selection of sensors has varying emphases; however, lidar is a necessary sensor for all types of intelligent driving vehicles. The main reason is that other sensors have their own defects to some extent, and they cannot independently undertake the environmental perception of intelligent driving vehicles.

In this paper we summarize the problems of intelligent vehicle navigation based on GPS and vision Simultaneous Localization and Mapping (SLAM) technology [5, 6]. (1) Navigation systems based on GPS have limited use scenarios, and signal loss is easily caused as a result of blockage. In addition, the GPS signal is unstable. Therefore, the application of this navigation scheme in intelligent driving vehicles has serious drawbacks and security problems. (2) The SLAM technology, which is based on vision, is greatly affected by light and weather. For example, in rainy days, foggy days, and strong and weak light conditions, the sensors' perception of the environment is affected, and there are also serious security problems. Compared with the vision sensor, the lidar sensor has fast response speed, strong anti-interference ability and high data accuracy, which solves the problems inherent to GPS and camera technology [7].

2 Related Work

At the present stage, generally speaking, the sensors used in lidar SLAM mainly include an inertial measurement unit, a wheel odometer and lidar. The map types constructed include a coverage grid map and a point cloud map. The coverage grid map has clearer divisions and annotation of the environment and is widely used. According to the assumption of the mapping environment, there are two types of SLAM technology: one is a dynamic environment, which means that there are moving objects (high dynamic objects) in the lidar field of vision, or that the position difference of the same object changes (low dynamic object) when lidar is observed twice; the other is a static environment, which is the type most SLAM algorithms widely use at present. In the latter, it is assumed that the environment is static in the process of mapping and navigation [8, 9]. On the basis of the static environment assumption, the environment is either divided into a scale map, a topological map or a hybrid map according to the output process. At present, almost all SLAMs are scale maps.

On the basis of a scale map, there are different branches varying in their main principles. At present, SLAM based on filters and SLAM based on graph optimization are widely used.

2.1 SLAM Based on Filters

According to the different filters, the SLAM method based on filters is divided into SLAM based on a Kalman filter and SLAM based on a particle filter. However, the main basis of the two filters is the same, and the main principle is recursive Bayesian state estimation. In order to avoid the problem of feature point definition and corresponding data association to a certain extent, the FastSLAM algorithm, as one of the most representative algorithms based on a particle filter SLAM algorithm, has become a hot topic of scholars at home and abroad. Therefore, the algorithm has been constantly improved by different scholars, which makes the algorithm capable of achieving good results in specific scenarios.

The core idea of the SLAM algorithm based on a recursive Bayesian estimation is to use the motion model and observation model of intelligent driving vehicles to forecast and observe the state of vehicles under the assumption of a hidden Markov model. Although this method has the advantages of online real-time map updating, due to its own characteristics, it inevitably has its disadvantages. Because the method of map construction is incremental, and sensors errors and other aspects of the vehicle are constantly accumulating during the driving process; this cumulative error will lead to inconsistency of the constructed map when the vehicle driving environment is large. Therefore, the application of SLAM based on recursive Bayesian state estimation in large-scale environments is not ideal.

2.2 SLAM Based on Graph Optimization

With the widening application of SLAM technology, its application scenarios are also growing. In order to adapt to large-scale application scenarios, more and more scholars have carried out research on SLAM based on graph optimization. SLAM based on graph optimization can correct the trajectory of intelligent driving vehicles through global optimization and build a more realistic map. At present, SLAM based on graph optimization is the most widely used and researched method, with good effect. This SLAM method can have absolute position information and can recover to a better state from the error accumulation process. Through the maximum likelihood estimation of the position and attitude, the local minimum value is non convex optimization, so as to obtain the position and attitude information of the vehicle at a certain time in the future.

Grisetti G et al. [11] proposed a solution based on least square error, and proposed optimization using the framework of SLAM problem W et al. [12] and others proposed to use the branch binding method to effectively solve the mapping problem of subgraphs, and has good loopback ability. It has high accuracy in building maps, and can solve slam problems in large environment. In 2016, vysotska et al. [13] and others will build new subgraphs, public maps and data from laser sensors So as to improve the drawing effect. Most of these graph optimization SLAM algorithms are basic nonlinear optimization problems, and the least squares method is also the most commonly used algorithm framework [14, 15].

Based on the lidar, we carry out the research and application of real-time positioning and map building technology in intelligent driving vehicles, including the preprocessing of raw data required by SLAM, the front-end algorithm of SLAM, the back-end optimization of SLAM and a final algorithm experiment. The main contributions of this paper are as follows: in the front-end algorithm of SLAM, based on the traditional curvature feature point extraction method and Random Sample Consensus (RANSAC) algorithm, a boundary line feature extraction scheme is proposed, and point cloud registration and pose estimation are realized based on the optimized Iterative Closest Point(ICP). In the back-end processing algorithm, the sparse algorithm of graph nodes is proposed to select, and the boundary test is proposed based on the improved loop detection and relocation strategy. Through a series of front-end and back-end algorithm optimization, the influence of noise on the matching algorithm is reduced, and the time consumed by loop frame determination algorithm is considerably reduced.

3 Design of SLAM Front End Processing Algorithm for Lidar

Due to the low density of lidar remote point cloud data, the effect and accuracy of these point cloud data in point cloud registration and other post-processing are usually not very good [16, 17]. Therefore, this paper sets conditions for the x-axis, y-axis and z-axis to remove the remote data [18]. In this paper, we set the filter to specify the value range from three dimensions, and then check whether a point is in the specified value domain of the specified dimension as the condition to traverse the cloud data, remove the external points and retain the internal points.

Suppose the midpoint P (x, y, z) of the original point cloud, if:

$$x \in (X_1, X_2) \cap y \in (Y_1, Y_2) \cap z \in (Z_1, Z_2) \tag{1}$$

When Eq. (1) is satisfied, the point is retained, otherwise it is deleted.

On the other hand, in order to ensure the processing speed and efficiency of the later point cloud data, the point cloud data must be downsampled in the process of preprocessing the original input point cloud. Considering the effect of down sampling and the fidelity of the original point cloud, the following methods are used to downsample the input point cloud.

The main idea of this method is as follows: firstly, the input 3D point cloud is divided into a series of 3D grids. Assuming that there are n point cloud data in a grid, the center of gravity is as follows:

$$(x, y, z) = \left(\frac{\sum_{i=1}^{n} x_i}{n}, \frac{\sum_{i=1}^{n} y_i}{n}, \frac{\sum_{i=1}^{n} z_i}{n} \right) \tag{2}$$

For each grid point cloud, the center of gravity of these point clouds is approximately replaced, and other point cloud data are removed and the center of gravity points are retained to achieve the purpose of down sampling.

3.1 Feature Point Extraction from Point Cloud Data

At present, the curvature-based feature point extraction method is mainly used. The theory of this method is relatively simple, the calculation speed is fast, and the extraction effect of feature points is relatively ideal. However, this method is sensitive to noise and does not have good robustness. Therefore, on this basis, this paper combines this method with the RANSAC algorithm, and proposes a boundary line feature extraction scheme to ensure the integrity of the method. The feature information of a point cloud is used to prepare for the later point cloud registration. The boundary line feature extraction scheme is as follows:

(1) Taking a grid point cloud Q_{data} as input, the model is set as linear model M, and two points in Q_{data} are randomly selected as sample points to fit model M. The schematic diagram is shown in Fig. 1.

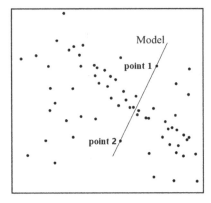

Fig. 1. Schematic diagram of any two points fitting model M.

(2) Because the point cloud data are not strictly in linear distribution, there are some fluctuations in the data points. The tolerance range is set as δ, and then it is found out if the point cloud Q_{data} falls within the tolerance range δ and the number of the points N is counted. Figure 2 is a schematic diagram of the points within the tolerance range.

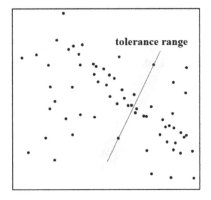

Fig. 2. Schematic diagram of points within tolerance range.

(3) In a point cloud Q_{data}, two points are randomly selected as sample points, and the steps in (1) and (2) are repeated K times. The number of iterations K is determined by the total number of data points N in the point cloud Q_{data} and the number of points within the tolerance range N_{in}. Suppose that the probability of n points out of all N points of point cloud Q_{data} falling within the tolerance range is P_{in}, while the probability of falling outside the tolerance range is P_{out}. Therefore, the probability that at least one of these N points falls outside the tolerance range is $1 - P_{in}$, while $P_{out} = \frac{1-N_{in}}{N}$, and then $(1 - P_{out})^n$ represents the probability that all points in point cloud Q_{data} fall within the tolerance range. Therefore, when a point in point cloud Q_{data} falls outside the tolerance range, the probability is $1 - (1 - P_{out})^n$. Therefore, in the process of K iterations, the probability that each point falls out of the tolerance range is $(1 - (1 - P_{out})^n)^K$, where

K is obtained by:

$$1 - P_{in} = (1 - (1 - P_{out})^n)^K \tag{3}$$

$$K = \frac{\log(1 - P_{in})}{\log(1 - (1 - P_{out})^n)} \tag{4}$$

Figure 3 is the schematic diagram of a certain iteration for reselecting sample points.

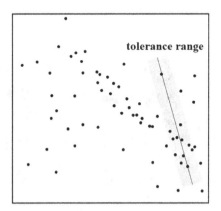

Fig. 3. Schematic diagram of a certain iteration for reselecting sample points.

(4) After each iterative fitting, there will be a corresponding number of local points N_{in} in the tolerance azimuth δ. After iteration, the line model M corresponding to the maximum value of N_{in} is the final extracted line feature. The schematic diagram is shown in Fig. 4.

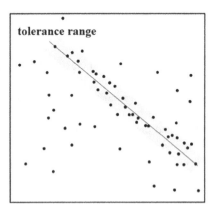

Fig. 4. Schematic diagram of line model corresponding to N_{in} Max in iteration process.

At the same time, according to whether there are point cloud data points in the grid, it can be divided into a real grid and an empty grid. We binarize these two kinds of grids and define that $f(x, y, z) = 1$ is the real grid and $f(x, y, z) = 0$ is the empty grid. Real grids can be expressed as:

$$g(x, y, z) = \sum_{-1 \le i \le 1} \sum_{-1 \le j \le 1} \sum_{-1 \le k \le 1} |f(x, y, z) - f(x + i, y + j, z + k)| \quad (5)$$

where I, J and K denote the topological directions of the grid, and satisfy the equation $i + j + k = \pm 1 \,\& \,(i = 0 \| j = 0 \| k = 0)$.

At this time, if $g(x, y, z) \ge 3$, we determine the real grid as the boundary grid, and use the RANSAC algorithm to calculate the straight line boundary in the same topological direction in all of the boundary grids. The calculation effect is shown in Fig. 5.

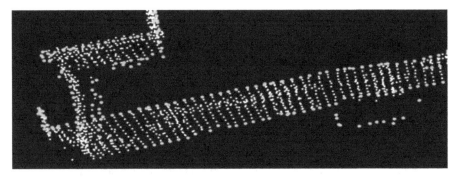

Fig. 5. Effect of boundary line feature extraction.

So far, the feature information has been extracted based on curvature and the RANSAC algorithm. The next step is to filter the feature information.

4   Design of Laser Radar SLAM Back-End Processing Algorithm

4.1   Selection and Extraction Strategy of Graph Nodes

Due to the low speed of intelligent driving vehicles at present, the speed is controlled below 30 km/h in complex environments, and the speed can reach 50–60 km/h only when the environment is simple and the road is straight. When the vehicle speed is low in complex environments, there will be a large amount of redundant data in the front-end of SLAM, while in a flat road environment, only a small amount of position and attitude data is needed. Therefore, in order to effectively simplify the data and reduce the complexity of the back-end optimization algorithm, this paper proposes a sparse algorithm to sample the vehicle trajectory.

The algorithm used in this paper is based on the vertical distance between a point and the line where two points are located, and it sets a threshold to screen the pose points. The specific algorithm process is described as follows.

(1)   A straight line is determined according to the starting position and pose point x_1 and the ending position and pose point x_n of the vehicle track.

(2) The position and pose points x_i on the vehicle track are detected one by one; then the distance d_{1i} between them and the straight line x_1x_n is calculated, and then the position and attitude point x_k corresponding to the maximum distance d_{1max} is determined.

(3) Comparing d_{1max} with the threshold value ε, if $d_{1max} < \varepsilon$, it can be considered that the trajectory of this segment is approximately equal to the segment, so it is replaced by this segment.

(4) If $d_{1max} \geq \varepsilon$, the vehicle trajectory is divided into two segments by taking the pose point x_k as the boundary, and the process of steps (1) to (3) is repeated separately for these two segments.

(5) In the same way, all parts of the vehicle track are processed in the same way, and the position and posture points on the track are compressed.

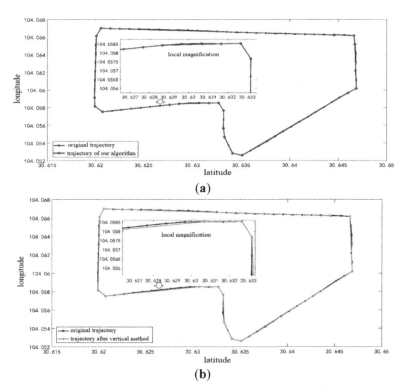

Fig. 6. Comparison of trajectory before and after using two kinds of thinning algorithms: (a) effect of thinning algorithm; (b) vertical pumping effect.

Another widely used thinning algorithm is the vertical distance limit method, but this method cannot control the fidelity of the original trajectory globally. Figure 6 shows the comparison of the two algorithms. It is obvious that the proposed algorithm has better fidelity while compressing the number of pose points.

4.2 Improved Loop Detection and Relocation Strategy Design

The framework of the loop detection method proposed in this paper is mainly composed of the following steps: 1. point cloud preprocessing; 2. feature point extraction; 3. preliminary determination of candidate loop frame; 4. descriptor extraction; 5. loop frame accurate determination; 6. target matching; 7. boundary verification.

This paper proposes boundary validation. When the target matching work is finished, due to the determination of the looping frame and a small amount of matching inaccuracy, in order to ensure the correctness of the whole process, the point cloud in the candidate matching list in (3) is further verified. The specific method is as follows: match the boundary line feature points extracted from two groups of point clouds based on the RANSAC algorithm to obtain the transformation matrix R_v and T_v. If R_m and T_m are consistent with R_v and T_v, it is judged that the loop detection match is consistent, that is, the vehicle returns to the historical position in the track after a period of time, and then a loop detection edge is added to the pose image; otherwise, when the loop frame appears in the case of false detection, the values of R_m, T_m and R_v, T_v will be very different, and the looping frame will be eliminated.

5 Experimental Verification and Result Analysis

The operating platform of the industrial control equipment is a 64 bit Ubuntu 16.04 system. The data processing and algorithm experiments involved in this paper are based on the Robot Operating System (ROS) robot operating system.

5.1 Experimental Analysis of Front End Processing

Feature Point Extraction Experiment
The strategy of feature point extraction in this paper is a curvature-based and RANSAC-based boundary line extraction method. The common curvature based feature point extraction method has fast calculation speed but is sensitive to noise. The reliability of feature points extracted in a complex environment will be greatly reduced. As shown in Fig. 10, the feature points extracted from the point cloud data of the experimental scene based on curvature extraction are shown in Fig. 7.

The red line in the above figure is the part with trees in the experimental scene. The scene of this part is more complex and changeable, which leads to the reliability of the feature points in this part to a certain extent. Therefore, based on this, this paper extracts the boundary line features of the scene based on RANSAC, and the extraction effect is shown in Fig. 8.

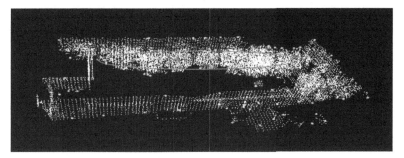

Fig. 7. Feature point extraction based on curvature. (Color figure online)

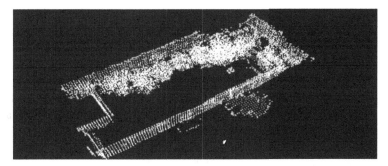

Fig. 8. Boundary line feature extraction based on Random Sample Consensus (RANSAC).

Point Cloud Matching Experiment

In this paper, the point cloud matching is optimized on the basis of the original classical iterative closest point (ICP) algorithm. After optimization, (1) when approaching the minimum value of the objective function, the descent direction of the iteration gradually approaches the Gauss Newton method, which is similar to the second derivative information, so as to effectively improve the convergence speed of the algorithm; (2) when far away from the minimum value of the objective function, the iterative descent method can search the global solution and avoid the local optimal solution.

In order to show the advantages of point cloud matching after optimization, we compared the two matching algorithms before and after optimization in terms of iterative efficiency and robustness to noise in the same experimental scene.

In the comparison experiment of iterative efficiency, this we iterated 10 times, 20 times, 40 times, 80 times, 160 times and 320 times to carry out the point cloud matching experiments of the two methods. The comparison of the time-consuming of the two methods is shown in Fig. 9. It can be seen from the graph that the efficiency of the classical algorithm was greatly improved after optimization, and with the increase of the number of iterations, the efficiency of the algorithm was increasingly different.

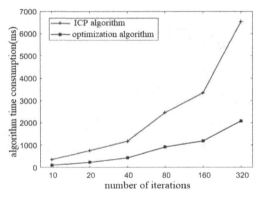

Fig. 9. Time consumption comparison of point cloud matching between classical Iterative Closest Point(ICP) algorithm and our algorithm.

In the contrast experiment of robustness to noise, Gaussian noise was added to the original data of the experimental scene to compare the matching accuracy of the two matching algorithms. The added Gaussian noise was divided into seven levels, from weak to strong. The first level did not add Gaussian noise, and then the standard deviation of each level increased by 0.5 mm until the seventh level. As shown in Fig. 10, the point cloud data with the third level of Gaussian noise were added. Green points are Gaussian noise points, and white points are original data points.

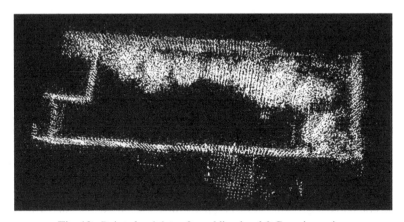

Fig. 10. Point cloud data after adding level 3 Gaussian noise.

The comparison of matching accuracy scores of the two matching algorithms under different levels of Gaussian noise is shown in Fig. 11. It can be clearly seen from the figure that the matching accuracy of the classical ICP algorithm for point cloud matching was significantly reduced when there was too much noise in the environment, while the optimized matching algorithm presented in this paper was less affected by the noise.

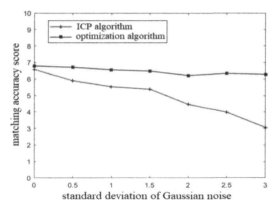

Fig. 11. Comparison of matching accuracy under different levels of Gaussian noise.

5.2 Back-End Optimization Experiment Analysis

The back-end of SLAM in this paper refers to the optimization of the pose map with loop constraints. For this part, a comparative experiment was set up to examine two aspects: the optimization degree of the algorithm to the trajectory of the pose map and the time consumption of the loop frame detection.

Regarding a comparative experiment of in situ pose map trajectory, we compared the effect before and after the optimization of the back-end pose map from two perspectives of the whole process of three-dimensional trajectory and of height change. In Fig. 12, the 3D trajectory comparison effect map of the pose map before and after the optimization of the rear end is shown. The coordinate point (0, 0, 0) in the figure is the starting point of the experiment, and the vehicle stopped at the entrance of the college after a circle around the college. It can be seen from the figure that the red and blue tracks basically coincided at the beginning of the journey. When entering the first corner, the errors of the two kinds of trajectories began to appear. The later trajectory for back-end optimization appeared more and more drift. When the red curve was close to the starting point of the experiment, a good closed-loop was formed for the red curve, while the error accumulation of the blue track was caused by the distance. There was a big deviation in the red trajectory.

On the other hand, the comparison effect of height error before and after optimization corresponding to the three-dimensional trajectory is shown in Fig. 13. The route of the experimental scene in this paper basically had no large height fluctuation. It can be seen from the figure that the height after the rear end optimization always fluctuated slightly up and down based on the starting position, while the height before the rear end optimization fluctuated greatly due to the impact of vehicle bumps and other factors.

In addition, in order to reflect the advantages of this algorithm in the back-end loop optimization, the running effect of large-scale environmental offline data sets containing loopback was compared with whether to carry out graph optimization and loop detection. As shown in Fig. 14, the trajectory had obvious drift without loop detection for pose optimization.

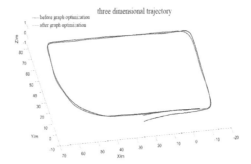

Fig. 12. Trajectory comparison before and after optimization. (Color figure online)

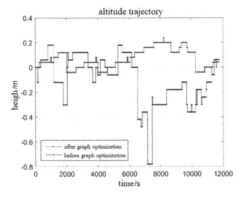

Fig. 13. Comparison of height error before and after rear end optimization.

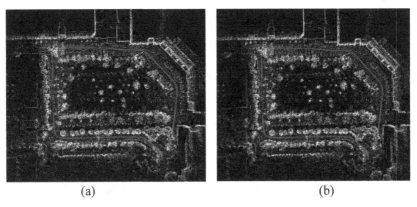

Fig. 14. Large scale environmental mapping effect including loop: (a) the Simultaneous Localization and Mapping (SLAM) algorithm presented in this paper; (b) SLAM algorithm without loop detection and graph optimization.

In this paper, the number of feature points is taken as the constraint condition to carry out the prescreening work, which greatly reduces the time consumption of the loop frame determination. In this regard, experiments were set to verify the optimization effect of the algorithm's time consumption by the number of feature points. The experimental comparison is shown in Fig. 15. Experimental results showed that when the vehicle passed through the straight road to a new environment, the time consumption of the loop frame detection was greatly reduced, the algorithm time consumption increased within the distance of less than 50 m at the beginning of the experiment, and the remaining parts significantly reduced the time consumption of the loop frame determination algorithm.

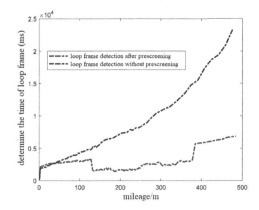

Fig. 15. Loop frame determination process time comparison.

6 Conclusions

The map and location technologies that intelligent driving vehicles depend on is one of the hot topics of research. In this paper, considering the advantages of lidar data stability and good development prospects of laser SLAM, the analysis and processing of raw data, front-end processing and back-end optimization of lidar SLAM were studied. In this paper, a boundary line feature extraction method was proposed to supplement the curvature-based feature points, so as to enhance their anti-interference ability to noise. Regarding graph nodes, reasonable sparse sampling was carried out on the nodes of the pose map through the environmental characteristics and trajectory characteristics of the intelligent driving vehicle. Regarding the constraint edge between nodes, the loop edge was determined through the determination of a candidate loop frame, the accurate determination of a loop frame and boundary verification. Finally, the back-end optimization algorithm was used to optimize the whole pose map to reduce the cumulative error caused by the large scale of the environment. The experimental results showed that the optimized matching algorithm was less affected by noise, and the loop frame detection optimization algorithm was reduced by 75%, which greatly reduced the time consumption of the loop frame determination algorithm and proves that the optimization algorithm in this paper is effective. The results provide ideas for the accurate mapping of intelligent vehicles in the process of driving, and improve the safety of vehicle driving.

References

1. Colak, H.E., Memisoglu, T., Erbas, Y.S., Bediroglu, S.: Hot spot analysis based on network spatial weights to determine spatial statistics of traffic accidents in Rize, Turkey. Arab. J. Geosci. **11**, 151 (2018)
2. Arif, F., Bayraktar, M.E.: Current practices of transportation infrastructure maintenance investment decision making in the United States. J. Transp. Eng. Part A. Syst. **144**, 4018021 (2018)
3. Pring-Mill, D.: Drone taxi service could impact urban infrastructure. Eng. News-record **280**, 49 (2018)
4. Gao, Y.B., Liu, S.F., Atia, M.M., Noureldin, A.: INS/GPS/LiDAR integrated navigation system for urban and indoor environments using hybrid scan matching algorithm. Sensors **15**, 23286–23302 (2015)
5. Nelson, G.: Car guys to Google: Move over - Mercedes' concept of a driverless car is no toy. Autom. News **89**, 1–42 (2015)
6. Goodwin, A.: Google reveals driverless car. Diesel Car: The UK's Leading Magazine for Diesel & Alternative Fuel Vehicles, pp. 64–65 (2014)
7. Crain, K.E.W.: Relax! This self-driving car is normal. Autom. News **92**, 46 (2018)
8. Ji, Z., Singh, S.: LOAM: lidar odometry and mapping in real-time. In: Robotics: Science and Systems Conference, vol. 6, pp. 12–19 (2019)
9. Dhiman, N.K., Deodhare, D.; Khemani, D.: Where am I? Creating spatial awareness in unmanned ground robots using SLAM: a survey. In: Sadhana: Academy Proceedings in Engineering Science, vol. 40, pp. 1385–1433 (2015)
10. Grisetti, G., Kummerle, R., Stachniss, C., et al.: A tutorial on graph-baesd SLAM. IEEE Intell. Transp. Syst. Mag. **2**(4), 31–43 (2010)
11. Hess, W., Kohler, D., Rapp, H., et al.: Real-time loop closure in 2D LIDAR ALAM. In: IEEE International Conference on Robotics and Automation. IEEE (2016)
12. Vysotska, S.: Exploiting building information from publicly available maps in graph-based SlAM. In: Intelligent Robots and Systems (2016)
13. Lenac, K., Cesic, J., Markovic, I., Petrovic, I.: Exactly sparse delayed state filter on Lie groups for long-term pose graph SLAM. Int. J. Robot. Res. **37**, 585–610 (2018)
14. Cheng, J.T., Kim, J., Shao, J.L., Zhang, W.H.: Robust linear pose graph-based SLAM. Robot. Autonom. Syst. **72**, 71–82 (2015)
15. Jaakkola, A., Hyyppa, J., Kaartinen, H.: Object classification and recognition from mobile laser scanning point clouds in a road environment. IEEE Trans. Geosci. Remote Sens. **54**, 1226–1239 (2016)
16. Macfaden, S.W., Pelletier, K.C., Royar, A.R.: An object-based system for LiDAR data fusion and feature extraction. Geocarto Int. **28**, 227–242 (2013)
17. Taie, S.A., Sayed, H.M., Abdelrahman, I.F.: Point clouds reduction model based on 3D feature extraction. Int. J. Embedded Syst. **11**, 78–83 (2019)
18. Marani, R., Renò, V., Nitti, M.: A modified iterative closest point algorithm for 3D point cloud registration. Comput.-Aided Civ. Infrastruct. Eng. **31**, 515–534 (2016)
19. Li, F., Hitchens, C., Stoddart, D.: A performance evaluation method to compare the multi-view point cloud data registration based on ICP algorithm and reference marker. J. Mod. Opt. **65**, 30–37 (2018)

A Problem-Driven Discussion Teaching Method Based on Progressive Cycle

Xiaoyi Zhou[1], Shaohua Duan[1], and Wei Li[2(✉)]

[1] School of Computer and Cyberspace Security, Hainan University, Haikou, China
[2] School of Computer Science and Engineering, Dalian Minzu University, Dalian, China

Abstract. The problem-driven discussion teaching method is that in the process of teaching, according to the objective law of the learning process, teachers adopt the methods of asking questions, inspiration and guidance, so as to make students think actively and analyze initiatively, and then jointly explore the teaching method to solve the problems raised. After discussing the significance of problem-driven discussion teaching, this paper analyzes the design of the teaching model, and takes the chapter "ranking" as an example to describe how to design problems for group discussion. This paper presents a problem-driven discussion teaching method based on progressive cycle, namely "from known to unknown and then to known". The specific idea is to design problems according to students' mastery of knowledge, so as to guide them to explore unknown knowledge, and then start from new knowledge, they compare the new with existing knowledge, so as to not only reviews the old knowledge, but also well master the new one. The comparison between the students' evaluation and the students' achievements of the two years proves that the problem-driven discussion teaching method can greatly improve the students' interest in learning, mobilize the students' ability of autonomous learning, and improve the teaching quality and learning effect of the data structure.

Keywords: Problem-driven teaching · Discussion teaching · Data structure · Teaching method

1 Introduction

One of the main advantages of object-oriented design is to encourage well-organized code development to build reusable, robust and adaptable software. However, designing high-quality object-oriented code requires not only understanding object-oriented design methods, but also effectively using these and other object-oriented technologies in a powerful and elegant way, and data structures are the effective way to use face-to-face object technology. The data structure focuses on some basic problems in the scheme design stage, simultaneous design coding and parsing stage in the process of software development. The purpose of this course is to enable students to have an in-depth understanding of the logical relationship between data elements, physical storage and logical storage of data, so as to implement the algorithm according to different storage structures, and be able to analyze the complexity of the algorithm. It is not only the first of the

J. Cheng et al. (Eds.): CSS 2020, LNCS 12653, pp. 225–235, 2021.
https://doi.org/10.1007/978-3-030-73671-2_20

core courses in the computer science curriculum system, but also in order to meet the needs of the wide application of computers in other disciplines, in order to improve students' programming ability, some schools set data structure as an important theoretical basic course for their information science-related majors. For example, apart from the Department of computer Science, the other departments of the School of Information Science and Technology of Hainan University, such as electronics, communications, information security and applied mathematics, all take data structure as a compulsory course.

However, there are a large number of students in the Chinese classroom, so on the whole, it is difficult to achieve teacher-student interaction. Students still listen passively in class and have little time to think, thus reducing the teaching effect. How to improve teaching from the perspective of students and improve their initiative and enthusiasm is a problem that every teacher must think about.

The innovation of this study is that the previous problem-driven method guides students from the unknown to the known knowledge, while this method runs through the classroom, allowing students to move from the known to the unknown and then to the known. Specifically, according to the knowledge that the students have mastered, the problem is guided to another knowledge that has not been taught, so as to achieve the purpose of "known to unknown"; Then the students explore the new knowledge and continue to explore the differences between the old knowledge, so as to achieve the purpose of "unknown to known", and consolidate the new knowledge.

2   The Meaning of Problem-Driven Discussion-Style Teaching

Through an in-depth study of hundreds of effects on student performance in the United States and other countries, American education researcher Robert J. Marzano believes that the impact on student performance at the school level, classroom level and student level accounts for 7%, 13% and 80% respectively. Therefore, there is no doubt that the student-led teaching method has important practical significance. However, at present, the attention of teaching and learning reform in colleges and universities is mostly focused on teachers. How to enhance the influence of students to deepen education and teaching reform is a problem that college teachers need to explore.

Problem-driven and discussion teaching methods are highly efficient teaching methods advocated in modern quality education [2–5]. Problem-driven discussion teaching means that teachers use the method of asking questions-inspiration and guidance to make students think actively and consciously to solve and understand problems according to the course content, so as to achieve the purpose of grasping the knowledge they have learned. This teaching method has made many achievements in teaching research and practice [6–10].

2.1   It is Helpful to Cultivate the Innovative Thinking of College Students

President Xi Jinping mentioned at the Pujiang Innovation Forum in 2014 that "innovation is an inexhaustible driving force for the prosperity of a nation." The "problem" is the starting point of innovation and the ideal carrier to arouse students' interest and motivation. Traditional classroom teaching puts too much emphasis on the imparting of knowledge. Teachers only focus on the excavation and interpretation of knowledge, ignoring the stimulation and cultivation of students' thinking. The more clearly they speak, the more restrictions on students' thinking. Over time, students are lazy or even unable to think, and regard the learning process of "class", which requires active participation, as a passive process that only needs to listen with their ears and take notes with their hands. Therefore, as a course teacher, to a large extent, we should take students as the center of teaching, so that students can maintain their initiative in the whole process of learning, and take the initiative to ask questions, think about problems, discover problems and explore problems.

2.2 It is Helpful to Cultivate the Students' Team Spirit and Strengthen the Democratic and Broad Mind

The level of students in the same class varies, with some students responding quickly and others slightly slower. This phenomenon is particularly prominent among the students of the information security department taught by the writers, because many students are transferred to this major. Therefore, students' entrance achievements vary greatly. At this time, teachers should let every student give full play to his or her ability in learning. for this reason, the method of "group discussion teaching" is adopted at a certain knowledge point, that is, students are freely combined into learning groups with roughly the same number (such as 4–5 people). In each group, a group leader is freely selected (usually by students who are good at learning), and the group leader is responsible for coordinating the learning tasks of the students in this group. After that, the members of the group are randomly selected to express their opinions in class. Through mutual communication, mutual complement and mutual improvement, the students' habit of cooperative exploration is cultivated, which is beneficial to the students' innovation and divergent thinking, and to the cultivation of students' innovation and divergent thinking. In order not to affect the scores of their respective groups when answering questions, each student's main role can be brought into full play, so that students can form the habit of being good at cooperation, critical self-enrichment and self-improvement in communication [11]. And in the discussion, students should not only be good at listening to the opinions of others, but also combine the opinions of others to form their own unique opinions, which helps to enhance the nature of democracy.

3 Design of Progressive-Cycle-Based Problem-Driven Teaching

The method proposed in this paper is that on the premise that the teacher fully understands the students' mastery of knowledge, the existing knowledge is taken as the starting point for question setting. Students acquire new knowledge through self-study, and then compare with the old knowledge, so as to review the old knowledge and consolidate the new one. Through consulting materials, the students discuss in groups, form a report and elaborate the views. Finally, classroom teaching is evaluated by team members, other students and teachers [12–16].

Taking data structure teaching as an example, we must design the teaching links and procedures of group discussion according to the characteristics of the course, so as to ensure the effective implementation of group discussion teaching method. Figure 1 depicts the link design of the problem driven discussion approach.

3.1 Discussion of Good Quality Topics

"The essence of a university is to bring together a group of outstanding young people to inspire each other's creativity and generate wisdom that will benefit them for life," wrote the book the concept of a first-class university in the United States. Therefore, it is very important for university teaching to create a more effective environment for young people to stimulate each other's wisdom and creativity. "How to break the choice of theme, how to break the traditional teaching methods, and turn the "full classroom" into an open forum of "group talk", and let young people's ideas blossom, so as to improve their innovative ability, they are challenges for students and teachers.

The topic is the basis of the discussion and the focus of the preparatory work. In order to implement problem-driven discussion teaching in classroom teaching, teachers should first of all be good at mining problems from the teaching content, which should not only be closely linked to knowledge points, but also be able to expand from knowledge points. inspire students to master basic principles and core concepts in the process of thinking. Not only that, but also need to read extracurricular literature to answer the questions that cannot be found in the textbook. Therefore, teaching depends to a large extent on teachers' skills in setting questions and their ability to expand their knowledge. Therefore, in the design of the discussion topic, teachers should design the discussion content according to the teaching objectives and students' knowledge mastery.

Since the quality of the questions set by teachers to students directly affects the effect of students' group discussion and learning, the topics chosen by teachers should have the following characteristics [12]:

1. The problems discussed are open to a certain extent. The data structure in books is only the tip of the iceberg of this subject, but it is impractical to explain all knowledge in class, so teachers should not rigidly adhere to the introduction and explanation of concepts and algorithms, but should pay attention to students' understanding of knowledge and guide how to use it. Access to literature to obtain knowledge that is not available in textbooks. Therefore, the design of topic discussion should be both flexible and interesting, which should not only arouse students' thinking and discussion, but also induce students to have learning motivation and strong desire for knowledge.
2. The solution to the problem is diversified. The data structure involves a variety of logical structures and storage structures, and sometimes the same problems can be solved with static tables or dynamic tables, which makes the solution to the problem not necessarily unique, but multiple solutions that can be solved from multiple perspectives, so teachers need to have the ability to set problems at a certain height. It causes students to collide with each other in the process of thinking, which leads to the debate on the solution to the problem.
3. The problem has practical application value. The data structure needs to construct the mathematical model of the problems in real life and solve them by programming. Although the course has strong theory, it is still closely related to practice, so the

closer the choice of subject is to the actual problem, the more students can put themselves in the shoes of thinking and exploring ways to solve the problem.

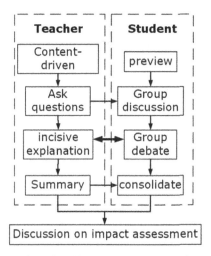

Fig. 1. The design of problem-driven discussion-based teaching.

3.2 Key Points of the Group Discussion

Mr. Meade, an American sociologist, believes that meaningful learning is produced through interpersonal interaction [12]. Interaction in group discussion can effectively promote young people with different knowledge structures and different ways of thinking to communicate with each other and develop together, and use collective strength to complete learning tasks. Through the comparison of the number of different groups, the author finds that the group size of group discussion teaching should be 4–5. If the number is too small and the thinking is not divergent enough, it is not easy to form an atmosphere of problem discussion; and if there are too many people, it is easy to make the differences among the adult members too big, making it difficult to co-ordinate. In order not to occupy too much class time, the pre-preparation of the group discussion is mainly completed in the form of extracurricular homework, leaving the reading literature and discussion time to the students to complete in their spare time, and then display the cooperation results in the classroom in small groups [12]. In order to make the students more motivated, the overall score of the group can be included in the overall evaluation as the usual performance of the individual. In this way, students can help each other to achieve common learning goals in group work.

3.3 Evaluation of the Effectiveness of Panel Discussions

In order to test the learning situation of the group, the teacher can randomly select a classmate or multiple members to share the results of the discussion in this group. In this link, teachers and other members of each group comment and question the research results of the members of the group by raising their hands freely, so as to help students find the omissions in the research, so as to critically absorb the views of others and train the openness and creativity of thinking, so as to improve their own innovative ability, communication ability, expression ability and teamwork ability. The teaching content is the leading group discussion, asking questions, extracurricular preparation, intensive lecture, inter-group debate, summarizing and consolidating the effect of knowledge and discussion. Teachers and students in each group after showing the learning results of the group, teachers guide students to sum up the gains and experience in the process of discussion, find and reflect on the deficiencies in problem analysis and scheme design [12].

4   Specific Case Study

4.1   Teaching Content and Class Hours

This section takes the sorting algorithm as an example to explore how to carry out the problem-driven discussion teaching method. The teaching contents and hours are arranged as follows:

1. The basic idea and algorithm implementation of direct insertion sorting, as well as the time performance analysis in the best, worst and average cases. Directly insert the role of the Sentinel in the sort. For a given input instance, it is necessary to be able to write a sorting process that is directly inserted into the sort (1 class hour).
2. The basic idea and algorithm implementation of bubbling and fast sorting, as well as the time performance analysis in the worst and average cases to understand the stability of the algorithm. The influence of the base element (partition element) in a quick sort on whether the partition is balanced or not. According to the given input example, the sorting process of quick sort can be written (1 class hour).
3. Pile, small root vertebra, large root pile, pile top and other related concepts and definitions. Heap properties and the relationship between heap and complete binary tree. The basic idea and algorithm implementation of direct selection sorting and heap sorting, as well as time performance analysis. Write out the sorting process of heap sorting (1 class hour) for a given input instance.
4. The basic idea and algorithm implementation of merge sorting, as well as time performance analysis. According to the given input example, the sorting process of merging sorting can be written, and the difference between allocating sorting and other kinds of sorting can be written (1 class hour).
5. Through the comparison of the number of records to be sorted, the amount of information recorded, the structure and initial state of keywords, stability requirements, the size of auxiliary space, various time performance and other aspects to grasp the advantages and disadvantages of various sorting. Choose the appropriate ranking method (2 class hours) according to the characteristics and requirements of the actual questions.

4.2   Question Settings

With regard to the problem setting discussed, it is divided into the problems that all algorithms must discuss and the problems that each algorithm must discuss separately.

The Problem Discussed by All Algorithms

1. Is your sorting algorithm easy to implement on linked lists (including single, double, and circular linked lists)? Why?
2. Is the algorithm suitable for cases where the record value is large? Why?
3. Is the algorithm stable? Does the algorithm save memory (i.e. spatial complexity) if unstable?
4. Discusses the time complexity of the algorithm at its best, worst, and average.
5. Is the algorithm you use more efficient in any case than the bubbling algorithm?
6. In three cases, the number of comparisons under the algorithm is discussed, and how many movements are recorded. i) 1, 2, 3, ..., 10, J, Q, K; ii) K, Q, J, ..., 4, 3, 2, 1; iii)5, 9, 3, 2, 6, J, 8, 1, 7, J, 4, 10

Directly Insert the Question of Sorting Discussion

1. Why did you introduce a lookout? What is its function?
2. What is the ideal situation for this sort?
3. What does the efficiency of the algorithm depend on?
4. Can the algorithm be further improved? What is the idea of improvement?

Hill Sorted the Issues Discussed

1. How to improve the efficiency of the algorithm?
2. $h1 = N/2, N/4, N/8..., h2 = 2^k - 1,..., 15, 7, 3, 1, h3 = (3^k - 1) ..., 13, 4, 1$ and other three groups of different step size values to sort a set of random numbers of Number 20, which group has the best performance? (need to be solved programmatically)
3. What is the best-known increment? (extra-curricular search and answer is required)

Quickly Sort the Issues Discussed

1. Why is it called "quick" sort? How fast is it?
2. Arrange the sequence QHCYPAMSRDFX in ascending order, what is the result of the first quick sort?
3. What does the execution time of quick sort depend on? In accordance with what characteristics of the sequence with the best quick sorting?
4. What is the worst-case scenario of sorting? How to choose a standard record to avoid the worst?

Directly Insert the Question of Sorting Discussion

1. What are the advantages of direct sorting?
2. What is the reason for restricting the efficiency of direct selection sorting? How to improve?

Heap Sorting Discusses the Issue

1. What is the key to 1 heap sorting?
2. can all binary trees become heaps?
3. do the keyword sequences {75, 38, 62, 15, 26, 49, 58, 17, 6} and {10, 15, 50, 25, 30, 80, 76, 38, 49} meet the heap conditions? 4 what are the main factors that affect the time efficiency of heap sorting?

Group and Sort the Issues Discussed

1. Why is the two-way merging sort suitable for internal and external sorting at the same time?
2. what if the length of the two child tables of the remaining records are not the same in the merge sort? What if the remaining records can only form one child table?

4.3   Discussion Session Settings

Take the information security majors of Hainan University in 2014 as an example, there are 59 students in the class. Considering that there are six sorting algorithms to be explained (bubbling sorting has been explained in detail in the "C language programming" class of freshmen, so the algorithm is not used as a group discussion), it is divided into five groups, and one algorithm is discussed by two groups respectively. If necessary, the members of the group are randomly selected to give lectures, and the achievements of each member of the group are used as the basis for the achievements of each member of the group. In this way, the uneven division of labor among individual members of the group can be avoided and work together to achieve common learning goals.

For the same algorithm, if the two groups have different opinions on the same problem, the two groups will debate, and then the whole class will discuss which group's answer is more accurate.

5   Student Evaluation and Two-Term Performance Comparison

For a long time, the teaching of "data structure" has been well received by the students. According to the score of the course evaluation over the years, the students' satisfaction with this course is very high. In the academic year 2012–2013, the students scored 92.867 on the data structure and 91.082 in 2013–2014. after the adoption of discussion teaching, the score for 2014–2015 suddenly increased to 96.482. Students generally believe that "data structure courseware has various forms, meticulous production, vivid content, combined with practical application cases, profound and simple," and the teaching process is "very devoted, passionate, clear about concepts, profound and simple, and contagious. The question is set properly".

With the support of the school's "discussion curriculum construction" project, the author has made greater efforts to reform the courses such as "data structure" and "discrete mathematics", introduce more discussion teaching methods into the classroom, and increase the topic and time of discussion. After several years of practice, not only the final grades of the students have been improved year by year compared with the unused discussion courses, but also the classroom activity has been significantly improved, which is rare in the more boring engineering theory courses. It can be found from Fig. 2 that the score of the paper is generally on the low side. This is because the volume of the paper set by the author is large and the difficulty is on the high side. At the same time, it can also be found that after a semester of classroom teaching practice, the excellent rate and good rate of the students of Grade 2014 have been greatly improved after a semester of classroom teaching practice, from 1.79% to 13.56% and 5.36% to 20.34% respectively. The failure rate dropped from 53.57% to 40.68%. In addition, through the calculation, the average class score of the final paper score rose from 53.3 to 63.6. These changes prove that the problem-driven discussion teaching method helps to improve the learning effect of students, which is greatly improved for middle and upper-class students, but not obvious for those students with weak learning ability and poor foundation. but it's just as effective. However, it is a pity that later, because of the curriculum reform, the School of Information of Hainan University adopted the mode of computer enrollment, and the "data structure" was opened to freshmen, thus reducing the theory class hours from the original 64 class hours to 48 class hours. therefore, in order to ensure the content of the theory course, reduce the class discussion time, resulting in a lower excellent and good rate.

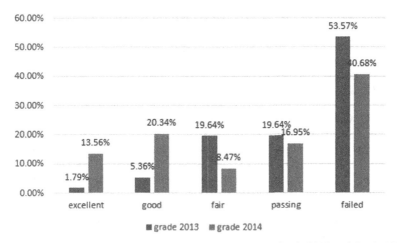

Fig. 2. Comparison of the results of data structure between Grade 2013 and Grade 2014

6 Conclusion

In our proposed teaching method, starting from the existing knowledge, set up problems, stimulate students to explore, form their own views, and make knowledge and skills become their wealth. The final exams prove that the proposed method has raised stutents' grades and improve their mastery of knowledge. This shows that our proposed method proposed has a positive effect and significance on computer science and Cyberspace Security Education. In addition, teachers should also improve the artistry of classroom teaching, so that students have time and space for independent learning, so that they have the opportunity to experience the accumulation of knowledge, so that the classroom can become a place that students look forward to.

Acknowledgement. The research was supported in part by Research project of Education and Teaching Reform of Hainan University (Grant No. hdjy2053) , "Golden Course" Construction Project of Hainan University (Grant No. hdjk2020040).

References

1. Qi, H., and other translations: Education Management (Fifth Edition). Chinese University Press, Beijing (2014)
2. Song, C.: Use heuristic discussion teaching methods to follow the cognitive law. Ideological Polit. Teach. (Z1), 35–36 (2002)
3. Li, M., Wu, W., Zhao, J., Chi, X.: The application of heuristic discussion teaching method in the teaching of signals and systems courses. High. Educ. J. **16**, 69–70 (2015)
4. Zhang, J.: Discussion-style teaching seminar research teaching - a little interpretation of the ministry of education's higher education document. J. Wuhan Inst. Sci. Technol. **09**(1), 86–87 (2005)
5. Jiang, A., Wei, W.: Discussion teaching and its operation process. J. Sichuan Inst. Educ. **12**, 14–16 (2005)
6. Zhang, C., Ye, P: Discussion-style teaching analysis. Educ. Res. Exper. New Course Res. **09**, 6–8 (2006)
7. Zhixuan, W.: Several strategies to improve the effectiveness of discussion - based teaching. J. Hetian Norm. Coll. **06**, 93–94 (2007)
8. Zhong for the group: Talk about discussion - style teaching. J. Minnan Med. Coll. **03**, 239–240 (1996)
9. Yanhui, Z., Wenmei, L.: Problems and countermeasures in postgraduate discussion teaching. China High. Educ. Assess. **04**, 74–75 (2006)
10. Jia, G.: The details that should be paid attention to in the group discussion teaching of colleges and universities. Continuing Educ. Res. **02**, 128–131 (2007)
11. Dingying, T., Chen, P., Liu, X.: Application of group cooperation in data structure and algorithm teaching. Sci. Technol. Inf. (17), 174 (2008)
12. Chen, Y., Jie, J.: Effect analysis of the use of group discussion teaching in classroom teaching of public administration. J. Hum. Inst. Sci. Technol. **36**(06), 141–145 (2015)
13. Xiaoyi, Z., Yihong, L., Honglei, L.: Application of suspense teaching in the design of C. J. Hainan Univ. (Natl. Sci. Ed.) **27**(03), 291–294 (2009)
14. Xiaoyi, Z., Longxuan, W., Jia, R.: The practice of Seminar teaching mode in data structure courses. J. Hainan Univ. (Natl. Sci. Ed.) **34**(01), 82–89 (2016)

15. Huizhen, Z., Shujiao, M.: Data Structure course teaching method improvement discussion. J. Shanghai Polytech. Univ. (Soc. Sci. Ed.) **40**(02), 173–178 (2018)
16. Haixia, L., Yuxuan, R., Juya, W.: Research on the teaching reform of data structure and algorithms, an independent college based on flash. Mod. Comput. (Prof. Ed.) **31**, 38–40 (2018)

The Detection and Segmentation of Pulmonary Nodules Based on U-Net

Guilai Han[1(✉)], Wei Liu[1(✉)], Benguo Yu[1], Lin Niu[1], Xiaoling Li[1], Lu Liu[1], and Haixia Li[2(✉)]

[1] College of Biomedical Information and Engineering, Hainan Medical University, Haikou, China
liuwei@hainmc.edu.cn
[2] College of Pharmacy, Hainan Medical University, Haikou, China

Abstract. Deep learning technology has been widely used in the classification and recognition of various kinds of images. In order to improve the speed of deep learning network and the accuracy of detection, the input images of deep learning network, especially convolution neural network, have fixed size, which usually is minuscule. However, the size of computed tomography (CT) images used for detecting pulmonary nodules is 512×512, which is usually difficult for ordinary convolution neural networks to detect directly. As a special full convolution network, U-net can be used directly for large-scale image detection by replacing the full connection layer with the convolution layer. The U-net network structure is adjusted and optimized in this paper, and the improved U-net is used for region detection and segmentation of pulmonary nodules. In order to avoid over fitting of deep learning network, the method of generating pulmonary Nodules image by deep convolutional generative adversarial networks (DCGAN) is used to enlarge the sample size of pulmonary. By comparing the segmented results with the labeled ground truth mask, the experimental results show that the proposed method based on U-net in this paper can obtain high sensitivity, which is of great significance for the recognition of pulmonary nodules and privacy protection of patients using deep learning technology.

Keywords: Pulmonary nodules · U-net · DCGAN · Deep learning

1 Introduction

The incidence rate of lung cancer is the highest, and it is worthy of the name of cancer killer [1]. Pulmonary nodule is an important early manifestation of lung cancer. Due to the large amount of chest CT images, it is easy to increase the probability of missed diagnosis and misdiagnosis. Computer aided diagnosis (CAD) technology can automatically analyze CT images and prompt suspected pulmonary nodules to radiology department to improve diagnostic efficiency.

Supported by the scientific research item of institutions of higher learning in Hainan Province (Grant No:Hnky2019ZD-21).

© Springer Nature Switzerland AG 2021
J. Cheng et al. (Eds.): CSS 2020, LNCS 12653, pp. 236–244, 2021.
https://doi.org/10.1007/978-3-030-73671-2_21

In the past, support vector machine (SVM) and boosting method were usually used in early medical image classification and recognition [2, 3]. This kind of method usually needs to segment the sample image, and needs to be designed manually to extract the visual features of the lesions, including gray, texture and shape, etc. through training and learning to generate a discriminant model, and then according to the generated discriminant model, each segmentation region of the image to be detected is classified and judged in turn. The advantage of this method is that it needs less sample data. The disadvantage is that the accuracy of image segmentation and the rationality of feature extraction seriously restrict the effect of medical image classification and recognition, leading to the accuracy of medical image classification and recognition has been difficult to have a qualitative breakthrough.

Since 2012, Hinton's research group, Alex krizhevsky, et al. proposed AlexNet, which was applied to the large-scale image dataset ImageNet, and won the 2012 ImageNet Large Scale Visual Recognition Challenge (ILSVRC) [4], the accuracy of deep learning technology in the field of image classification and recognition continues to improve, and has made a breakthrough. Since 2013, the best teams have adopted convolution neural network and its related improved methods. However, deep learning technology needs a large number of sample image data, and the lack of sample data will lead to the weak generalization ability of deep learning, which seriously restricts the effect of deep learning classification and recognition. However, due to personal privacy and other reasons, it is difficult to collect enough sample data from medical images.In addition,whether it is the classic AlexNet or visual geometry group (VGG) network [5], the size of the input images in each network is not only fixed but also small. The input image size of AlexNet and VGG network is 224×224, while the size of chest CT image is usually 512×512. Therefore, how to detect pulmonary nodules from a large CT image is a difficult problem.

As a special full convolution network, U-net uses convolution layer instead of full connection layer. At the beginning, u-net was proposed to solve the biomedical problems of small samples. And it can not only be used for large-scale image detection, but also segmentation of the position of the target object. Therefore, in order to solve the problem of small sample and large size of pulmonary noduless image recognition, this paper proposes a method of detection and segmentation of pulmonary nodules based on U-net. At the same time, in order to solve the problem of weak generalization ability caused by too few sample data in deep learning network training, DCGAN image generation technology is used to expand the sample data of pulmonary nodules.

The main contributions of this paper are as follows:

1. By adjusting and optimizing the U-net network structure, U-net is used for regional prediction and segmentation of pulmonary nodules.
2. In order to avoid over fitting of deep learning network, the method of generating pulmonary Nodules image by DCGAN is used to enlarge the sample size of pulmonary Nodules image.
3. By comparing the segmented mask with the labeled ground truth mask, the experimental results show that the detection and segmentation of pulmonary nodules based on U-net can obtain high sensitivity.

This paper is organized as follows:

Section 1: The background and current situation of computer-aided detection of pulmonary nodules using deep learning are introduced.

Section 2: The network structure of U-net is introduced. And the network composition of pulmonary nodules area detection and image segmentation based on U-net is elaborated.

Section 3: The U-net training data set, the method of expanding the data set and some parameters setting of the training network are described in detail. The predicted pulmonary nodule mask and the labeled pulmonary nodules mask are compared and analyzed.

Section 4: In order to avoid over fitting of deep learning network, the method of generating pulmonary Nodules image by DCGAN is used to enlarge the sample size of pulmonary Nodules image.

Section 5: The methods of pulmonary nodules region detection and image segmentation based on U-net are summarized, and the problems to be solved in the next step are puts forward.

2   The Pulmonary Nodule Regions Detection Based on U-net

2.1   Overview of U-net

U-net is a deep learning model proposed by Olaf Ronneberger, which won the International Biomedical Imaging Symposium (ISBI) competition in 2015 [6]. The U-net adopts the Encode-Decode structure, which can be divided into down-sampling and up-sampling. There are only convolution and pooling layers in the network structure, but no full connection layers. There is an intermediate stitching operation between the up-sampling and the down-sampling, that is, the skip connection. The convolution of the same number of layers is used in both up-sampling and down-sampling of the U-net, and skip connection is used to connect the up-sampling and the down-sampling layer so that the features obtained by the down-sampling layer can be transferred to the up-sampling layer.

The U-net was first proposed for cell wall segmentation, and it has excellent performance in the detection of pulmonary nodules and the extraction of blood vessels from the retina. U- net has been widely used in retinal vascular segmentation [7], rectal tumor segmentation [8] and so on.

2.2   The Structure Design of Pulmonary Nodule Detection Based on U-net

The detection structure of pulmonary nodules based on U-net is shown (see Fig. 1). In the application based on U-net network, the whole image is usually the input. After passing through the U-net network, the segmented mask image is the output. In order to reduce the influence of noise on the results, the lung parenchyma was extracted. The size of the input CT image will not be changed after dataset preprocessing. Therefore, the input is $512 \times 512 \times 1$ Gy-scale image of lung parenchyma. After two convolution operations with $3 \times 3 \times 32$ convolution kernel, $512 \times 512 \times 32$ feature data is obtained.

Each 3×3 convolution is followed with a Relu nonlinear transformation. And then the maximum pooling operation of 2×2 is performed to obtain the feature data with the size of $256 \times 256 \times 32$. The above process has to be repeated 4 times, that is, (3×3 convolution + 2×2 maximum pooling) $\times 4$ times. After each pooling, the number of 3×3 convolution kernels increases exponentially. At the lowest level, after the fourth maximum pooling, the image becomes $32 \times 32 \times 512$.

After two convolution operations of 3×3, it enters the up sampling process of deconvolution layer. Firstly, the image is changed to $64 \times 64 \times 256$ by 2×2 deconvolution, and then the image before the corresponding maximum pooling layer is copied and cropped. The arrows connecting the middle part of the U-net network indicate that the feature image is clipped and copied. Clipping is due to the loss of boundary pixels caused by convolution, so clipping is needed. Copying is to provide detailed information of the object during the above sampling process, forming a new feature map, and then to convolute horizontally. The image is spliced with the deconvolution image to get a $64 \times 64 \times 512$ image, and then the convolution operation of $3 \times 3 \times 256$ is performed. Repeat the process four times to obtain a $512 \times 512 \times 32$-sized image at the top level, and then perform a 1×1 convolution operation to obtain a mask for a $512 \times 512 \times$ 1sized pulmonary nodule segmentation image.

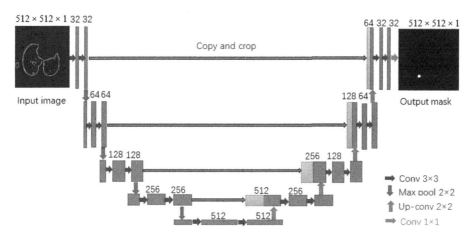

Fig. 1. The detection structure of pulmonary nodules based on U-net.

3 The Data Amplification of Pulmonary Nodules Based on DCGAN

Although U-net is more suitable for deep learning of small sample data, too little data will lead to low accuracy of network segmentation and recognition. Therefore, a technology based on Generative adversarial networks(GAN) is used to amplify the sample data of pulmonary nodules. Automatic image generation has always been a key research direction in the field of computer vision. The development of deep learning technology also makes a breakthrough in image automatic generation technology. Generative adversarial networks, which was proposed by Goodfellow in 2014 [9], has become a hot technology in the field of deep learning. However, the original GAN method has some problems such as the problem of non convergence and training difficulty. In order to solve the problems of the original GAN model, such as difficult convergence, unstable training and poor quality of generated samples, Alec Radford et al. Introduced convolution operation on the basis of GAN network, used the strong feature extraction ability of convolution layer to improve the effect of GAN, and pro-posed deep convolution generation countermeasure network (DCGAN) in 2015 [10]. After that, some improved methods have been put forward and used in various image generation tasks, such as image synthesis [11], style transfer [12], restoration of incomplete image [13].

GAN includes a generator G and a discriminator D. Generator G and discriminator D in DCGAN are realized by two convolutional neural networks. DCGAN cancels the pooling layer in convolutional neural networks (CNN) and uses deconvolution in generator G for up sampling; DCGAN cancels the full connection layer in CNN and uses convolution layer to connect the output of generator G and the input of discriminator D. The generator used in this paper to generate pulmonary nodule data is shown (see Fig. 2). The input of the generator is a uniform onedimensional random noise with a length of 8192. After reshape, the 512 dimensional data with a size of 4×4 is obtained. After seven deconvolution up sampling operations, pulmonary nodule image is generated. Among them, the first six deconvolution up sampling layers in the generator all use the relu activation function, while the last deconvolution up sampling layer in the generator uses the Tanh activation function to get the generated image of pulmonary nodule with size of $512 \times 512 \times 1$.

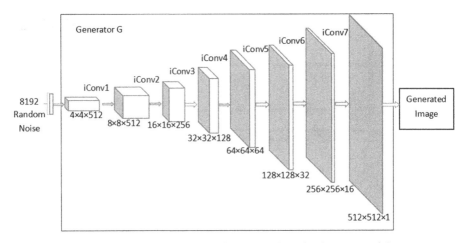

Fig. 2. The generator for generating Image data of pulmonary nodules.

The discriminator judges whether the input image data is a real pulmonary nodule image or a fake pulmonary nodule image. The structure of the discriminator is shown (see Fig. 3). The discriminator for distinguishing true and false images of pulmonary nodules has seven convolution operations. In addition to the last fully connected layer, the Leaky Relu activation function is used for each convolution layer in the discriminator. The discrimination result is converted into true and false value with length of 1 through a full connection layer with the help of Sigmoid activation function.

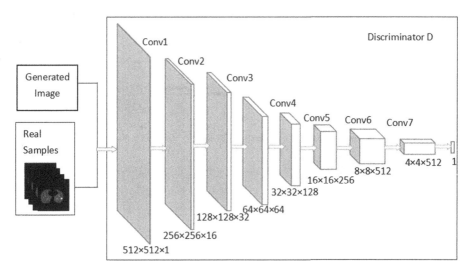

Fig. 3. The discriminator structure for true and false images of pulmonary nodules.

After one round of training, the generator and discriminator in DCGAN will calculate their respective loss functions according to the judgment results, and update their respective parameters according to the loss value, so as to carry out the next round of game.

4 Experiments

This experiment is based on LIDC-IDRI dataset. Among them, 2632 samples with pulmonary nodules marked by experts were extracted as the sample data of U-net training. In order to reduce the interference of chest contour and noise, the lung parenchyma is segmented before training U-net. Two adjacent slices of the pulmonary noduless and some good images of pulmonary nodules generated by DCGAN were added to the data set to enlarge the sample set of pulmonary nodules. The processed data is divided into two parts: training data and test data. Among them, 80% of datasets are training sets and 20% are test sets.

The experiment uses Windows 10 operating system, python as programming language, and implements the algorithm in keras framework. The computer is configured with Intel Xeon 2.40 GHz CPU, NVIDIA GTX1080 8 G GPU and 32 G memory. In each round of training, the sample data is divided into four batches. After 50 rounds of training, the dice coefficients of training and verification obtained in the u-net training process are shown (see Fig. 4). The evaluation was performed on 1007 pulmonary nodules, and the result was 64%. The comparison between the predicted results of some pulmonary nodules and the ground truth pulmonary nodules mask is shown in Table 1. Through comparison, it can be found that U-net can better segment the area of pulmonary nodules.

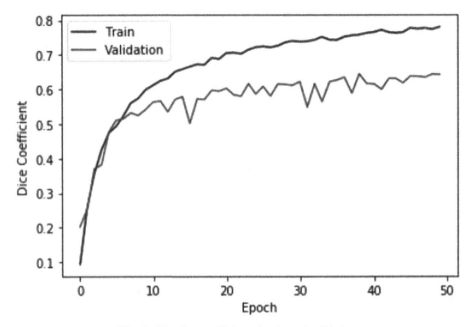

Fig. 4. The dice coefficient of train and validation

Table 1. The comparison of the mask of predicted and the mask of ground truth.

The image of lung parenchyma	The predicted results of pulmonary nodules	The ground truth pulmonary nodules mask

5 Conclusion

By adjusting and optimizing the U-net network structure, the improved U-net is used for regional prediction and segmentation of pulmonary nodules in this paper. When training the model, 512×512 images of lung parenchyma were used as the input of the network. In order to avoid over fitting of deep learning network, the method of generating pulmonary nodules image by DCGAN is used to enlarge the sample size of pulmonary nodules image. By comparing the segmented mask with the labeled ground truth mask, the experimental results show that the method presented in this paper, which is based on U-net, can obtain high sensitivity. By comparing the segmented mask with the labeled ground truth mask, the experimental results show that the U-net based pulmonary nodules prediction and segmentation method proposed in this paper can obtain high sensitivity. However, this method still produce some false positive pulmonary nodules, which will be the research content of our future work.

References

1. Chen, W., et al.: Cancer statistics in China, 2015. CA: a cancer. J. Clin. **66**(2), 115–132 (2016)
2. Informatik, F., Joachims, T.: Making Large-Scale SVM Learning Practical (1998)
3. Grabner, H., Bischof, H.: On-line boosting and vision. In: Proceedings of the IEEE Computer Society Conference on Computer Vision and Pattern Recognition, vol. 1, pp. 260–267 (2006)
4. Hinton, G.E., Srivastava, N., Krizhevsky, A., Sutskever, I., Salakhutdinov, R.R.: Improving neural networks by preventing co-adaptation of feature detectors. 1–18 (2012)
5. Simonyan, K., Zisserman, A.: Very deep convolutional networks for large-scale image recognition. In: 3rd International Conference on Learning Representations, ICLR 2015 - Conference Track Proceedings, pp. 1–12 (2015)
6. Ronneberger, O., Fischer, P., Brox, T.: U-net: Convolutional networks for biomedical image segmentation. In: Navab, N., Hornegger, J., Wells, W.M., Frangi, A.F. (eds.) MICCAI 2015. LNCS, vol. 9351, pp. 234–241. Springer, Cham (2015). https://doi.org/10.1007/978-3-319-24574-4_28
7. Wenxuan, X., Jianxia, L., Ran, L., Xiaohui, Y.: AnImproved method for retinal vascular segmentation in U-Net. Acta Optica Sin. **40**(12), 1210001 (2020)
8. Haijun, G., Xiangyin, Z., Dazhi, P., Bochuan, Z.: Rectal tumor segmentation method based on improved U-Net model. J. Comput. Appl. **40**(8), 2392–2397 (2020)
9. Goodfellow, I., et al.: Generative adversarial networks. Commun. ACM, **63**(11), 139–144 (2020)
10. Radford, A., Metz, L., Chintala, S.: Unsupervised representation learning with deep convolutional generative adversarial networks. In: 4th International Conference on Learning Representations, ICLR 2016 - Conference Track Proceedings, pp. 1–16 (2016)
11. Chen, W., Hays, J.: SketchyGAN: towards diverse and realistic sketch to image synthesis. In: Proceedings of the IEEE Computer Society Conference on Computer Vision and Pattern Recognition, pp. 9416–9425 (2018)
12. Chang, H., Lu, J., Yu, F., Finkelstein, A.: PairedCycleGAN: asymmetric style transfer for applying and removing makeup. In: Proceedings of the IEEE Computer Society Conference on Computer Vision and Pattern Recognition, pp. 40–48 (2018)
13. Mi, J., et al.: A method of plant root image restoration based on GAN. IFAC-PapersOnLine. **52**, 219–224 (2019)

Trajectory Shaping Guidance Law of Homing Missile with High Maneuver and Low Overload and Its Database Security

Li Miao$^{(\boxtimes)}$, Wang Lei, and Xu Chao

Beijing Institute of Special Mechanic-Electric, Beijing 100012, China
limiaopla@sina.com

Abstract. Under the condition of large maneuvering and small overload, the improved trajectory shaping guidance law is easy to implement in engineering, so that the medium and long range missile can not only attack from the front, but also attack vertically from the top or even from the tail or side with large maneuvering, obtain a reasonable impact angle and a small angle of attack, and achieve the best hit effect. Also, maintaining the database security and the capacity of resisting disturbance during the use of trajectory shaping guidance law is an important issue. In this paper, the trajectory shaping guidance law in the case of large maneuvering and small overload is derived and studied, the mathematical model of the remain flight time is derived and the influence of its deviation on the flight trajectory is analyzed. It provides theoretical and simulation support for the missile to complete the mission of high maneuverability and precision attack under the condition of small overload. The security of using database is discussed.

Keywords: Trajectory shaping · Fall angle constraint · Overload constraint

1 Introduction

Modern battlefield environment is extremely complex, many high-value fortifications are located on the reverse slope of the hillside, while the top and front protection is the strongest, if the missile can attack its weak links from the tail, it will undoubtedly be more conducive to the formation of effective damage to the fortifications. The front armor protection of tanks and armored vehicles is particularly strong, and with the development of active protection system, the active protection formed in a certain area in front of and above the armored vehicle can interfere with or even destroy the incoming missile. In addition, in the process of moving in the battlefield, tanks are prone to produce a large amount of dust, which will shield the target in some directions. Therefore, when the missile attacks the moving target, it can not only attack from the front, but also maneuver around the protection area or shelter area, attack vertically from the top or even from the tail or side, which can greatly improve the damage effect to the target. Under the condition of large maneuvering and small overload, the guidance law of trajectory shaping is improved for medium and long range precision strike weapons, so that the missile can obtain a reasonable impact angle and a small angle of attack to achieve the best hit effect.

© Springer Nature Switzerland AG 2021
J. Cheng et al. (Eds.): CSS 2020, LNCS 12653, pp. 245–260, 2021.
https://doi.org/10.1007/978-3-030-73671-2_22

2 Modeling

2.1 Coordinate System Description

(1) Terrestrial coordinate system $Axyz$: the terrestrial coordinate system Axyz is a coordinate system fixed to the surface of the earth. The coordinate system origin A is selected as the missile launching point; the Ax axis is that line of intersection of the ballistic plane with the horizontal plane, which is positive toward the target; the Ay axis goes up along the vertical line, and the Az axis is perpendicular to the other two axes and forms a right-hand coordinate system.

(2) Body coordinate system $Ox_1y_1z_1$: the origin of the coordinate system O is chosen as the center of mass of the missile (the center of mass is here taken as the center of inertia); the Ox_1 axis coincides with the longitudinal axis of the projectile and is positive towards the nose; the Oy_1 axis is located in the longitudinal symmetry plane of the missile body and is perpendicular to the Ox_1 axis, and the upward direction is positive; the Oz_1 axis is perpendicular to the Ox_1y_1 plane and is oriented in a right-handed coordinate system.

(3) Velocity coordinate system $Ox_3y_3z_3$: the origin of the coordinate system O is chosen as the center of mass of the missile; the Ox_3 axis coincides with the velocity vector V of the missile's center of mass; the Oy_3 axis is located in the longitudinal symmetry plane of the missile body and is perpendicular to the Ox_3 axis, and the upward direction is positive; the Oz_3 axis is perpendicular to the Ox_3y_3 plane and is oriented in a right-handed coordinate system.

(4) Ballistic coordinate system $Ox_2y_2z_2$: the origin of the coordinate system O is selected as the instantaneous centroid of the trajectory; the Ox_2 axis coincides with the missile velocity vector V; the Oy_2 axis lies in the vertical plane containing the velocity vector V, perpendicular to the Ox_2 axis, and points upward to be positive; the Oz_2 axis is perpendicular to the other two axes and forms the right-hand coordinate system [1–4].

2.2 Missile Structure and Function Brief Introduction

Refer to Fig. 1 for the structural outline of the missile. The missile has a " $+ - +$ " configuration. A seeker, a direct lateral force control mechanism, a warhead cabin section, a missile wing mechanism, an electronic cabin, a drag increasing device, an aerodynamic rudder and an endurance engine nozzle. Initial mass of missile $m_0 = 120$ kg.

A direct lateral force control mechanism is installed in front of the mass center position of the missile to control the large angle steering of the missile body at low speed (≤ 60 m/s). The fuel gas ejected from the engine is communicated to the control mechanism through a conduit, a control signal is generated by a missile-mounted computer, and the fuel gas is ejected through four axisymmetrically distributed nozzles to change the attitude of the missile.

The drag increasing device consists of four wings controlled by a pulley. When the missile is about to enter the terminal guidance phase, the fins of the drag increasing device are fully opened, the drag coefficient of the missile body is increased by more than 1.5 times of the normal value, and the speed of the missile is rapidly reduced.

When the missile is in the boost phase, the aerodynamic rudder installed on the tail of the missile completes the guidance and control of the missile, and the aerodynamic force provides lift, drag and lateral force for the missile.

The missile consists of three stages of engines, namely, take-off engine, acceleration engine and endurance engine. At the end of the takeoff engine, the missile is leaving the canister at a speed of 21.6 m/s, the thrust of the acceleration engine is 6 KN, the endurance engine is a variable thrust engine. When the missile is in endurance flight and terminal guidance flight, the thrust is 5 KN, when the missile needs large maneuver flight, the thrust is reduced to 3.5 KN and the thrust ratio is 10:7.

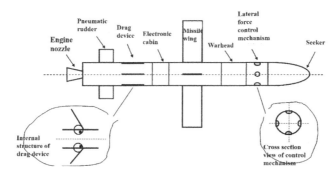

Fig. 1. Sketch map of missile structure layout in endurance flight

2.3 Missile Flight and Guidance Constraint

Missile Motion Equation. Establish the kinematic and dynamic equations for the missile in the longitudinal plane as follows [1−3].

$$
\begin{cases}
m\dfrac{dV}{dt} = F + P \\[6pt]
\dfrac{dH}{dt} = M + M_P \\[6pt]
\dfrac{dx}{dt} = V \cos\theta \cos\psi_V \\[6pt]
\dfrac{dy}{dt} = V \sin\theta \\[6pt]
\dfrac{dz}{dt} = -V \cos\theta \sin\psi_V \\[6pt]
\dfrac{d\vartheta}{dt} = \omega_y \sin\gamma + \omega_z \cos\gamma \\[6pt]
\dfrac{d\varphi}{dt} = (\omega_y \cos\gamma - \omega_z \sin\gamma)/\cos\vartheta \\[6pt]
\dfrac{d\gamma}{dt} = \omega_x - \tan\vartheta\,(\omega_y \cos\gamma - \omega_z \sin\gamma) \\[6pt]
\dfrac{dm}{dt} = -m_c
\end{cases}
$$

Where t is the missile flight times, m is the instantaneous mass of the missile, F is the resultant of the total aerodynamic and gravitational forces, P is the engine thrust, v is the missile instantaneous velocity, θ is the missile flight trajectory inclination, ϑ is the missile pitch angle, φ is the missile yaw angle, γ is the missile bank angle, ω is the rotational angular velocity of the missile body relative to the ground coordinate system.

Constraint Condition

(1) In the process of missile flight, considering the recognition distance of image seeker, the maximum flight altitude is limited to 3 km.
(2) The overload of anti-tank missile should not be too large, and the overload required by guidance law should be less than 7 g.
(3) Considering the damage effect of the missile to the target, the terminal angle of attack is within $\pm 3°$.

3 Research on Improvement of Trajectory Shaping Guidance Law with Large Maneuver and Small Overload

3.1 Purpose and Method of Improvement

The traditional trajectory shaping guidance law can only control the impact angle within $0° \sim -90°$. If we want to realize great maneuver, we must have great overload. However, for the traditional anti-tank missile, in order to ensure low cost and mass production, the missile structure can not withstand large lateral overload. The improved trajectory shaping guidance law can realize the large angle turn flight of the missile on the premise of retaining the advantages of low overload near the impact point of the traditional trajectory shaping guidance law. The variable thrust endurance engine, the direct lateral force control device and the drag increasing device are comprehensively utilized, before turning at a large angle, the variable thrust endurance engine reduces thrust, opens the wing of the resistance increasing device, reduces the flight speed of the missile to less than 60 m/s, retracts the wing of the resistance increasing device, controls the missile body to rotate at a large angle to a preset angle by the direct lateral force control device, increases thrust to about 6 KN, and accelerates the missile to normal endurance. Thereby realizing large maneuvering and small overload.

The availability of the trajectory shaping guidance law in the case of high maneuvering and small overload is derived and studied, the mathematical model of the remaining flight time is derived and the influence of its deviation on the flight trajectory is analyzed.

3.2 Theoretical Derivation of Trajectory Shaping Guidance Law

If the relative velocity V_r is constant and the relative distance R between the missile and the target is known at the initial time, the terminal time T is known. v(t) is the missile normal velocity. Because the greater the normal velocity of the missile at the end of the trajectory, the greater the impact angle of the missile, so the limit for the impact angle of the missile can be transformed into the limit for the normal velocity at the end of the trajectory. The geometric relationship between the missile falling angle and the missile normal velocity at the terminal point is shown in Fig. 2. In Fig. 2, v(T) is the normal velocity at the end of the trajectory and σ is the missile falling angle.

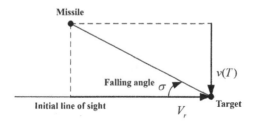

Fig. 2. Geometric relationship between missile impact angle and normal velocity at the end of trajectory

According to the characteristics of different targets, the best falling angle value can be found. To simplify the problem, the normal velocity at the end of the missile can be used instead of the impact angle. According to the relative velocity between missile and target Vr and the initial angle of sight between missile and target q_0, the limit condition of the impact angle can be transformed into the normal velocity value Ve at the end of the trajectory. At the same time, the limitation condition of the angle of attack of the missile is that the angle of attack value α_e at the end of the trajectory is expected to approach 0. Here, the initial missile-target line-of-sight angle is a constant, and $q_0 = 0$ may be set, that is, the missile and the target are in the same horizontal plane at the initial time. Generally, the error of the impact point is required to be $y_e = 0$ at the terminal point of the missile. For ease of study, only the case where the missile and the target are always in the same vertical plane is considered.

That is, the end point constraint condition is:

$$y(T) = y_e \tag{1}$$

$$v(T) = v_e \tag{2}$$

$$\alpha(T) = \alpha_e \tag{3}$$

Derivation by means of variational method:
System state equation:

$$\dot{y} = v \tag{4}$$

$$\dot{v} = a \tag{5}$$

The control variable for this problem is normal overload a(t).

Objective function:

$$J(t_0) = c_y \frac{(y(T) - y_e)^2}{2} + c_v \frac{(v(T) - v_e)^2}{2} + \int_{t_0}^{T} \frac{1}{2} a^2(t) \, dt \tag{6}$$

Among,

$$\varphi(x(T), T) = c_y \frac{(y(T) - y_e)^2}{2} + c_v \frac{(v(T) - v_e)^2}{2}$$

Where y is the displacement normal to the missile (i.e., perpendicular to the initial target line), v is the missile normal velocity, and a is the missile normal overload. The objective function is selected to minimize that integral of the square of the normal overload, which means to minimize the control energy and the velocity loss caused by the induced drag. Appropriate selection of the coefficients c_y and c_v can make the end point constraint condition (1) or (2) both be satisfied as far as possible. The greater the value of c_y and c_v is, the higher the degree of satisfaction of the end point constraint condition is. If c_y and c_v is infinite, the end point restriction condition can be strictly satisfied.

To study the optimal guidance law is to find the law of controlling the normal overload a to minimize the objective function J.

Hamiltonian function: [1−2]

$$H = \frac{1}{2} a^2 + v\lambda_y + a\lambda_v \tag{7}$$

Co-state equation:

$$-\dot{\lambda}_y = \frac{\partial H}{\partial y} = \frac{\partial}{\partial y} (\frac{1}{2} a^2 + v\lambda_y + a\lambda_v) = 0$$

$$-\dot{\lambda}_v = \frac{\partial H}{\partial v} = \frac{\partial}{\partial v} (\frac{1}{2} a^2 + v\lambda_y + a\lambda_v) = \lambda_y$$

Extremum condition:

$$0 = \frac{\partial H}{\partial a} = \frac{\partial}{\partial a} (\frac{1}{2} a^2 + v\lambda_y + a\lambda_v) = a + \lambda_v \tag{8}$$

From the extremum conditions, the conditions of the optimal control are:

$$a(t) = -\lambda_v(t) \tag{9}$$

If can be known from the end point constraint condition,

$$\begin{bmatrix} \frac{\partial \varphi(T)}{\partial y} \\ \frac{\partial \varphi(T)}{\partial v} \end{bmatrix} - \begin{bmatrix} \lambda_y(T) \\ \lambda_v(T) \end{bmatrix} = 0 \tag{10}$$

Expand Eq. (10):

$$\lambda_y(T) = \frac{\partial \varphi(T)}{\partial y} = \frac{\partial}{\partial y} (c_y(y(T) - y_e)^2/2 + c_v(v(T) - v_e)^2/2) = c_y(y(T) - y_e)$$

$$\lambda_v(T) = \frac{\partial \varphi(T)}{\partial v} = \frac{\partial}{\partial v}(c_y(y(T) - y_e)^2/2 + c_v(v(T) - v_e)^2/2) = c_v(v(T) - v_e)$$

Integrating $\dot{\lambda}_y = 0$ over the interval [t,T] yields:

$$\lambda_y(t) \equiv \lambda_y(T) \tag{11}$$

Substituting Eq. (11) into the covariant equation of state yields $\dot{\lambda}_v = -\lambda_y(T)$, and integrating this equation in the interval [t, T] yields:

$$\lambda_v(T) - \lambda_v(t) = -(T - t)\lambda_y(T) \tag{12}$$

Substituting Eq. (9) into equation of state (5) yields:

$$\dot{v} = -\lambda_v(t) \tag{13}$$

Substituting Eq. (12) into Eq. (13) and integrating over the interval [0,t] yields:

$$v(t) = v(0) - t(\lambda_v(T) + T\lambda_y(T)) + t^2\lambda_y(T)/2 \tag{14}$$

Integrating Eq. (14),

$$y(t) = y(0) + v(0)t - t^2(\lambda_v(T) + T\lambda_y(T))/2 + t^3\lambda_y(T)/6 \tag{15}$$

When t = T, there is the following relationship,

$$c_y y(0) + c_y T v(0) = (1 + c_y T^3/3)\lambda_y(T) + c_y T^2\lambda_v(T)/2 + c_y y_e$$
$$c_v v(0) = c_v T^2\lambda_y(T)/2 + (1 + c_v T)\lambda_v(T) + c_v v_e$$

Represented in matrix form as:

$$\begin{bmatrix} 1 + c_y T^3/3 & c_y T^2/2 \\ c_v T^2/2 & 1 + c_v T \end{bmatrix} \begin{bmatrix} \lambda_y(T) \\ \lambda_v(T) \end{bmatrix} + \begin{bmatrix} c_y y_e \\ c_v v_e \end{bmatrix} = \begin{bmatrix} c_y & c_y T \\ 0 & c_v \end{bmatrix} \begin{bmatrix} y(0) \\ v(0) \end{bmatrix} \tag{16}$$

Solving matrix Eqs. (16), at the same time, in order to obtain the closed-loop guidance law, we should take the system state $y(t)$ as the feedback quantity. Therefore, in the integral process of formula (14), (15), we can take the current time as 0, then the initial value of the state integral becomes the current state value $y(t)$, $v(t)$ and the integral time becomes $T - t$. Thus, we can obtain the relationship between the current value of the system state and the terminal value of the adjoint state.

$$\begin{bmatrix} \lambda_y(T) \\ \lambda_v(T) \end{bmatrix} = \frac{1}{\Delta(T-t)} \begin{bmatrix} (T-t) + \bar{c}_v & (T-t)^2/2 + \bar{c}_v(T-t) \\ -(T-t)^2/2 & -(T-t)^3/6 + \bar{c}_y \end{bmatrix} \begin{bmatrix} y(t) \\ v(t) \end{bmatrix}$$
$$- \frac{1}{\Delta(T-t)} \begin{bmatrix} (T-t)y_e + \bar{c}_v y_e - (T-t)^2 v_e/2 \\ -(T-t)^2 y_e/2 + (T-t)^3 v_e/3 + \bar{c}_y v_e \end{bmatrix} \tag{17}$$

Among,

$$\Delta(T-t) = (T-t)^4/12 + \bar{c}_v(T-t)^3/3 + \bar{c}_y(T-t) + \bar{c}_v\bar{c}_y$$
$$= ((T-t)^3/3 + \bar{c}_y)((T-t) + \bar{c}_v) - (T-t)^4/4$$

The control law is known from the previous derivation,

$$a(t) = -\lambda_v(t) = -\left(\lambda_v(T) + (T - t)\lambda_y(T)\right) \tag{18}$$

Substituting Eq. (17) into Eq. (18) yields:

$$
\begin{aligned}
a(t) = &-\frac{(T - t)^2/2 + \bar{c}_v(T - t)}{\Delta(T - t)}y(t) - \frac{(T - t)^3/3 + (T - t)^2\bar{c}_v + \bar{c}_y}{\Delta(T - t)}v(t) \\
&+ \frac{(T - t)^2/2 + \bar{c}_v(T - t)}{\Delta(T - t)}y_e + \frac{-(T - t)^3/6 + \bar{c}_y}{\Delta(T - t)}v_e
\end{aligned} \tag{19}
$$

Where $\Delta(T - t) = (T - t)^4/12 + \bar{c}_v(T - t)^3/3 + \bar{c}_y(T - t) + \bar{c}_v\bar{c}_y$, the bigger the coefficient c_y, c_v is, that is, the smaller the $\bar{c}_y$, $\bar{c}_v$ is, the more the parameters of the terminal trajectory are close to the terminal constraint conditions. When the terminal condition $y(T) = y_e, v(T) = v_e$ is strictly satisfied, we can take $c_y, c_v \to \infty$, namely $\bar{c}_y = 0, \bar{c}_v = 0$, and substitute it into the expression of optimal guidance law a(t) to obtain,

$$a(t) = -\frac{6}{(T - t)^2}y(t) - \frac{4}{(T - t)}v(t) + \frac{6}{(T - t)^2}y_e - \frac{2}{T - t}v_e \tag{20}$$

Equation (20) is the guidance law in terms of two states y(t), v(t), remaining flight time (T-t), and terminal constraint y_e, v_e.

Let $t_{go} = $ T-t, substitute formula (20) to get,

$$a(t) = -\frac{6}{t_{go}^2}y(t) - \frac{4}{t_{go}}v(t) + \frac{6}{t_{go}^2}y_e - \frac{2}{t_{go}}v_e \tag{21}$$

Equation (21) is the optimal guidance law expressed by the two states of normal displacement y(t) and normal velocity v(t), the remaining flight time t_{go} and the terminal constraint y_e, v_e. Because the normal displacement and normal velocity of the missile at each moment are not easy to be measured directly during the flight of the missile, the optimal guidance law expressed by Eq. (21) is not easy to be realized in engineering. However, when the missile-target line-of-sight angle is relatively small, the tangent value of the missile-target line-of-sight angle can be approximately considered to be equal to the missile-target line-of-sight angle, so that the normal displacement y(t) and the normal velocity v(t) can be replaced by two states, i.e. The missile-target ling-of-sight angle and the missile-targets ling-of-sight angular velocity.

When the line-of-sight angle q is small, there exists the following approximation,

$$q(t) \approx \tan q(t) = -\frac{y(t)}{(T - t)V_r} = -\frac{y(t)}{t_{go}V_r} \tag{22}$$

$$\dot{q}(t) \approx -\frac{\dot{y}(t)}{(T - t)V_r} - \frac{y(t)}{(T - t)^2V_r} = -\frac{\dot{y}(t)}{t_{go}V_r} - \frac{y(t)}{t_{go}^2V_r} \tag{23}$$

It can be concluded that,

$$a(t) = \frac{6}{t_{go}^2}q(t)t_{go}V_r - \frac{4}{t_{go}}(-\dot{q}(t)t_{go}V_r + q(t)V_r) + \frac{6}{t_{go}^2}y_e - \frac{2}{t_{go}}v_e$$

That is,

$$a(t) = 4V_r\dot{q}(t) + \frac{2V_r}{t_{go}}q(t) + \frac{6}{t_{go}^2}y_e - \frac{2}{t_{go}}v_e \tag{24}$$

Equation (24) is an optimal guidance law expressed by using the missile-target line-of-sight angle q and the missile-target line-of-sight angular velocity $\dot{q}$ instead of the missile lateral velocity and lateral displacement. The angular velocity of line of sight between missile and target can be measured directly by seeker, the angular velocity of line of sight between missile and target can be obtained by adding the frame angle of seeker and the attitude angle of missile body measured by attitude gyroscope on the missile, the remaining flight time can be estimated, the velocity V_r of missile along the line of sight can be measured by inertial navigation system, and the terminal limit condition y_e, v_e is a known constant. Therefore, the optimal guidance law can be realized.

At the end point, $t_{go} = 0$, the end line-of-sight angle constraint is q_F, and $q_F < 0$, under the small angle, substituting Eq. (23),

$$v_e = v(T) = q_F V_r \tag{25}$$

As shown in Eq. (25), the constraint on the terminal normal velocity can be translated into a constraint on the missile-to-target line of sight angle q_F at the terminal. Substituting Eq. (25) into Eq. (24), then get,

$$a(t) = 4V_r\dot{q}(t) + \frac{2V_r(q(t) - q_F)}{t_{go}} + \frac{6}{t_{go}^2}y_e \tag{26}$$

Equation (26) is the optimal guidance law of limited impact angle and impact point expressed by missile-target line-of-sight angle, missile-target line-of-sight angular velocity, remaining flight time t_{go}, terminal normal displacement limit condition y_e and terminal line-of sight angle limit condition q_F. wherein the terminal line-of-sight constraint q_F is approximately equal to the terminal angle constraint.

When the constraint condition for the normal displacement of the end point is 0, that is, $y_e = 0$, it is obtained by substituting Eq. (26).

$$a(t) = 4V_r\dot{q}(t) + \frac{2V_r(q(t) - q_F)}{t_{go}} \tag{27}$$

Equation (27) is the optimal guidance law derived on the premise of linear assumption and small angle assumption. Whether the guidance law can still meet the impact point and impact angle constraints in the case of large maneuvering and small overload, the following mathematical simulation to verify the availability of the guidance law in the case of large maneuvering and small overload.

3.3 Emulation Verification of Large Angle Turn of Missile

The simulation conditions are as follows: the missile only considers the movement of the vertical plane and ignores the dynamic link; the target is stationary, and the guidance

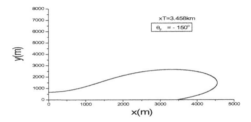

Fig. 3. Terminal guidance phase trajectory shaping trajectory

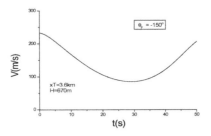

Fig. 4. Terminal guidance phase velocity curve

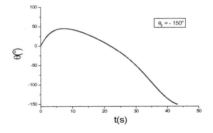

Fig. 5. Terminal guidance phase trajectory inclination curve

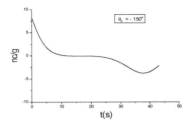

Fig. 6. Terminal guidance phase overload command curve

is started at the initial moment of the terminal guidance stage; the altitude of the missile at the beginning of the terminal guidance phase was 670 m, the distance to the target was 3600 m, and the missile impact angle q_F was $-150°$. The trajectory curve is shown in Fig. 3, Fig. 4, Fig. 5 and Fig. 6.

From the above trajectory simulation results, it can be seen that the guidance law can not only meet the impact point accuracy requirements, but also achieve the desired impact angle. Therefore, it can be proved that the optimal guidance law with limited impact angle and impact point based on the assumption of small angle is suitable for the case of large target line-of-sight angle.

3.4   Research on Realization of Trajectory Shaping Guidance

Realization of Traditional Trajectory Shaping Guidance Law. After the end of the boost phase, the missile enters the terminal guidance phase, and begins to guide with the trajectory shaping guidance law, ensuring the impact point accuracy and the impact angle range of $0° \sim -90°$. Due to the high velocity of the missile, the required overload of the missile in the guidance and control process is relatively large. In that guidance process, the sight line angular velocity of the missile and the target is directly measured by a guidance head or calculate by inertial navigation information; and that sight angle of the missile and the target can be calculated by the inertial navigation information.

Realization of Improved Trajectory Shaping Guidance Law. When the missile is about to enter the terminal guidance stage, the speed of the missile is reduced to the magnitude of tens of meters by using the variable thrust characteristic of the engine and the action of a drag increasing device, and then the attitude of the missile is adjusted under the action of a direct lateral force control mechanism to complete a large maneuvering turn; at this time, because the speed of the missile is not large, the overload required is not large. After the attitude adjustment is completed and the seeker locks on the targets, the missile attacks the target. In the whole terminal guidance phase, the impact point constraint, overload constraint and angle of attack constraint are implemented by the improved trajectory shaping guidance law in the low speed state.

The implementation scheme is as follow:

1) The angular velocity of line of sight $\dot{q}(t)$ can be measured directly by seeker or calculated by inertial navigation system.
2) The missile-target sight angle $q(t)$ can be calculated by the inertial navigation information; when the missile is equipped with a seeker, the line of sight angle $q(t)$ can be calculated from the frame angle of the seeker and the attitude angle of the missile body measured by the attitude gyro on the missile.
3) V_r is the average relative velocity between the missile and the target along the missile-target line. Because the target is stationary, V_r is replaced by the current velocity V_m of the missile, V_m can be calculated by inertial navigation system.
4) Computational model of remaining flight time t_{go} is $t_{go} \approx R_{tm}/V_r$, where R_{tm} is the distance between the missile and the target, $R_{tm} = \sqrt{(X_m - X_t)^2 + (Y_m - Y_t)^2 + (Z_m - Z_t)^2}$, the target position (X_t, Y_t, Z_t) is known, and the missile position (X_m, Y_m, Z_m) is calculated by inertial navigation.

From the above analysis, we can see that the trajectory shaping guidance law can be realized in engineering.

Due to the measurement error of inertial navigation system, R_{tm}, V_m will have an error, which will lead to the calculation error of the remaining flight time, and the deviation of t_{go} will affect the overload command. The influence of the deviation of t_{go} on the deviation of impact point and the miss distance is analyzed by simulation. Let a certain moment, the remaining flight time $t_{go} = R_{tm}/V_r$ without considering the deviation; considering the remaining flight time $t_{go}' = kt_{go} + \Delta t_{go}$ after deviation, the influence of remaining flight time deviation on miss distance and impact angle deviation is analyzed below.

Effect of Δt_{go}.
Let $k = 1$, that is, $t_{go}' = t_{go} + \Delta t_{go}$, the curves of fall angle deviation and miss distance versus Δt_{go} are shown in the figure below. As can be seen from the figure below, the influence of Δt_{go} on the miss distance is very small, and the main influence is the falling angle, and the falling angle deviation increases with the increase of Δt_{go} absolute value (Fig. 7 and Fig. 8).

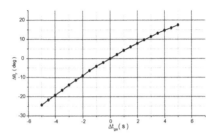

Fig. 7. Variation curve of falling angle deviation with Δt_{go}

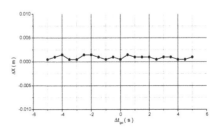

Fig. 8. Curve of miss distance versus Δt_{go}

Effect of k.
Let $\Delta t_{go} = 0$, that is, $t_{go}' = kt_{go}$, the variation curves of fall angle deviation and miss distance with Δt_{go} are shown in figures below. It can be seen from Fig. 9 that when $k < 1.1$, the size of k has almost no effect on the falling angle and the miss distance. When $k > 1.1$, the falling angle deviation and the miss distance increase with the increase of k (Fig. 10).

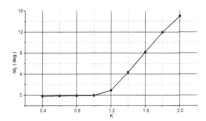

Fig. 9. Variation curve of falling angle deviation with k

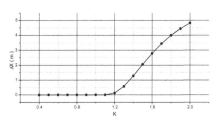

Fig. 10. Curve of miss distance versus k

Effect of Δt_{go},k.

Let $t'_{go}, = kt_{go} + \Delta t_{go}$ the curves of fall angle deviation and miss displace corresponding to different values of Δt_{go},k are shown in Fig. 11 and Fig. 12. It can be seen from the figure that the fall angle deviation of $\Delta t_{go} < 0$ is large, and when k takes some values, the fall angle deviation and the miss distance diverge.

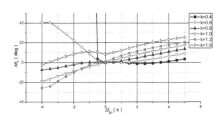

Fig. 11. Curve of falling angle deviation corresponding to different Δt_{go} and k

Introduce ε.

In order to reduce the fall angle deviation and miss distance caused by the measurement error of the remaining flight time, a small quantity of $\varepsilon(\varepsilon > 0)$is introduced. When $t_{go} < \varepsilon$, let $t_{go} = \varepsilon$.

Let $k = 1$, that is $t'_{go} = t_{go} + \Delta t_{go}$. The variation curves of falling angle deviation and miss distance with Δt_{go} corresponding to different ε are shown in the figure below. It can be seen from the figure that the falling angle deviation of the $\Delta t_{go} < 0$ part after the ε is introduced is smaller than the falling angle deviation of the $\Delta t_{go} < 0$ part without introducing the ε, but with the increase of ε, the falling angle deviation are also increased (Fig. 13 and Fig. 14).

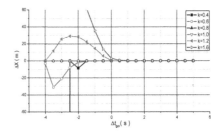

Fig. 12. Curve of miss displace corresponding to different Δt_{go} and k

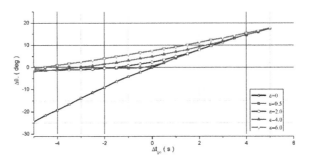

Fig. 13. Curve of falling angle deviation corresponding to different Δt_{go}

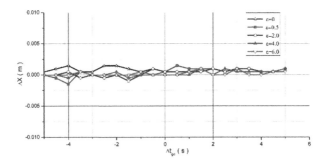

Fig. 14. Variation curve of miss displace versus Δtgo

Let $\Delta t_{go} = 0$, that is $t'_{go} = kt_{go}$. The variation curves of falling angle deviation and miss distance with k corresponding to different ε are shown in the Fig. 15 and 16. It can be seen from the figure that the falling angle deviation after the ε is introduced is bigger than the falling angle deviation without introducing the ε, but the introduction of ε can reduce the miss distance, and with the increase of ε, the reduction of miss distance is greater.

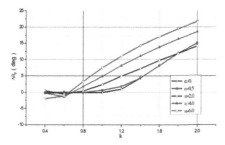

Fig. 15. Variation curve of falling angle deviation with k

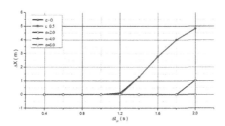

Fig. 16. Variation curve of miss distance with k

4 Conclusion

Under the condition of large maneuvering and small overload, the improved trajectory shaping guidance law can reach the impact angle of $0° \sim -180°$ while ensuring the impact point accuracy. The ballistic characteristics of medium and long range precision strike weapons are more conductive to the formation of effective damage to high-value solid fortifications located on the reverse slope of the hillside. At the same time, the moving target can not only attack from the front, but also maneuver around the active protection area or shelter area, attack vertically from the top or even from the tail or side, which greatly improves the damage effect to the target. The concept of large maneuver and small overload is put forward for the first time, and the overload is no more than 6 g. Traditionally, the realization of large maneuvering ballistic characteristics will produce large demand overload, which requires high design requirements for missile overall, structure and aerodynamics. With the development of variable thrust motor technology and direct lateral force control technology, combined with the improved trajectory shaping guidance law, the missile can complete the large maneuvering attack on the target in the middle and long range under the condition of small overload. It must be realized that the database security during the transportation of signals between missile and controlling center, which uses the guidance law, must be confirmed in order to keep the capacity of resisting disturbance.

References

1. Zarchan, P.: Tactical and strategic Missile Guidance Four Edition in AIAA Tactical Missile (2004)

2. Garnell, P.: Guided Weapon Control Systems revision by Qi zai-kang. Beijing: Beijing institute of technology (2004)

3. Qianxingfang. Missile Flight Mechanics. Beijing Institute of Technology, Beijing (2000)

4. Qianxingfang, Y.: Controlled Flight Dynamics and Computer Simulation. National Defense industry Press, Beijing

5. Anwar, W., Khan, M.Z., Israr, A., Mehmood, S., Nazeer, A.: Anjum. Effect of structural dynamic characteristics on fatigue and damage tolerance of aerospace grade composite materials. Aerospace Sci. Technol. **64**, 39–51 (2017)

6. Taguchi, G.: Taguchi on Robust Technology Development: Bringing Quality Engineering Up stream. ASME Press, New York (1993)

7. Du, X., Chen, W.: Towards a better understanding of modeling feasibility robustness in engineering design. J. Mech. Des. **122**(4), 385–394 (1999)

8. Gao, C.W., Liu, M., Green, W.H.: Uncertainty analysis of correlated parameters in automated reaction mechanism generation. Int. J. Chem. Kinet. **52**(4), 266–282 (2020)

9. Yu, H., Gillot, F., Ichchou, M.: A polynomial chaos expansion based reliability method for linear random structures. **15**(12), 2097–2111 (2012)

10. Xiu, D., Karniadakis, G.: The Wiener-Askey polynomial chaos for stochastic differential equations. SIAM J. Sci. Comput. **24**(2), 619–644 (2002)

11. Rackwitz, R., Flessler, B.: Structural reliability under combined random load sequences. Comput. Struct. **9**(5), 489–494 (1978)

Bibliometric and Graph Analysis in Document Data Mining Based on the Cultivation of New Type Professional Farmers

Chaosheng Tang$^{(\boxtimes)}$ (iD) and Lijin Qin (iD)

Hainan University, Haikou 570228, China

Abstract. In order to further enhance the depth and breadth of literature mining, this paper meets the needs of researchers to improve the efficiency of resource utilization and strengthen the visualization effect, and understand the research status and trends related to the cultivation of new-type professional farmers in China. According to CNKI academic research literature in the field of cultivation and research of new professional farmers in China, from the perspective of bibliometrics and social network map, this paper comprehensively uses CiteSpace + Gephi + UCINET knowledge map software. Qualitative analysis and quantitative statistics are carried out on the time series, research field and organization distribution, research hotspots and research trends of literature publication. The analysis results show that the current cultivation of farmers has a wide range of topics and rich content, but the lack of information literacy, especially the cultivation of information security literacy, so it is necessary to continue to expand the scope of cultivation to adapt to the development of The Times.

Keywords: Bibliometric · Social network map · Knowledge map software · Information security literacy

1 Introduction

In 2012, the No. 1 document of the Central Committee of the Communist Party of China clearly stated for the first time that it is necessary to vigorously cultivate new types of professional farmers as the backbone of promoting the development of agricultural industry, realizing agricultural modernization, and then improving the quality of urbanization. Since then, the Central Committee No. 1 document from 2013 to 2016 has emphasized the need to vigorously cultivate new-type professional farmers, and establish the core and basic position of cultivating new-type professional farmers as the core and foundation of promoting modern agricultural construction. In this context, the academic circle has successively carried out a series of research and practice on the cultivation of new-type professional farmers.

In the literature review, it is found that the qualitative analysis method is mostly used in the literature on the cultivation of new-type professional farmers and related topics, involving policy interpretation [1, 2], connotation extraction [3, 4], problem disclosure

© Springer Nature Switzerland AG 2021
J. Cheng et al. (Eds.): CSS 2020, LNCS 12653, pp. 261–274, 2021.
https://doi.org/10.1007/978-3-030-73671-2_23

[5–7] and path analysis [8, 9] In some literatures, quantitative and visual analysis methods are used in the course review [10] and hot-spot tracking [11], reflecting the diversity of current research methods and forms. However, there are some problems in the research process, such as insufficient combination of qualitative and quantitative analysis, superficial use of tool software, insufficient correlation and support. In order to accurately clarify the research context of the cultivation of new-type professional farmers, clarify the development status and existing problems, further deepen the research content, broaden the scope of research, and explore the unknown areas, we need to explore more analytical methods and tools.

In the research, the author found that the combination of CiteSpace + gephi + UCINET can link up and strengthen the results of qualitative and quantitative analysis from multiple levels and angles, and give full play to the advantages of these software: (1) as one of the most popular mapping tools, CiteSpace software is used to construct knowledge map and track research hotspots and development trends in the field Potential [12, 13], outline user portrait [14], etc. (2) Gephi is an open source free cross platform software, which is suitable for various network and complex system analysis, can provide a variety of symbiotic graphs and cluster graphs [15], support dynamic graph data analysis [16], and is widely used in hot research in many fields [17–19]. (3) UCINET, as one of the social network analysis software, has complete supporting tools and supports the quantitative analysis of the whole and detailed network. It can be analyzed from the sub network structure, network density, network distance, centrality and small groups [20]; it supports seamless docking with Netdraw software to build the domain knowledge map [21].

Drawing on the previous research results, this paper intends to use bibliometrics and social network graph analysis technology to analyze and explore it from the perspectives of keyword change, hot spot distribution and edge clustering in the form of visualization, trying to reveal its development trend and provide beneficial reference for the sustainable development of the cultivation of new professional farmers in the future. At the same time, through summarizing the advantages and disadvantages of the two methods, it provides guidance and ideas for researchers to mine literature information.

2 Bibliometric Analysis

2.1 Literature Sources

In order to more accurately and comprehensively reflect the research status in related fields in China, the author adopts the theme of "new professional farmers" and ("cultivation" or "training") in CNKI "China academic literature online publishing general database", with the time span of 2006–2019 (retrieval time: November 15, 2019), and a total of 926 articles with fund support were selected. The author carefully combs the above literature, and on this basis, carries on the statistical analysis to the research results in this field.

2.2 Analysis Methods and Means

In order to fully integrate and give full play to the advantages of various analysis software and tools, the author, on the one hand, uses the statistical function of CNKI and the co word analysis technology of CiteSpace [22], a scientific and technological text mining software, to complete basic econometric analysis such as literature publication time series statistics, research field and research institution statistics. On the other hand, with the help of social network graph analysis, the co-word matrix is further mined: (1) the original co word matrix is obtained by reverse calculation of the co word matrix obtained by CiteSpace; (2) the keyword co-occurrence network map is generated by gephi software, from which the current research hotspots can be found; (3) Using UCINET software, the centrality of the original matrix is calculated and the core edge matrix is divided, and the central words and marginal words are screened out. (4) The edge matrix is divided into subgraphs and clustered to extract new research hotspots and topics.

2.3 Bibliometric Analysis Results

Quantitative and qualitative analysis can be carried out from time series, distribution of disciplines and journals, distribution of high-yield authors and research institutions. This paper mainly considers the statistics on time series.

Time series involves two aspects: one is the time series of literature publication quantity change, the other is the time series of literature keyword change. Key words as the concentration of the main content of the article, its statistical analysis can extract the idea and theme of the article to a certain extent [11].

From the time of publication, the research literature on the cultivation or training of new-type professional farmers can be divided into two stages: the first stage is from 2006 to 2012, which is the initial stage of research in this field. The number of published papers is relatively small (about 10 articles), and the research scope is also narrow. This is mainly because China is in the early stage of transformation from traditional agriculture to modern agriculture, the concept of new professional farmers has not been clear, the relevant policies have not been issued, and the research papers are basically in the initial stage of exploration. The second stage is the 2013–2019 year blowout period, which mainly stems from 2012–2016 years' central 1 document, which has promulgated relevant policies for training new occupation farmers. The 13th five year plan for the cultivation and development of new professional farmers in China was issued in 2017, which clarified the development ideas, main tasks, key projects and specific measures of cultivating new-type professional farmers in China during the 13th five-year plan. It was proposed that the total number of new-type professional farmers in China would reach 20 million by 2020, becoming the leading force in the construction of modern agriculture. Driven by a series of policies, the number of research literature at this stage has been increasing, and the research upsurge has continued to rise.

From the perspective of time change of keywords, the author uses cite space In the software, co-occurrence analysis was conducted on the keywords retrieved from the previous 926 articles on the cultivation of new-type professional farmers, and the time series map of keywords was drawn (Fig. 1). The size of the circle around the key words in the figure reflected the heat of the research on the word, and the connection curve reflected the relationship between the keywords The first stage (2006–2012) only focuses on the basic vocabulary of new-type farmers and cultivation; the second stage (after 2012) has a wider range of literature research and more diversified subject contents (from cultivation of new professional farmers, training of new professional farmers, training countermeasures, agricultural modernization, training willingness, cultivation mode, cultivation path to precision training, Rural Revitalization and mutual promotion) Networking + open education, etc.). In addition to some key words such as new professional farmers and cultivation, there are few central nodes in the map, which indicates that the relevant research has not formed a clear direction and goal.

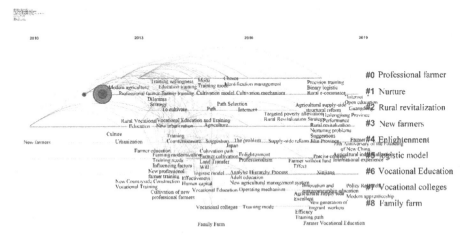

Fig. 1. Time series graph of keywords

3   Social Network Analysis

In order to understand the current research hotspots and possible research directions in the future, the author uses the analysis method and means of social network graph to further mine. Since the co word matrix generated by CiteSpace is not the original matrix, it is calculated by cosine algorithm. The internal standard value of the matrix is 0–1. The algorithm is shown in Formula 1:

$$cosine\left(c_{ij}, s_j, s_j\right) = \frac{c_{ij}}{\sqrt{s_i s_j}} \tag{1}$$

Where c_{ij} is the co-word frequency of i and j, s_i is the frequency of i and j, and s_j is the frequency of J. Since the co word matrix is in CSV format, it can be easily imported into the table software for further processing. Therefore, the author compiles VBA code in Excel software, and calculates the original matrix by combining with frequency statistical matrix. The value of VBA code can reflect the common word frequency of each keyword, which is convenient for subsequent graph network analysis.

3.1   Co-word Network Map Display

The drawing of the co-word network map relies on the natural connection between the keyword data, which three-dimensionally and intuitively presents the relationship between the keywords and the overall characteristics of the co-word network [23]. In order to highlight the characteristics, the author uses Gephi software to import the.net file exported by CiteSpace into the system and build a common word network map (Fig. 2). The 134 keywords in the figure are marked with dots. The larger the dots and labels, the greater the centrality and the more they are located in the core of the network.The lines between dots indicate that there are co-words between keywords, and the thicker the lines indicate these two key points The frequency of co-occurrence of words is higher. Except for the search terms "new professional farmer cultivation" and "new professional farmer training", keywords such as "professional farmer", "new professional farmer", "countermeasures" and "agricultural modernization" are relatively central, with rich surrounding relationships and located in the center of the network The location reflects their importance in the research field or research perspective, and is a research hotspot in this field. However, most of the vocabulary has a small centrality, the correlation curve is relatively sparse and thin, and the profile also reflects that the overall research direction is relatively scattered.

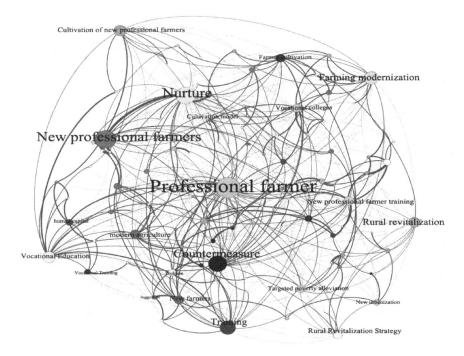

Fig. 2. Co-word network map

3.2   Network Density Measurement and Centrality Analysis

The network map can let us intuitively feel the status of various keywords from a qualitative perspective. In order to further explore the relationship, we need to do quantitative calculation and analysis. Through the measurement of network density, a quantitative description of the overall situation of the network diagram can be obtained. Density describes the closeness of the relationship between the key words in the network graph, that is, the cohesion. The value range of this measure is [0,1]. The closer the value is to 1, the closer the relationship between nodes is, that is, the cross influence of research sub fields represented by keywords in the network graph is stronger [24]. According to the operation line of network/cohesion/density, the density of the network is 0.2691 calculated by UCINET software. This shows that most of the keywords in the co word network are not closely related to each other, reflecting that the research direction in this field is relatively scattered. In addition, in the study of social network, centrality is to evaluate whether a person is important or not, to measure the superiority or privilege of his position, status, and social prestige [25]. Drawing on this idea, the centrality of the network map in the field of literature analysis reflects the status and role of a keyword node in the co word network, and reflects the degree of attention and cross influence in the research field.

Around the measurement of centrality, Freeman divided the centrality of networks into several categories: degree centrality, intermediate centrality and proximity centrality [26], and then added centrality of eigenvectors. The intermediate centrality can be used to measure whether a node is in the core position of the network. If the middle centrality of a node is higher, the dependence of other nodes on it is stronger. Therefore, in the co word network, the middle centrality of a keyword can be used as an index to measure the ability of the keyword to influence the co-occurrence of other keywords in a journal paper. According to the operation line of network/centrality/multiple measures, the centrality values of 134 keywords can be obtained by importing the co word matrix (Fig. 3). The summary is shown in Table 1 (only 9 keywords with the highest middle centrality are listed in the table due to space limitation).

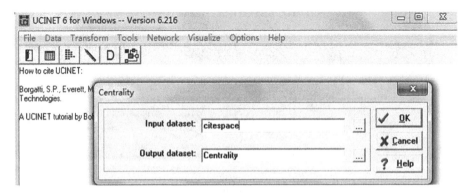

Fig. 3. Centrality operation interface

Table 1. The centrality table of keywords

Key words	Betweenness centrality	Eigenvector centrality	Closeness centrality
Professional farmer	17.951	42.293	9.353
New professional farmers	13.212	40.895	9.333
Nurture	11.715	36.09	9.281
Countermeasure	10.467	37.028	9.294
Training	7.361	29.754	9.198
farming modernization	7.246	29.053	9.217
Cultivation of new professional farmers	6.553	20.596	9.103
Rural revitalization	5.571	24.362	9.185
Vocational education	4.230	28.359	9.141

From Table 1, it can be found that several keywords such as "professional farmer" and "new professional farmer" are relatively high (the centrality is above 10), and the core position is relatively prominent, which is consistent with the situation presented by the previous network map. In general, the centrality of keywords shows a gradual and gradual decline, but statistics show that there are still 30 keywords with zero centrality, which indicates that the transmission of information in the co-word network is more dependent on a few Keywords, lack of information flow between some keywords, independent and scattered. In order to visually show the closeness between the core keywords and between the core words and other edge keywords, the author will use the core edge measure to divide the core word area and the edge word area, which can reflect the current research on the distribution of cold and hot, but also Pave the way for subsequent optimization and screening of potential keywords.

3.3 Core-edge Matrix Analysis

The core-edge matrix divides the nodes in the network into core areas and edge areas according to the closeness of the connections between nodes in the network. This method divides keywords into two types according to the density of network relationships: the core is a cluster of keyword nodes with a closely related pattern, which represents a high degree of structure; the edge is a cluster of keyword nodes with a sparse relationship, which represents association Loose. With UCINET, the core-edge matrix is constructed on the input co-word matrix (Fig. 4). The dense matrix in the upper left corner of the figure is the core area, and the keywords in the area are closely related; the remaining keywords are distributed in the edge area, and the sparse matrix in the lower right corner reflects the looseness of their mutual connections. On the one hand, keywords in the marginal zone reflect their low level of attention and lack of relevant research; on the other hand, they also show that they have a certain research potential. If combined with the current policy orientation, they may become a new round Research hotspots.

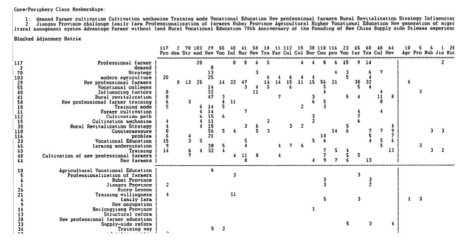

Fig. 4. Core-edge matrix

3.4 New Research Hotspots and Trend Analysis

In order to dig out some potential keywords and focus on new research directions, it is necessary to further filter the edge vocabulary: (1) the core edge matrix is successively divided into subsets and sub graphs, which can be split to obtain the core and edge. Two different matrices; (2) Use the previous set of intermediate centrality as the separation set and then divide the edge matrix into sub-graphs to obtain a matrix M0 with a keyword intermediate degree of zero and a non-zero edge matrix M1; (3) The M1 matrix is processed twice to eliminate the keywords that do not meet the conditions to obtain new research hotspots.

The first two steps mentioned above can be completed by the sub-set division and sub-graph division functions of the UCINET software, which will not be repeated here. So how to define which keywords should be eliminated in the third step? The author considers from two levels: (1) from the perspective of time, keywords with a closer year are more likely to become hotspots. According to the time when the keywords first appeared, remove those that appeared before 2015 in the M1 matrix. Keywords; (2) from the perspective of centrality, the centrality of a point is closely related to the centrality of its neighbors. For example, in a school, if some students are very popular and they like another student very much, then this student must also be very popular. In the social network, those actors who themselves receive a lot of information are also more valuable information. Source [25]. The eigenvector centrality measurement proposed by Bonacich is based on this idea. He believes that if a point is related to other points that are at the core of itself, the point is also at the core, and the status of an actor is related to other points. A linear function of the status of the actor [27]. According to the centrality of the keyword feature vector in Table 1, sort the keywords appearing in the M1 matrix, and then eliminate the keywords with little meaning, such as "revelation", "challenge" and other words, the final word The table is shown in Table 2:

Table 2. Feature vector centrality screening table

Key words	Eigenvector centrality
Targeted poverty alleviation	19.927
Internet+	11.547
Agricultural supply-side structural reform	9.355
family farm	6.186
logistic model	5.338
New agricultural management system	5.287
Binary logistics	4.67
Modern apprenticeship	4.458
Professionalism	3.815
Analytic hierarchy process	3.488
Performance	3.047
efficacy	3.039
Precision cultivation	2.94
Open education	2.94
Training mode	2.099
Innovation and entrepreneurship education	1.481
Micro lesson	1.226
Training path	0.712

The above research mainly focuses on individual marginal words and excavates the status of individuals in the group in which they belong. However, sometimes our research may focus more on the relationship between these words. How can they be brought together to condense new research topics? For this reason, the author makes further discussion from the perspective of cohesive subgroup.

3.5 Cluster Analysis

The cohesive subgroup satisfies the following conditions-a subset of actors, that is, the actors in this set have relatively strong, direct, close, frequent, or positive relationships. The applied research on agglomerated subgroups has gone deep into various fields. For example, agglomerated subgroups are used to reveal the hierarchical characteristics of urban network link strength [28]; the influence of the strength of agglomerated subgroups on the speed of word-of-mouth information is used to improve the communication model [29]; Take the main path as the seed document to extract the condensed subgroups to show the domain evolution structure [30] and so on.

Condensed subgroups are a broad concept of subgroups, including a variety of specific types, such as factions, k-nuclei, lambda sets, and the aforementioned core-periphery, etc. The "component" subgroups can target multiple polarities. The network graph of large connected sub-graphs is divided into sets. Although simple, it can sometimes provide us with sufficient useful information. Select Network/Regions/Components/Simple graphs to operate the line, the result is shown in Fig. 5. It can be seen that these edge words have been divided into 5 sets, which is basically the same as the visualization results displayed when the edge matrix M1 is imported into Visualize/NetDraw (Fig. 6). Although the keywords in the cohesive subgroup are not as popular as the previous core keywords, they belong to the same set, indicating that they have a strong dependence. For example, words such as "modern apprenticeship" and "micro lessons" reflect farmers Changes in training and education methods; "precise poverty alleviation" is inseparable from the support of policies and systems such as "supply side", "structural reforms", "vocational colleges" and "Internet+"; "dual logistic" is the current "training More methods are used in modeling research of "willingness".

Sometimes we should not only focus on the nature of the relationship within the subgroup, but also analyze the characteristics of the relationship within and outside the subgroup. Therefore, it is necessary to promote the concept of "components", which is a condensed subgroup. "Block" is such a concept. It divides each actor in a network into discrete subsets according to certain standards, and calls these subsets "Location" can also be called "clustering" [25]. Before clustering, I first streamline the matrix M1, remove some words with similar edges or similar meanings, and finally get a new matrix M2 with only 19 words, expand along the path of Network → Roles & Positions → Structural → CONCOR, Cluster analysis of words (Fig. 7) can group the 19 marginal words into four groups, and summarize them into four themes of cultivation model exploration, cultivation mechanism reform, cultivation policy support, and cultivation demand change, which shows that the current research The shortcomings also point out the future research direction.

```
Components with 2 or more members
  1   family farm Professionalization of farmers Agricultural Vocational Education efficacy Training path
  2   Structural reform Micro Lesson mode Lifelong education Cultivation model logistic model Rural Vocational Education Supply side Vocational College Urbanization Vocational Education a:
  3   Training willingness New agricultural management system human capital Professionalism Farmer education Binary logistics New Countryside Construction Operating mechanism
  4   Recognition standard Identification management
  5   Beautiful village Cultural quality

Component size heterogeneity  0.870
Normalized heterogeneity  0.886
Entropy  2.675
Normalized entropy  0.665
Fragmentation  0.886 (prop. of nodes that cannot reach each other)
```

Fig. 5. Results of component subgroups

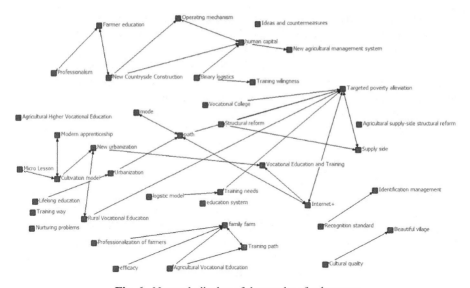

Fig. 6. Network display of the results of subgroups

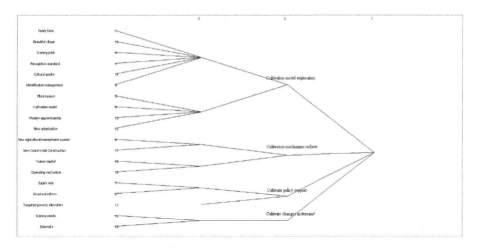

Fig. 7. Cluster analysis results

4 Conclusion

This article uses bibliometrics and graph analysis methods to analyze the literature on new occupations in my country at multiple levels and angles. Summarizing the results of the statistical analysis, the following conclusions are drawn: (1) The research topics related to farmer cultivation are extensive and the content is rich. Excluding the core keywords such as "professional farmer", "new professional farmer" and "new professional farmer training (training)" obtained from the literature search, there are more than 120 keywords, indicating the wide range of research. In addition, the keywords include words related to "cultivation policy", "cultivation path", "cultivation mode", "training demand", "training willingness", etc., indicating that it is enriching cultivation connotation, optimizing cultivation policies, improving cultivation methods, and quantifying cultivation factors. Corresponding research has been conducted in other aspects. (2) The research direction is scattered and the correlation strength is not enough. The measured value of co-word network density is 0.2691. In addition, the core matrix vocabulary in the core-edge partition is small (only 21), and the edge matrix is relatively sparse, indicating that the research direction is too scattered and the cohesion is insufficient. (3) The research method is relatively simple and the depth is not enough. Among the many keyword vocabularies, there are relatively few research methods involved, and there are only keywords such as "dual logistics", "logistics model", "analytic hierarchy process", "factor analysis" and other keywords, and these words are related to other words. Lower. It shows that a large number of studies still prefer to conduct purely descriptive analysis of cases, and insufficient exploration of quantitative analysis and new research methods. There is a lack of research depth for analyzing the causes of cases from a more macro perspective or predicting the future development direction from the time dimension [5]. (4) The scope of research needs to be expanded. Analyzing the intensity of hot keywords, it is found that the research on countermeasures to problems and cultivation paths is relatively concentrated. However, the exploration of the cultivation mode under the Internet and big data environment is still slightly weak, although there are also new cultivation methods such as "open education", "micro-classes", and "modern apprenticeship".

Summarizing the techniques and methods used in the analysis process can be obtained: (1) CNKI has a good support for the statistical functions of the document's table time, organization distribution, and personnel distribution, while the CiteSpace software can provide the themes and key points contained in the literature. The words are displayed over time. In addition, the keyword emergence detection function of CiteSpace can also characterize the change of the subject in time, so as to provide a certain basis for the future development of the field. (2) Using VBA programming in EXCEL can convert the co-word matrix output by CiteSpace into the original co-word matrix, and Gephi software can display the overall status of the co-word network map in a visual form. (3) UCINET can perform qualitative and quantitative analysis of the co-word network, such as density measurement to reflect the overall degree of relevance; use the middle centrality function to further quantify the central position of keywords; divide two types of keywords based on core-periphery subgroups Matrix; use the component analysis in the agglomerated subgroup to obtain the correlation between keywords in the edge matrix; use the block agglomerated subgroup to cluster these keywords to condense the topic.

Through the quantitative keyword analysis, it is found that there is almost no training on Farmers' information literacy. With the rapid development of information technology, we need to improve the quality of new occupation farmers, besides building a new mode of cultivation suitable for Internet plus environment, we should also optimize training contents and scientifically set up courses. That is to say, the training content should not only include professional skills courses, but also include public basic courses. The public basic courses not only involve policies and regulations, green development concept and other contents, but also include new professional farmers' information literacy, especially information security literacy. Through the education of information security, the new professional farmers can have a strong awareness of information security, understand the information security situation, clarify the importance of information security to their own development, improve their own information security skills, standardize the use of mobile phones and other electronic devices to participate in training, prevent the leakage of personal information, and how to prevent criminals from using the name of training for fraud.

Acknowledgments. This work was supported by the Hainan Provincial Natural Science Foundation (618ms025); the Hainan Higher Education and Teaching Reform Research (hnjg2020-12).

References

1. Wu, Z.: On the cultivation of new-type professional farmers under the new situation. Agric. Econ. **04**, 67–69 (2018)
2. Zhang, Y., Zhu, Q., Cao, Y.: Analysis of influencing factors and policy recommendations on the effect of new-type vocational farmer training. Vocat. Educ. Forum **03**, 108–112 (2018)
3. Chen, J., Zhu, Y.: A review of domestic scholars' research on the cultivation of new-type professional farmers. South. Agric. **12**(29), 139–141 (2018)
4. Liang, C., Huang, X.: The historical origin and connotation interpretation of Xi Jinping's vocational farmer training thought. Qinghai Soc. Sci. **04**, 20–26 (2018)
5. Wang, H., Sun, Z.: Review and prospects of the research on new-type professional farmers in China. Adult Educ. **39**(08), 52–59 (2019)
6. Li, Y., Zhou, J., Zhang, L., et al.: Analysis of the needs and directions of the cultivation of new-type vocational farmers in the future–based on the survey of demand for training of new-type vocational farmers in my country. High. Agric. Educ. **309**(03), 121–125 (2018)
7. Liu, Y., Feng, J.: Research on the issue of cultivating new-type professional farmers under the background of migrant workers returning to their hometowns to start businesses. Rural Econ. Technol. **28**(23), 200–203 (2017)
8. Qu, K., Zuo, D.: Research on the internal construction path of rural revitalization–based on the perspective of village community rationality. J. Southwest Univ. (Soc. Sci. Ed.) **45**(01), 55–61 (2019)
9. Guo, Y.: Analysis of the path of training new-type professional farmers. Contin. Educ. Res. **06**, 38–39 (2016)
10. Liang, C., Shu, H.: Retrospect and prospect of the research on professional farmers in china since the reform and opening-up–based on the perspective of quantitative visual analysis method. J. Southwest Univ. (Soc. Sci. Ed.) **45**(04), 36–46 (2019)
11. Zuo, J., Sun, G., Wu, J.: The hotspots and frontiers of farmer education research in the 70 years since the founding of new China-visual analysis based on knowledge graphs. Contemp. Vocat. Educ. **05**, 89–98 (2019)
12. Wang, X., Jia, R., Wang, D., et al.: Research on the research hotspots and development trends of artificial intelligence in the field of library and information. Libr. Inf. Serv. **63**(01), 70–80 (2019)
13. An, J., Liang, Z., Chen, X.: Research on cyberspace security knowledge graph. Cybersp. Secur. **9**(01), 30–35 (2018)
14. Zhang, H., Xu, H., Zhang, X., et al.: Current status and prospects of user portrait research in the field of library and information at home and abroad. Libr. Inf. Serv. **63**(07), 127–134 (2019)
15. Yang, J., Cheng, C., Shen, S., et al.: Comparison of complex network analysis software: CiteSpace, SCI^2 and Gephi. IEEE (2017)

16. Liu, P., Li, X., Wang, L.: Research on social network analysis software. Comput. Sci. **42**(12), 171–174 (2015)
17. Zhao, S., Long, J., Fan, X., et al.: Visual analysis of new retail model research based on Gephi. E-commerce **04**, 50–52 (2019)
18. Yang, R., Jiang, X.: From the citation perspective of disciplines and journals, the knowledge structure and evolution of interdisciplinary research–an empirical study of library and information disciplines. Libr. Inf. Serv. **62**(05), 30–39 (2018)
19. Huang, S., He, C., Xu, H.: Visualized research on R&D investment and company growth based on Gephi. Electron. Commer. **11**, 30–31 (2019)
20. Lu, W.: Research on author's co-authorship in the field of book collection culture–based on social network analysis. Libr. Res. Work **05**, 43–47 (2019)
21. Liu, H., Li, Y.: research on the academic contributions of important countries in the field of library and information from the time series perspective. Libr. Inf. Serv. **62**(23), 87–96 (2018)
22. Chen, Y., Chen, C., Liu, Z., et al.: Methodological function of CiteSpace knowledge graph. Stud. Sci. Sci. **33**(2), 242–253 (2015)
23. Huang, J., Liu, W.: Literature review and prospects of the study of land-lost farmers in my country–based on bibliometric methods and social network analysis techniques. Local Gov. Res. **3**, 58–70 (2017)
24. John, C.: Social Network Analysis Method. Chongqing University Press, Chongqing (2007)
25. Liu, J.: Lecture Notes on Whole Network Analysis: A Practical Guide to UCINET Software. Gezhi Publishing House, Shanghai (2009)
26. Freeman, L.C.: Centrality in social networks' conceptual clarification. Soc. Netw. **1**(3), 215–239 (1979)
27. Bonacich, P., Holdren, A.C., Johnston, M.: Hyper-edges and multidimensional centrality. Soc. Netw. **26**(3), 189–203 (2004)
28. Sheng, K., Yang, Y., Zhang, H.: Research on the cohesive subgroups and influencing factors of China's urban network. Geogr. Res. **38**(11), 2639–2652 (2019)
29. Liu, X., Qian, X.: Research on word-of-mouth communication mechanism based on agglomerated subgroups. Appl. Res. Comput. **35**(12), 70–73 (2018)
30. Han, Y., Zhou, C., Liu, J.: The domain evolution context of the main path as the seed document and the identification of agglomerated subgroups. Libr. Inf. Serv. **57**(3), 22–26 (2013)

Privacy-Preserving Movie Scoring Algorithm Based on Deep Neural Network

Weinan Song[1], Xinyu Fan[1], Jing Li[2], Aslam Niaz Khan[1], and Lei Wang[1(✉)]

[1] Hainan University, Hainan 570228, China
wanglei@hainanu.edu.cn
[2] Capital Medical University School, Beijing 100050, China

Abstract. The development of modern technology has made the movie recommendation system more and more diverse. However, it will also violate users' privacy and lack the accuracy of recommendation information.This paper proposes a movie scoring algorithm based on deep neural networks. Firstly,user data is processed through homomorphic encryption. The pre-processed user data and movie data are embedded, and at the same time, the natural language text information of the movie name is embedded using word vectors. Then the text convolutional neural network is used to extract the local feature of the movie name vector sequence, and the feature is obtained after semantic fusion. Finally, the fully connected layer was used to jointly model user data and movie data to obtain the user's score prediction for the movie. This method was 0.237, 0.043, 0.057 lower than the user-based collaborative filtering algorithm, Slop one algorithm, and SVD++ algorithm on the MSE. Besides, after using the multi-scale convolution regression proposed in this paper, the MSE further decreases the rate by 0.027 based on the fully connected layer regression model.

Keywords: Movie scoring algorithm · Data privacy · DNN · Text CNN · Fully connected layer

1 Introduction

The recommendation system is one of the most effective ways to solve the problem of information overload. By combining with traditional classification, search engine, and other technologies, it can effectively improve the efficiency of users in obtaining information and bring people a good experience. However, user information leakage and inaccurate recommendation information also affect the trust of users and the development of the industry. Face with a large number of videos, on the one hand, it better protects user privacy, on the other hand, it promotes the evolution and development of scoring algorithm.The research of Chenchen et al. [1] has been able to protect the privacy of the recommendation system well. Currently, the most widely used scoring algorithm is the collaborative filtering algorithm [2]. However, the recommendation accuracy of the traditional collaborative filtering algorithm is still not good,. At present, deep learning technology has achieved great success in the fields of computer vision and natural

© Springer Nature Switzerland AG 2021
J. Cheng et al. (Eds.): CSS 2020, LNCS 12653, pp. 275–289, 2021.
https://doi.org/10.1007/978-3-030-73671-2_24

language processing. In 2012, in the Image Net Image classification competition, the Alex net model proposed by Hilton [3] team achieved amazing results. Aaron proposed a deep music audio content recommendation system by predicting potential factors in 2013 [4]. These papers show that deep convolutional neural networks are significantly better than traditional methods.

To further improve the recommendation accuracy, this paper designs and implements a movie scoring algorithm based on deep neural networks. Firstly, user data is processed through homomorphic encryption. The preprocessed user data and movie data are embedded to map to a feature vector high-dimensional space and each dimension of the vector has its unique semantics. At the same time, the natural language text information of movie names is embedded using word vectors to map movie names to natural language word feature semantic spaces. Then the text convolutional neural network is used to extract the local features of the word vector sequence of movie names, and the features are obtained by semantic fusion. Finally, the fully connected layer is used to jointly model the user data and movie data to obtain the user's scoring prediction for the movie. The mean square error is used to regression fit the predicted value to the true value. This method has significantly improved accuracy compared with the traditional method. To further improve the accuracy of movie score regression prediction; this paper proposes a regression algorithm based on multi-scale convolution, which further improves the model accuracy during the regression prediction stage of the model.

2 Text Convolutional Neural Network

Convolutional neural networks were originally mainly used in the field of computer vision to extract the visual features of images. Convolutional neural networks have strong non-linear mapping capabilities, high self-adaptability, and weight sharing. More and more scholars have explored the application of convolutional neural networks to the field of natural language processing. Neural networks came into being. The core of the text convolutional neural network is to organically combine the "word vector" and the "deep convolutional neural network", and use the word vector as the input of the deep convolutional network.

2.1 Word Vector Embedding

CBOW Language Model
CBOW [5, 6] (Continuous Bag-of-Words Model) is a similar model to forward NNLM, except that CBOW removes the most time-consuming non-linear hidden layer and all words share the hidden layer. As shown in Fig. 1 below, the CBOW model is a prediction $p(w_t|w_{t-k}, w_{t-(k-1)}, \ldots, w_{t-1}, w_{t+1}, \ldots, w_{t+k})$.

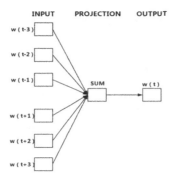

Fig. 1. CBOW language model example

Skip-Gram Language Model [7, 8]

The graph of the Skip-Gram model is exactly the opposite of CBOW. As shown in Fig. 2, Skip-Gram predicts the probability p (wi/wt) (t $-$ c $\leq$ i $\leq$ t $+$ c&i $\neq$ t), c is a constant that determines the size of the context window. The larger c is, the more pairs need to be considered, which can generally bring more accurate results, but the training time will also increase. Assuming a phrase sequence $w_1, w_2, w_3, \ldots, w_T$ exists, the goal of Skip-gram is to maximize:

$$\frac{1}{T}\sum\nolimits_{t=1}^{T}\sum\nolimits_{-c\leq j\leq c, j\neq 0} logp\left(w_{t+j}|w_t\right) \tag{1}$$

Basic Skip-Gram model definition is:

$$p(w_O|w_I) = \frac{e^{v_{w_O}^T v_{w_I}}}{\sum_{w=1}^{W} e^{v_{w_O}^T v_{w_I}}} \tag{2}$$

It is not difficult to see from the formula that Skip-gram is an asymmetric model. If w_k is in its window when w_t is the central word, then w_t must be in the same size window with w_k as the central word. That is:

$$\frac{1}{T}\sum\nolimits_{t=1}^{T}\sum\nolimits_{-c\leq j\leq c, j\neq 0} logp(w_{t+j}|w_t) = \frac{1}{T}\sum\nolimits_{t=1}^{T}\sum\nolimits_{-c\leq j\leq c, j\neq 0} logp(w_t|w_{t+j}) \tag{3}$$

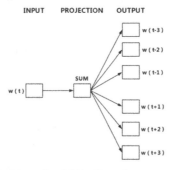

Fig. 2. Example of Skip-Gram language model

At the same time, each word vector in the Skip-gram represents the distribution of the context.

2.2 Text Convolutional Neural Network

Convolutional neural networks were the first algorithms applied to images. In 2014 Yoon Kim proposed a text convolutional neural network for text classification [9]. There is not much difference in structure from the ordinary convolutional neural network for image processing. The main difference is that the input to the network is a word embedding vector, and the convolution kernel is not a square $n * n$ like in a convolutional neural network that processes images.

As shown in Fig. 3, the input layer of the network is a word embedding layer, and the input is a matrix of two-word vectors (a matrix composed of "word-word vectors") of a sentence. The two matrices are identical at first, one of which is defined as *static* and the other as *non-static*. The difference is that the word vector in *non-static* will be changed by "backpropagation" during model training, while the *static* matrix is will not. The purpose of doing this is to better adapt to the vectors in the data set and improve the classification efficiency.

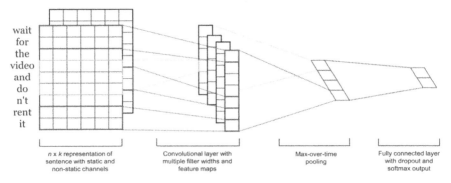

Fig. 3. Example of a text CNN

3   User Information Encryption Design of Movie Scoring Model

3.1 Homomorphic Encryption

According to the types and operations of supported mathematical operations, homomorphic encryption algorithms can be divided into: partial homomorphic encryption algorithm which supports one mathematical operation and does not limit the number of operations; SW homomorphic encryption algorithm which supports specific mathematical operation and limited number of operations; Supports full homomorphic encryption algorithm without restriction of mathematical operation types and unlimited number of operations. Paillier homomorphic Encryption algorithm is adopted in this study, which includes four steps (key generation KeyGen, Encryption, Decryption and verification) [10–12]:

(1) The secret key generated $keyGen() \rightarrow (pk, sk)$.

Two large prime numbers p and q of the same length are randomly selected, and they satisfy $gcd(pq, (p-1)(q-1)) = 1$.

To calculate $N = pq, \lambda = lcm(p-1, q-1)$, Randomly selected $g \in Z_{N^2}^*$. The public key is $pk = (N, g)$, and the private key is $sk = \lambda$.

(2) Encryption algorithm $Encryption(pk, m) \rightarrow c$.

Input public key pk and plaintext information m, randomly selected $r \in Z_N^*$. Calculation ciphertextr is

$$c = g^m r^N (\mathrm{mod} N^2) \tag{4}$$

(3) Decryption algorithm $Decryption(sk, c) \rightarrow m$.

Enter the private key sk and the ciphertext message c, where $L(x) = \frac{x-1}{N}$. Calculate plaintex is

$$m = \frac{L(c^\lambda (\mathrm{mod} N^2))}{L(g^\lambda (\mathrm{mod} N^2))} \mod N \tag{5}$$

(4) Verification algorithm:

$$
\begin{aligned}
E(m_1) \times E(m_2) &= \left(g^{m_1} r_1^n \left(\mathrm{mod} N^2\right)\right) \times \left(g^{m_2} r_2^n \left(\mathrm{mod} N^2\right)\right) \\
&= \left(g^{m_1+m_2} (r_1 \times r_2)^N \left(\mathrm{mod} N^2\right)\right) \\
&= E(m_1 + m_2)
\end{aligned} \tag{6}
$$

3.2 Fully-Connected Layer Regression Scored for Movie Scoring

The movie recommendation system contains a large amount of user data and movie data. When calculating the similarity between users or movies, it is difficult for traditional methods to quickly and efficiently extract features with sufficient recognition from complex massive data. However, neural networks can better extract data features to complete recommendation due to its modeling and prediction ability far beyond the algorithm. The movie scoring model based on deep neural network mainly uses the training data set to model the relationship between user information and movie information, so that a fully connected layer is used to perform regression forecasting using both user features and movie features to get scores. The movie scoring model based on deep neural network designed in this paper is shown in Fig. 4.

The training data set contains user data of user ID, gender, age, and occupation, as well as movie data of movie ID, movie type, and movie name. Among them,the movie name is composed of several words,and the others can use numbers to indicate categories. The first four dates and the last two are embedded with feature vector respectively to extract the corresponding features. The principle of the embedding layer is similar to the principle of word vector embedding. One-hot data is transformed into a dense vector to represent its characteristics, and the implementation of embedded layer function *tf.nn. Embedding_lookup* can be directly called in the tensor flow environment for the movie name data composed of words; the text convolutional neural network is used to extract its features. Then, all features are jointly modeled using a fully connected layer, and user features and movie features are obtained. Thereafter, a fully connected layer with a *sigmoid* function is used for regression forecasting to obtain the final score.

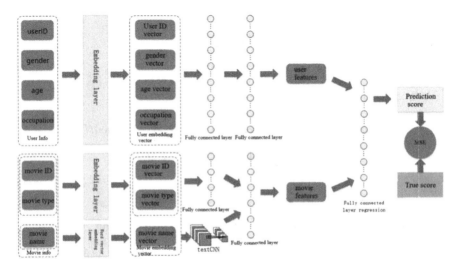

Fig. 4. Movie scoring model based on deep neural network

The algorithm for training the model is mainly as follows, the flowchart is shown in Fig. 5.

(1)　The data set is divided into a training set and a test set, and n samples are selected from the training set and input into the network as a batch:

$$X(n) = (x_1(n), x_2(n), \ldots, x_k(n)) \tag{7}$$

$$Y(n) = y_1(n) \tag{8}$$

X(n) the training data, k is the number of data contained in a sample, and Y(n) is the true label.

(2)　Randomly initialize all parameters of the network.

(3) The batch is fed into the network, and each neuron in the network automatically computes the input and output until the entire network runs. The calculation of neurons can use the following formula:

$$f_{out}(x_{in}) = \sum_{i=1}^{n} (wx_{in} + b)$$ (9)

w is the weight of the neuron and b is the bias of the neuron.

(4) After the final result is calculated by the neural network, the loss function *loss* is established by using the neural network result and the label value. *Loss* is a function of weight and bias. This article uses the *MSE* loss function (mean square error). Then, the partial derivatives of the loss function concerning the weight and the bias are obtained, and the corresponding parameters are updated by using the gradient descent method [13] for backpropagation [14]. The formula of *MSE* is as follows:

$$\text{loss} = \frac{1}{2} \sum \left(y_{pred} - y_{true} \right)^2$$ (10)

The formula for gradient descent backpropagation is as follows:

$$w = w - \alpha \frac{\partial loss}{w}$$ (11)

$$b = b - \alpha \frac{\partial loss}{b}$$ (12)

α is the learning rate.

(5) When the number of iteration steps reaches the set maximum number of iterations or the *loss* drops to a reasonable stable value, the training ends, otherwise return to step (3).

(6) The test set is entered into the network for testing, and the algorithm ends.

3.3 Multi-scale Convolution Regression Scored Movie Scorings

Movie score prediction is a typical regression problem, that is, it is desirable to design a movie score prediction model so that the predicted score of the model is as close as possible to the real movie score. Commonly used regression methods include linear regression [15], Logistic regression [16], support vector machine regression (SVM) [17], etc. In recent years, due to the rise of neural networks, some scholars began to use neural networks for regression prediction [18, 19]. Due to the powerful modeling ability of the neural network, it can achieve better results than traditional regression methods. The most common neural network regression method is to use fully connected neural networks for regression prediction. Regression prediction is a key step for the movie scoring system to get the final score, so the quality of the regression model directly affects the performance of the final score. The previous section used the simplest fully connected neural network regression method. This section improved it. This section proposes a regression prediction algorithm based on multi-scale convolution, as shown in Fig. 6.

Fig. 5. Flow chart of movie scoring model based on deep neural network

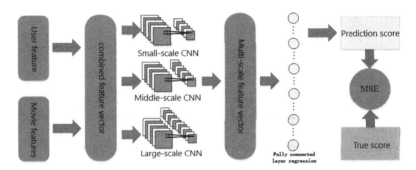

Fig. 6. Regression forecasting algorithm based on multi-scale convolution

4   Experimental Design and Analysis

4.1   Introduction to Data Set and Experimental Environment

Data Set Introduction

The data used in this article has been encrypted.

This article uses *MovieLens1M*. This data set is collected by *Movie Lens* [20] movie video website user scorings given to the movie, and then organized by the *Group lens* group. Now it is widely used in the research of movie recommendation algorithm. The details of the data set are shown in Table 1.

Users rate the video as an integer between 1 and 5. A score of 1 indicates that the user does not like the movie, and a score of 5 indicates that the user particularly likes the movie.

The data set consists of three files: users.dat, movies.dat, and scoings.dat.

Table 1. Details of the MovieLens1M dataset

Dataset	User data	Number of movies	Number of scorings
MovieLens1M	6040	3544	993482

(1) User data

User data includes user ID, gender, age, occupation ID, zip code, and the data format is User ID: Gender: Age: Occupation: Zip-code. Among the age data, 0 represents below 18, 1 represents 19–24, 2 represents 25–34, 3 represents 35–44, 4 represents 45–49, 5 represents 50–55, and 6 represents 56 or more. Career data 0: "other" or not specified, 1: "academic/educator", 2: "artist", 3: "clerical/admin", 4: "college/grad student", 5: "customer service", 6: "doctor/health care", 7: "executive/managerial", 8: "farmer", 9: "homemaker", 10: "K-12 student", 11: "lawyer", 12: "programmer", 13: "retired", 14: "sales/marketing", 15: "scientist", 16: "self-employed", 17: "technician/engineer", 18: "tradesman/craftsman", 19: "unemployed", 20: "writer". Part of the data is shown in Fig. 7:

```
101::F::18::3::33314
102::M::35::19::20871
103::M::45::7::92104
104::M::25::12::00926
105::M::45::12::90277
106::F::35::11::79101
107::M::45::18::63129
108::M::25::12::30316
109::M::45::15::92028
110::M::25::2::90803
111::M::35::15::55416
112::M::25::16::97209
113::M::18::12::37032
114::F::25::2::83712
115::M::25::17::28083
116::M::25::17::55744
117::M::25::17::33314
118::M::35::17::22315
119::F::1::10::77515
120::M::25::11::27106
```

Fig. 7. Example of user data

(2) Movie data

Movie data contains movie ID, movie name, and movie type. The data format is Movie ID: Title: Genres. Part of the data is shown in Fig. 8:

(3) Scoring data

The scoring data includes user ID, movie ID, scoring, time stamp, and the data format is User ID: Movie ID: scoring: Timestamp. Part of the data is shown in Fig. 9:

Introduction to the Experimental Environment

The experiment was performed in *Ubuntu 16.04* environment, and the running memory

```
1::Toy Story (1995)::Animation|Children's|Comedy
2::Jumanji (1995)::Adventure|Children's|Fantasy
3::Grumpier Old Men (1995)::Comedy|Romance
4::Waiting to Exhale (1995)::Comedy|Drama
5::Father of the Bride Part II (1995)::Comedy
6::Heat (1995)::Action|Crime|Thriller
7::Sabrina (1995)::Comedy|Romance
8::Tom and Huck (1995)::Adventure|Children's
9::Sudden Death (1995)::Action
10::GoldenEye (1995)::Action|Adventure|Thriller
```

Fig. 8. Movie data example

```
1::Toy Story (1995)::Animation|Children's|Comedy
2::Jumanji (1995)::Adventure|Children's|Fantasy
3::Grumpier Old Men (1995)::Comedy|Romance
4::Waiting to Exhale (1995)::Comedy|Drama
5::Father of the Bride Part II (1995)::Comedy
6::Heat (1995)::Action|Crime|Thriller
7::Sabrina (1995)::Comedy|Romance
8::Tom and Huck (1995)::Adventure|Children's
9::Sudden Death (1995)::Action
10::GoldenEye (1995)::Action|Adventure|Thriller
```

Fig. 9. Example of scoring data

was 8G. The development language is *python3.6*, and the deep learning platform used is *tensor flow* developed by *Google* [21]. Also, some Python toolkits such as *jumpy, pandas, sklearn*, etc. are also used.

4.2 Data Set Preprocessing and Network Hyperparameter setting

Data Set Preprocessing

Zip code data and timestamp data were not used in the experiment, and the user ID, occupation, and movie ID remained in the original data form. For the gender field, this article converts F and M into computer-process able 0 and 1. For the age field, this paper divides it into 7 consecutive ages from 0 to 6. For the movie category field, first convert the categories in it to a dictionary mapping of strings to numbers, and then turn the category field of each movie into a list of numbers. Some movies are combinations of multiple categories. For the movie name field, first remove the year from the movie name, then create a dictionary of text to Numbers, and finally turn the description in the movie name into a list of Numbers. The length of the field of movie category and movie name needs to be uniform for neural network processing. The missing part is filled with the number corresponding to <PAD> in this article. Partially processed data is shown in Tables 2 and 3:

Table 2. Partially processed user data

Date	User ID	Gender	Age	Occupation
1	1	0	0	10
2	2	1	5	16
3	3	1	6	15
4	4	1	2	7
5	5	1	6	20

Table 3. Partially processed movie data

Date	Movie ID	Movie name	Movie type
1	1	[310, 2184, 634, 634, 634, 634, 634, 634, 634,...	[0, 18, 7, 17, 17, 17, 17, 17, 17, 17, 17, 17, ...
2	2	[1182, 634, 634, 634, 634, 634, , 634, 634, 634, ...	[3, 18, 8, 17, 17, 17, 17, 17, 17, 17, 17, 17, ...
3	3	[5011, 4744, 2629, 634, 634, 634, 634, 634, 63...	[7, 9, 17, 17, 17, 17, 17, 17, 17, 17, 17, 17, ...
4	4	[4095, 1535, 1886, 634, 634, 634, 634, 634, 63...	[7, 5, 17, 17, 17, 17, 17, 17, 17, 17, 17, 17, ...
5	5	[3563, 1725, 3790, 3727, 838, 343, 634, 634, 6...	[7, 17, 17, 17, 17, 17, 17, 17, 17, 17, 17, 17...

Network Hyperparameter Setting

The hyperparameters of the deep neural network will have some influence on the experimental results, so the reasonable selection of hyperparameters is a very important issue. For example, if the dimension of the feature vector is too large, the network training time will be too long, and it is so difficult to fit; if the dimension of the feature vector is too small, which will lead to the lack of feature information and the bad learning effect of network. If the number of neurons is too much, the training time of the network will be longer; if the number of neurons is too little, the fitting ability of the network will be insufficient. The iteration cycle is the number of times that the entire network learns completely over the entire data set. The *batch size* [19] is the number of data samples sent into the network at one time. Too much of it will lead to too much computation of network training, and too little will make the network training fluctuate greatly and affect the training effect. Dropout is a parameter to prevent network overfitting. If it is too large, too much noise in the network will make the network fitting more difficult. The Learning rate is the step size of the network using a gradient descent method to find the optimal solution. If it is too large, the network will cross the optimal solution, while if it is too small, it will not only slow the training speed, but also make the network fall into the local optimal, which will affect the final network performance. After experimental adjustments, the final hyperparameters of the network structure are shown in Table 4, and the training hyper-parameters of the network are shown in Table 5:

Table 4. Network structure hyperparameters

Parameter	Setting value
User ID feature embedding dimension	32
Gender feature embedding dimension	16
Age feature embedding dimension	16
Occupational characteristics embedded dimension	16
Movie ID feature embedding dimension	32
Movie genre feature embedding dimension	32
Movie name feature embedding dimension	32
Number of neurons in the first fully connected layer of user data	128
Number of neurons in the second fully connected layer of user data	200
Movie name text convolution network convolution kernel	8
Number of neurons in the first fully connected layer of movie data	64
Number of neurons in the second fully connected layer of movie data	200

Table 5. Training hyperparameters

Parameter	Setting value
Iteration cycle	10
Batch size	256
Dropout proportion	0.25
Learning rate	0.001

4.3 Experimental Results and Analysis

In this paper, a movie scoring prediction model based on deep neural networks is designed and trained, and verified on the *MoiveLen1M* dataset. The network randomly selects 256 samples from the processed data set for training each time. During the training process, the *tensor board* visualization tool that comes with the *tensor flow* can observe the change trend of training loss. As shown in Fig. 10, the training loss of the network decreases continuously with the iteration of the network. Finally stabilize at a level that the training is complete.

To verify the performance of the movie scoring prediction model based on a deep neural network designed in this chapter, this paper compares it with several classic traditional methods. This paper uses the existing algorithm design comparison experiment in the open-source software package Mahout and directly calls its API. The methods used include a user-based collaborative filtering algorithm, the Slop one algorithm, and SVD++ algorithm.

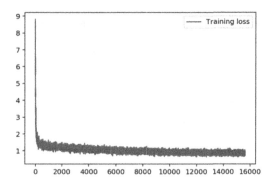

Fig. 10. Training loss change

In the comparison experiment, each algorithm uses the same divided training and test sets. The indicator for evaluating the quality of the algorithm is MSE on the test set [22–24]. MSE represents the mean square error between the predicted value and the real value. The smaller the MSE is, the closer the predicted value of the algorithm is to the true value, and the better the algorithm's effect is. The results of the comparison experiment are shown in Table 6. Since there are some dirty and difficult to fit special data in the data set itself, when the MSE of the algorithm drops to a certain level, due to the reason of the data set, the space for MSE to drop becomes more and more limited and the difficulty becomes greater and greater.

Table 6. Comparative experimental results

Algorithm	MSE
The User-based collaborative filtering algorithm	1.092
Slop one algorithm	0.898
SVD++ algorithm	0.912
Movie scoring model based on deep neural network (fully connected layer regression)	0.855
Movie scoring model based on deep neural network (Multiscale convolution regression)	0.828

5 Conclusions

This paper designs and implements a movie scoring algorithm based on deep neural networks. Firstly, user data is processed through homomorphic encryption to protect user privacy. The pre-processed user data and movie data are embedded to map to a feature vector high dimensional space. At the same time, the word vector is used to embed the movie name into the feature semantic space of the natural language word. Then, the text convolutional neural network is used to extract the local features of the word vector sequence of movie names and obtain the features after semantic fusion Finally, the full connection layer is used to conduct joint modeling of user data and movie data to obtain the user's rating prediction of the movie. The mean square error is used to regression fit the predicted value to the true value. This method is better than the comparison method on MSE. In addition, MSE declines further after using the multi-scale convolution regression proposed in this paper.In the future, the undifferentiated local feature extraction by convolution can be considered to further introduce the attention mechanism of deep learning and focus the model on the extraction of a specific effective feature, to further improve its performance.The robust federated recommendation system can also be studied to further protect user information data.

Acknowledgment. This work was supported by the High-Level Talent Project of the Natural Science Foundation of Hainan Province of China (grant number 2019RC117); Hainan Provincial Scientific Research Funding Projects for Colleges and Universities of China (Hnky2018-95); the National Key Research and Development Program of China (grant number 2016YFC0700804).

References

1. Chen, C., Zhang, J, Anthony, K.H.T., Kankanhalli, M., Chen, G.: Robust federated recommendation system. arXiv:2006.08259 [cs.LG]
2. Jiang, M., Zhang, Z., Jiang, J., Wang, Q., Pei, Z.: A collaborative filtering recommendation algorithm based on information theory and bi-clustering. Neural Comput. Appl. 31(12), 8279–8287 (2019)
3. Montavon, G., Lapuschkin, S., Binder, A., et al.: Explaining nonlinear classification decisions with deep Taylor decomposition. Pattern Recogn. 65, 211–222 (2017)
4. Oord, A.V.D., Dieleman, S., Schrauwen, B.: Deep content-based music recommendation. Adv. Neural Inf. Process. Syst. 26, 2643–2651 (2013)
5. Zhao, R., Mao, K.: Fuzzy bag-of-words model for document representation. IEEE Trans. Fuzzy Syst. 26(2), 794–804 (2017)
6. Xie, R., Liu, Z., Jia, J., et al.: Representation learning of knowledge graphs with entity descriptions. In: Thirtieth AAAI Conference on Artificial Intelligence (2016)
7. Hollis, G., Westbury, C., Lefsrud, L.: Extrapolating human judgments from skip-gram vector representations of word meaning. Q. J. Exp. Psychol. 70(8), 1603–1619 (2017)
8. Bražinskas, A., Havrylov, S., Titov, I.: Embedding words as distributions with a Bayesian skip-gram model. arXiv preprint arXiv:1711.11027 (2017)
9. Kim, Y.: Convolutional neural networks for sentence classification. Eprint Arxiv (2014)
10. Wang, R.B., Li, Y.N., Xu, H.Y., Feng, Y., Zhang, Y.G.: Electronic scoring scheme based on real paillier encryption algorithms. IEEE Access 7, 128043–128053 (2019)

11. Ganesan, I., Balasubramanian, A.A.A., Muthusamy, R.: An efficient implementation of novel paillier encryption with polar encoder for 5G systems in VLSI. Comput. Electr. Eng. **65**, 153–164 (2018)
12. Wu, H.T., Cheung, Y.M., Huang, J.W.: Reversible data hiding in Paillier cryptosystem. J. Vis. Commun. Image Represent. **40**, 765–771 (2016)
13. Bottou, L.: Stochastic gradient descent tricks. In: Montavon, G., Orr, G.B., Müller, K.-R. (eds.) Neural Networks: Tricks of the Trade. LNCS, vol. 7700, pp. 421–436. Springer, Heidelberg (2012). https://doi.org/10.1007/978-3-642-35289-8_25
14. Hecht-Nielsen, R.: Theory of the backpropagation neural network. In: Neural Networks for Perception, pp. 65–93. Academic Press (1992)
15. Tibshirani, R.: Regression shrinkage and selection via the lasso: a retrospective. J. R. Stat. Soc. Ser. B (Stat. Methodol.) **73**(3), 273–282 (2011)
16. Ouyed, O., Allili, M.S.: Group-of-features relevance in multinomial kernel logistic regression and application to human interaction recognition. Expert Syst. Appl. **48**, 113247 (2020)
17. Cortes, C., Vapnik, V.: Support-Vector Networks. Mach. Learn. **20**(3), 273–297 (1995)
18. Qiu, X., Zhang, L., Ren, Y., et al.: Ensemble deep learning for regression and time series forecasting. In: 2014 IEEE Symposium on Computational Intelligence in Ensemble Learning (CIEL), pp. 1–6. IEEE (2014)
19. Sateesh Babu, G., Zhao, P., Li, X.-L.: Deep convolutional neural network based regression approach for estimation of remaining useful life. In: Navathe, S.B., Wu, W., Shekhar, S., Du, X., Wang, X.S., Xiong, H. (eds.) DASFAA 2016. LNCS, vol. 9642, pp. 214–228. Springer, Cham (2016). https://doi.org/10.1007/978-3-319-32025-0_14
20. Harper, F.M., Konstan, J.A.: The movielens datasets: history and context (2015)
21. Abadi, M., Barham, P., Chen, J., et al.: TensorFlow: a system for large-scale machine learning (2016)
22. Smith, S.L., Kindermans, P.J., Ying, C., et al.: Don't decay the learning rate, increase the batch size. arXiv preprint arXiv:1711.00489 (2017)
23. Hahn, J., Hausman, J., Kuersteiner, G.: Estimation with weak instruments: accuracy of higher-order bias and MSE approximations. Econom. J. **7**(1), 272–306 (2010)
24. Mathieu, M., Couprie, C., LeCun, Y.: Deep multi-scale video prediction beyond mean square error. arXiv preprint arXiv:1511.05440 (2015)

Research on a Malicious Code Detection Method Based on Convolutional Neural Network in a Domestic Sandbox Environment

Jianhua Xing[1,2(✉)], Hong Sheng[3], Yuning Zheng[1,2], and Wei Li[1,2]

[1] Beijing Jinghang Computation and Communication Research Institute, Beijing, China
[2] The Classified Information Carrier Safety Management Engineering Technology Research Center of Beijing, Beijing, China
[3] School of Cyber Science and Technology, Beihang University, No. 37, Xue Yuan Road, Beijing 100191, China

Abstract. For malicious code detection, the paper proposes an improved serialization detection method based on convolutional neural network algorithm, it adopts the architecture of "domestic environment virtual sandbox + convolutional neural network detection model + dynamic simulation". First, extract the features of the API sequence, use the Densenet model to detect on the basis of redundant information preprocessing, and then use the characteristics of the convolutional neural network in deep learning to process time series data to directly model and learn the sequence. Finally, based on virtualization technology, a simulation experiment is carried out in the virtual sandbox environment of a domestic safe and reliable operating system. Through three comparative experiments of malicious code detection accuracy, missed detection rate and efficiency, The results show that the improved method has high efficiency and accuracy in detecting a large number of malicious codes, and it can be applied to the detection of malicious codes in a safe and controllable operating system.

Keywords: Industrial information security · Virtualization · Sandbox · Malicious code · Convolutional neural network

1 Introduction

With the in-depth integration of new-generation information technology with key infrastructure industries such as aerospace and power, the Industrial Internet has become a new network infrastructure that promotes the transformation and upgrading of industrial industries and develops the real economy. An important carrier of globalization, industrial information security has become an important component of national security [1]. At the same time, industrial information security faces the influence and threats of a variety of targeted, concealed, and anti-kill malicious attack technologies, among which malicious programs are the most important source of threats in the Internet [2]. There are more and more malicious code attacks against national key infrastructures and industrial control companies, and CNVD contains as many as 2,306 vulnerabilities

J. Cheng et al. (Eds.): CSS 2020, LNCS 12653, pp. 290–298, 2021.
https://doi.org/10.1007/978-3-030-73671-2_25

related to industrial control systems [3]. Most of the current research on malicious code detection is based on feature extraction methods, through feature extraction of the byte-code, assembly code, PE structure or dynamic execution results of the malicious code, and various machine learning algorithms are used to complete the variant detection of the malicious code. For example, a malicious code detection method that extracts the opcode sequence of a malicious code disassembly file and converts it into a dot matrix graph [4], unknown threat code detection method based on partial least squares and nuclear vector machines [5]. Traditional information security protection methods are no longer sufficient to effectively protect industrial information security. Therefore, it is necessary to adopt safe and controllable malicious code detection technology to solve industrial information security problems [6].

This paper adopts the architecture of "domestic environment virtual sandbox + convolutional neural network detection model + dynamic simulation". By constructing a domestic safe and controllable virtual sandbox environment, it captures the API call behavior, network behavior, and files in the running process of malicious code. Dynamic behaviors, such as behaviors, analyze the behavior characteristics of the entire life cycle of the file program to identify threats and vulnerabilities and expose hidden attacks.

2 Principle and Methods

2.1 Virtual Sandbox Simulation of Domestic Environment

Safe and Controllable Environment
This paper combines the operating system and hardware to compile and transplant multiple systems. During the compilation process, the basic libraries needed by the system are constructed first, such as Glibc library, graphics library QT, NGINX/PHP/SSL, etc., to compile and build a static appraiser, Basic equipment components such as dynamic sandbox identification system. Install the selected operating system on the hardware platform, and then compile and build the malicious code detection model on the domestic platform, modify the compilation errors, and install the domestic security and controllable office software into the sandbox to simulate the environment. The behavior rule module conducts dynamic testing and optimizes the simulation environment [7].

Virtual Sandbox
The sandbox is a security mechanism that isolates and executes untrusted software with unknown threats [8]. The virtual sandbox scene simulation is based on a virtualized environment to realize the restoration of attack behaviors of domestically made independent controllable software and scenes [9]. Any known or unknown program that accesses resources in the cloud sandbox system will be strictly controlled and recorded. The virtual sandbox system will adopt redirection technology to virtualize its attack behavior and transfer the harm of unknown threat code to the local computer to the cloud. The shadow resources in the sandbox system directory can prevent the real host operating system of the local computer from being infringed.

Based on virtualization technology, the paper realizes the simulation of the characteristics and application scenarios of the domestically made safe and controllable operating system and office software in the virtual sandbox system, and traps malicious code behavior materials by trapping. By simulating the real user's computer environment and simulating mainstream security and controllable software application scenarios, more comprehensive sample behaviors can be collected. The restored samples that have been recorded to the truest level should have all behaviors. The technical architecture is as follows (Fig. 1):

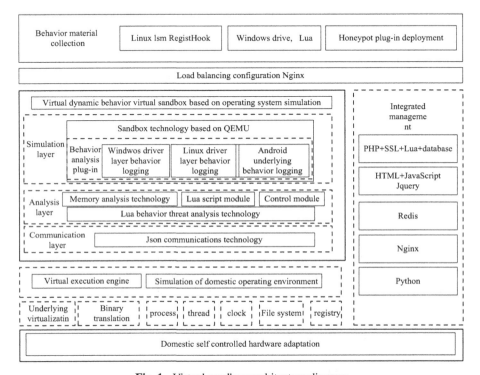

Fig. 1. Virtual sandbox architecture diagram

2.2 Malicious Code Detection Model Based on Convolutional Neural Network Algorithm

The paper mainly focuses on API sequence data, improves the serialization detection scheme based on the convolutional neural network algorithm, uses the improved convolutional neural network model to model and analyze the API sequence, and mines more local related information of the variant sequence, thereby Realize the detection of malicious code variants [10].

Dynamic API Sequence Extraction and Preprocessing

In the malicious code dynamic sequence task, each line in the dynamic behavior file can be regarded as a dynamic behavior, and all the dynamic behaviors obtained by traversing the dynamic behavior logs in all files can be used as the lexicon [11]. The construction of the thesaurus is essentially to encode all the prototype functions of the Windows API, label the words in the thesaurus with consecutive numbers, obtain the mapping from dynamic behavior to the label ID and add an Unknown label to handle future occurrences. Dynamic behavior that has occurred. The following figure shows the process of building and labeling the thesaurus (Fig. 2):

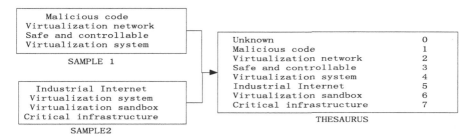

Fig. 2. Schematic diagram of sample dynamic behavior building word database

For the constructed thesaurus, map it to a serialization mode. Each word in the data set, that is, each Windows API, can be represented as a vector, which is generated by random numbers in the initial stage and used in the algorithm process [12]. Forwarding dynamically updates the sequence matrix. If the word vector is already a trained model, it can also be directly input to the next layer in a static manner without updating. The generation and selection process of the lexicon matrix is shown in the figure (Fig. 3).

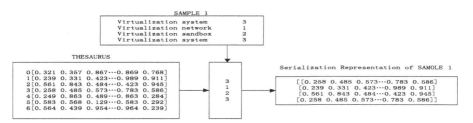

Fig. 3. The sample dynamic behavior log is converted to a full matrix diagram

Improved Malicious Code Detection Method Based on Convolutional Neural Network

The paper first embeds the API vocabulary into a low-dimensional vector in the embedding layer. The convolutional layer uses multiple convolutional checks of different sizes to perform convolution on the embedded word vector. The pooling layer converts the result of the convolutional layer into a long feature vector. And add dropout regularity. The fully connected layer performs backpropagation to update the word vector and convolution kernel parameters according to the penalty agreement of the penalty layer, and finally classifies the results according to the output of the softmax layer.

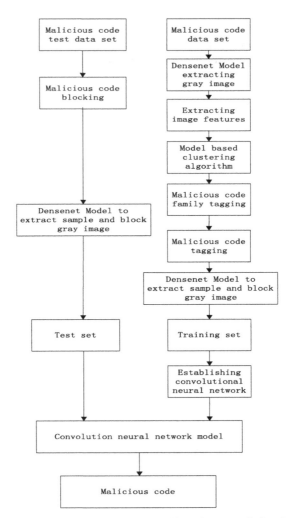

Fig. 4. Improved malicious code detection model based on convolutional neural network

Wherein, the method includes:

a) Use the Densenet model to process the malicious code library, map the malicious code in the library to a file gray image, and extract its gray image features;

b) Use general clustering algorithms, such as hierarchical clustering, density clustering, K-means clustering, etc., to cluster the features of the gray-scale image of malicious code, and perform clustering results based on the Microsoft MSE malicious code analysis equipment Malicious code family annotation;

c) Construct a convolutional neural network to train the gray-scale image recognition model, and set the network structure parameters and training parameters;

d) In the data preprocessing stage, the Densenet model is used to divide the malicious code file into multiple sections. Then, map each section of the malicious code to grayscale images;

e) In the training stage, the convolutional neural network model is trained using the labeled malicious code family files and the file segmented gray-scale image collection, and the classification model is cross-validated and evaluated;

f) In the detection stage, according to the input PE file to be detected, the malicious code file is divided into multiple section sections using the Densenet model, and each section section is converted into a gray image, and the file and its divided gray image are input In the convolutional neural network CNN classification model, it is determined whether the malicious code to be tested is malicious code according to the output result of the model, and the malicious code family is determined (Fig. 4).

3 Experiments and Results

This experiment selects 12,000 unknown threat codes in the CNCERT data set as the experimental objects, and uses detection accuracy and detection time as standards to test the improved malicious code detection method based on convolutional neural networks in this article, and test the performance of each method on this data set [13, 14]. Malicious code detection capabilities. Conclusions can be drawn through the following experiments:

3.1 Comparative Analysis Experiment of Malicious Code Detection Accuracy

The literature [4] method extracts the operation code sequence of the malicious code disassembly file, and transforms it into a bitmap malicious code detection method. The detection accuracy decreases with the increasing number of unknown threat codes in the data set. When there are 10,000 unknown codes, the detection accuracy is less than 30%; the method in literature [5] is a method of converting the malicious code binary executable file into a gray-scale image, and the detection accuracy is poor and has large errors. The detection accuracy of the method in this paper is the highest and most stable. At the same time, because the method is implemented in a virtual sandbox, it is least affected by the number of unknown threat codes, and it can prevent the computer's real host operating system from being infringed (Fig. 5).

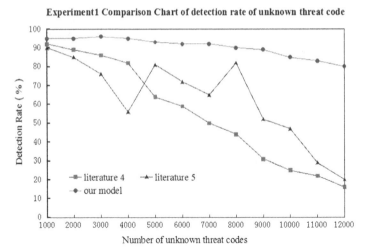

Fig. 5. Comparison Chart of detection rate of unknown threat code

3.2 Comparative Analysis Experiment of Malicious Code Detection Efficiency

Contrast with literature [4] method and literature [5] method. The method in this paper has the faster detection efficiency for unknown threat codes in the data set. This is because the proposed method uses the bag-of-words model method to process the analysis report to eliminate some of them. Redundant and interfering structural information effectively improves the detection efficiency of unknown threat codes (Fig. 6).

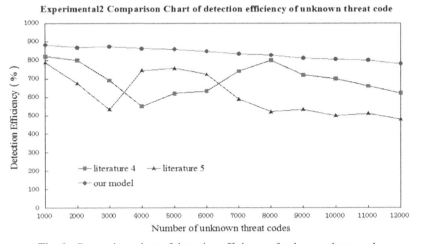

Fig. 6. Comparison chart of detection efficiency of unknown threat code

3.3 Comparative Analysis Experiment on the Missed Detection Rate of Malicious Code

With the increase in the number of malicious codes, the missed detection rate of the methods proposed in [4] and [5] both exceeded 5%. The model in this paper has a lower missed detection rate because of the unknown code analysis in the virtual sandbox, This method can greatly reduce the missed detection rate (Fig. 7).

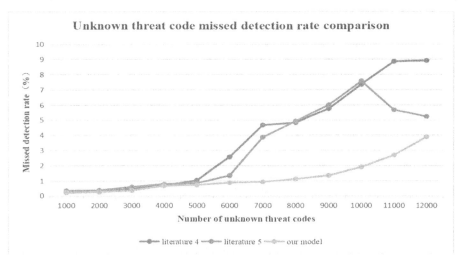

Fig. 7. Comparative analysis experiment on the missed detection rate of malicious code

4 Conclusions

Unknown threat analysis of malicious code is a key technology for realizing network security emergency response, which is of great significance to maintaining national security and stability [15]. Based on a virtualized environment, this paper realizes the behavior collection of running samples in a multi-platform simulation environment, and adapts autonomous controllable application software, scenarios and a variety of safe and controllable application software. Through the simulation of the virtual environment, this article can achieve better triggering malicious strategies for unknown files, expose the behavioral characteristics of malicious code, build a highly realistic honeypot scene, and improve the use of algorithms based on convolutional neural network for API sequence data. The serialization detection program uses an improved convolutional neural network model to model and analyze the API sequence, and mine more local related information of the variant sequence, thereby realizing the detection of malicious code variants.

Acknowledgment. First of all, I would like to thank all the authors for their joint efforts to complete this paper. Second, the authors are highly thankful for National Key Research Program (2019YFB1706001), National Natural Science Foundation of China (61773001), Industrial Internet Innovation Development Project (TC190H46B). And this project supported by Chinese National Key Laboratory of Science and Technology on Information System Security.

References

1. Ahmadi, M., Ulyanov, D., Semenov, S., et al.: Novel feature extraction' selection and fusion for effective malware family classification. In: Proceedings of the Sixth ACM Conference on Data and Application Security and Privacy, pp. 183–194. ACM (2018)
2. Lian, S.: Data backup mechanism based on virtualization. Comput. Syst. Appl. **8**(24), 247–251 (2017)
3. Linn, C., Debray, S.: Obfuscation of executable code to improve resistance to static disassembly. In: Proceedings of the 10th ACM Conference on Computer and Communications Security, pp. 290–299. ACM (2017)
4. Kolbitsch, C., Kirda, E., Kruegel, C.: The power of procrastination: detection and mitigation of execution-stalling malicious code. In: Proceedings of the 18th ACM Conference on Computer and Communications Security, pp. 285–296. ACM (2019)
5. Metz, J.: VMware Virtual Disk (VMDK) format specification [DB/OL], December 2018
6. Kumar, R., Gupta, N., Charu, S., et al.: Open source solution for cloud computing platform using OpenStack. Int. J. Comput. Sci. Mob. Comput. **3**(5), 89–98 (2018)
7. Hong, S., Lv, C., Zhao, T., et al.: Cascading failure analysis and restoration strategy in an interdependent network. J. Phys. A Math. Theor. **49**(19), 195101 (2016)
8. Michail, H., Kakarountas, A.P., Koufopavlou, O., Goutis, C.E.: A low-power and high-throughput implementation of the SHA-1 hash function. In: Kobe, IEEE International Symposium on Circuits and Systems (ISCAS), Japan, pp. 23–26 (2019)
9. Han, K.S., Lim, J.H., Kang, B.J., et al.: Malware analysis using visualized images and entropy graphs. Int. J. Inf. Secur. **14**(6), 1–14 (2019)
10. Lu, X., Jiang, F., Zhou, X., Cui, B., Yi, S., Sha, J.: API based sequence and statistical features in a combined malware detection architecture. J. Tsinghua Univ. (Sci. Technol.) **58**(5), 500–508 (2018)
11. Hong, S., Yue, T., Liu, H.: Vehicle energy system active defense: a health assessment of lithium-ion batteries. Int. J. Intell. Syst. (2020). https://doi.org/10.1002/int.22309
12. Liao, G.H., Liu, J.Y.: A malicious code detection method based on data mining and machine learning. J. Inf. Secur. Res. **2**, 74–79 (2016)
13. Kolosnjaji, B., Zarras, A., Webster, G., Eckert, C.: Deep learning for classification of malware system call sequences. In: Kang, B.H., Bai, Q. (eds.) AI 2016. LNCS (LNAI), vol. 9992, pp. 137–149. Springer, Cham (2016). https://doi.org/10.1007/978-3-319-50127-7_11
14. Tobiyama, S., Yamaguchi, Y., Shimada, H., et al.: Malware detection with deep neural network using process behavior. In: 40th Annual IEEE Conference on Computer Software and Applications (COMPSAC), Atlanta, GA, USA, pp. 577–582. IEEE (2016)
15. Hong, S., Zhu, J., Braunstein, L.A., Zhao, T., You, Q.: Cascading failure and recovery of spatially interdependent networks. J. Stat. Mech. Theor. Exp. **2017**(10), 103208 (2017)

Electricity Sales Forecasting Based on Model Fusion and Prophet Model

Kai Li[1], Jian Li[1], Jun Tang[1], Siming Chen[2], Jiao Wu[1], Yaoheng Xie[1], and Kejiang Xiao[3]([✉])

[1] State Grid Hunan Electric Power Company Limited, Changsha 410004, China
[2] China Southern Power Grid Corporation Kunming Power Supply Bureau, Kunming 650000, China
[3] Hubei Research Center for Educational Informationization, Faculty of Artificial Intelligence in Education, Central China Normal University, Wuhan 430079, China

Abstract. Accurate forecast of electricity sales is a very meaningful task for both electricity companies, security and government departments. This paper proposes a forecasting model for short-term, mid-term and long-term electricity sales respectively. For short-term and mid-term forecasting, we use multiple base models to make predictions and use model fusion methods to get the final prediction results. As for long-term forecasting, the tuned Prophet is used to make a prediction. Through experiments, we found that XGBoost as the base model can achieve the best prediction effect, in which the short-term prediction error can reach 1.97% and the average error of the mid-term prediction is 1.472%. In the long-term forecasting, the MAPE of the entire month of June 2020 is 3.64%. It can be seen that they have achieved good prediction results.

Keywords: Electricity sales forecasting · Model fusion · Prophet · X11

1 Introduction

Electricity plays an important role on human production, data security and life. With the rapid development of China, electricity consumption is increasing rapidly [1]. Electricity consumption is an important indicator to measure the development level of a certain area [2]. Accurate forecasting of electricity consumption is of great significance for managers to make policy. Therefore, electricity consumption forecasting is one of the most important tasks for electric power systems. Electricity sales is an important part of electricity consumption. Forecasting electricity sales can also help electric companies estimate electricity generation. So the forecast of electricity sales is a very meaningful work.

Since the electricity sales data is in the form of a sequence, time series analysis methods are commonly used to analyze electricity sales data in the past studies [3–5]. In order to make more accurate predictions, some researchers used some simple machine learning methods such as linear regression and SVM to predict the electricity sales [6–8].

© Springer Nature Switzerland AG 2021
J. Cheng et al. (Eds.): CSS 2020, LNCS 12653, pp. 299–315, 2021.
https://doi.org/10.1007/978-3-030-73671-2_26

But these simple methods need some real-time features as input data to make predictions and the real-time features are difficult to collect real-time.

In this paper, we first use feature engineering with the decomposed electric load data and the preprocessed electricity data to transform them into the input data of forecasting models. For short-term forecasting and mid-term forecasting, we perform model fusion to several base models. As for long-term forecasting, use the adjusted Prophet to make prediction.

The contribution of this paper is summarized as follows:

(1) We proposed a short-term and mid-term electricity sales forecast model based on an Integrated learning method stacking, which can simultaneously reduce the impact of variance and bias, thereby improving model performance.
(2) We proposed a long-term electricity forecast model based on tuned Prophet model. The tuned Prophet model can work well on electricity sales data with strong volatility and sensitivity.

2 Related Works

There are been many previous researches on electricity sales or consumption based on time series algorithms. Zhang et al. [3] used seasonal adjustment algorithm to decompose the electricity sales curve and predicted the electricity by linear regression. Zheng et al. [4] used LSTM recurrent neural network to predict the household electricity and used the prediction model to home energy management system they proposed. Yang et al. [5] combined with the economic index analysis method and the adjustment of holiday factors to analyze and forecast the time series of electricity sales. These time series analysis algorithms can well control temporal changes and periodic laws, but electricity sales are affected by many factors. So just analyzing the time series of electricity sales is not enough.

There are also simple machine learning models for research. Bianco et al. [6] develop different regression model by using historical electricity consumption, gross domestic product (GDP), gross domestic product per capita (GDP per capita) and population. Cao et al. [7] hybridizes support vector regression (SVR) with fruit fly optimization algorithm and the seasonal index adjustment to forecast monthly electricity consumption. Al-Musaylh et al. [8] made short-term electricity demand forecasting based on Multivariate Adaptive Regression Spline (MARS), SVR, and Autoregressive Integrated Moving Average (ARIMA). These models have obtained high accuracy. But many important factors related to electricity sales are real-time factors and cannot be obtained in real time. In order to solve this problem, some studies directly predict those related factors first, and then predict electricity sales. Liu et al. [9] used X13 seasonal adjustment algorithm to decompose electricity sales, and respectively predicted the decomposition items and merged them to obtain the final prediction result. The work of Sun et al. is more detailed [10]. They forecast monthly electricity consumption based on X12 and Loess (STL) decomposition model, and made more detailed predictions for different influencing factors. However, there are errors in directly predicting related factors, and these errors will accumulate in the final electricity sales forecast.

This paper uses X11 to process electric load data to obtain data that can be input to the machine learning model. At the same time, other relevant observable factor data are processed and used as input at the same time. And use different methods to forecast long-term, short-term and medium-term electricity sales respectively.

3 Overview

The overview of our electricity sales forecasting model is shown in Fig. 1. The overall electricity sales forecast model is divided into five processes, including data preprocessing, feature engineering, electric load curve decomposition and itemized processing, grid optimization, model fusion and Prophet model tuning. They are introduced separately below.

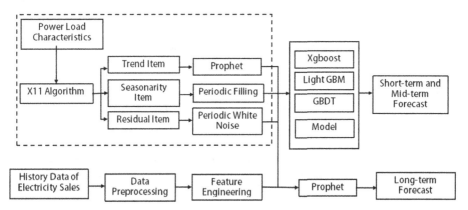

Fig. 1. Overall structure of electricity sales forecasting model.

- Data preprocessing: Data outlier identification and outlier processing.
- Feature engineering: Select and extract relevant features (such as power load, date, temperature, etc.) for modeling data, and perform correlation coefficient or chi-square test on the features to optimize.
- Power load curve decomposition and itemized processing: Use the X11 decomposition algorithm to decompose the power load curve, and decompose to get the trend item, the seasonal item and the residual item. We use Prophet model to predict the trend item. The seasonal item has strong regularity, so we fill it according to the periodic item. And perform LB test on the residual item, if it is judged as a white noise sequence, use random Gaussian model to fill it with white noise.

- Grid optimization: The strong learner model for short-term and mid-term forecasting of electricity sales contains a large number of parameters. Use GridSearchCV to perform a grid search on the parameters to select the optimal parameter combination.
- Model fusion: Use the stacking method for model fusion to further improve the accuracy of the model.
- Prophet model tuning: For long-term forecasting of electricity sales, tuning Prophet model by setting breakpoints, increasing disturbances, setting thresholds and other tuning methods, the electricity sales curve in the long sequence is more realistic.

4 Electricity Forecasting Model

4.1 Data Preprocessing and Feature Engineering

The research extracts 12 features from feature engineering, including electric load (purchase_elecqt), day of year (day_of_year), day of week (day_of_week), year (year), month (month), the id of total week (week_total_id), the id of week of year (week_year_id), whether the day is a holiday (if_holiday), the id of month of year (month_year_id), the id of total month (month_total_id) and the number of holiday (holiday_num).

In addition to date and load, the project also considers relevant weather factors, which are one of the main factors that affect electricity sales. How to deal with weather data is very important to the results of electricity sales forecasts. In this study we preprocess weather data by setting a comfortable temperature range. Generally, people will not take cooling or heating measures at a comfortable temperature. Therefore, this project sets a low temperature threshold temperature and a high temperature threshold temperature for each industry, and only when the actual temperature is lower than the low temperature threshold temperature or higher than the high temperature threshold temperature. When heating or cooling measures are generated, the corresponding heating coefficient and refrigeration coefficient are set, and their quantified value is included as an influencing factor of monthly electricity sales into the prediction model.

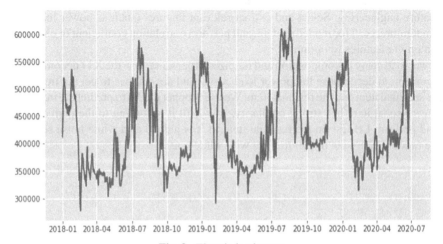

Fig. 2. Electric load curve.

4.2 Electric Load Curve Decomposition

Electric load is a real-time feature. To use electric load to forecast electricity sales, it is necessary to estimate the electricity load first, and use the estimated electricity load as a feature of future electricity sales.

Figure 2 is the electric load curve from January 2018 to July 2019. It can be observed that the cyclic trend of the load curve is relatively stable, and the estimated error will not be too large.

Putting the electricity sales and the electricity load together as Fig. 3 shown, we can find that the curves of the two are very similar. Therefore, it is concluded that power load is a strong correlation real-time feature of electricity sales forecast, which can be accurately estimated.

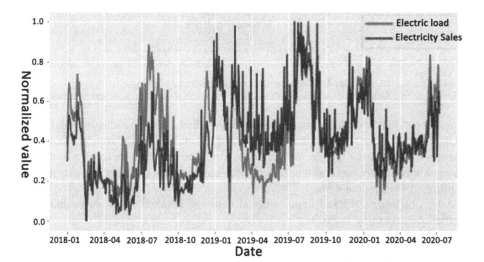

Fig. 3. Relationship diagram between electricity sales and power load.

We use X11 to decompose the curve of electric load. The formula of the additive model of X11 decomposition is as follows:

$$Y = T + S + R \tag{1}$$

i.e., divide the electric load data series Y into a trend item T, a seasonal item S, and the residual item (residual error item) R for the next forecast. [11].

And we will forecast the trend item, the seasonal item and the residual item respectively.

The method used to predict trend items is the Prophet model proposed by Facebook [12]. Compared with other traditional time series models, the Prophet model has the following advantages: (1) More flexible; (2) Don't worry about missing values; (3) The fitting is very fast, making interactive exploration possible; (4) The parameters of the prediction model are very easy to explain, so the analyst can set some parameters based on experience.

The seasonal item is a periodic component decomposed by the curve. Therefore, the seasonal term does not need to be predicted by complicated methods, but only needs to be filled according to the period.

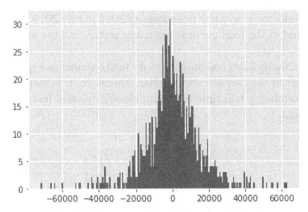

Fig. 4. Histogram of remaining electric load.

As for residual item, according to the probability distribution in its histogram (Fig. 4) and the LB test, it can be found that the residual data conforms to the standard Gaussian noise model. This means that the residual items cannot be predicted (because it is random data), and accordingly, just continue to generate Gaussian noise (white noise) to complete the filling of the residual items.

After obtaining the trend item, seasonal item and residual item, we estimate the electric load according to Eq. 1.

4.3 Short-term and Mid-term Electricity Sales Forecasting

The estimated power load is added as a new feature to the short-term and mid-term forecasts of electricity sales. The selected forecasting models are Gradient Boosting Decision Tree (GBDT) [13], XGBoost [14] and Light Gradient Boosting Machine (LightGBM) [15].

GBDT is an algorithm implemented by multiple decision trees based on Boosting. It consists of multiple decision trees, and the conclusions of all trees are added together to make the final answer. When it was proposed, it was considered as an algorithm with strong generalization ability together with SVM. The model has the advantages of good training effect and not easy to overfit.

XGBoost is an efficient implementation of GBDT. It mainly optimizes the following three aspects of GBDT. One is the optimization of the algorithm itself. XGBoost adds regularization to the loss function, and unlike the loss function of GBDT, only the first-order Taylor expansion is performed on the error part, and the XGBoost loss function is the second-order Taylor expansion on the error part. The second is the optimization of algorithm operation efficiency. Make parallel selections for each weak learner, such as the process of decision tree building, to find suitable subtree split features and eigenvalues.

The third is the optimization of algorithm robustness. The third is the optimization of algorithm robustness. For the features of missing values, the processing method of missing values is determined by enumerating whether all missing values enter the left subtree or the right subtree at the current node. The regularization term is added to prevent over-fitting and has a stronger generalization ability.

LightGBM is a framework that implements the GBDT algorithm, supports high-efficiency parallel training, and has the advantages of faster training, lower memory consumption, and better accuracy. At the same time, LightGBM has distributed support and can quickly process massive data.

After obtaining these three forecasting models, we perform model fusion to these models. Model fusion is to train multiple models, and then integrate multiple models according to a certain method, such as voting, averaging, stacking, etc. We choose stacking as the method of model fusion. Simply put, stacking is to design several separate models, perform K-fold cross-validation to output the prediction results, then merge the prediction results output by each model into new features, and train the base model, so as to improve the accuracy of the model.

4.4 Long-term Electricity Sales Forecasting

In this study, we use the improved Prophet model to predict long-term electricity sales. The Prophet model has been used in the forecast of the trend item of the electric load. Compared with electricity load, the volatility and sensitivity of electricity sales data are stronger, so Prophet model needs to be optimized. For seasonal disturbances, weekly (7 days), monthly (30.5 days) and annual (365.5 days) variables are added, and weekend and holiday fluctuations are added. The growth trend line and threshold are set to make the overall trend as realistic as possible.

5 Experiment

5.1 Data Set

The data used in this study are the daily electricity sales from January 2018 to June 2020, the monthly electricity sales and power load data from January 2011 to June 2020 in a province in China. We use the data of April, May, and June in 2020 as the test set.

5.2 Data Preprocessing

The first step is to set the low temperature and high temperature threshold temperature. First, we count the daily electricity sales and daily average temperature in Hunan Province in 2019, then draws the daily average temperature-daily electricity sales scatter diagram and draws the fitting curve, and finally analyzes the curve trend to set the threshold. Figure 5 is a scatter diagram of the relationship between daily average temperature and total electricity sales. According to the analysis, it can be concluded that the low and high temperature thresholds for residential electricity consumption are 15 °C and 25 °C respectively.

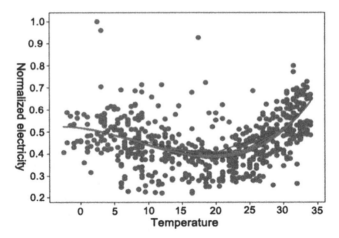

Fig. 5. Daily average temperature-daily electricity sales scatter plot.

After setting the high temperature and low temperature thresholds, the heating coefficient and cooling coefficient are calculated according to the thresholds. The heating coefficient represents the average temperature below the low temperature threshold temperature. The larger the heating coefficient, the lower the temperature and the greater the heating intensity required. And the refrigeration coefficient indicates the magnitude of the average temperature above the high temperature threshold temperature. The larger the refrigeration coefficient, the higher the temperature and the greater the refrigeration intensity required. When the temperature is higher than the low temperature threshold temperature or lower than the high temperature threshold temperature, it is in the comfort zone, and no heating or cooling measures are taken. The calculation formula of daily heating coefficient and refrigeration coefficient is as follows:

$$hd_i = max\ (T_{low} - T_i, 0) \tag{2}$$

$$cd_i = max\ (T_i - T_{high}, 0) \tag{3}$$

hd_i and cd_i are denoted as the heating coefficient and cooling coefficient respectively in day i. T_{low} and T_{high} are denoted as low temperature threshold temperature and high temperature threshold temperature respectively, and the value of them can be determined according to the daily average temperature-daily electricity sales scatter diagram and its fitting curve diagram for each industry. T_i is the daily average temperature of the day.

After obtaining the daily heating coefficient and refrigeration coefficient, the corresponding temperature coefficient is obtained:

$$HCD_i = \alpha * hd_i + cd_i \tag{4}$$

Where hd_i and cd_i are the heating and cooling coefficients on the i-th day, respectively. And α is calculated by the following formula:

$$\alpha = \frac{\sum_{X=2018}^{2019} S_{7:8}/S_{1:2}}{X} \tag{5}$$

The electricity sales in the m-th month of the X year are recorded as $S_{m:m+1}$. The peak electricity sales are generally in January and July, so it is $S_{7:8}/S_{1:2}$. α is the average value of the ratio of peak electricity sales in 2018 and 2019.

After extracting and sorting out relevant feature information, filter the features and adopt the spearman correlation coefficient. The correlation coefficient is shown in Table 1. The features with a correlation coefficient greater than 0.05 are selected as the features of the final data set.

Table 1. Spearman correlation coefficients of all Features and electricity sales.

Feature name	Spearman
day_of_week	0.033597
month_year_id	0.040365
day_of_year	0.042342
month	0.049902
week_year_id	0.058902
if_holiday	0.082758
day_of_month	0.085564
holiday_num	0.095444
month_total_id	0.426949
week_total_id	0.429911
year	0.468665
purchase_elecqt	0.733308
conselecqt	1.000000

5.3 Electric Load Curve Decomposition

Decompose the original electric load data series into a trend item, a seasonal item, and a remaining item (residual error item) by using X11 for the next forecast. The decomposition effect is shown in Fig. 6.

For the trend item, we use Prophet model to perform the forecasting. And Prophet uses the default parameters when predicting the electric load here. Prophet's prediction curve is shown in Fig. 7. Among them, the MAPE in April was 6.379%, the MAPE in May was 5.929%, and the MAPE in June was 0.761%. From the curve and error, we can see that there was an abnormal decrease during the epidemic. The overall trend item is accurate.

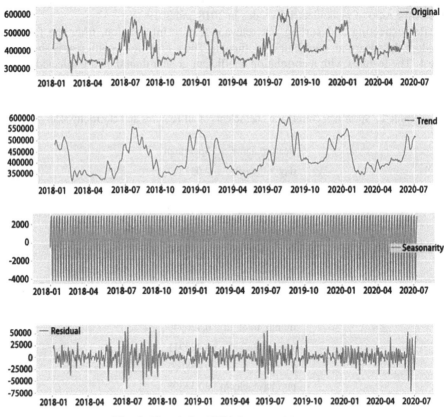

Fig. 6. Electric load X11 decomposition curve.

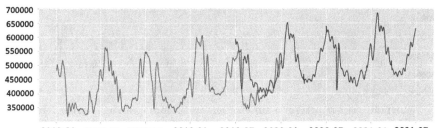

Fig. 7. Electric load trend item forecast curve.

The filling effect of seasonal item is shown in the Fig. 8.

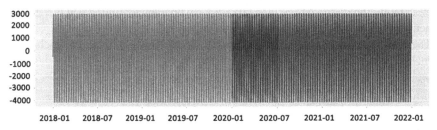

Fig. 8. Filling curve diagram of power load seasonal item.

We fill in the residual item by generating Gaussian noise. And the filling effect is shown in the Fig. 9.

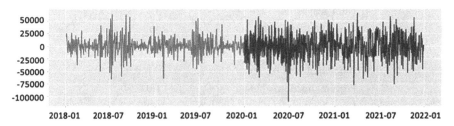

Fig. 9. Filling curve diagram of residual items of electric load.

After forecasting and filling the trend items, seasonal items and residual items, we restore the electric load data by calculate the sum of them according to Eq. 8. The restoring effect is shown in Fig. 10. Among them, MAPE in April was 5.93%, MAPE in May was 3.38%, and MAPE in June was 0.761%. According to the monthly error of the second quarter, it can be proved that the load evaluation is feasible.

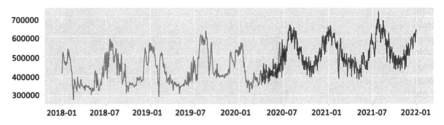

Fig. 10. Electric load forecast curve.

5.4 Short-term and Mid-term Electricity Sales Forecasting

We use GridSearchCV to select the optimal parameters of GBDT, XGBoost and Light-GBM. GridSearchCV uses the current parameter tuning that has the greatest impact on the model until the optimization; then takes the next parameter tuning that has the most impact, and so on, until all the parameters are adjusted.

The parameters determined by GridSearchCV are shown in Table 2, which are the optimal parameters of each model to the training set.

Table 2. The optimal parameters of GBDT, XGBoost and LightGBM.

	GBDT	XGBoost	LightGBM
Learning rate	0.2	0.1	0.005
n_estimators	1030	170	5157
Metric	–	–	Mae
Max_depth	3	4	4
Num_leaves	–	–	5
Min_child_samples	–	–	20
Min_child_weight	–	8	0
Bagging_fraction	–	–	0.5
Feature_fraction	–	–	1.0
Reg_alpha	–	0.5	0.08
Reg_lambda	–	1	0
Min_samples_split	130	–	–
Min_samples_leaf	60	–	–
Gamma	–	0	
subsample	–	0.8	–

And Next, we perform model fusion on the optimal models obtained by Grid-SearchCV. Figure 11 is the curve chart of short-term and mid-term forecasting results. And the detailed forecasting results are shown in the Table 3.

According to Table 3, the daily error of each model is about 6.5–7%, the 7-day error is about 3.5–4%, the 15-day error is about 1.8–2.8%, and the monthly error is about 0–3%. The model fusion method with xgboost as the base model has the best effect. The error in 15 days can reach 1.97%, and the average error in April, May, and June can be reduced to 1.472%.

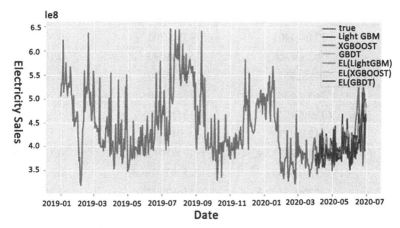

Fig. 11. Curve chart of short-term and mid-term forecasting.

Table 3. Short-term and mid-term electricity sales forecast errors of each model.

Mape (%)	Daily	7 days	15 days	4 months	5 months	6 months	Second quarter
LightGBM	7.002	3.963	2.815	2.553	2.615	0.366	1.845
XGBoost	6.465	3.604	2.240	0.972	1.071	4.178	2.074
GBDT	7.014	3.993	2.110	1.715	1.238	2.407	1.786
EL(lgb)	6.845	4.041	2.165	0.566	0.292	4.624	1.828
EL(xgb)	6.905	4.027	1.970	0.133	0.014	4.269	1.472
EL(gbdt)	6.886	3.902	2.316	0.257	0.507	5.390	2.051

According to the forecast error, the selected model is based on XGBoost, and XGBoost, LightGBM and GBDT are combined. The model uses a 15-day cycle, monthly electricity consumption for three months from April to June, and the overall quarter of the second quarter. The electricity sales short-term and mid-term forecast results are shown in Table 4.

Table 4. Forecast results of short and medium-term electricity sales in April, May, and June in 2020.

Date	Real electricity sales	Forecast electricity sales	MAPE
4.1–4.15	5721915407	5743509700	0.377396229
4.16–4.30	5762598366	5756301090	0.109278411
5.1–5.15	5908824579	5778365800	2.207863472
5.16–5.30	5965766882	6071295130	1.768896608
5.31–6.14	6179979786	5813112060	5.936390385
6.15–6.29	6812189773	6640018480	2.527400122
April	11484513772.9	11499810790.0	0.133196907
June	12254688369	12252921830.0	0.014415209
July	13075093129.5	12516875020.0	4.269324157
Second quarter	36814295271.4	36269607640.0	1.479554688

5.5   Long-term Electricity Sales Forecasting

For long-term forecasting, we adjust the parameters of Prophet. The Prophet parameter component curve is shown in the Fig. 12. From top to bottom, it is trend component, holiday component, weekly component, annual component, monthly component, and weekend (holiday) component.

In addition, Prophet can manually set mutation points to more accurately capture the overall trend of the data. The mutation point setting curve is shown in Fig. 13. And the long-term forecast is currently judged based on the forecast results in June and July 1–8 in 2020 and the overall curve fitting trend. The average error for 7 days is 8.24%, the error for 15 days is 7.49%, MAPE for June is 3.64%, and MAPE for July 1–8 is 0.29%. The long-term forecast curve of electricity sales is shown in Fig. 14.

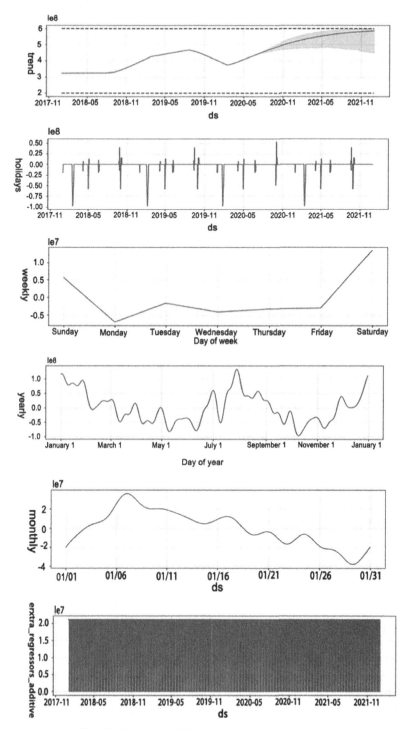

Fig. 12. Prophet model parameter component curve.

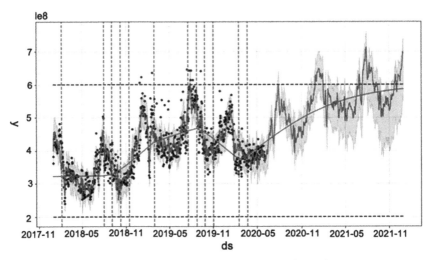

Fig. 13. Prophet model manually set mutation points.

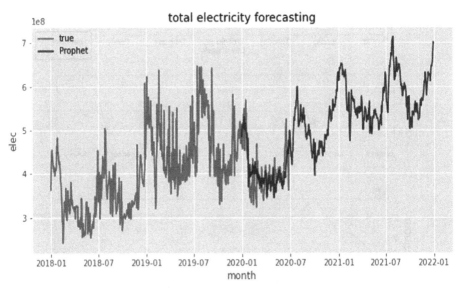

Fig. 14. Curve chart of Prophet model long-term electricity sales forecasting.

6   Conclusion

The electricity sales forecasting model that proposed in this paper can achieve good accuracy whether in the short-term, mid-term or the long-term electricity sales forecasting. Even after experiencing the new crown epidemic in 2020, it has achieved good prediction results, which shows that it can accurately capture the trend of electricity sales.

Acknowledgement. This work was supported in part by the National Natural Science Foundation of China under Grant No. 61803391, and in part by the Hunan Provincial Natural Science Foundation of China under Grant No. 2019JJ50803.

References

1. Zhou, S., Teng, F.: Estimation of urban residential electricity demand in China using household survey data. Energy Policy **61**, 394–402 (2013)
2. Burney, N.: Socioeconomic development and electricity consumption A cross-country analysis using the random coefficient method. Energy Econ. **17**(3), 185–195 (1995)
3. Zhang, Y., Han, X., Yang, G.: A novel analysis and forecast method of electricity business expanding based on seasonal adjustment. In: 2016 IEEE PES Asia-Pacific Power and Energy Engineering Conference (APPEEC), pp. 707–711 (2016)
4. Zheng, Z., Chen, H., Luo, X.: Spatial granularity analysis on electricity consumption prediction using LSTM recurrent neural network. Energy Procedia **158**, 2713–2718 (2019)
5. Yang, Z., Liu, Y., Wu, G.: Improved time series electricity sales forecast based on economic prosperity method. In: IOP Conference Series: Earth and Environmental Science, p. 062042. IOP Publishing (2019)
6. Bianco, V., Manca, O., Nardini, S.: Electricity consumption forecasting in Italy using linear regression models. Energy **34**(9), 1413–1421 (2009)
7. Cao, G., Wu, L.: Support vector regression with fruit fly optimization algorithm for seasonal electricity consumption forecasting. Energy **115**, 734–745 (2016)
8. Al-Musaylh, M., Deo, R., Adamowski, J., et al.: Short-term electricity demand forecasting with MARS, SVR and ARIMA models using aggregated demand data in Queensland Australia. Adv. Eng. Inform. **35**, 1–16 (2018)
9. Liu, J., Zhao, J., Chen, Y., et al.: Efficient electricity sales forecasting based on curve decomposition and factor regression. In: 2017 13th International Conference on Natural Computation, Fuzzy Systems and Knowledge Discovery (ICNC-FSKD), pp. 2411–2418 (2017)
10. Sun, T., Zhang, T., Teng, Y., et al.: Monthly electricity consumption forecasting method based on X12 and STL decomposition model in an integrated energy system. Math. Probl. Eng. (2019)
11. Fagen, Z.: Electrical coal demand forecasting model and case studies based on improved X-12-ARIMA. Electric Power **47**(2), 140–145 (2014)
12. Taylor, S., Letham, B.: Forecasting at scale. Am. Stat. **72**(1), 37–45 (2018)
13. Friedman, J.: Greedy function approximation: a gradient boosting machine. Ann. Stat. 1189–1232 (2001)
14. Chen, T., Guestrin, C.: Xgboost: A scalable tree boosting system. In: Proceedings of the 22nd ACM SIGKDD International Conference on Knowledge Discovery and Data Mining, pp. 785–794 (2016)
15. Ke, G., Meng, Q., Finley, T., et al.: Lightgbm: a highly efficient gradient boosting decision tree. In: Advances in Neural Information Processing Systems, Long beach, USA, pp. 3146–3154 (2017)

Research on Electricity Sales Forecast Model Based on Big Data

Kai Li[1], Jian Li[1], Siming Chen[2], Jun Tang[1], Jiao Wu[1], Yingping Zhang[1], and Kejiang Xiao[3](✉)

[1] State Grid Hunan Electric Power Company Limited, Changsha 410004, China
[2] China Southern Power Grid Corporation Kunming Power Supply Bureau, Kunming 650000, China
[3] Hubei Research Center for Educational Informationization, Faculty of Artificial Intelligence in Education, Central China Normal University, Wuhan 430079, China

Abstract. Electricity plays a leading role in reflecting macroeconomic trends. It is sensitive and closely related to the implementation of national policies, industry development, data security and electricity demand of various users. In this paper, X13-ARIMA-SEATS is used to decompose the original electricity sales curve, combined with immediacy factors and leading factors, to use a variety of machine learning algorithms to establish forecast models for the trend, seasonal and random items obtained from the decomposition to predict. Finally, we use AHP to select the optimal curve and reconstruct the curve, and get the final prediction curve after the Spring Festival adjustment. This work has solved the problem of messy electricity sales forecast data and huge amount of calculation. We used this model to predict and verify the historical data of the five types of electricity sales of industry, residents, agriculture, industry and commerce, and bulk sales of a provincial power company. The forecast results obtained by this model in each month are generally better than the industry-wide error. And after segmented modeling and the Spring Festival adjustment algorithm is optimized, the error can be reduced.

Keywords: Electricity sales · Big data · X13-ARIMA-SEATS

1 Introduction

As the core indicator of power grid business, electricity sales directly reflect the achievement of the company's business goals and data security [1]. Some electricity companies have carried out some related work on electricity sales forecast, but the following problems still exist: (1) Lack of power sales forecasting system support. (2) Lack of analysis methods for the influence of internal and external factors on electricity sales. (3) Lack of support for electricity sales forecasting methods based on big data analysis.

With the development of emerging technologies such as big data and artificial intelligence, traditional electricity sales analysis and forecasting methods can no longer meet the requirements of electricity market development [2, 3]. There is an urgent need for big data technology to empower the electricity sales forecasting business and deeply analysis of the changing law of power company sales growth.

© Springer Nature Switzerland AG 2021
J. Cheng et al. (Eds.): CSS 2020, LNCS 12653, pp. 316–328, 2021.
https://doi.org/10.1007/978-3-030-73671-2_27

Usually in research, a combination of multiple forecasting methods is usually used to obtain higher-precision forecasts. Big data analysis methods, regression algorithms, time series algorithms, etc. are often used for forecasting. These methods all use the historical data at the corresponding time point as the basis. However, as the month of the launch is different, the amount of electricity sold in the known month continues to increase, and the month that needs to be predicted decreases accordingly. In addition, historical data often has jumps, especially near the jump point, which easily leads to large errors in the predicted value.

In summary, in order to improve the forecast accuracy of annual electricity sales, this paper proposes a model. First, based on the X13-ARIMA-SEATS (X13) algorithm, the original electricity curve is decomposed into trend term, seasonal term and random term, considering the immediacy and leading indicators. Under the circumstances, the use of machine learning methods to carry out the construction of predictive models.

The contributions are summarized as follows: (1) We proposed an electricity sales prediction framework based on big data which can improves the model's perception of data; (2) We merged multiple machine learning methods to obtain the prediction of electricity sales and select the best result based on the analytic hierarchy process (AHP); (3) The result is optimized based on the influence of seasonal factors and Spring Festival factors.

2   Related Work

There are already many studies on electricity forecasting. Ding and etc. [4] used the grey model (GM) based on particle swarm optimization to forecast China's overall and industrial electricity consumption. Hu [5] used a neural-network-based GM (NNGM) to predict the electricity consumption of Taiwan because GM's developing coefficient and control variable were dependent on the background value that is not easy to be determined. GM is a commonly used electricity related forecasting model and a lot of improvement methods have been proposed for it. But the data that the GM relies when the model makes predictions is only the historical data, the accuracy of prediction results is difficult to guarantee. Zheng and etc. [6] use LSTM recurrent neural network to forecast individual household electric power consumption. Bedi and etc. [7] propose a deep learning framework to forecast electricity demand based on historical electricity consumption data. These methods achieved a higher accuracy but the data they used is still only historical data of electricity consumption, which is still its limitation.

With the development of big data related technologies and security requirement, the means of obtaining data become varied, researchers begin to incorporate more data into the study. Marvuglia and etc. [8] use recurrent artificial neural networks (RANN) base on the dry bulb air temperature, the air relative humidity and the other data to forecast household electricity consumption. Tang and etc. [9] proposed an electricity consumption farecasting method based on expert prediction and Fuzzy Bayesian theory by using the per capita gross domestic product, the electricity intensity, the adjustment of the industrial structure and the other data. Liu and etc. [10] forecast the annual electricity sales based on co-integration theory, which effectively solve the problem of false regression caused by the instability of time series. These studies incorporate a variety of data into the research, but none of them consider the influence of seasonal factors.

3   An Overview

The electricity sales forecasting model based on big data analysis proposed in this paper is based on the investigation of the electricity sales analysis methods that have been carried out by power companies and security department. It is constructed by combining more than ten kinds of big data algorithms. The scheme used for electricity sales forecasting is as follows. The prediction model is mainly composed of the following parts.

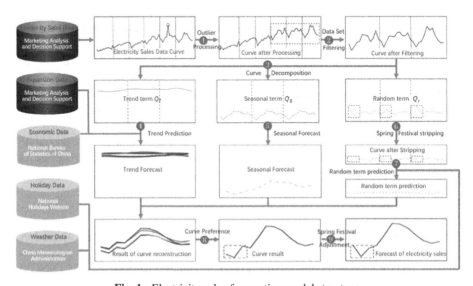

Fig. 1. Electricity sales forecasting model structure.

(1) Data Preprocessing. The content of this part mainly includes outlier processing and data screening. The work of outlier processing is to identify the abnormal data in the data set and deal with it accordingly. The work of data set screening is to filter out the optimal modeling data set and improve the quality of modeling data.

(2) Curve Decomposition. In this part, we use the X13-ARIMA-SEATS algorithm to decompose the original electricity sales data. This can grasp the rules of data details and improve the scientific of the model.

(3) Itemized Forecasting. Combining immediacy factors and leading factors to construct forecast models for trend term, seasonal term and random term. And then reconstructing them and obtain the prediction result.

(4) Curve Reconstructing. Sum the forecast results of the trend term, seasonal term and random term. Since there are four forecast results for the trend term, four forecast results will be generated after the addition; comprehensively consider the forecast error, trend reliability, forecast trend similarity, etc. Index, combined with AHP to get the best prediction result.

4 Forecasting Model

4.1 Curve Decomposition

X-13-ARIMA-SEAT is a seasonal adjustment program issued by U.S. Census Bureau. The basis is X-11, which is a series of centralized moving averages. Because it is a centralized moving average, X-11 has difficulties in processing the data at both ends of the sequence. X-13-ARIMA-SEAT uses ARIMA (reg-ARIMA) with regression independent variables to predict and expand the series, thereby partially solving the moving average of the latest data. In addition, reg-ARIMA can also identify outliers, calendar effects, mobile holidays, etc. Due to factors such as seasons, weather, etc., the shape of the electricity sales curve changes diversified, which has drowned the trend of electricity sales to a certain extent. In this paper, we use X13 to decompose the original electricity sales curve to obtain the trend term, seasonal term and random term. The following is the steps of decomposing the original electricity sales curve. At first, we perform linear filtering on the original time series data Et and obtain the trend term T_t. And this is the formula for linear filtering computed by:

$$T_t = \left(E_{t-6}/2 + E_{t-5} + \ldots + E_{t+5} + E_{t+6}/2\right)/12 \tag{1}$$

Q_t minus T_t gets SE_t, use the moving average method of SE_t to get the seasonal term S_t. The formula is as the following.

$$S_t^* = \left(SE_{t-24} + 2SE_{t-12} + 3SE_t + 2SE_{t+12} + SE_{t+24}\right) \tag{2}$$

$$S_t = S_t^* - \left(S_{t-6}^*/2 + S_{t-5}^* + \ldots + S_{t+5}^* + S_{t+6}^*/2\right)/24 \tag{3}$$

And we let T_t minus S_t and obtain the random term R_t. After the above calculation, we decompose the original electricity sales data into trend term, seasonal term and random term. And their relationship can be expressed as:

$$E_t = SUM\left(T_t,\ S_t,\ R_t\right) \tag{4}$$

By using the X13 algorithm, we have effectively extracted the change trend term, seasonal term and random term of electricity sales, which improves the model's ability to perceive the electricity sales trends.

4.2 Itemized Forecasting

We forecast trend items and random items separately based on immediacy factors and leading factors. The immediacy factors include temperature, disposable income per capita, rainfall, etc. And the leading factors refer to factors that have a leading or lagging influence on electricity sales, including manufacturing PMI, non-manufacturing PMI, and the net added capacity of industry expansion.

1) *Trend Term*
   The monthly electricity sales trend item curve is relatively smooth, which is mainly affected by economic factors. We use the following steps to predict the trend term of electricity sales.

Mark the data sequence of the known electricity sales trend term data as $\{T(t)|t = 1, 2, ..., N\}$. The immediacy factor is marked as $\{F(t)|t = 1, 2, ..., N\}$, and $F(t) = \{F^1(t), F^2(t)| t = 1, 2, ..., N\}$ if there are 2 factors. The leading factor is marked as $\{L(t)| t = 1, 2, ..., N\}$, and $L(t) = \{L^1(t), L^2(t)| t = 1, 2, ..., N\}$ if there are two factors. If these two leading factors are the net added capacity of industry expansion and PMI, then $L^1(t) = \{net(t-1), net(t-2), ..., net(t-m)\}$ and $L^2(t) = \{PMI(t-1), PMI(t-2), ..., PMI(t-m)\}$, m is the number of months in which the trend term of net increase in business expansion leads in front of the trend item of electricity sales, $net(t)$ is the trend term of net increase in business expansion in month t, n is the number of months in which the PMI leads in front of the trend item of electricity sales, $PMI(t)$ is the PMI in month t. Other leading factors and so on.

Then use Principal Component Analysis (PCA) to remove the correlation between the leading factors and the immediacy factors [11].

$$P(t) = PCA(F(t), L(t)), \ t = 1, 2, \ldots, N \tag{5}$$

$P(t)$ is the data that has been removed the correlation, so we use it as the input data of model.

Finally, the trend term forecasting model is established. Since the trend item accounts for a relatively large proportion, in order to ensure the prediction accuracy, four algorithms, Support Vector Machines (SVM) [12], Sparse Logistic Regression with L1/2 (SLR), Echo State Network (ESN) [13] and Extreme Learning Machine (ELM) [14] are used to predict separately.

2) *Seasonal Term*

The seasonal term of electricity sales has strong regularity, with small fluctuations in the same month value each year and relatively stable trend changes. In this paper, SLR is used to predict the seasonal term of electricity sales.

We use SLR to forecast the seasonal term and obtain the result of seasonal term forecasting.

3) *Random Term*

The random term of electricity sales fluctuates greatly but has a small amplitude, which is mainly affected by holidays and temperature. The prediction steps are as follows. We use the mixture of experts model whose every expert in the model uses SVM, the number of holidays and the monthly average temperature is the input data of the model. Then we obtain the prediction of factors. The number of holidays can be obtained directly through the national government website. And the monthly average temperature can be predicted by SLR. Finally, we can obtain the result of random term prediction.

4.3 Curve Reconstruction

After the above calculation, we obtain the prediction of trend term, seasonal term and random term within 1 prediction steps. Because there are four algorithms in the trend term forecasting process, we have four prediction results. We reconstruct electricity sales curve by adding them together according to Eq. 4 and get four prediction results of electricity sales. Then use AHP to obtain the best prediction result. According to the hierarchical structure of AHP, the problem of selecting the best results of electricity sales forecast is divided into target layer, criterion layer and scheme layer.

The target layer includes one target, which is to select the prediction curve with the most predictive performance.

$$a_1 = 1 - \frac{1}{n} \sum_{i=1}^{n} \left(\left| Y_h^i - Y_p^i \right| \right) \Big/ Y_h^i, i = 1, 2, \ldots, n \tag{6}$$

Y_h^i, Y_p^i are the actual electricity sales and forecast electricity sales in the i-th month respectively. Forecast trend similarity reflects the similarity between the current forecast results of the forecast model and the historical electricity sales curve shape.

$$a_2 = cor\left(\left\{ Y_h^i, \ldots, Y_h^{i+12} \right\}, \left\{ Y_p^i, \ldots, Y_p^{i+12} \right\} \right), i = 1, 2, \ldots, n \tag{7}$$

Y_h^i, Y_p^i are the predicted electricity sales in the i-th month and the corresponding actual electricity sales in the month of the previous year. The length of $\{Y_h^i, \ldots, Y_h^{12}\}$ is 12, which can avoid the problem of index failure when the curve length is shortened to 2.

Forecast trend credibility is a measure of the current forecast results of the forecast model in line with historical curve trend changes.

$$a_3 = \begin{cases} \frac{1}{1+(r_{min}-r)}, & r \in (-1, r_{min}) \\ x, & r \in [r_{min}, r_{max}] \\ \frac{1}{1+(r-r_{max})}, & r \in (r_{max}, +\infty) \end{cases} \tag{8}$$

r_{min}, r, r_{max} are annual growth rates of electricity sales.

The scheme layer includes 4 schemes, namely the forecast results of electricity sales of the four algorithms SVM, SLR, ELM and ESN. Then construct the judgment matrix of the target layer to the criterion layer, obtain the weight vector. It should be noted that the AHP judgment matrix needs to be tested for consistency.

4.4 Spring Festival Adjustment

The Spring Festival adjustment model uses the number of days between the first day of the historical Spring Festival from January to March and the historical quarterly ratio of electricity sales from January to March as input data. Secondly, a polynomial is used to fit the input data to obtain the fitting function of the number of days between the first day of the historical Spring Festival from January to March and the quarterly ratio of electricity sales from January to March.

$$w_t = f(x_t) \tag{9}$$

Combining the fitting function and the number of days from the first day of January to March during the Spring Festival of the year to be predicted, calculate the forecasted quarterly ratio from January to March of the forecast year. Finally allocate the forecast value of electricity sales in each month of the first quarter, obtain the output result of the Spring Festival adjustment model.

5 Experiment

5.1 Data Set

This paper uses the electricity sales data of a certain province from January 2015 to December 2019 as the data set, which is divided into total electricity sales forecast, residential electricity sales forecast, large industrial electricity sales forecast, general industrial and commercial electricity sales forecast, agricultural electricity sales forecast, and bulk sales electricity forecast.

We use the electricity sales data from January 2015 to December 2018 as the training set, and the electricity sales data from January 2019 to December 2019 as the verification set to conduct the forecast of electricity sales in 2019. This paper uses the Mean Absolute Percentage Error (MAPE) as the criterion of the model. And the value range of MAPE is $[0, +\infty]$. When the value of MAPE is 0, the model is perfect. When the value of MAPE value is greater than 100%, the model is bad.

5.2 Electricity Sales Forecasting

Figures 2, 3, 4, 5 and 6 show the forecast curves of electricity sales from January to November in 2019 for residential, large industrial, general industrial and agriculture respectively.

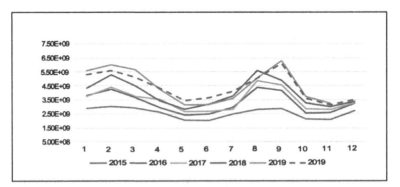

Fig. 2. Forecast curve of residential electricity sales from January to November in 2019 of the electricity.

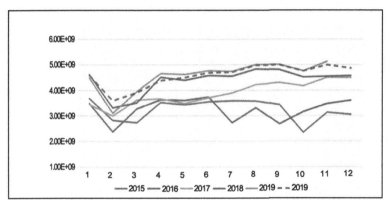

Fig. 3. Forecast curve of large industrial electricity sales from January to November in 2019 of the electricity company.

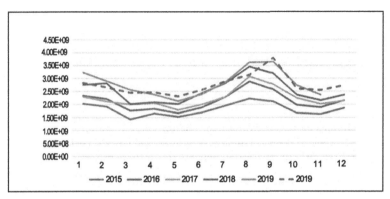

Fig. 4. Forecast curve of general industrial electricity sales from January to November in 2019 of the electricity company.

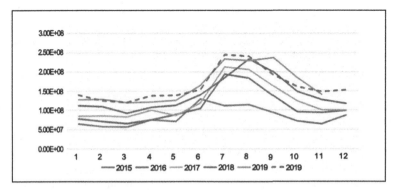

Fig. 5. Forecast curve of agricultural electricity sales from January to November in 2019 of the electricity company.

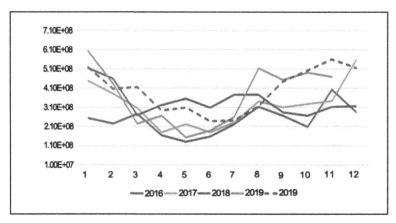

Fig. 6. Forecast curve of bulk sales from January to November in 2019 of the electricity company.

5.3 Error Analysis

Table 1 is the error analysis of the above forecast results using MAPE. The average MAPE of the total electricity sales in 2019 is 3.14%, the residential electricity sales is 6.61%, the large industrial electricity sales is 3.10%, the general industrial electricity sales is 6.81%, the agricultural electricity sales is 6.81%, the bulk electricity sales is 28.60%.

Through error analysis, we found that average error of the bulk electricity sales is large, reaching 28.60%. By observing Fig. 6, we can find that the bulk sales of electricity fluctuate greatly, and its value is small, which is likely to cause large forecast errors.

From the perspective of bulk sales forecasting, more consideration needs to be given to the business reasons that affect bulk sales, especially the impact of temporary event factors on bulk sales, so as to reduce the model prediction error of bulk sales.

Through the analysis of the total amount and the forecast error of the electricity sales of each electricity consumption category, the forecast error distribution and model verification from January to November are mastered. In order to analyze the main reasons for the total error, the error contribution analysis of each electricity consumption category is carried out. The meaning of the error contribution is the error contribution of the sub-industry that causes the total forecast deviation.

The main calculation method is as follows:

(1) Calculate the difference A between the predicted value of each electricity consumption category and the true value of each electricity consumption category;
(2) The total real power sales is Q, and $A/Q = M$ is defined, and M is the error contribution degree of each power consumption category.

We verified the total electricity sales of a provincial company from January to November in 2019 and the electricity sales forecast of each electricity consumption category. And the contribution of each electricity consumption category is calculated to the total forecast error from January to November in 2019. The result is shown in Table 2.

5.4 Model Improvement and Optimization

(1) *Segmented Modeling*

Through the analysis of the verification errors in 2019, there is a certain degree of optimization space for the verification errors of the residents' electricity sales forecast during the non-peak period. For the forecast in April and May, considering that it has not been affected by low or high temperature in the past few months, the two-stage modeling method is considered for forecasting. The main ideas are as follows:

Calculate the average electricity in April and May from 2015 to 2018. And use the least squares algorithm to fit the function on the basis of drawing a scatter plot.

It can be seen from Fig. 8 that the average electricity consumption in these months has been regularly increased year by year because it has not been affected by extreme high temperatures and low temperatures. Therefore, the average electricity (Basic electricity) in these months can be directly established as a function of time, or with per capita A function of disposable income. Take the function of time as an example. The function we get is as follows:

$$y = 313140835.70 * x + 1757794358.00 \tag{10}$$

And the Coefficient of determination (R^2) is 0.99. Using the function (14), it can be predicted that the basic electricity for the two months of 2019 will be 3323498537 kWh. Then combine the three variables of the basic electricity (a) in April and May 2019, the monthly average temperature (b), and the year-on-year temperature change (c) to construct a functional relationship with the total electricity in each month. The resulting function is as follows:

$$y = -273154428.51 + 0.99131998 * a + 13303887.21 * b + 16653134.49 * c \tag{11}$$

And R^2 is 0.9677, which shows that the model can track the amount of power change well. In this way, the forecast optimization of residential electricity sales in 2019 can be realized.

From the analysis results in Table 3, it can be seen that the two-stage modeling forecast adjustment for residents can effectively reduce the residents' electricity sales forecast errors in April and May in 2019. Explains the effectiveness of using the segmented modeling for the optimization of residential electricity sales during non-peak periods.

Forecasting optimization during the Spring Festival Since the Spring Festival is usually in the middle of late January or February in the first quarter, it mainly affects the electricity sales from January to March, but has a small impact on the total electricity sales in the first quarter, so the available electricity sales account for the quarterly ratio (The proportion of electricity sold in each month to the total electricity sold in the quarter) is to redistribute the forecast results for the first quarter, and then obtain the forecast results of electricity sales in each month after the Spring Festival adjustment. Figure 9 is an analysis of the impact of the Spring Festival on the electricity sales of large industries.

As can be seen from the above figure, the Spring Festival has a obvious impact on the electricity sales of large industries. And the relationship function is is

$$y = 0.000066 * x^2 + 0.000458 * x + 0.289276 \qquad (12)$$

The coefficient of determination of the function is 0.85, and the model fits well.

We calculated the quarterly ratio of monthly electricity sales in the first quarter based on the fitting relationship between the number of days before the Spring Festival and the electricity sales of large industries. After obtaining the quarterly ratio, redistribute the monthly electricity sales in the first quarter and obtain the adjusted electricity sales forecast results after the Spring Festival.

Take the first quarter of 2019 as an example to illustrate the impact of the Spring Festival adjustment on the forecast of electricity sales. The results are shown in Table 4. After the above analysis, it can be seen that after the Spring Festival adjustment, the total electricity sales forecast error rate in the first quarter of 2019 will be reduced by 1.09%, of which the forecast error rate of large industrial and general industrial and commercial electricity sales will be reduced by 3.89% and 4.14%. This proves that the Spring Festival adjustment algorithm has a good effect on reducing errors.

Table 1. Forecast error of electricity sales from January to November in 2019.

	Residential	Large industrial	General industrial	Agricultural	Bulk sales	Total sales
January	−5.16%	2.51%	−12.50%	8.84%	−14.15%	−4.66%
February	−7.11%	15.7%	−8.42%	−2.76%	−6.08%	−1.69%
March	−9.45%	−1.07%	−4.18%	0.52%	86.57%	−3.91%
April	−1.66%	−6.05%	3.35%	12.76%	10.28%	−0.78%
May	9.93%	−2.80%	8.27%	10.43%	103.30%	5.20%
June	14.8%	−1.66%	7.34%	−6.78%	25.39%	5.66%
July	14.3%	−0.60%	0.91%	4.84%	−6.58%	4.33%
August	−0.63%	−8.58%	−13.60%	5.00%	−38.15%	−5.07%
September	−2.99%	−0.45%	4.25%	−18.64%	2.14%	−0.64%
October	−3.40%	−0.24%	−4.65%	−12.55%	1.99%	−2.33%
November	−3.24%	−0.20%	7.50%	5.28%	19.94%	−0.28%
Average	6.61%	3.10%	6.81%	8.04%	28.60%	3.14%

Table 2. The company's total error from January to November 2019 and the error contribution of each electricity sales category.

	Large industry	Residential	Agricultural	General industrial	Bulk sales	Industrywide error
January	0.80%	−2.05%	0.08%	−2.88%	−0.61%	−4.66%
February	3.89%	−3.40%	−0.03%	−1.94%	−0.21%	−1.69%
March	−0.34%	−4.27%	0.00%	−0.86%	1.55%	−3.91%
April	−2.43%	0.60%	0.13%	0.69%	0.23%	−0.78%
May	−1.27%	3.06%	0.13%	1.74%	1.54%	5.66%
June	−0.74%	4.40%	−0.10%	1.65%	0.45%	5.20%
July	−0.24%	4.40%	0.10%	0.22%	−0.15%	4.33%
August	−0.15%	−0.22%	0.08%	−3.42%	−1.36%	−5.07%
September	−0.08%	−1.20%	−0.28%	0.99%	−0.06%	−0.64%
October	−0.08%	−1.07%	−0.20%	−1.07%	0.08%	−2.33%
November	−1.24%	−0.93%	0.07%	1.56%	0.82%	0.28%

Table 3. Comparison of errors before and after adjustment of residential electricity sales forecast in April and May 2019.

Period	Ground truth	Prediction before optimization	Prediction after optimization	MAPE before optimization	MAPE after optimization	Reduced value of MAPE
201904	31.44	36.96	34.56	17.56%	9.92%	7.63%
201905	31.63	38.07	36.33	20.36%	14.86%	5.50%

Table 4. Based on the average error of the first quarter electricity sales before and after the Spring Festival adjustment.

	MAPE before adjustment	MAPE after adjustment	Decrease value
Total sales	4.51%	3.42%	1.09%
Large industrial	10.31%	6.45%	3.87%
Residential	7.24%	7.24%	0.00%
Agriculture	2.87%	4.04%	−1.17%
General industrial	12.50%	8.37%	4.14%

6 Conclusion

This paper proposes a model with higher accuracy that can predict electricity sales. This model has good perception of data, and through the non-peak period and peak period segmented modeling and adjusted according to the impact of the Spring Festival, the accuracy of the model is effectively improved.

Acknowledgement. This work was supported in part by the National Natural Science Foundation of China under Grant No. 61803391, and in part by the Hunan Provincial Natural Science Foundation of China under Grant No. 2019JJ50803.

References

1. Pan, Y., Wei, Y.: Strategy of electricity sales and retail based on double-layer game. In: 2020 International Symposium on Frontiers of Economics and Management Science (FEMS 2020), Dalian, Liaoning, China, pp. 172–177. Institute of Management Science and Industrial Engineering (2020)
2. Liu, Y., Song, K., Wang, X.: Analysis of economic prosperity index based on big data of electricity. Telecommun. Sci. **36**(06), 166–171 (2020)
3. Siuly, S., Zhang, X.: Guest Editorial: special issue on "Application of artificial intelligence in health research." Health Inf. Sci. Syst. **8**(1), 1 (2020)
4. Ding, S., Hipel, K., Dang, Y.: Forecasting China's electricity consumption using a new grey prediction model. Energy **149**, 314–328 (2018)
5. Hu, Y.: Electricity consumption prediction using a neural-network-based grey forecasting approach. J. Oper. Res. Soc. **68**(10), 1259–1264 (2017)
6. Zheng, Z., Chen, H., Luo, X.: Spatial granularity analysis on electricity consumption prediction using LSTM recurrent neural network. Energy Proc. **158**, 2713–2718 (2019)
7. Bedi, J., Toshniwal, D.: Deep learning framework to forecast electricity demand. Appl. Energy **238**, 1312–1326 (2019)
8. Marvuglia, A., Messineo, A.: Using recurrent artificial neural networks to forecast household electricity consumption. Energy Proc. **14**, 45–55 (2012)
9. Tang, L., Wang, X., Wang, X., Shao, C., Liu, S., Tian, S.: Long-term electricity consumption forecasting based on expert prediction and fuzzy Bayesian theory. Energy **167**, 1144–1154 (2019)
10. Liu, J., et al.: Research on the method of forecasting annual electricity sales based on co-integration theory. In: IOP Conference Series Materials Science and Engineering, vol. 394, no. 4 (2018)
11. Yu, Y., Peng, M., Wang, H., Ma, Z., Li, W.: Improved PCA model for multiple fault detection, isolation and reconstruction of sensors in nuclear power plant. Ann. Nucl. Energy **148**, 107662 (2020)
12. Soumaya, Z., Taoufiq, B., Benayad, N., Yunus, K., Abdelkrim, A.: The detection of Parkinson disease using the genetic algorithm and SVM classifier. Appl. Acoust. **171**, 107528 (2021)
13. Allen, H., James, H., Jonathan, D.: Embedding and approximation theorems for echo state networks. Neural Netw. Off. J. Int. Neural Netw. Soc. **128**, 234–247 (2020)
14. Chen, Y., Xie, X., Zhang, T., Bai, J., Hou, M.: A deep residual compensation extreme learning machine and applications. J. Forecast. **39**(6), 986–999 (2020)

Author Index

330 Author Index

Printed in the United States
by Baker & Taylor Publisher Services